## STRUCTURE AND IMPROVISATION IN CREATIVE TEACHING

With an increasing emphasis on creativity and innovation in the twenty-first century, teachers need to be creative professionals just as students must learn to be creative. And yet, schools are institutions with many important structures and guidelines that teachers must follow. Effective creative teaching strikes a delicate balance between structure and improvisation. The authors draw on studies of jazz, theater improvisation, and dance improvisation to demonstrate that the most creative performers work within similar structures and guidelines. By looking to these creative genres, the book provides practical advice for teachers who wish to become more creative professionals.

Dr. R. Keith Sawyer is internationally known as an expert in the learning sciences and in the psychology of creativity. He is the editor or author of more than eighty scholarly articles and ten books, including *The Cambridge Handbook of the Learning Sciences* (2006), *Explaining Creativity: The Science of Human Innovation* (2006), and *Group Genius: The Creative Power of Collaboration* (2007).

D1260001

# Structure and Improvisation in Creative Teaching

Edited by

## R. Keith Sawyer

*Washington University in St. Louis*

CAMBRIDGE UNIVERSITY PRESS
Cambridge, New York, Melbourne, Madrid, Cape Town,
Singapore, São Paulo, Delhi, Tokyo, Mexico City

Cambridge University Press
32 Avenue of the Americas, New York, NY 10013–2473, USA

www.cambridge.org
Information on this title: www.cambridge.org/9780521746328

First published 2011

Printed in the United States of America

*A catalog record for this publication is available from the British Library.*

*Library of Congress Cataloging in Publication data*
Structure and improvisation in creative teaching / [edited by] R. Keith Sawyer.
p.   cm.
Includes bibliographical references and index.
ISBN 978-0-521-76251-9 (hardback) – ISBN 978-0-521-74632-8 (paperback)
1. Student-centered learning.   2. Active learning.   3. Creative teaching.
4. Motivation in education.   I. Sawyer, R. Keith (Robert Keith)
LB1027.23S77   2011
371.102–dc22        2011010351

ISBN 978-0-521-76251-9 Hardback
ISBN 978-0-521-74632-8 Paperback

# CONTENTS

PART 3    THE CURRICULUM PARADOX

# TABLE AND FIGURES

# NOTES ON CONTRIBUTORS

LISA BARKER is a doctoral candidate in teacher education at Stanford University. A former K–12 English and drama teacher, she is an instructor in the Stanford Teacher Education Program and the Center to Support Excellence in Teaching. Her research centers on the ways in which improvisational theater training can engage teachers in thinking actively about notions of presence, classroom discourse, and relationship-building with young people and colleagues.

RONALD A. BEGHETTO is an Associate Professor of Education Studies at the University of Oregon. His research focuses on supporting creativity in classrooms and teacher development. He has published more than 50 articles and book chapters on these topics. His latest book (with James C. Kaufman) is *Nurturing Creativity in the Classroom*.

DAVID C. BERLINER is Regents' Professor Emeritus at Arizona State University. His interests are in the study of teaching and educational policy. He is the author or co-author of more than two hundred books, chapters, and journal articles; a former president of the American Educational Research Association; and a member of the National Academy of Education.

HILDA BORKO is a Professor of Education at Stanford University. Her research explores the process of learning to teach, with an emphasis on changes in novice and experienced teachers' knowledge and beliefs about teaching and learning, and their classroom practices, as they participate in teacher education and professional development programs. She is also designing and studying a program to prepare math educational leaders.

PAMELA BURNARD is a Senior Lecturer at the University of Cambridge, UK, where she manages Higher Degree courses in Educational Research and Arts, Culture, and Education. Her books include *Music's Creativities*, *Reflective*

*Practices in Arts Education, Creative Learning 3–11,* and *Music Education with Digital Technology.* She is co-convenor of the British Education Research Association SIG Creativity in Education.

STACY DEZUTTER is an Assistant Professor of Education at Millsaps College. Her research builds on insights from sociocultural theory to examine two separate, but related, areas of interest: the social formation of teacher cognition and the distributed creative processes of groups. She holds a PhD in the Learning Sciences from Washington University in St. Louis.

FREDERICK ERICKSON is the George F. Kneller Professor of Anthropology of Education at the University of California, Los Angeles, where he is also appointed as Professor of Applied Linguistics. He is a pioneer in the video-based study of face-to-face interaction, with special attention to the musicality of speech and of listening behavior, and he also writes on qualitative research methods. His most recent book is titled *Talk and Social Theory: Ecologies of Speaking and Listening in Everyday Life.*

JANICE E. FOURNIER is a Research Scientist for UW Information Technology at the University of Washington. She also teaches in the UW College of Education and is an education consultant to arts organizations. Her research interests include the arts and learning, arts literacy, and educational technology.

A. SUSAN JUROW is an Assistant Professor of Educational Psychological Studies at the University of Colorado, Boulder. She studies the interrelations between identity, interaction, and culture in and across learning environments. Her research has been published in journals including *Journal of the Learning Sciences*; *Mind, Culture, and Activity*; and *Journal of Teacher Education.*

JAMES C. KAUFMAN is an Associate Professor of Psychology at the California State University at San Bernardino, where he directs the Learning Research Institute. His past books on creativity include *Creativity 101* and *The Cambridge Handbook of Creativity.* He is active in APA's Division 10 as president-elect and co-editor of their journal, *Psychology of Aesthetics, Creativity, and the Arts.*

JÜRGEN KURTZ is Professor of English and Teaching English as a Foreign Language at Justus Liebig University Giessen, Germany. He previously taught at the University of Dortmund and at Karlsruhe University of Education. His current research focuses on the role of improvisation in enhancing oral proficiency in EFL classrooms, on EFL textbook analysis and use, and on culture-sensitive foreign language education in all-day schools.

CARRIE LOBMAN is an Associate Professor in the Rutgers Graduate School of Education. Her research interests include teacher education and the relationship between play, performance, learning, and development. She is a co-author of *Unscripted Learning: Using Improv Activities Across the K–8 Curriculum*.

LYNDON C. MARTIN is an Associate Professor in the Faculty of Education at York University. His research interests are in mathematical thinking and learning with a particular emphasis on understanding and how this can be characterized and described. He is also concerned with mathematical understanding in the workplace and in how adults working in construction trades understand and use mathematical concepts in formal and informal ways.

LAURA CREIGHTON MCFADDEN received her PhD in science education at the University of Colorado at Boulder. She has taught junior high school science and was an Assistant Professor of Science Education at Rhode Island College. Laura is currently pursuing a career in fiction writing and is working on her first young-adult novel.

ANTHONY PERONE is a doctoral candidate at the University of Illinois at Chicago. His research focuses on the life-span presence, development, and benefits of imaginative play activity and the role of improvisational theater activities in formal and informal learning environments and in teacher education.

ANNETTE SASSI is an independent education researcher and evaluator based in the greater Boston area. She currently works as a consultant at TERC in Cambridge, MA, and has worked at Education Matters, Inc., in Cambridge, MA, and Education Development Center in Newton, MA. She is a co-author of *The Effective Principal: Instructional Leadership for High-Quality Learning*.

R. KEITH SAWYER studies creativity, collaboration, and learning. He has published more than eighty scholarly articles and is author or editor of ten books, including *The Cambridge Handbook of the Learning Sciences*, *Explaining Creativity: The Science of Human Innovation*, and *Group Genius: The Creative Power of Collaboration*.

JO TOWERS is a Professor in the Faculty of Education at the University of Calgary. Her research interests center on the phenomenon of mathematical understanding. Bringing to bear conceptions of learning drawn from the domains of ecology, complexity theory, and improvisational theory, she studies students' growing understandings of mathematics, the role of the teacher in occasioning such understandings, and the implications for teacher education structures and pedagogies.

# FOREWORD

## DAVID C. BERLINER

The first and last chapters of this book provide both a forward and a backward glance at the important contributions each author has made to right a great wrong. This wrong has been promoted and supported by many politicians, business people, and school administrators. This wrong has made it more difficult for America's teachers to be effective.

This wrong is the imposition of structures on teachers, in the belief that structures such as algorithms, procedures, scripts, and protocols for conducting instruction will improve teaching and learning. In areas like airline travel, manufacturing, or finance, tried-and-true protocols – routines and scripts for accomplishing one's job – make businesses more efficient and profitable, allow workers to achieve competency sooner, and often make customers happier. In these industries, structures have a proven ability to enhance efficiency and increase quality control. But it is misguided to apply these same ideas in the much more uncertain environment of a classroom with thirty diverse students.

Although the airline industry and its pilots depend on routines, checklists, and protocols for doing many things, when a plane's engines fail – as they did in 2009 over the Hudson river – there was no procedure to follow. The pilot improvised, saving everyone's life, and reminding us that protocols, scripts, and checklists for performing a job simply cannot cover everything that happens on the job.

And in spite of the demonstrated power of structures in many businesses, there is plenty of contrary evidence that overadherence to routines, scripts, protocols, and the like can act as a straightjacket, restricting reflection and creativity. For example, when the future of the gasoline engine began to be questioned, and the environmental hazards associated with its use became clear, General Motors continued to make the same cars they had made for decades. Apparently no one in command could stop and reflect, and change the course of this giant American company. The managers could not, or would not, respond to changing conditions. The creativity that had brought our auto industry into worldwide prominence was nowhere to be found. Similarly, banks continued to offer mortgages as their risks escalated and even as respected members of their community issued warnings about the unsustainability of the housing market. Their actions caused an international economic recession because they could not stop what they were doing. Reliance on the routines that served them so well in the past overwhelmed good sense: The routines they used blocked the reflection they needed.

To be sure, the power of routines, scripts, and all kinds of established procedures to guide action in environments that are stable and predictable is not to be questioned. Semmelweis, who taught physicians to wash their hands before and after every contact with a patient, dramatically taught us that! And business process techniques like Six Sigma have increased quality and efficiency, lowering product costs and increasing value for everyone.

But as events become less certain, and the outcomes desired less standardized, adherence to those same routines can be ineffectual, if not dangerous. That is the paradox addressed in this book. Too much of classroom life has become too routinized. In both the United Kingdom and the United States, this is due partly to powerful accountability policies that demand that certain student outcomes be achieved, greatly constraining what teachers do in classrooms. But another reason for this increase in demand for uniformity and routines in our schools arises from the increasing dominance of business models applied to education. The protocols, routines, and scripts that can be helpful in business settings are believed to apply easily to classroom life, so they are promoted by school administrators without regard for their effects on teaching and the outcomes of education.

The imposition of structure and efficiency approaches to schools is resulting in what I call *creaticide*. "Creaticide" is a national movement to kill literary, scientific, and mathematical creativity in the school-age population of the United States of America, particularly among impoverished youth. While all of public education feels the impact of accountability policies and policies that promote business models to improve education, it is the schools with the most impoverished students that feel these pressures the most. Schools with poor children often have the lowest test scores, and so policies thought to improve test performance are implemented with greater fervor. But it is now recognized that contemporary educational policy in both the United Kingdom and the United States, particularly for impoverished youth, has resulted in four outcomes: curriculum narrowing, narrowing of the assessments used to judge the quality of schooling, narrowing of the schools' conceptions of what it means to be smart in school, and narrowing of the ways we judge teacher competency. With a few notable exceptions, policies designed to improve schools in both countries have resulted in a diminution of those classroom activities that are more likely to promote higher levels of thought, problem solving, and creativity in academic areas. It is not that the research community can agree on how to produce higher-order thinking and creative responses among youth. Far from it! But there is remarkable agreement about how *not* to produce the outcomes we desire. And by constraining what teachers and students can do in classrooms we do just that.

I have been in schools that were heavily routinized. It always sounds so simple to engineer and so it is so easy to garner support for these practices: Turn over to teachers an approved curriculum (often a text, workbook, and teacher's manual with test questions), train the teachers or aides in "good" classroom practice (have them learn scripts such as "Repeat: C, A, T, spells CAT. Say it again, C, A, T! Good. Is the C in CAT a hard C sound or a soft C sound? Everybody: It is a hard C sound"), and the students will magically learn all that they should. In fact, the children in this class did seem to be learning through this kind of direct instruction – in part, because some aspects of reading, such as phonemic awareness and spelling, can be routinized. I am sure there are other, and perhaps better, ways to teach phonemic awareness, but the predictability in this aspect of reading, or in learning some mathematics, or for composing a letter to an editor, all can be routinized to some degree. So teachers can learn to be better at their craft by learning about best practices for teaching certain curricula to students x, y, or z, just as physicians can learn best practices for treating patients x, y, or z.

But in those same scripted classrooms, there is Juanito, the student who cannot learn the way the teacher taught that lesson. There is Johnny, the student who refuses to learn. There is Sarah, who expresses a wonderful idea that leads the class off in a different direction from what the curriculum demands, but it is a pleasant path to follow for a while. For the physician, there is Juanito's father, who does not respond to the cholesterol-lowering drug that is recommended for his condition. There is Johnny's mother, who will not follow her prescribed regimen of therapy. And there is Sarah's mother, who refuses to get treatment because she now heals herself with herbs. Routines, best practices, approved protocols for acting in certain ways – all are useful, *except when they are not!* And that is the problem with those who wish to see more standardization in teaching and in educational outcomes. Like clinical medicine, teaching is highly unpredictable. And if it were not, it would need to be made so to develop in our students skills for dealing with uncertainty and to provide the nation with variation in the outcomes of schooling.

By failing to build and honor the improvisational repertoires of teachers so they can respond in educative ways to the unique opportunities afforded during interaction with students and curriculum, we chip away at their love of teaching. And we also restrain student growth in creative responding. Neither of these outcomes is desirable for a nation that must compete with its wits, and through its schools, in the knowledge age.

Not the teachers' mastery and love for the curriculum they teach, nor the students' desire (and right) to communicate what they think and feel in each subject, nor the nation's need for a creative citizenry is served if all that is taught is what is needed to answer test items on high-stakes examinations tapping relatively low cognitive levels of knowledge. Of course, in teaching as in any professional practice, there is a necessary balance between structure and creativity. Doctors follow repeatable scripts and protocols throughout much of their day, and health care is improved as a result. That is why there will always be a tension as a teacher enacts the required curriculum. This book reminds us, indeed implores us, to remember that whatever else classrooms have to be, they should also always be places for lively, often spontaneous interactions. This book convincingly argues that spontaneity and improvisation in classrooms may be no less exhilarating, and certainly requires no less skill than improvisation does in jazz, dance, and theater.

In this brief foreword, I've acknowledged the potential value of scripts and routines to improve medical care and aspects of business, and in teaching some parts of the desired curriculum. And yet, I've argued that schools today are excessively reliant on structuring techniques. If we want our students to learn higher-level skills, including creativity and critical thinking, structures and scripts cannot get us there. So are you confused? Wondering what is the best balance between structure, improvisation, and creativity? That is why this book should be widely read and discussed! These chapters speak directly to that confusion: They give us the clarity we need to negotiate the necessary tensions of teaching in an age that must pay more attention to creativity.

# What Makes Good Teachers Great?
# The Artful Balance of Structure and Improvisation

R. KEITH SAWYER

In the 1970s and 1980s, educational researchers began to study what makes good teachers great. One common approach of these early researchers was to compare experienced teachers with novice teachers; they found that experienced teachers have a greater repertoire of *scripts* than novice teachers – standard sequences of activities, or responses to students, that work in specific situations. Researchers also found, however, that experienced teachers were better at *improvising* in response to each class's unique flow; in fact, they tended to spend less advance time planning than novice teachers (Berliner & Tikunoff, 1976; Borko & Livingston, 1989; Yinger, 1987). Experienced teachers do two apparently contradictory things: They use more structures, and yet they improvise more.

These early studies of teacher expertise focused on the structures that teachers created themselves, as ways to enhance teaching, manage classrooms, and handle problems that may arise. In addition, many of the structures that guide teaching are mandated by law, administration, or state and federal guidelines. Modern schools are complex organizations, with relatively rigid structures and bureaucratic and administrative frameworks that constrain what teachers can do in classrooms (Olson, 2003). Many education researchers have explored the tension between teachers' professional autonomy and reflective practice on the one hand and the many policies that constrain teachers on the other (e.g., Cochrane-Smith & Lytle, 1999; Darling-Hammond, 1997; Ingersoll, 2003). In the United States, one of these constraining policies is the No Child Left Behind Act (NCLB), which has mandated that states develop tests to assess yearly progress; these tests

---

In R. K. Sawyer (Ed.) (2011). *Structure and improvisation in creative teaching* (pp. 1–24). Cambridge: Cambridge University Press.

have typically had the effect of increasing the amount of structure and the number of constraints that teachers must satisfy (O'Day, 2008).

An active debate rages about how to improve schools: Should we invest in the professional expertise of our teachers, and then grant them autonomy to exercise that expertise? Or should we structure and script teachers' work in classrooms, as a way of ensuring standardization of desired curricular goals and learning outcomes?

This book provides a new voice in this debate. We accept the need for structures in the classroom; after all, research on teacher expertise shows that all good teaching involves structuring elements. Teachers are rarely allowed to do whatever they want, even in schools committed to constructivist and creative learning. The challenge facing every teacher and every  school is to find the balance of creativity and structure that will optimize student learning. Great teaching involves many structuring elements, and at the same time requires improvisational brilliance. Balancing structure and improvisation is the essence of the art of teaching. The contributors to this book are deeply concerned about the increasing constraints placed on teachers, because there is a risk that too much additional structure could interfere with the creative improvisation associated with expert teaching. The increasing use of scripted teaching methods, sometimes called *direct instruction*, is particularly disturbing, because it risks disrupting the balance associated with great teaching. Scripted instruction is opposed to constructivist, inquiry-based, and dialogic teaching methods that emphasize creativity in the classroom. Many educators are concerned that the recent emphasis on standardized testing has resulted in less creative teaching and learning.

This book proposes that we view teaching as an *improvisational* activity. Conceiving of teaching as improvisation highlights the collaborative and emergent nature of effective classroom practice, helps us understand how curriculum materials relate to classroom practice, and shows why teaching is a creative art. The best teaching is *disciplined* improvisation because it always occurs within broad structures and frameworks (Sawyer, 2004). Expert teachers use routines and activity structures more than novice teachers, but they are able to invoke and apply these routines in a creative, improvisational fashion (Berliner, 1987; Leinhardt & Greeno, 1986). Several researchers have noted that the most effective classroom interaction balances structure and script with flexibility and improvisation (Borko & Livingston, 1989; Brown & Edelson, 2001; Erickson, 1982; Mehan, 1979; Yinger, 1987). Effective teachers act as directors, orchestrating learning experiences (Park-Fuller, 1991); their students participate in a collective improvisation, guided by and along with the teacher.

The chapters in this volume each focus on one or more manifestations of the tension between structure and improvisation:

- *The teacher paradox*: Teacher expertise must weave together a large knowledge base of plans, routines, and structures, within improvised practice.
- *The learning paradox*: In effective constructivist classrooms, students are provided with scaffolds – loose structures that are carefully designed to guide the students as they improvise toward content knowledge, skills, and deeper conceptual understanding.
- *The curriculum paradox*: Good curricula and lesson plans are necessary to guide teachers and students down the most effective learning trajectory toward the desired learning outcomes. Yet, the most effective curricula are those designed to foster improvisational learning within the curricula.

Like most education scholars, the contributors to this book are committed to the use of constructivist, inquiry-based, and dialogic teaching methods. Contemporary research in the learning sciences has repeatedly shown the superiority of constructivist methods for teaching the kinds of deeper understanding needed by knowledge workers in the innovation economy (Sawyer, 2006a); constructivist methods result in deeper understanding among learners (Bereiter, 2002; Palincsar, 1998; Rogoff, 1998; Sawyer, 2004, 2006d). However, today's constructivism is not a free-wheeling, student-centered caricature; rather, learning scientists have repeatedly demonstrated that constructivist learning proceeds more effectively in the presence of *scaffolds*, loose structures that guide students (Mayer, 2004; Sawyer, 2006a). Effective constructivist learning must constantly negotiate the learning paradox.

In the most effective classrooms, all three paradoxes are balanced through improvisational processes. To address the teacher paradox, teachers constantly improvise a balance between creativity and constraint. To address the learning paradox, teachers create and adapt structures of just the right sort to scaffold students' effective learning improvisations. To address the curriculum paradox, teachers adapt textbooks and develop lesson plans that enable students to participate in classroom improvisations. In great classes, all three paradoxes are addressed through an artful dance; the direction of the class emerges from collaborative improvisation between the teacher and the students.

## THREE RESEARCH TRADITIONS

This book builds on three traditions of previous scholarship: teaching as performance, teacher expertise, and creativity in teaching.

### Teaching as Performance

Beginning in the 1980s, several educators explored the implications of the "teaching as performance" metaphor (McLaren, 1986; Pineau, 1994; Rubin, 1983, 1985; Sarason, 1999; Timpson & Tobin, 1982). These scholars noted many obvious similarities between theater and teaching. Teachers stand at the front of the classroom, "on stage," and they perform for their "audience," the students. Effective teachers master many skills that actors must also master. If a teacher is entertaining and animated, students will be more attentive. If a teacher speaks clearly and projects the voice, students are more likely to hear and understand. Effective teaching, like theater acting, involves rehearsal, scripting, timing, and stage presence.

One of the first uses of the "teaching as performance" metaphor was to emphasize the artistry of teaching (Barrell, 1991; Dawe, 1984; Eisner, 1983; Hill, 1985; Rubin, 1985). These writers argued that, like improvising stage actors, teachers are artists who operate on intuition and creativity. Barrell (1991) emphasized the improvisational elements of classroom artistry: Expert teachers "forego the insistence upon clear-cut behavioral objectives and predictable learning outcomes for the freedom to adjust and to explore new avenues with unpredictable outcomes" (p. 338).

Eisner (1979) argued that teaching is an art, in four ways. First, some teachers perform with such skill that students perceive the experience of the classroom to be aesthetic. This is quite similar to the experience of a skillful symphony orchestra, or a mesmerizing reading of a Shakespearean monologue. Second, teachers "make judgments based largely on qualities that unfold during the course of action" (p. 176). This is the improvisational element of teaching. Third, teaching should not be limited to routines; rather, teachers should also creatively respond to the unique contingencies of each classroom. Fourth, the ends that teachers achieve are often "emergent ... found in the course of interaction with students" (p. 176–177) rather than predetermined.

These writers make the important point that good teaching has an undeniably aesthetic dimension. Unfortunately, there are two problems with many of these "performance artistry" metaphors. First, in their advocacy for an aesthetic conception of teaching in opposition to an instrumental conception, they tend to emphasize what Pineau (1994) called an "instinctive, nebulous" creativity. For example, Hill (1985) argued that artistic teachers are guided by instinct and intuition as they use an "unconscious competence" (p. 184). This conception of teaching neglects the large body of structures that underlie teacher expertise, and makes teaching seem like an innate, intuitive ability that resists analysis.

Second, "performance artistry" metaphors tend to emphasize performance as a set of techniques that can enhance instructional communication. This has two unfortunate implications. First, it emphasizes the teacher's actions in isolation, as a "sage on the stage," and thus offers fewer practical insights as to what teachers should do when they are interacting with students. It is dangerously close to a view of teaching as a form of public speaking rather than a view of teaching as the scaffolding of students' learning improvisations. Thus it provides little insight into how teachers might resolve the learning paradox. Second, it leads to a conception of the teacher as a reader of scripts – highly detailed curricula developed by others. Performance is reduced to style (as in Timpson and Tobin, 1982). As Smith (1979) pointed out, "if the acting analogy were carried to its logical extreme, a teacher who took it seriously would never have to understand anything" (p. 33). Thus it provides little insight into how teachers might resolve the curriculum paradox.

This book extends the teaching-as-performance metaphor by shifting the focus to *improvisational* performance. Skillful improvisation always resides at the tension between structure and freedom. Of course, expert teachers have deep intuition and are talented performers, but their performance is rooted in structures and skills. The improvisation metaphor  emphasizes that teachers and students together are collectively generating the classroom performance; in this way, it is consistent with constructivist learning principles rather than the transmission-and-acquisition model implied by earlier performance metaphors.

## Teacher Expertise

In the 1970s and 1980s, a distinct and parallel group of researchers began to analyze the knowledge structures that underlie expert teaching. These researchers took an opposite approach from the performance artistry tradition; instead of an intuitive, inexplicable art, these researchers analyzed expert teachers to better understand exactly what they know that makes them good teachers.

Teacher expertise research emerged from the 1970s "cognitive revolution" in psychology (e.g., Chi, Glaser, & Farr, 1988; Ericsson, et al., 2006). Cognitive scientists study the internal mental structures that are responsible for observed human behavior. From the 1970s onward, cognitive scientists have been particularly interested in expert performance – initially, because they were collaborating with computer scientists who were attempting to capture expertise in artificial intelligence (AI) computer programs. Among AI researchers, these software applications were called *expert systems* – computer programs that codified and captured professional expertise.

Much of this research explicitly contrasted novices with experts (Ericsson, et al., 2006). In one classic study, novice and expert chess players were shown chess positions that had occurred in the middle of a game. Experts were much better at remembering the locations of all of the pieces. Emerging from this research, the cognitive elements of expertise were thought to be some combination of learned rules, plans, routines, conceptual frameworks, and schemas. The cognitivist roots of the teacher expertise tradition are most obvious in the widely cited article "The Cognitive Skill of Teaching" by Gaea Leinhardt and James G. Greeno (1986).

Developing the "knowledge base" of teacher expertise has been the focus of teacher expertise research, as represented by David Berliner (1986, 1987), Leinhardt and Greeno (1986), and Lee Shulman (1987). To take one example, Richard Shavelson (1986) described three types of "schemata" that characterize teacher expertise: scripts (with temporal event sequences), scenes (common classroom events; the relationships in these schemata are spatial), and propositional structures (factual knowledge). In a second example, Leinhardt and Greeno (1986) argued that expertise is based on operational plans they call "agendas," which are specific versions of their schemata. Experts' cognitive schemata are more elaborate, more complex, more interconnected, and more accessible than those of novices.

In a third example, Robert Yinger (1980) described two types of structure used in planning: *activity* and *routine*. The activity was the basic structural unit of planning; the features were "location, structure and sequence, duration, participants, acceptable student behavior, teacher's instructional moves, and content and materials" (p. 111). Routines came in four types: activity (coordinate the activity), instructional (questioning, giving instructions), management (controlling behavior not associated with an activity – e.g., transition between activities, handing out materials), executive planning (not during instruction, but during preactivity planning). Yinger further proposed that planning occurred at five different time scales: year, term, unit, week, and day (also see Clark & Yinger, 1977 and Yinger 1979).

Like cognitive science more generally, the focus on teacher expertise tended to emphasize the fixed structures – plans, routines, and scripts – that supported expert performance. In exchange, this tradition of research on teacher expertise largely downplayed teacher improvisation and decision making in the classroom. For example, Shulman's (1987) list of the teacher knowledge base did not include improvisational practice (p. 8). The focus on the fixed structures of teacher expertise was valuable, given the tendency in the broader culture to devalue the teaching profession. Shulman (1987) argued that "[t]his emphasis is justified by the resoluteness with which research and policy have so blatantly ignored those aspects of teaching in the past" (p. 13). Shulman and others presented brilliant examples of teachers demonstrating astonishing expertise.

One goal of these researchers was to demonstrate that content knowledge alone is not enough to make a good teacher. A second goal was to identify a set of skills and competencies that could be used in a national board exam for the teaching profession. Berliner (1987) noted that his research argued against granting teaching certificates on the basis of content knowledge alone, because this policy "denies that there is any sophisticated knowledge base needed for classroom teaching" (p. 77). The research of Shulman, Berliner, and others, showing that teaching depends on a knowledge base of expertise, was used to argue that teaching was not just an art based on intuition.

Yet, the structuralist and cognitivist background of this research had the unintended effect of downplaying the improvisational artistry of teaching – even though these early scholars of teaching expertise realized that fixed cognitive structures had to be implemented in practice, and that this practice would involve some sense of improvisation. Schön's (1983) concept of *reflective practice* is essentially improvisational – and his notion of what it means to be a "professional" is, essentially, the ability to improvise effectively within structures. Eisner (1979) emphasized the uncertainty of classrooms and the need for teachers to develop an "educational imagination" that would enable them to balance structure and spontaneity. Shulman (1987) noted that the "wisdom of practice" was poorly understood; he said its study should be a "major portion of the research agenda for the next decade" (p. 12).

In one of the first studies of how the structures of expertise are improvisationally applied in practice, Clark and Yinger (1977) analyzed "interactive decision making." They concluded that teachers "rarely changed their strategy from what they had planned, even when instruction was going poorly. That is, interactive decision making rarely resulted in an immediate change in the course of instruction" (p. 293). It was "more a process of fine tuning and adapting to aspects of the situation that were unpredictable in principle, such as specific student responses." They concluded that teacher improvisation was rare:

> The few findings available indicate that teacher interactive decision making occurs primarily at times when there are interruptions of the ongoing instructional process by students. The teachers studied seem to be monitoring student involvement as their primary index of smoothness of the instructional process. When interruptions of the instructional process occur, teachers occasionally consider alternatives but hardly ever implement those alternatives. That is, for various reasons, teachers tend not to change the instructional process in midstream, even when it is going poorly. (Clark & Yinger, 1977, p. 301)

At about the same time, several scholars began to analyze improvisational, opportunistic action by teachers in the moment. These studies observed quite a bit more classroom improvisation than did Clark and Yinger (1977). In studies of classroom discourse, Hugh Mehan (1979) and Frederick Erickson (1982) noted that classroom discourse was often improvisational. One of the first studies to apply these insights to teacher practice was a study of physical education teachers; it found that experienced teachers are more opportunistic than novices; and that experts planned for adaptation twice as often as the novices (Housner & Griffey, 1985). One of the first scholars to use the term "improvisation" to describe teachers' classroom practice was Yinger (1987); in this influential article, Yinger explicitly noted the parallels between classroom instruction and live jazz improvisation. Borko and Livingston (1989), building on both the teacher expertise tradition and Yinger's improvisational metaphor, presented the first explicit statement of the teacher paradox: What is the relationship between knowledge structures and the improvisational characteristics of practice? As Borko and Livingston wrote, "Expert teachers notice different aspects of classrooms than do novices, are more selective in their use of information during planning and interactive teaching, and make greater use of instructional and management routines" (1989, p. 474).

The improvisation metaphor also provides insights into what I have called the curriculum paradox. Boote (2004) wrote: "All curricula are inherently vague, requiring a teacher to interpret the intentions" (p. 2); thus there is always some teacher discretion. Boote identified three levels of teacher discretion. *Procedural professional discretion* is simply the ability to devise a coherent curriculum and teach it. At the next higher level of expertise, *substantive professional discretion* is demonstrated by a teacher's "ability to recognize that their actions are inadequate for achieving the intended results or that their intended results need modification and their ability to make appropriate changes" (p. 5) Haworth (1986) called it *critical competence*: A person who has it "creatively seizes the opportunities that come his way" (p. 46). The highest level of expertise is *innovative professional discretion* or "the ability to go beyond merely choosing among established and sanctioned curriculum options to creating new curricular-instructional practices that ameliorate the dilemmas of their domain of curriculum practice" (p. 6). At this level of expertise, teachers are creating curriculum and assessment, not merely implementing them. Boote recommended that novice teachers "should generally be expected to follow prescribed curricula until they demonstrate adequate professional discretion" (p. 8). Novice and expert teachers resolve the curriculum paradox in very different ways, and increasing expertise is reflected by a shift in how this paradox is resolved, as demonstrated by Borko and Livingston (1989).

This book extends teacher expertise research by acknowledging that both structures and improvisation are essential to good teaching. Expert teachers engage in *disciplined improvisation* – they have mastered the knowledge base of expertise identified by these scholars, and at the same time, they know how to apply this expertise in improvisational practice.

## Creative Teaching and Learning

The study of creative teaching and learning has traditionally been associated with arts educators, but many contemporary scholars have argued that creative learning should be embedded in all subject areas (e.g., Craft, Jeffrey, & Leibling, 2001; Gardner, 2007). This is not a new idea; one of the core features of the progressive education movement has always been an emphasis on student creativity throughout the curriculum. Creativity is an important component of the kindergarten movement of Pestalozzi, of the Montessori method, and of Dewey's emphasis on inquiry and experience.

One of the most influential modern scholars to study creativity in education was the late E. Paul Torrance, a psychologist who worked in the "first wave" of creativity research in the 1950s and 1960s (Sawyer, 2006b). Torrance developed an influential test to measure creative potential, known as the Torrance Tests for Creative Thinking (TTCT: Torrance, 2008). This test was based on J. P. Guilford's proposal that a key component of creativity is *divergent thinking*, the ability to generate a large number of possible solutions to open-ended problems. The Torrance test resulted in several scores. The three most important ones are *ideational fluency*, the sheer number of ideas generated; *originality*, the number of ideas generated that were not usually suggested by similar-aged students; and *flexibility*, the number of different categories that the ideas fell into. Torrance also developed several different curricular units to teach creativity, with the goal of helping students increase their scores on the TTCT, such as the Future Problem Solving Program (Torrance, Bruch, & Torrance, 1976).

In the 1990s, an important group of scholars in the United Kingdom began to study creative teaching and learning, based on the broader societal recognition that creativity is required to succeed in the modern world (see the papers collected in Craft, Jeffrey, & Leibling, 2001). First, these scholars emphasized that creativity was not limited to arts classes, but that it was important to all subjects, including mathematics and sciences. Second, these scholars argued that creativity was not limited to gifted and talented students, but that creative potential should be nurtured in all students.

These scholars studied two distinct, but related, elements of creativity in education: the creativity of teachers, or "creative teaching"; and the types of learning environments that foster creativity in students, or "teaching for creativity." These studies were contributions to both the teacher paradox and the learning paradox. Both of these were emphasized in the UK National Advisory Committee on Creative and Cultural Education report (NACCCE, 1999; Joubert, 2001). According to this report, teaching for creativity involves encouraging beliefs and attitudes, motivation and risk taking; persistence; identifying across subjects; and fostering the experiential and experimental. Creative teaching involves using imagination, fashioning processes, pursuing processes, being original, and judging value.

Cremin, Burnard, and Craft (2006) defined creativity as *possibility thinking*, which includes seven habits of mind: posing questions, play, immersion, innovation, risk taking, being imaginative, and self-determination. A report by the UK government's Qualifications and Curriculum Authority (2005) mentions six quite similar habits of mind: questioning and challenging; making connections and seeing relationships; envisaging what might be; exploring ideas, keeping options open; and reflecting critically on ideas, actions, and outcomes.

These writings are closely related to the "thinking skills" movement in the United Kingdom, and the "twenty-first-century skills" movement in the United States. Twenty-first-century skills are thought to include creativity and innovation (creative thinking, collaboration, and implementation);

critical thinking and problem solving (reasoning, systems thinking, decision making, and problem solving); and communication and collaboration (Partnership for 21st Century Skills, 2007; Trilling & Fadel, 2009).

The chapters in this book extend this research by providing concrete, specific examples of classrooms and techniques that experienced teachers use to teach creatively, and to teach for creativity.

## Extending Previous Research

This book is meant to be a contribution to all three of these existing strands of research. First, we extend the "teaching as performance" tradition by shifting the focus from conventional, scripted theater to improvisational theater. Our shift to improvisation also moves us away from the teacher as a solo performer, to a conception of teacher and students improvising together. Second, we extend the teacher expertise tradition by examining how the "knowledge base" of teaching – the repertoire of plans, routines, and scripts – is contingently used in the always-shifting demands of each class session. Third, we extend the creative teaching and learning tradition by providing specific theories and empirical examples of exactly what teachers and students do in creative classrooms.

Every teacher knows that great teaching is more than simply intuition and empathy – more than instinctive artistry. Great teaching involves a knowledge base of rules, plans, and structures that are developed over years, even decades. And every teacher likewise knows that great teaching is more than this knowledge base of rules, plans, and routines. Great teaching involves *both* the possession of a large knowledge base of expertise and a knowledge of improvisational practice – of how and when to use that knowledge. But there remains a gap in our understanding of good teaching: How do good teachers use their fixed knowledge and implement it in a given classroom situation? In other words, how do the fixed structures of expertise become realized in the everyday improvisation of a real-world classroom practice?

### IMPROVISATION AND CREATIVE TEACHING

The chapters in this book are unified by their belief that *improvisation* provides an invaluable perspective on creative teaching. Improvisation is generally defined as a performance (music, theater, or dance) in which the performers are not following a script or score, but are spontaneously creating their material as it is performed. Improvisation can be as basic as a performer's elaboration or variation of an existing framework – a song, melody, or plot outline. At the other extreme, in some forms of improvisation, the performers start without any advance framework and create the entire work on stage (Sawyer, 2003).

There is a common misconception that improvisation means anything goes; for example, that jazz musicians simply play from instinct and intuition, without conscious analysis or understanding. There are parallels between this misconception and the teacher artistry perspective I reviewed earlier. In fact, jazz requires a great deal of training, practice, and expertise – it requires many years simply to play at a novice level (Berliner, 1994). Jazz requires of the performer a deep knowledge of complex harmonic structures and a profound familiarity with the large body of *standards* – pieces that have been played by jazz bands for decades. Standards are typically based on the thirty-two-bar pop song, with four subsections of eight bars each. Usually one or two of the eight-bar sections is repeated, resulting in song forms such as AABA – a song where the first eight bars are the same as the second and fourth eight bars. A standard is outlined on a *lead sheet*, a shorthand version of the song, with only the melody and the chord changes written.

In addition to these shared understandings, most jazz performers also develop their own personal structuring elements. In private rehearsals, they develop *licks*, melodic motifs that can be inserted into a solo for a wide range of different songs. Still, the choice of when to use one of these motifs, and how to weave these fragments with completely original melodic lines, is made on the spot. In group rehearsals, jazz groups often work out ensemble parts that can be played by the entire band at the end of a solo.

Improvisation provides a valuable perspective because both staged improvisation and teaching require an artful balance between structure and creativity. In a general sense, improvisation is characteristic of any human action that is not fully scripted and determined – which is the case in most of our daily encounters. The study of human action in social context is typically associated with the discipline of sociology, and several scholars have explored the ways in which human social action is improvised (Bourdieu 1977 [1972]; de Certeau, 1984 [1980]; Erickson, 2004; Sawyer, 2001). These scholars all explore the theoretical tension between the structures that guide human action and the creativity and freedom that result in unpredictability. After all, no one ever acts with complete freedom; in everyday conversation, for example, we talk in ways that are appropriate to our context and to those people with whom we are speaking. We use idioms to communicate meaning, and we make subtle points using shared cultural references.

The authors in this volume have all studied the staged, improvisational performances of music, theater, or dance. Each chapter explores a specific form of staged improvisation – whether jazz, theater, or dance – and then applies lessons from that form to help improve creative teaching. These concrete examples help provide explicit clarity to the "teaching is improvisation" metaphor, above and beyond such truisms as "good teachers are responsive to students" or "good teachers listen to students." The chapters in this book go beyond these truisms by working through exactly how expert teachers resolve the tension between structure and improvisation.

The concrete examples of jazz, theater, and dance are used in this book to shed light on the questions left unanswered by these three previous research traditions:

- Improvisation helps us resolve *the teacher paradox*: It shows us that teaching is a form of expertise and then presents us with a new conception of what that expertise consists of, namely mastery of a toolbox, but in a manner that it can be executed in practice through improvisational creativity.
- Improvisation helps us resolve *the learning paradox*: It incorporates student improvisations as they construct their own knowledge, but guided by the teacher so that those constructions proceed in the most effective manner.
- Improvisation helps us resolve *the curriculum paradox*: It is a productive way of thinking about the relation between curriculum as planned and curriculum as enacted.

The chapters in this book, in various combinations and ways, elaborate the improvisation metaphor to foster creative teaching. Our goal is, ultimately, to develop a new theory of professional pedagogical practice. This volume is a step in that direction.

### Differences between Teaching and Staged Improvisation

The main similarity between staged improvisation and expert teaching is that both are characterized by an unavoidable tension between structure and freedom. But of course, there are many differences between staged improvisation and classroom teaching. Several of these chapters explore one or more of the following four differences; acknowledging these differences makes the improvisation metaphor more useful to practicing teachers.

(1) Staged improvisation is focused on the process and on the moment of performance; there is no product that remains after the performance is

finished. In contrast, teaching performances have a desired outcome: the student's learning. This outcome will be assessed. In contrast, staged improvisers do not have the responsibility of causing some mental state change in their audience (beyond some broad hope that the audience will be entertained). The teacher as performer has a more explicitly articulated responsibility to the students: they must learn the required material. Stage improvisers do not have this sort of responsibility.

This leads to a very different balance of structure and improvisation in classrooms than in performance genres like jazz. The balance shifts toward a greater degree of structure and a lesser degree of improvisation.

The authors in this book argue that too many classrooms are overly structured and scripted. In these classrooms, the three paradoxes are resolved by making them go away altogether – by choosing the extreme of complete structure, predictability, standardization, and regularity. Yet the research presented in this book demonstrates that when teachers become skilled at improvisational practice, their students learn more effectively.

(2) The relation between the performer and the audience is different in a classroom. In staged improvisation, the audience does not participate actively in the performance; they are relatively passive. In contrast, decades of research have shown that learning is more effective when students participate actively, and all experienced teachers involve students in some way. Sawyer (2004) has suggested that teachers conceive of their students as fellow ensemble members, in a collective improvisation, rather than as an audience for their performance.

This difference leads to what I called above *the learning paradox*: Students improvise within structures, and a key aspect of good teaching is the teacher knowing exactly what structures, and what degree of structuring, are appropriate at each moment in the classroom's learning trajectory.

The authors in this book argue for a vision of classrooms in which students participate actively, and not just in a rote manner – that students be given opportunities to improvisationally construct their own knowledge. And yet, research shows that these classroom improvisations result in more effective learning when they are carefully guided by structures provided by the teacher.

(3) Teachers occupy a position within an elaborated institution, and the structures of the classroom are often developed and then imposed by an administrative structure. In staged improv, in contrast, the structures are the collective and emergent property of the community of performers; they can optionally be adopted or rejected by performers. As Pineau (1994) pointed out, the improvisation metaphor is hard to reconcile with

institutionalized conceptions of teaching, in which teachers are viewed as semi-skilled technicians.

The authors in this book advocate a radically different conception: Teachers are skilled, creative professionals. Some institutional constraints and structures are necessary, but we argue that in too many schools, these structures are overly constraining and prevent creative teaching and learning from occurring.

(4) Students are required to attend class, whereas a theater audience has chosen to attend the performance. This results in fundamental power and authority differences. In a theater, in some sense, the performers and the audience members are peers. In improv theater, part of the reason the audience likes it is that they identify with the performers, they recognize themselves in the performance. This is less likely to happen in a classroom due to age, status, and expertise differences.

The authors in this book argue that creative learning is more likely to occur when the rigid division between teacher and student is somewhat relaxed, creating an environment where teacher and students jointly construct the improvisational flow of the classroom.

While remaining cognizant of these very real differences, an exploration of the similarities can help teachers resolve the three teaching paradoxes: the teacher paradox, the learning paradox, and the curriculum paradox. Many chapters in this book argue that knowing a bit about how improvisation works in jazz and theater could help teachers creatively foster more effective learning. Several chapters present examples from jazz or improv theater, and then identify exactly how those performers balance the tensions between structure and freedom, drawing lessons for practicing teachers.

Many of the chapters argue that teachers and students will benefit if they are taught how to participate in theater improvisations themselves. Most major U.S. cities have at least one improv acting coach, and these coaches are often experienced at working with non-professional actors as a way of helping them develop communication or teamwork skills. Thus, school districts might consider integrating improv activities in continuing professional development.

The improvisation metaphor leads to a new conception of professional expertise. It is a mastery of a corpus of knowledge – ready-made, known solutions to standard problems – but in a special way that supports improvisational practice. Creative teachers are experts at disciplined improvisation, balancing the structures of curricula and their own plans and routines, with the constant need to improvisationally apply those structures. They create improvisational learning experiences for their students by implementing scaffolds that are appropriate to both the content knowledge and to the students' current level of understanding.

In classrooms with expert teachers, students attain their learning outcomes more quickly and more thoroughly. Students gain a deeper conceptual understanding of the material and retain it longer. Their learning results in adaptive expertise (Bransford, Brown, & Cocking, 2000) – an increased ability to transfer the knowledge to new situations, thus preparing learners to engage in creative activity. In addition to an enhanced learning of content knowledge, when teachers are skilled at disciplined improvisation, students learn more than the content knowledge: They learn a broad range of thinking skills that have been widely identified to be essential in today's world.

## THE CHAPTERS

The chapters each address one or more of the three teaching paradoxes: the teacher paradox, the learning paradox, and the curriculum paradox. The chapters are grouped according to which paradox is primary, although many of the chapters are relevant to more than one of these paradoxes. The book concludes with an integrative discussion chapter by Lisa Barker and Hilda Borko.

### The Teacher Paradox

The preceding brief summary of research on teacher expertise shows that experienced teachers have a larger repertoire of structures that they use in the classrooms, yet at the same time, they are more effective improvisers. This is the *teacher paradox*: the fact that expert teachers constantly negotiate the balance between structure and improvisation.

Stacy DeZutter draws on her experience as an improvisational theater actor and director to elaborate the potential uses of improvisation in teacher education. She begins by arguing that constructivist learning requires a learning environment in which students are given opportunities to improvise. In her chapter, she conducted a content analysis of fourteen general-methods textbooks that are widely used in preservice teacher education programs. She found, first of all, that all fourteen textbooks advocate constructivist learning theory. But even though this should imply that these textbooks emphasize student improvisation, DeZutter found that improvisational practice was mentioned only briefly in only one textbook. Based on this content analysis, she concludes that these textbooks present an instructionist view of teaching expertise that seems to be in opposition to constructivist learning theory.

Pam Burnard's chapter examines an important UK government schools initiative, *Creative Partnerships*, created in 2002. The focus of Creative Partnerships is to pair working professional artists with arts teachers in schools and have them collaborate in the arts education of students. This is the UK government's flagship creative learning educational program. As of 2010, the UK government had spent £247 million and in 2009–2011, an additional £100 million was budgeted. Burnard's chapter provides evidence of how the teacher paradox is resolved in these collaborative pedagogic practices between teachers and artists working in partnership in schools. One of her findings is that teachers' pedagogical practices tend to be toward the more structured end of the spectrum, whereas their artist collaborators tend to work toward the more improvisational end.

Carrie Lobman's chapter analyzes a teacher professional development program in New York City called the Developing Teachers Fellowship Program (DTFP). DTFP is based on a Vygotskian framework that emphasizes everyday life as performance, and emphasizes *developmental learning*, or a conception of learning and development as inseparable. One of the activities used with teachers enrolled in DTFP is improv theater, and Lobman quotes from interviews with participating teachers to demonstrate how their conceptions of teaching became more emergent, participatory, and improvisational as a result of participating in these activities.

Ronald Beghetto and James Kaufman's chapter focuses on the challenge faced by teachers who value creativity but who must avoid disciplinary or curricular chaos in the classroom. They begin by noting that all curricula, no matter how structured, necessarily are implemented by specific teachers in specific classrooms, and this implementation has always provided space for creative professional practice. They consider teacher expertise as *disciplined improvisation*: creativity guided by the constraints of prior planning. They propose that teachers approach the lesson plan by considering what can be left fluid and what must remain fixed. The challenge facing all teachers is getting the balance just right.

## The Learning Paradox

Decades of research on constructivism in education have demonstrated that the most effective learning occurs when the learners' discovery and exploration are guided by scaffolds – structures put in place by the teacher. This is the *learning paradox*: the always-difficult task of identifying just the right degree and type of scaffolds, so that the learner's creative process of knowledge building is most effective.

In a 1982 paper, Frederick Erickson was the first scholar to analyze student classroom conversation as a form of improvisation. In his chapter, he presents several transcripts of student conversation to discuss four versions of the learning paradox – the difficult balance faced by teachers of using just the right degree of structures to foster maximally effective improvisational conversations among students. These examples demonstrate (1) the important role of *implicit metacommunication* – when teachers provide structure through their tone, rhythm, or wording but that is not explicitly stated; (2) the essential role of improvisation when teachers respond effectively to "teachable moments"; (3) the ways that students improvise on classroom structures to accomplish their own personal goals, but in ways that ultimately foster their learning; and (4) the ways that teachers can structure exploratory science learning that proceeds in an improvisational manner.

Two chapters analyze the use of improvisation with language learners. Jürgen Kurtz reports on his use of guided improvisation in English as a Foreign Language (EFL) classes in Germany. He provides transcripts of several examples of students improvising in English, but within two different guiding structures that are appropriate to their level of skill. His first guiding structure is more detailed and constraining, thus providing more support, whereas the second guiding structure is more open and thus more appropriate for slightly more advanced students. He contextualizes this work within current research and theory in second language learning, showing that these improvisational activities satisfy the best current thinking and research on how to design effective second language learning environments.

Anthony Perone's chapter analyzes the use of improvisational games with adult immigrant English language learners in Chicago. An improv actor himself, he begins his chapter by describing the "improv rules" that inform the activities he uses with his students. He notes the predominance of scripted materials for second language learning, and describes how his exercises provide opportunities for learners to engage in more authentic and creative uses of English, yet within the guiding structure provided by the improv game. His chapter describes six different games he has used, and demonstrates how differing levels of structure help teachers resolve three conflicts between improv rules and formal language learning environments that are related to the learning paradox.

Janice Fournier's chapter extends the improvisation metaphor to dance choreography. She describes how contemporary dance choreographers typically work collaboratively with dancers to develop new dances. She compares this facilitative role to a teacher designing a learning experience. Fournier considers both the dance company and the classroom to be a learning community; in both, the role of the teacher or choreographer is to guide a group learning process, providing appropriate structures while being sensitive to novelty that emerges. In her studies of dance choreography, she has identified three uses of improvisation: to generate ideas, to explore material and deepen understanding, and to bring the work to life in performance. By analogy, she applies these three uses to the "learning arc" that one finds in a creative, constructivist classroom.

## The Curriculum Paradox

Designed instruction always has a desired learning outcome. The term "curriculum" represents the structures that are designed to ensure that learners reach those learning outcomes – whether textbooks, lists of learning objectives, or lesson plans. Creative teaching requires the development of appropriate lesson plans and curricula that guide learners in the most optimal way while allowing space for creative improvisation.

Annette Sassi's chapter asks the question: Which learning environments are most likely to result in learning for understanding? She argues that scripted curricula – specific instructions for the teacher, word-for-word prompts, and with pedagogical decisions specified – often are more effective at fostering learning for understanding. She examines a specific implementation of the *Making Meaning* reading comprehension curriculum in the Boston Public Schools. Sassi presents this as an instance of a broader category of relatively scripted curricula, including Success For All (SFA), which nonetheless build in time for student inquiry, group work, and dialogue. Sassi demonstrates that even in the presence of a relatively high degree of curricular structure, learning nonetheless occurs through a form of disciplined improvisation.

Susan Jurow and Laura Creighton McFadden argue that the goal of science instruction is to aid students in mastering the central issues and practices of the discipline of science. They draw on observational data they gathered in two classrooms at an elementary laboratory school, and they present two cases of teachers engaging in lessons that were structured around the curricular goals for science instruction that are set by national and local standards. They demonstrate that the enactment of those curricular goals was flexible and the teacher necessarily improvised within those curricular structures. The paradox faced by science teachers is one of allowing children opportunities to creatively articulate and explore their own emerging ideas, while providing the guiding structures that will lead those students into the appropriate disciplinary practices and understandings of science.

Lyndon Martin and Jo Towers's chapter argues for reconceptualizing the goal of mathematics instruction as a form of mathematical understanding that is both improvisational and collective. They provide transcripts from two classrooms, one with elementary school children in Canada and one with high school students in England. Both transcripts demonstrate that the students' unfolding and emergent mathematical understanding occurs through collective improvisation. Their chapter concludes with recommendations for how teachers can provide the appropriate structures to guide learners' improvisations.

### CONCLUSION

In today's knowledge societies, schools need to teach content knowledge in a way that prepares students to use that knowledge creatively; they also need to impart thinking skills, twenty-first-century skills, to students. Teaching in this way requires disciplined improvisation. And yet, schools are complex organizations with many structures and constraints; these structures serve important functions and cannot simply be abandoned. The tension between structure and improvisation cannot be avoided – it is fundamental to the institution of schooling in the knowledge age.

Effective creative learning involves teachers and students improvising together, collaboratively, within the structures provided by the curriculum and the teachers. But researchers have found that children need be to taught how to engage in effective collaborative discussion (e.g., Azmitia, 1996). Here is a place where arts education can contribute – because arts educators have long emphasized the importance of collaboration and creativity. The performing arts are fundamentally ensemble art forms. Music educators are increasingly realizing the importance of using musical collaboration in their classes (Sawyer, 2006c). Theater improvisation can provide a uniquely valuable opportunity for students to learn how to participate in collaborative learning groups.

Many schools have already transformed their curricula to emphasize creative teaching. However, these transformations have often been occurring in the wealthiest countries and the wealthiest school districts, potentially leading to a knowledge society that is run by children of privilege. In many large U.S. urban school districts, schools have taken an opposite tack – toward scripted curricula that are teacher-proofed, preventing improvisation altogether. This removes the need for teachers to balance structure and improvisation – but at the cost of also removing the improvised, creative, collaborative learning that, learning sciences researchers have demonstrated, results in more effective learning for today's knowledge society. Imagine the immense benefits if we unlocked the creative potential of the world's population by systematically implementing creative teaching and learning throughout all schools.

## REFERENCES

Azmitia, M. (1996). Peer interactive minds: Developmental, theoretical, and methodological issues. In P. B. Baltes & U. M. Staudinger (Eds.), *Interactive Minds: Life-span Perspectives on the Social Foundation of Cognition* (pp. 133–162). New York: Cambridge.

Barrell, B. (1991). Classroom artistry. *The Educational Forum, 55,* 333–342.

Bereiter, C. (2002). *Education and mind in the knowledge age.* Mahwah, NJ: Erlbaum.

Berliner, D. C. (1986). In pursuit of the expert pedagogue. *Educational Researcher, 15*(7), 5–13.

(1987). Ways of thinking about students and classrooms by more and less experienced teachers. In J. Calderhead (Ed.), *Exploring Teachers' Thinking* (pp. 60–83). London: Cassell Education Limited.

Berliner, D. C. & Tikunoff, W. J. (1976). The California beginning teacher study. *Journal of Teacher Education, 27*(1), 24–30.

Berliner, P. (1994). *Thinking in jazz: The infinite art of improvisation.* Chicago: University of Chicago Press.

Boote, D. N. (2004). *Teachers' professional discretion and the curricula.* Paper presented at the American Educational Research Association. Retrieved.

Borko, H. & Livingston, C. (1989). Cognition and improvisation: Differences in mathematics instruction by expert and novice teachers. *American Educational Research Journal, 26*(4), 473–498.

Bourdieu, P. (1972/1977). *Outline of a theory of practice.* New York: Press Syndicate of the University of Cambridge. Originally published as *Esquisse d'une théorie de la pratique* (Genève: Droz, 1972).

Bransford, J. D., Brown, A. L., & Cocking, R. R. (Eds.). (2000). *How people learn: Brain, mind, experience, and school.* Washington, DC: National Academy Press.

Brown, M. & Edelson, D. C. (2001). *Teaching by design: Curriculum design as a lens on instructional practice.* Paper presented at the Annual Meeting of the American Educational Research Association, April, Seattle, WA.

Chi, M. T. H., Glaser, R., & Farr, M. J. (1988). *The nature of expertise.* Hillsdale, NJ: Erlbaum.

Clark, C. M. & Yinger, R. J. (1977). Research on teacher thinking. *Curriculum Inquiry, 7*(4), 279–304.

Cochrane-Smith, M. & Lytle, S. L. (1999). The teacher research movement: A decade later. *Educational Researcher, 28*(7), 15–25.

Craft, A., Jeffrey, B., & Leibling, M. (Eds.). (2001). *Creativity in education.* London: Continuum.

Cremin, T., Burnard, P., & Craft, A. (2006). Pedagogy and possibility thinking in the early years. *Thinking Skills and Creativity, 1,* 108–119.

Darling-Hammond, L. (1997). *The right to learn: A blueprint for creating schools that work.* San Francisco, CA: Jossey-Bass.

Dawe, H. A. (1984). Teaching: A performing art. *Phi Delta Kappan,* 548–552.

de Certeau, M. (1984). *The practice of everyday life.* Berkeley, CA: University of California Press. (Original work published 1980).

Eisner, E. W. (1979). *The educational imagination: On the design and evaluation of school programs.* New York: Macmillan.

   (1983). The art and craft of teaching. *Educational Leadership, 40*(4), 4–13.

Erickson, F. (1982). Classroom discourse as improvisation: Relationships between academic task structure and social participation structure in lessons. In L. C. Wilkinson (Ed.), *Communicating in the Classroom* (pp. 153–181). New York: Academic Press.

   (2004). *Talk and social theory: Ecologies of speaking and listening in everyday life.* Cambridge: Polity Press.

Ericsson, K. A., Charness, N., Feltovich, P. J., & Hoffman, R. R. (Eds.). (2006). *The Cambridge handbook of expertise and expert performance.* New York: Cambridge University Press.

Gardner, H. (2007). *Five minds for the future.* Boston, MA: Harvard Business School Press.

Haworth, L. (1986). *Autonomy: An essay in philosophical psychology and ethics.* New Haven, CT: Yale University Press.

Hill, J. C. (1985). The teacher as artist: A case for peripheral supervision. *The Educational Forum, 49*(2), 183–187.

Housner, L. D. & Griffey, D. C. (1985). Teacher cognition: Differences in planning and interactive decision making between experienced and inexperienced teachers. *Research Quarterly for Exercise and Sport, 56*(1), 45–53.

Ingersoll, R. M. (2003). *Who controls teachers' work? Power and accountability in America's schools.* Cambridge, MA: Harvard University Press.

Joubert, M. M. (2001). The art of creative teaching: NACCCE and beyond. In A. Craft, B. Jeffrey & M. Leibling (Eds.), *Creativity in Education* (pp. 17–34). London: Continuum.

Leinhardt, G. & Greeno, J. G. (1986). The cognitive skill of teaching. *Journal of Educational Psychology, 78*(2), 75–95.

Mayer, R. E. (2004). Should there be a three-strikes rule against pure discovery learning? The case for guided methods of instruction. *American Psychologist, 59*(1), 14–19.

McLaren, P. (1986). *Schooling as a ritual performance: Towards a political economy of educational symbols and gestures.* London: Routledge & Kegan Paul.

Mehan, H. (1979). *Learning lessons.* Cambridge, MA: Harvard.

National Advisory Committee on Creative and Cultural Education (NACCCE) (1999). *All our futures: Creativity, culture and education.* London: DFEE.

O'Day, J. (2008). Standards-based reform: Promises, pitfalls, and potential lessons from the U.S. In W. Böttcher, W. Bos, H. Döbert & H. G. n. Holtappels (Eds.), *Bidungsmonitoring und Bildungscontrolling in nationaler und internationaler Perspektive* (pp. 107–127). Münster, Germany: Waxmann.

Olson, D. R. (2003). *Psychological theory and educational reform.* New York: Cambridge University Press.

Palincsar, A. S. (1998). Social constructivist perspectives on teaching and learning. In J. T. Spence, J. M. Darley & D. J. Foss (Eds.), *Annual Review of Psychology* (Vol. 49, pp. 345–375). Palo Alto, CA: Annual Reviews.

Park-Fuller, L. (1991). *Learning to stage a learning experience: The teacher as director.* Paper presented at the National Convention of the Speech Communication Association, November, Atlanta, GA.

Partnership for 21st Century Skills. (2007). *The intellectual and policy foundations of the 21st century skills framework.* Tucson, AZ: Partnership for 21st Century Skills.

Pineau, E. L. (1994). Teaching is performance: Reconceptualizing a problematic metaphor. *American Educational Research Journal, 31*(1), 3–25.

Qualifications and Curriculum Authority (QCA) (2005). *Creativity: Find it, promote, promoting pupils' creative thinking and behaviour across the curriculum at key stages 1 and 2, practical materials for schools.* London: Qualifications and Curriculum Authority.

Rogoff, B. (1998). Cognition as a collaborative process. In D. Kuhn & R. S. Siegler (Eds.), *Handbook of Child Psychology, 5th edition, Volume 2: Cognition, Perception, and Language* (pp. 679–744). New York: Wiley.

Rubin, L. J. (1983). Artistry in teaching. *Educational Leadership, 40*(4), 44–49.

(1985). *Artistry in teaching.* New York: Random House.

Sarason, S. B. (1999). *Teaching as a performing art.* New York: Teachers College Press.

Sawyer, R. K. (2001). *Creating conversations: Improvisation in everyday discourse.* Cresskill, NJ: Hampton Press.

(2003). *Improvised dialogues: Emergence and creativity in conversation.* Westport, CT: Greenwood.

(2004). Creative teaching: Collaborative discussion as disciplined improvisation. *Educational Researcher, 33*(2), 12–20.

(Ed.). (2006a). *Cambridge handbook of the learning sciences.* New York: Cambridge University Press.

(2006b). *Explaining creativity: The science of human innovation.* New York: Oxford.

(2006c). Group creativity: Musical performance and collaboration. *Psychology of Music, 34*(2), 148–165.

(2006d). The new science of learning. In R. K. Sawyer (Ed.), *Cambridge Handbook of the Learning Sciences* (pp. 1–16). New York: Cambridge.

Schön, D. (1983). *The reflective practitioner: How professionals think in action.* New York: Basic Books.

Shavelson, R. J. (1986). *Interactive decision making: Some thoughts on teacher cognition.* Paper presented at the Invited address, I Congreso Internacional, "Pensamientos de los Profesores y Toma de Decisiones." Retrieved.

Shulman, L. S. (1987). Knowledge and teaching: Foundations of the new reform. *Harvard Educational Review, 57*(1), 1–22.

Smith, R. A. (1979). Is teaching really a performing art? *Contemporary Education, 51*(1), 31–35.

Timpson, W. M. & Tobin, D. N. (1982). *Teaching as performing: A guide to energizing your public presentation.* Englewood Cliffs, NJ: Prentice-Hall.

Torrance, E. P. (2008). *The Torrance tests of creative thinking: Norms-technical manual.* Bensenville, IL: Scholastic Testing Service.

Torrance, E. P., Bruch, C. B., & Torrance, J. P. (1976). Interscholastic futuristic creative problem solving. *Journal of Creative Behavior, 10*, 117–125.

Trilling, B. & Fadel, C. (2009). *21st century skills: Learning for life in our times.* San Francisco, CA: Jossey-Bass.

Yinger, R. J. (1979). Routines in teacher planning. *Theory into Practice, 18*(3), 163–169.

  (1980). A study of teacher planning. *The Elementary School Journal, 80*(3), 107–127.

  (1987). *By the seat of your pants: An inquiry into improvisation and teaching.* Paper presented at the Annual Meeting of the American Educational Research Association, April, Washington, DC.

# PART 1

# THE TEACHER PARADOX

## 2

## Professional Improvisation and Teacher Education: Opening the Conversation

STACY DEZUTTER

In this chapter, I argue that teacher educators should help their students understand that teaching is inherently improvisational. I propose this as part of a larger shift that, I believe, needs to occur in teaching: We need to redefine our profession as an improvisational one. By this I mean that we should liken teaching to other explicitly improvisational professions such as unscripted theater and jazz music, where conscious efforts are made to develop improvisational expertise, and where a body of knowledge has been built up for doing so. This chapter uses the improvisation metaphor to extend the tradition of research on teacher expertise (summarized in Sawyer's introduction) that has found that expert teachers have mastered a large repertoire of scripts, plans, and routines, while at the same time becoming experts at appropriate and disciplined improvisation in practice. This reconceptualization of teacher expertise will be an important move toward supporting the kinds of teaching that are needed to meet the demands of our society in the twenty-first century.

The assertion that good teaching involves improvisation is a statement of the obvious to any experienced classroom teacher. But improvisation has rarely been an explicit part of conversations about teaching, and because we do not talk much about our improvisation, we limit our ability as a profession to advance our knowledge and capacity for improvising well. Unlike other improvisational professions, we do not have a well-elaborated, shared notion of what constitutes excellent improvisation, nor do we know much about how teachers learn to improvise or what teacher educators can do to facilitate that learning. Yet, as I explain later in the chapter, many scholars

In R. K. Sawyer (Ed.) (2011). *Structure and improvisation in creative teaching* (pp. 27–50). Cambridge: Cambridge University Press.

believe that improvisation will be ever more important to teaching in our increasingly knowledge-based society.

This chapter focuses on teacher education because these programs are important sites for conversations about teaching; this is where we can pass on to our next generation of teachers ideas about what we hope teaching will be. I identify two barriers to the reconceptualization of teaching as disciplined improvisation. First, I show that few teacher educators have thought systematically about the role of improvisation in teaching or have adopted it as a learning goal for their students. Second, I argue that teacher education students do not naturally come to the view that teaching should be improvisational, due to certain deeply held, culturally based beliefs about teaching that I identify in this chapter. To overcome these two barriers, I describe how familiar methods in teacher education can be easily adapted for the purpose of helping future teachers understand the improvisational nature of teaching.

I begin the chapter by explaining the importance of an improvisational view of teaching to the educational needs of the twenty-first century. I then discuss what we can expect to gain by viewing teaching as not just improvisational, but as professionally improvisational. Next, I examine how improvisation currently figures in conversations within teacher education, as evidenced by a content analysis of methods textbooks; this content analysis helps us understand why the improvisational dimension of teaching may be less obvious to pre-service teachers than it is to those with experience in the classroom. In the final section of the chapter, I propose strategies that teacher educators can use to help their students think productively and professionally about the improvisation that teachers do. Throughout the chapter, I operate from a view of teaching derived from constructivist learning theory, in which teaching must be improvisational – because to teach effectively, teachers must improvisationally scaffold evolving student thinking.

This chapter speaks to one of the primary questions explored in this volume: What are the implications of improvisation for our understanding of teacher expertise? I join with other authors in the volume in arguing for a new conception of teacher expertise that includes expertise in improvisation. However, I focus on teacher expertise as seen not through the eyes of scholars but through the eyes of pre-service teachers. I examine the tension between teaching viewed as a form of professional improvisation and the planning-centric view of teaching that teacher education students often bring to their programs, and that those programs implicitly reinforce. I address this tension by presenting strategies for moving pre-service teachers away from a view of teaching as desirably scripted toward a view of teaching as desirably improvisational.

In addition, the chapter touches on a second question explored in this volume: What is the relationship between teaching and other forms of professional improvisation? Like many authors, I use the improvisational metaphor to analyze teacher expertise. As Sawyer points out (2004, this volume), this metaphor has limits, because there are important ways in which the aims and circumstances of teaching differ from those of artistic performance. In this chapter, my assertion is that the key feature that teaching *should* share with jazz music and theatrical improvisation, although it currently does not, is the availability of an explicitly held and deliberately taught body of knowledge about how to successfully improvise in order to accomplish the intended aims of the profession. This is the teaching paradox: the always-present balance between knowledge structures and improvisational practice. It is my hope that this chapter and this volume will serve as catalysts for the development of explicit professional knowledge for improvisational teaching.

## IMPROVISATIONAL TEACHING AND THE KNOWLEDGE SOCIETY

Beginning in the 1970s, scholars began to refer to the United States as a "knowledge society" (Bereiter, 2002; Hargreaves, 2003; Sawyer, 2006a) because, more and more, our economy, culture, and daily lives turn on our ability to generate and manage new knowledge. Education scholars writing about the knowledge society note that many of our current schooling practices emerged in response to the needs of the industrial economy of the late nineteenth and early twentieth centuries, when the emphasis was on acquisition of text-based knowledge and rote procedures (Bransford, Brown, & Cocking, 2003; Rogoff, et al. 2003; Sawyer, 2006a). The schooling needs of the knowledge society, however, are different from those of an industrial society. To prepare our young people to participate in the knowledge society, we need to develop more than just their factual knowledge base. For today's young people, the ability to think critically and flexibly and to develop new ways of solving problems will prove far more important than the ability to algorithmically apply learned procedures or recall information. Successful critical thinking, along with the increasingly important ability to think creatively and to innovate, depends on deep conceptual knowledge that goes beyond rote memorization or basic comprehension of facts (Bereiter, 2002; Bransford, Brown, & Cocking, 2003; Hargreaves, 2003; Sawyer, 2006a). Today's school graduates will also need the ability to collaborate productively, as work teams and complex collaborative enterprises become fixtures of knowledge-oriented industries (Sawyer, 2006a). To meet the needs of the knowledge society, then, instructional time in schools should not be focused on transmitting information to students, but rather on creating opportunities for students to generate – for themselves but with teacher guidance – increasingly sophisticated ways of thinking (Bransford, Brown, & Cocking, 2003; Hargreaves, 2003; Sawyer, 2004, 2006a). In addition, students need to have many experiences involving collaborative work. In these respects, schooling for the knowledge society rests firmly on a constructivist vision of teaching.

In recent decades, scholars who study learning have reached a consensus about the robustness of constructivist theory for understanding how people learn, particularly how people learn deep conceptual knowledge (Bransford, Brown, & Cocking, 2003; Sawyer, 2006b; Siegler, 1998). Constructivist learning theory views learning as a process in which individuals construct new knowledge by reorganizing their existing knowledge in light of experiences that challenge their present understandings. Whereas constructivism is a descriptive theory of the learning process, and therefore makes no prescriptions for teaching, there is a wealth of scholarship that considers how we might leverage a constructivist understanding of learning in order to optimize the teaching process. Specific recommendations vary across content areas, but there are some general features that have emerged as hallmarks of constructivist-based teaching (Richardson, 2003; Windschitl, 2002). To begin, the core idea behind constructivist-inspired teaching is that students should be placed in situations that challenge their prior conceptions and press them to develop more sophisticated ones. The teacher's role is to design and facilitate situations and instructional activities that will trigger this process, and to revise those activities as needed to move students toward more successful ways of thinking. To do this successfully, teachers need lots of opportunities to find out what and how students are thinking, and this in turn means that instructional time should involve a great deal of teacher-student interaction. Constructivist-based teaching also includes an emphasis on group work, a commitment that stems both from the Piagetian observation that students will stimulate each other's learning, and the Vygotskian concern with involving students in a process of collaborative meaning making (Windschitl, 2002). In addition, constructivist-based teaching emphasizes that teachers should support students to take charge of their own learning by developing students' metacognitive and evaluative abilities.

Improvisation is implicated in constructivist-based teaching in a number of ways. Interactive teaching methods make lessons inherently unpredictable because it is not possible to precisely determine in advance what students' contributions to lessons will be. This will depend on how they connect the new aspects of the lesson to their prior knowledge. In addition, when students are given opportunities to interact with each other, it is not possible to predict how they will respond to each other's contributions or what thinking will emerge as a product of the interactions of the group. Teaching in a constructivist classroom, then, must be improvisationally responsive to students' evolving understandings. Teachers must make instructional decisions on the fly, based on careful observation and diagnosis of student thinking.

To clarify the role of improvisation in constructivist-based teaching, consider the "mathematics teaching cycle" articulated by Simon (1995). Although Simon observed this teaching cycle in the context of a mathematics classroom, the basic features of the teaching process he describes would hold for constructivist-based teaching in other disciplines. The teaching cycle begins with the teacher's formulation of a "hypothetical learning trajectory" – hypothetical because the teacher cannot know in advance what students' actual learning trajectory will be. Based on this hypothesis, the teacher selects learning goals for the lesson and chooses activities designed to accomplish these goals. Then, as the teacher interacts with and observes students during the lesson, two things happen simultaneously and continuously. The teacher and students, together through their dialogue, "collectively constitute an experience" of the mathematical concepts at hand (Simon, 1995, p. 137). At the same time, the teacher observes what is happening in the interactions and assesses student thinking. Based on these assessments, she modifies her hypothetical learning trajectory, which in turn requires modification of the immediate learning goals and activities. Thus, the teaching cycle hinges on the teacher's ability to improvise: The teacher must respond to evolving student thinking, which requires constant in-the-moment decision making and the flexibility to teach without rigid adherence to a predetermined plan.

In Simon's model, students as well as teachers are improvising. To develop new, more sophisticated ways of thinking, students need opportunities to encounter the limitations of their existing understandings, to actively work with unfamiliar ideas, and to generate and explore new possibilities for their own thought. Learning is an inherently creative act, defined by the learner's improvisational construction of new understandings (Sawyer, 2003). The teacher's role in this process is to establish and maintain conditions in the classroom that allow students to engage in the most robust intellectual improvisation possible. This is not just a matter of providing activities in which students can improvise new understandings, but also of establishing certain social and intellectual norms in the classroom. For example, students should feel safe and supported to take intellectual risks and make mistakes (Lobman & Lindquist, 2007).

Sawyer (2004) emphasizes that improvisational teaching is valuable because it allows for *co-construction* of knowledge. Many constructivist-based approaches to teaching have been influenced by insights from socio-cultural psychologists who emphasize that learning is a social process, dependent on conceptual interaction between the learner and others (who may also be learners or may be in the role of a teacher; Tudge & Rogoff, 1989). On this view, the aim of teaching should not be simply for individual students to do individual thinking, but rather for students to engage in conceptual interchange with their peers and their teacher. Through collaborative dialogue, students work collectively toward more robust understandings. The flow of the lesson needs to be collaboratively determined, perhaps guided in strategic ways by the teacher, but at the same time necessarily emergent from the interactive give-and-take between teacher and students and between students and each other. It is important for teachers to think of teaching as improvisational so that they do not attempt to control too tightly the flow of the lesson; this would circumvent the co-construction process (Sawyer, 2004).

Teaching improvisationally emphasizes knowledge generation rather than knowledge acquisition. For example, Kelley, Brown, and Crawford (2000) argue that teaching improvisationally is crucial in science education because students need to experience science as a process rather than as a product. Improvisational teaching methods such as inquiry-based science advance a view of science as interactionally accomplished, resulting from the ongoing, collaborative activity of scientists, rather than the view of science that has traditionally been offered in science classrooms, in which science is approached as a received set of static facts (Kelly, Brown, & Crawford, 2000). This same principle holds for other subjects as well. In recent decades, education scholars have emphasized the importance to contemporary schooling of helping students understand that subjects such as mathematics and history are dynamic products of human knowledge-generating processes (Bransford, Brown, & Cocking, 2003; Lobman & Lundquist, 2007). Teaching such subjects using open-ended, improvisational methods such as problem-based learning can help students become more aware of the processes by which disciplinary knowledge is generated, and begin to see themselves as participants in these processes (Scardamalia & Bereiter, 2006).

In descriptions of constructivist-based teaching, the themes of teacher flexibility and responsiveness appear frequently. In fact, it is far more common to see the improvisational elements of teaching discussed in these terms than to see teaching linked to the word "improvisation." There are a number of reasons, though, why it is important for us to think about improvisational teaching explicitly as improvisation rather than using more common terms like "flexibility" and "responsiveness". First, as Sawyer (2004) points out, referring to teaching as improvisation allows us to draw direct contrast with scripted instruction – an approach that is problematic because of its focus on knowledge acquisition without sufficient attention to knowledge generation, and because scripted instruction does not allow teaching to emerge from the intellectual activities of students. Second, considering teaching in terms of improvisation can help teachers think not only about their own responsiveness and flexibility, but also about generating successful student improvisation and effective collaboration between teachers and students. Third, thinking of teaching as improvisation may be more productive within teacher education than simply asserting that teachers need to be flexible and responsive. Telling someone to be responsive is not very useful; professional improvisation is a valuable model because improvisers in jazz and theater are taught exactly *how* to be flexible and responsive. Fourth, applying the concept of improvisation to teaching helps us see teachers as creative, knowledgeable, and autonomous professionals (Sawyer, 2004) rather than as technicians whose work mainly involves implementing procedures prepared by others – a view that has plagued the profession for over a century (Rogoff et al., 2003).

## TEACHING IMPROVISATION AS PROFESSIONAL IMPROVISATION

For the previously outlined reasons, it is important that we begin to attend explicitly to the improvisational nature of teaching. Simply becoming aware that teaching is improvisational is not enough, however. When seen from the perspective of constructivist learning theory and the educational demands of the knowledge society, improvisation is not something that is incidental in teaching; it is central, and therefore we need to focus our efforts on doing it expertly. We need to think of ourselves as professional, rather than incidental, improvisers.

Consider what might be gained for the teaching profession if we begin to think of ourselves as professional improvisers. To begin, seeing ourselves as professional improvisers creates an imperative to take our improvisation seriously, to attend to our successes and failures, and to strategize about how to improvise better. Further, viewing teaching as an improvisational profession will lead to the development of a body of professional knowledge to support our improvisation. Established improvisation communities such as jazz music and unscripted acting have well-elaborated, shared notions of what constitutes successful improvisation, from which are derived clear learning goals for newcomers and accompanying techniques for helping learners accomplish those goals.

For example, in the theatrical improv world (which is where my background lies) "good improv" is far more than simply "winging" a performance without using a script. Improv actors have a detailed set of criteria for evaluating the success of a performance. Among them are:

- The performance should be fully collaborative, with no one person "driving" the narrative. Players should not ignore or contradict each other's contributions to the scene, which is called "blocking" or "denial."
- The "platform," or narrative elements such as setting, character, and conflict, should become clearly defined as the performance progresses, and scenes should be steadily "advanced," meaning that new information and events should be added with each turn of dialogue.
- Although most improv is meant to be funny, the humor should not derive from jokes and one-liners but from the reactions of well-developed characters to well-developed situations.
- No matter how outrageous things may get, scenes should still be "honest" or "truthful," which means that audiences should be able to relate to something about the situation and/or the characters.

As this list suggests, alongside an elaborated vision of what constitutes successful improv comes a vocabulary that provides a shorthand for talking about the components of that success (and for talking about failures). These things then translate into learning goals for those who are new to the profession. For example, improv actors learn the rule of "yes, and," which says that with each turn of dialogue, the performer should accept what has been established in the previous turn and add something to it. The rule of "yes, and" helps improv actors work collaboratively to advance a scene and avoid behaviors that are problematic, such as denial. The improv community has several of these "rules of improv," and all new performers learn to follow them. These guidelines reflect the accumulated wisdom of the community about what works to make a satisfying experience for the audience. And because the guidelines are teachable, they prevent newcomers from having to create from scratch the strategies and skills needed for success.

No one expects novice actors to be good at improv right away. It takes time, practice and – most especially – training to acquire the professional knowledge that expert improv performers rely on. Over its sixty-year history, the improv community has developed a wealth of methods for teaching improv acting, and the great improv teachers (such as Paul Sills and Del Close) are venerated as much, if not more, than the great performers. Methods books for teaching improv abound (e.g., Spolin, 1983; Johnstone, 1987), and most improv teachers draw from a widely shared repertoire of exercises and strategies. These exercises encode the pedagogical knowledge of the improv community and make it easier for improv teachers to advance their students' learning. (Similar types of knowledge can be found in the jazz community; see Berliner, 1994).

We need a similar body of knowledge in the teaching profession, including a well-elaborated vision of good improvisational teaching, a shared vocabulary, learning goals for new teachers, and accompanying techniques for developing improvisational ability. One way to make progress toward these ends is to mine the wisdom of other improvisational communities. Several scholars have already begun work of this type. Donmoyer (1983) used Viola Spolin's classic manual on theatrical improvisation to analyze a successful example of problem-based teaching. For example, Donmoyer looks at the class's "point of concentration" (Spolin, 1983) to understand how the various problem-based activities the teacher had devised serve as overlapping opportunities for students, allowing them to strengthen a focused set of cognitive skills through intellectual improvisation. Donmoyer's work demonstrates how useful it might be to have a repertoire of concepts relating to improvisation through which to examine teaching activities. Sawyer (2004) views teaching as "disciplined improvisation," noting that theatrical improvisation is not simply "anything goes" but rather involves a strategic balancing of structure and open-endedness. Improv actors use games and other frameworks as scaffolds for successful improvisational performances. Such structures impose parameters within which the improvisation occurs, and this serves to cut down to a manageable range the amount of improvisation necessary to produce a coherent performance. Sawyer suggests that teachers need to design classroom activities with a similar idea in mind. Activities need to allow students intellectual space to construct their own knowledge while at the same time scaffolding the construction process. Sawyer notes that an observation derived from theatrical improvisation – that improvisation involves discipline as well as freedom – helps us move beyond simply viewing classrooms in terms of whether they are improvisational or not. We can instead ask more sophisticated questions such as "What sorts of guiding structures are appropriate in what kinds of settings and subjects?" and "How can teachers learn to improvise effectively within structures?" including those imposed by a set curriculum (Sawyer, 2004, p. 16). Sawyer

(2004) also notes that it will be helpful to train teachers in some of the techniques used by theatrical improvisers. There are a few such efforts currently underway. The legendary Second City theatre in Chicago offers a series of workshops for teachers on "improvisation for creative pedagogy" (http://www.secondcity.com/). The Developing Teachers Fellowship Program (DTFP) at the Eastside Institute in New York City teaches improvisational skills that educators can incorporate into their teaching, as well as improv games that can be used as learning activities in the classroom (Lobman, this volume; also see Lobman, 2007; Lobman & Lundquist, 2007). The DTFP has been shown to help teachers become more collaborative with their students and become skilled "environment builders" – a concept derived from an analogy between theatrical improvisation and the Vygostkian notion of a "zone of proximal development" (Lobman, 2007).

The work of Sawyer, Donmeyer, and Lobman demonstrates the value in attending to the knowledge for improvisation found in the theater community. (There is also some interesting work using insights from dance improvisation; see Fournier, this volume). However, drawing wisdom from other improvisational professions should not be our only strategy. As Sawyer (2004) notes, the demands of teaching in a K-12 school differ significantly from the demands of creating a performance in the arts. The stakes are much higher in schooling: Failure to improvise well (or to do it at all) will have serious consequences for our children's learning. If we are to advance the ability of the teaching profession to improvise, we will need to develop a vision, a vocabulary, and pedagogical techniques that are specific to teaching. Indeed, that is where much of the current scholarship on teaching-as-improvisation will likely lead. At the same time, though, we need to engage in a parallel effort that will establish an audience for such scholarship, and extend the conversation about improvisation to others besides education scholars. We need to take steps to help teachers understand why such scholarship matters, why it is important to understand teaching as improvisational, and why we should strive to improvise well.

## IMPROVISATIONAL TEACHING IN TEACHER EDUCATION: AN ASSESSMENT OF THE MESSAGE

To get a sense of how improvisation figures into conversations in teacher education, I examined numerous teacher education textbooks. Textbooks offer a reasonable proxy for the topics that are included in teacher education classes because to be adopted, a textbook must present the ideas and concepts that teacher educators deem important. I analyzed fourteen general-methods texts (see Table 2.1) to determine how each text dealt with the issue of teacher improvisation. Texts were selected by reviewing the online catalogs of the major publishers of education textbooks for use in the United States (Cengage, Houghton Mifflin, McGraw Hill, Pearson/ Allyn& Bacon, Pearson/Merrill Prentice-Hall, and Sage). All general-methods texts (texts not focused on a particular grade level or content area) were included, except for one text from Cengage that could not be acquired at the time of the study. Texts devoted only to a single aspect of teaching, such as classroom management, were not included.

The textbooks I examined treat constructivism in a variety of ways. Several (e.g., Jacobsen, Eggen, & Kauchak, 2009; Kauchak & Eggen, 2006; Ornstein & Lasley, 2004) make direct reference to constructivist learning theory early in the text and use this to inform discussions throughout the book. Others mention constructivism only long enough to link it to other terms or ideas that are used more frequently. For example, Eby, Herrell, & Jordan (2006) link constructivism to reflective action, the central theme of their text, noting that constructivism involves customizing teaching to each student's cognitive processes, which is one of the aims of reflective action as they define it. Still others (e.g., Lang & Evans, 2006) describe constructivism as a collection of teaching strategies rather than a theory of human learning that would inform all teaching situations (see Davis & Sumara, 2003 for discussion on this common misinterpretation of constructivism). Yet even in texts that do not name constructivism as a guiding theory of learning, there is a thorough commitment to many of the recommendations that arise from constructivist research, such as teaching in ways that require students to be intellectually active, linking new content to students' prior experiences, and creating opportunities for social interaction. It would be reasonable, then, to expect these texts to deal with teacher improvisation as a necessary feature of teaching that accomplishes such aims.

Surprisingly, only one text, Ornstein and Lasley (2004), mentions the word "improvisation" in reference to the act of teaching. In a discussion of differences between expert and novice teachers, in which they cite Borko and Livingston (1989, see below), Ornstein and Lasley explain,

> Experts engage in a good deal of intuitive and improvisational teaching. They begin with a simple plan or outline and fill in the details as the teaching-learning process unfolds. Novices spend much more time planning, stay glued to the content, and are less inclined to deviate or respond to students' needs or interests while the lesson unfolds. (2004, p. 80)

TABLE 2.1: *General-methods textbooks used in content analysis*

|   | Author(s) | Year | Title | Publisher |
|---|-----------|------|-------|-----------|
| 1 | Arends | 2009 | *Learning to teach* | McGraw Hill |
| 2 | Borich | 2007 | *Effective teaching methods: Research-based practice (6th ed.)* | Pearson Merrill/ Prentice Hall |
| 3 | Burden Byrd | 2007 | *Methods for effective teaching: Promoting K-12 student understanding (4th ed.)* | Pearson/ Allyn and Bacon |
| 4 | Cruickshank Jenkins Metcalf | 2009 | *The act of teaching (5th ed.)* | McGraw Hill |
| 5 | Eby Herrell Jordan | 2006 | *Teaching in K-12 schools: A reflective action approach (4th ed.)* | Pearson Merrill/ Prentice Hall |
| 6 | Freiberg Driscoll | 2005 | *Universal teaching strategies (4th ed.)* | Pearson/ Allyn and Bacon |
| 7 | Good Brophy | 2008 | *Looking in classrooms (10th ed.)* | Pearson/ Allyn and Bacon |
| 8 | Jacobsen, Eggen Kauchak | 2009 | *Methods for teaching: Promoting student learning in K-12 classrooms (8th ed.)* | Allyn and Bacon |
| 9 | Kauchak Eggen | 2006 | *Learning and teaching: Research-based methods (5th ed.)* | Allyn & Bacon |
| 10 | Lang Evans | 2006 | *Models, strategies, and methods for effective teaching* | Pearson/ Allyn and Bacon |
| 11 | Moore | 2009 | *Effective instructional strategies: From theory to practice* | Sage |
| 12 | Orlich Harder Callahan Trevisan Brown | 2004 | *Teaching strategies: A guide to effective instruction (7th ed.)* | Houghton Mifflin |
| 13 | Ornstein Lasley II | 2004 | *Strategies for effective teaching (4th ed.)* | McGraw Hill |
| 14 | Wandberg Rohwer | 2003 | *Teaching to the standards of effective practice: A guide to becoming a successful teacher* | Allyn and Bacon |

The section goes on to discuss additional differences between expert and novice teachers without further consideration of teacher improvisation. Another text, Frieberg and Driscoll (2005), includes a section on using theatrical improvisation as a teaching technique but does not mention or suggest that improvisation should be an integral part of every teaching process. In fact, the presence of this section may contribute to an impression that improvisation is *not* a normal part of teaching, but rather a special technique to be employed only in certain situations.

I then examined the possibility that teaching-as-improvisation is present in these texts, even though the term is not used. Even though all of the texts give at least passing nods to concepts such as teacher flexibility, responsiveness, and in-the-moment revision of plans, the lack of sustained discussion of such issues, accompanied by an emphasis on detailed lesson planning and vignettes of teaching in which the improvisational elements are not made salient, means that readers new to the profession are unlikely to take away the message that teaching is necessarily and always improvisational.

For example, in 597 pages of Ornstein and Lasley (2004), there are only four short allusions to the improvisational nature of teaching:

- The quote given earlier, about expert teachers being more improvisational (p. 80).
- A reference, on page 143, as a part of a discussion on why some experienced teachers do not use instructional objectives, to an assertion by Elliot Eisner that much of teaching cannot be planned in advance.
- A paragraph on flexibility, on page 186, within a section on guidelines for implementing lessons, in which the authors explain, "The teacher must be flexible – that is, prepared to develop a lesson along a different path from the one set down in the plan. Student reactions may make it necessary or desirable to elaborate on something included in the plan or to pursue something unexpected that arises as the lesson proceeds."
- A section on questioning techniques in the chapter on instructional strategies that implies, but does not directly state, that teachers will need to engage in online decision making in order to respond to unpredictable student contributions and in order to advance student thinking during classroom discussion.

Contrast these four brief mentions with one hundred pages that are devoted to teacher planning and fifty pages on "instructional strategies." The other texts I examined have similarly skewed emphases on planning and instructional strategies. Topics that we might expect to be associated with teacher improvisation, such as attending to individual student needs, teaching students with differing rates of learning, and accounting for diverse student backgrounds, tend to be addressed with advice on how lessons should be planned, and that advice rarely includes planning for improvisational teaching. All of the texts do at least mention that lesson plans must at times be revised on the fly, but there is an absence of sustained discussion about the necessary give-and-take between pre-lesson work and during-the-lesson decision making. To be clear, I would not argue against an emphasis on planning – teacher planning is critical to success. But the fact that there is at the same time so little discussion of how plans might be revised during a lesson, or of how one might plan for improvisation, creates a sense that what is most important is to have one's lesson carefully planned out, perhaps even scripted, prior to engaging with students.

All fourteen texts include case studies and/or vignettes of classroom teaching to illustrate important concepts. But the vignettes and case studies presented in these books rarely demonstrate the improvisational essence of teaching. For the most part, these examples detail the events of a lesson without letting us in to the teacher's in-the-moment thinking. This gives the impression that the important teacher's decision making is in the past, having occurred when the lesson was planned. Such descriptions also create the sense that the teacher is the only one who is shaping the direction of the lesson, because it is almost never made explicit that the flow of the lesson emerges from collaborative classroom dialogue.

These books do not show pre-service teachers the essential improvisational nature of teaching. And we know that pre-service teachers do not start teacher education programs with improvisational beliefs about teaching. Most pre-service teachers hold transmissionist views of teaching, in which teaching is seen as a fairly unproblematic matter of transferring information from the mind of the teacher to the mind of the student (Patrick & Pintrich, 2001; Richardson, 1996; Wideen, Mayer-Smith, & Moon, 1998; Woolfolk- Hoy & Murphy, 2001). This is done chiefly by telling the information to the students. This "transmission model" is linked to the history of western schooling and has been shown to be the dominant "folk pedagogy," or implicit model of teaching, in our culture (Olson & Bruner, 1996; Rogoff, et al., 2003; Torff, 1999). In one interesting example of research on this issue, Weber and Mitchell (1995) asked children, pre-service teachers, and practicing teachers to draw a picture of a teacher. The images they received were for the most part quite traditional: a woman standing in front of a blackboard or desk, "pointing or expounding" (p. 28). Weber and Mitchell concluded that this traditional image was widespread among not only pre-service teachers but most people in our culture (p. 28). To determine whether such images persisted in 2008, I replicated Weber and Mitchell's task with my own college students, asking them to draw a picture of "a school teacher in the process of teaching." I obtained nearly identical results: In almost every picture the teacher stood in front of the class, providing information by speaking and/or pointing to a blackboard. Students, if depicted, were shown sitting passively, in orderly rows, eyes on the teacher.

This experiment reveals the dominant image of teaching that teacher education students bring with them to their education classes. It is a problematic image because it resolutely positions the teacher as the intellectual authority and defines the teacher's role as the source of information to be learned, while remaining silent on the role of students' own intellectual activity in the teaching-learning process. Indeed, such transmissionist views have been shown to conflict with the learning of constructivist-based principles of teaching. When teaching is assumed to be a matter of simply transferring knowledge from teacher to student, there is no need to attend to what sort of thinking a lesson requires of students – but this is the key consideration in lesson design from a constructivist perspective (Anderson, 2001; Bryan, 2003; Holt-Reynolds, 2000; Windschitl, 2002). The main consideration from a transmissionist perspective, on the other hand, is what knowledge to present, and how and in what order to present it (Bryan, 2003; Lobato, Clarke, & Ellis, 2005; Strauss, 2001). It makes sense under the transmission model to depict a teacher speaking in the front of a classroom to a group of silent (or invisible) students. It makes far less sense, however, to depict a teacher this way under a constructivist-inspired model of teaching. From a constructivist perspective, the act of teaching cannot be depicted without including the students in the image, because the intellectual activity of the students is what is important.

There is a wealth of research literature establishing that most preservice teachers hold implicit transmissionist views of teaching (see Patrick & Pintrich, 2001; Richardson, 1996; Wideen, Mayer-Smith, & Moon, 1998; and Woolfolk Hoy & Murphy, 2001 for reviews). Research has also shown that transmissionist beliefs act as a lens through which teacher education students interpret the ideas presented in their courses (Anderson, 2001; Bryan, 2003; Holt-Reynolds, 1992; Patrick & Pintrich, 2001; Richardson, 1996). Such beliefs often act as a barrier to accurately understanding constructivist-inspired approaches to teaching, and will very likely also be a barrier to inferring the improvisational nature of teaching. From the transmissionist perspective, there is little reason for improvisation in teaching. Rather, planning exactly what the teacher will say and do during a lesson, even down to the minute details, seems advisable to ensure that all the important ideas get said and in the right order. Without explicit discussion of improvisation and its importance, teacher education students are likely to read their textbooks, and to understand the conversations around that reading, as endorsements of careful planning – even scripting – of a lesson, and to miss the few implied or passing references to the value of improvisation in teaching.

Getting explicit about improvisation in teacher education is an important step in advancing our profession's ability to improvise. If new teachers understand the value of improvisational teaching to student learning, they are more likely to plan for improvisation instead of planning a script. If they learn to think critically about the role of improvisation in teaching and to reflect on their own successes and failures in improvisation, they will become better classroom improvisers, and therefore, better teachers. In addition, such conversations may generate a demand for more scholarly work on teaching as improvisation, which can then be incorporated into teacher education, further advancing the cause of excellence in improvisational teaching. I would like to see improvisation addressed directly and substantively in forthcoming teacher education textbooks, but in the absence of such discussions, teacher educators should fill in the gaps by exploring the topic with their students.

## BRINGING IMPROVISATION INTO CONVERSATIONS WITHIN TEACHER EDUCATION

For guidance on incorporating conversations about improvisation into teacher education, we can turn first to the already well-developed body of literature on addressing teaching beliefs in teacher education. As suggested by the earlier discussion, the initial step in helping pre-service teachers understand the role of improvisation in teaching will be to address their assumptions about the teaching-learning process, some of which may conflict with the idea that effective teaching involves successful improvisation.

One of the insights gained from research on teaching beliefs is that it is not only the content of teacher education students' beliefs that make them problematic, but also the fact that the beliefs are implicit. When they begin their programs, students often do not realize they already have assumptions about teaching and learning, so they are not aware that their assumptions differ from the research-based understandings advanced by their professors (Patrick & Pintrick, 2001; Strauss 2001; Woolfolk Hoy & Murphy, 2001). Researchers such as Anderson (2001), Patrick and Pintrick (2001), and Woolfolk Hoy and Murphy (2001) therefore advocate addressing pre-service teachers' beliefs – directly, so that they can become aware of their own conceptions of teaching and engage explicitly with how those conceptions compare with the ideas being presented in their programs. Asking students to articulate and examine their beliefs about teaching helps them be more deliberate learners as they encounter new, challenging ideas, and it sets the stage for the career-long reflective consideration of the teaching-learning process that many teacher education programs strive to foster.

As a part of this process, teacher education students can be asked to think about their assumptions with regard to the improvisational nature of teaching, starting with such basic questions as "Should teachers improvise?" or "In what ways is teaching improvisational?" As Anderson (2001) points out, the aim in discussions of teaching beliefs is not to convince students that their beliefs are wrong (which is unlikely to work) but rather for the teacher educator to understand how her students are thinking about teaching in order to find ways to leverage their existing understandings in the service of new concepts. The skillful teacher educator will listen carefully to the notions of teaching that her students express and then find ways to link those notions to the ideas she hopes they will come to understand. With regard to improvisation, teacher educators can examine their students' thinking on a number of issues including:

- Do they think of planning in terms of scripting?
- How much control do they believe a teacher should have over the flow of a lesson and why?
- Do they expect effective teachers to engage in more or less improvisation than less effective teachers?
- Do they see a role for intellectual improvisation on the part of students?
- How are they understanding the collaborative relationship between teacher and student?

Teacher educators can listen for these and other issues and use their observations to inform class discussions and activities that will advance their students' thinking about the nature of improvisation in teaching.

Researchers have recommended a number of activities designed to generate dialogue around pre-service teachers' beliefs. Such activities can be used as opportunities to open conversations about the improvisational nature of teaching as well. Patrick and Pintrich (2001) note that having students create concept maps or other physical representations of how they view the teaching process provides an opportunity for them to examine their beliefs, and also makes students' beliefs available to each other, so that they can confront and challenge each others' ideas. Renninger (1996) describes a series of activities designed to unearth students' assumptions about learning, beginning with small group discussion of the question, "Which is the better metaphor for learning, snorkeling or carpentry?" and continuing with groups drawing models of the learning process that will be revisited and revised later in the course. Blumenfeld, Hicks, and Kracjik (1996) suggest that lesson-planning activities, which are a mainstay of methods courses, can be an important site for students to articulate and examine beliefs about the relationship between particular pedagogical choices and student learning. Woolfolk Hoy and Murphy (2001) note that having students write philosophies of learning can be a valuable tool for unearthing assumptions. Students can be asked to revise these at later points in their preparation, and can thereby track the evolution of their beliefs. As students' assumptions about the teaching process are explored in the context of activities like these, teacher educators can be on the lookout for themes relating to the improvisational nature of teaching. Such themes can then be included in the discussions that arise around these activities, so that students not only begin to unearth their assumptions relating to teacher improvisation, but also begin to learn that improvisation is an important issue in teaching.

Research has also revealed that teaching beliefs are quite resistant to change (Wideen, Mayer-Smith, & Moon, 1998). Programs that address beliefs only briefly or in a piecemeal fashion are unlikely to be effective in moving students toward robust, research-based understandings. Instead, sustained conversations are needed about students' evolving teaching beliefs throughout a program. These conversations should occur in each component of a program (including coursework and field experiences) to avoid fragmentation of the program's message and to limit opportunities for students to engage in unreflective thinking based on problematic assumptions such as transmissionism (Wideen, Mayer-Smith, & Moon, 1998). Thus, conversations about the improvisational nature of teaching should be integrated throughout a teacher education program as well, so that teacher education students have multiple, recurring opportunities to reflect on this aspect of their teaching beliefs.

In inviting pre-service teachers to think about teaching as improvisation, teacher educators can expect to encounter certain challenges. I have mentioned that transmissionist beliefs held by many pre-service teachers are likely to create difficulties for thinking about teaching as improvisation, because teaching understood as transmission seems to require scripting more than improvising. Thus, teacher educators should to look for opportunities to identify and problematize transmissionist beliefs that circumvent students' appreciation of the value of teaching improvisationally. Another challenge derives from the "apprenticeship of observation" that pre-service teachers have had. Lortie (1975) makes the point that upon entering a teacher education program, pre-service teachers have had twelve or more years of observing teaching from the vantage point of the student. As apprentice observers, people gain many images of teachers that they carry into preparation programs, but these images only include the parts of teaching a student can see. Teacher planning and on-the-fly decision making are mostly invisible to the student, and this masks the nature of teaching as skilled improvisation. Without access to teachers' initial intentions and their evolving strategies, we cannot be aware of their improvisations. From the student perspective, routines and order are salient, but improvisation is not (Labaree, 2005). This is why it is especially important to discuss teaching as improvisation not just in the context of pre-service teachers' own beliefs but in connection to instances of actual teaching, so that the improvisation that teachers do can become more salient.

A third challenge stems from teacher education students' conceptions of improvisation. The aim is not just that they understand that teaching is improvisational, but that they begin to think of themselves as professional improvisers who are deliberate about developing and employing improvisational skill. Attaining this understanding is likely to be difficult, because teacher education students are not likely to have a well-developed sense of what might constitute improvisational excellence or what might be involved in achieving it. Along with the other authors represented in this book, I argue that teacher educators can make an analogy to other professional improvisational communities, although this will require more than simply pointing out the commonalities between teaching and, for example, theatrical improvisation. Television shows like *Whose Line Is It Anyway*, along with the proliferation of improvisational comedy theaters in recent decades, have brought theatrical improvisation into mainstream awareness, but – much like teaching – when improv is done well, it looks easy. It is not obvious that professional improv performers engage in substantial training and preparation to become successful at their craft. Therefore, teacher educators might ask students to consider such questions as what might be involved in learning to improvise at a professional level and what kinds of knowledge professional improvisers draw on. It may even be useful to have students investigate some of the many books available on learning to improvise, and ask them to draw their own analogies between the skills explored in those texts and the skills involved in teaching. Above all, teacher education students should become aware that professional improvisers make conscious and sustained efforts to improve their skills, and that reflection about improvisational success will be an important component in students' own progress as teachers.

It has long been understood that the more teacher education students can observe actual teaching, the better. Many teacher education programs include numerous field experiences prior to student teaching, and the use of video case studies is gaining in popularity (Fishman & Davis, 2006). In addition, narrative case studies are a common feature in methods texts. Many teacher education programs also involve students in various hands-on teaching experiences, such as tutoring opportunities and "micro-teaches." With all of these methods, the value comes not simply from students' exposure to the complexities of teaching, but from the conversations they have around that exposure. By discussing these examples of teaching with their peers and their professors, education students learn to think analytically about teaching, which is an important step toward becoming a professional educator. As a part of these conversations, students should be invited to think about improvisation. When discussing their own teaching experiences, students can be asked about the role of improvisation in their teaching, and challenged to consider ways to make their teaching more successfully improvisational. When discussing observations and case studies, the role of improvisation may be less apparent, and so it may be useful for teacher educators to pose questions that will make this more salient. For example, a video case study can be paused to ask the viewers what the teacher is likely thinking about at a given moment and how she might respond to different contingencies, or to brainstorm about many possible directions in which the lesson may go depending on student responses. Cases can also be evaluated in terms of what kinds of improvisational demands were placed on students (What sort of knowledge construction opportunities were present?) or in terms of the teacher's success in establishing norms in the classroom to support successful improvisation (Do the students seem to feel safe taking intellectual risks?).

In addition to including improvisation in discussions of examples of teaching, it should also be included in discussions of lesson planning. Borko and Livingston (1989) established that experienced teachers teach more improvisationally than novices do because experienced teachers have more highly integrated knowledge structures relating to pedagogical strategies and content knowledge. This finding cautions us that to some degree, improvisational skill may be a function of classroom experience. On the other hand, this work has implications for how we teach new teachers to plan their lessons. Specifically, it might be valuable for teacher education students to consider what it means to plan to improvise. Planning time might be spent developing one's content knowledge rather than precisely scripting a lesson, given that better-elaborated content knowledge will allow teachers to be flexible and to understand their students' evolving thinking.

In addition, teachers may wish to attend more to the design of activities than to predetermining the flow of a lesson; this would help them attend to what kinds of explorations students will be supported to do. Conversations about these issues can be opened with some basic questions such as "How would the expectation to improvise vs. follow a script impact your approach to planning?" or "How might planning time be spent if you want to be prepared to let the lesson unfold improvisationally?"

## CONCLUSION

Improvisational teaching is key to meeting the educational demands of the knowledge society. As constructivist approaches to teaching emphasize, in order to build deep, conceptual understandings, students need opportunities for supported intellectual exploration. Not only does teaching need to allow space for teachers to respond to evolving student thinking; it must be designed to allow teachers and students to improvise new understandings together. Teachers need to be willing and effective improvisers, and this means that, as a profession, we must begin to explicitly examine the improvisation that we do. The authors represented in this book are developing a body of knowledge for expert teaching improvisation that will parallel the kinds of knowledge found in other professional improvisation communities. But at the same time as this work proceeds, we need to open the conversation about improvisational teaching to our next generation of teachers. Future teachers will need to embrace improvisation as an important component in their professional work, and think deliberately and analytically about how to improvise better. The idea that teaching is a form of professional improvisation may be a challenging one for many pre-service teachers, due to implicit transmissionist beliefs that make scripting a lesson seem more desirable than improvisation. Therefore, it will be important for teacher educators to help future teachers unearth their assumptions about teaching, including those related to improvisation, and to create opportunities for them to develop more robust understandings of the teaching process and of why improvisation is central to it.

## REFERENCES

Anderson, L. M. (2001). Nine prospective teachers and their experiences in teacher education: The role of entering conceptions of teaching and learning. In B. Torff & R. J. Sternberg (Eds.), *Understanding and teaching the intuitive mind: Student and teacher learning* (pp. 187–215). Mahwah, NJ: Lawrence Erlbaum Associates Publishers.

Bereiter, C. (2002). *Education and mind in the knowledge age*. Hillsdale, NJ: Lawrence Erlbaum Associates.

Berliner, P. F. (1994). *Thinking in jazz: The infinite art of improvisation*. Chicago: University of Chicago Press.

Blumenfeld, P., Hicks, L., & Kracjik, J. S. (1996). Teaching educational psychology through instructional planning. *Educational Psychologist, 31*, 51–62.

Borko, H. & Livingston, C. (1989). Cognition and improvisation: Differences in mathematics instruction by expert and novice teachers. *American Educational Research Journal, 26*, 474–498.

Bransford, J., Brown, A. L., & Cocking, R. R. (Eds.). (2003). *How people learn: Brain, mind, experience, and school*. Washington, DC: National Academy Press.

Bryan, L. A. (2003). Nestedness of beliefs: Examining a prospective elementary teacher's belief system about science teaching and learning. *Journal of Research in Science Teaching, 40*(9), 835–868.

Davis, B. & Sumara, D. (2003). Why aren't they getting this? Working through the regressive myths of constructivist pedagogy. *Teaching Education, 14*(2), 123–140.

Donmoyer, R. (1983, January). Pedagogical improvisation. *Educational Leadership, 40*(4), 39–43.

Fishman, B. J. & Davis, E. A. (2006). Teacher learning research and the learning sciences. In R. K. Sawyer (Ed.), *The Cambridge handbook of the learning sciences* (pp. 535–550). Cambridge: Cambridge University Press.

Hargreaves, A. (2003). *Teaching in the knowledge society: Education in the age of insecurity*. New York: Teachers College Press.

Holt-Reynolds, D. (1992). Personal history-based beliefs as relevant prior knowledge in course work. *American Educational Research Journal, 29*(2), 325–349.

(2000). What does the teacher do? Constructivist pedagogies and prospective teachers' beliefs about the role of a teacher. *Teaching and Teacher Education, 16*(1), 21–32.

Johnstone, K. (1987). *Impro: Improvisation and the theatre*. New York: Routledge

Kelly, G. J., Brown, C., & Crawford, T. (2000). Experiments, contingencies, and curriculum: providing opportunities for learning through improvisation in science teaching. *Science Education, 84*, 624–657.

Labaree, D. (2005). Life on the margins. *Journal of Teacher Education, 56*, 186–191.

Lobato, J., Clarke, D., & Ellis, A. B. (2005). Initiating and eliciting in teaching: A reformulation of telling. *Journal for Research in Mathematics Education, 36*(2), 36.

Lobman, C. (2007, April). The Developing Teachers Fellowship Program: Exploring the use of improv theatre for the professional development of inner city teachers. Paper presented at the annual meeting of the American Educational Research Association, Chicago, IL.

Lobman, C. & Lindquist, M. (2007). *Unscripted learning: Using improv activities across the K-8 curriculum*. New York: Teachers College Press.

Lortie, D. C. (1975). *Schoolteacher: A sociological study*. Chicago: University of Chicago Press.

Olson, D. R. & Bruner, J. S. (1996). Folk psychology and folk pedagogy. In D. R. Olson & N. Torrance (Eds.), *The handbook of education and human development: New models of learning, teaching and schooling* (pp. 9–27). Malden, MA: Blackwell Publishing.

Patrick, H. & Pintrich, P. R. (2001). Conceptual change in teachers' intuitive conceptions of learning, motivation, and instruction: The role of motivational and epistemological beliefs. In B. Torff & R. J. Sternberg (Eds.), *Understanding and teaching the intuitive mind: Student and teacher learning* (pp. 117–143). Mahwah, NJ: Lawrence Erlbaum Associates.

Renninger, A. (1996). Learning as the focus of an educational psychology course. *Educational Psychologist, 31*, 63–76.

Richardson, V. (1996). The role of attitudes and beliefs in learning to teach. In J. Sikula, T. J. Buttery, & E. Guyton (Eds.), *Handbook of research on teacher education* (2nd ed., pp. 102–119). New York: MacMillan.

(2003). Constructivist pedagogy. *Teachers College Record, 105*(9), 1623–1640.

Rogoff, B., Paradise, R., Arauz, R., Correa-Chávez, M., & Angelillo, C. U. (2003). Firsthand learning through intent participation. *Annual Review of Psychology, 54*, 175–203.

Sawyer, R. K. (2003). Emergence in creativity and development. In R. K. Sawyer (Ed.), *Creativity and development* (pp. 12–60). New York: Oxford.

(2004). Creative teaching: Collaborative discussion as disciplined improvisation. *Educational Researcher, 33*(2), 12–20.

(2006a). Educating for innovation. *Journal of thinking skills and creativity, 1*(1), 41–48.

(2006b). Introduction: The new science of learning. In R. K. Sawyer (Ed.), *The Cambridge handbook of the learning sciences* (pp. 1–17). Cambridge: Cambridge University Press.

Scardamalia, M. & Bereiter, C. (2006). Knowledge building: Theory, pedagogy, and technology. In K. Sawyer (Ed.), *Cambridge handbook of the learning sciences* (pp. 97–118). New York: Cambridge University Press.

Siegler, R. S. (1998). *Children's thinking* (3rd ed.). Upper Saddle River, NJ: Prentice Hall.

Simon, M. A. (1995). Reconstructing mathematics pedagogy from a constructivist perspective. *Journal for Research in Mathematics Education, 26*(2), 114–146.

Spolin, V. (1983). *Improvisation for the theater*. Chicago, IL: Northwestern University Press.

Strauss, S. (2001). Folk psychology, folk pedagogy, and their relations to subject-matter knowledge. In B. Torff & R. J. Sternberg (Eds.), *Understanding and teaching the intuitive mind: Student and teacher learning* (pp. 217–242). Mahwah, NJ: Lawrence Erlbaum Associates.

Torff, B. (1999). Tacit knowledge in teaching: Folk pedagogy and teacher education. In R. J. Sternberg & J. A. Horvath, (Eds.), *Tacit knowledge in professional practice: Researcher and practitioner perspectives* (195–213). Hillsdale, NJ: Lawrence Erlbaum Associates.

Tudge, J. & Rogoff, B. (1989). Peer influences on cognitive development: Piagetian and Vygotskian perspectives. In M. H. Bornsten & J. S. Bruner, (Eds.), *Interaction in human development* (pp. 17–40). Hillsdale, NJ: Lawrence Erlbaum Associates.

Weber, S. & Mitchell, C. (1995). *That's funny you don't look like a teacher: Interrogating images and identity in popular culture.* Washington, DC: Routledge.

Wideen, M., Mayer-Smith, J., & Moon, B. (1998). A critical analysis of the research on learning to teach: Making the case for an ecological perspective on inquiry. *Review of Educational Research, 68*(2), 130–178.

Windschitl, M. (2002). Framing constructivism in practice as the negotiation of dilemmas: An analysis of the conceptual, pedagogical, cultural, and political challenges facing teachers. *Review of Educational Research, 72*(2), 131.

Woolfolk Hoy, A. & Murphy, P. K. (2001). Teaching educational psychology to the implicit mind. In B. Torff & R. J. Sternberg (Eds.), *Understanding and teaching the intuitive mind: Student and teacher learning* (pp. 145–186). Mahwah, NJ: Lawrence Erlbaum Associates.

# 3

# Creativity, Pedagogic Partnerships, and the Improvisatory Space of Teaching

PAMELA BURNARD

There is a tension between two prominent agendas for school reform: the accountability agenda and the creativity agenda (see Burnard, 2008). Under the accountability agenda, teachers are required to measure and test students, to report using mandated standards and systems, and to teach in state sanctioned ways. Under the creativity agenda, teachers are expected to act effortlessly, fluidly, to take risks, be adventurous, and to develop pedagogy and classroom creativity in order to develop their own knowledge and skills as creative professionals. They are expected to develop creative learners who can succeed in a twenty-first-century economy that rewards creativity and innovation.

The accountability agenda makes it difficult for teachers to work more creatively. Teachers get overwhelmed by a constant barrage of accountability demands (standards, tests, targets, and tables) by government. There is general agreement that governments are increasingly taking control of the teaching profession (Alexander, 2004). Teachers are expected to perform in specific and regulated ways. In contrast, the creativity agenda encourages teachers to take risks, be adventurous, and explore creativity themselves. Yet, what constitutes creativity in education remains ambiguous. Slippage in language is confusing and common between "teacher creativity," "creative teaching," "teaching for creativity," and "creative learning." In this chapter, by "teaching for creativity" I mean creating a positive learning environment in which students can take risks, engage in imaginative activity, and do things differently.

Whereas important research conducted a decade ago by Woods and Jeffrey (1996) identified how teachers cope with tensions surrounding

In R. K. Sawyer (Ed.) (2011). *Structure and improvisation in creative teaching* (pp. 51–72). Cambridge: Cambridge University Press.

reforms, although more than ten years have passed, it still remains the case that the translation of education policy into pedagogic practice is neither straightforward nor unproblematic. The conflict between the creativity and accountability agendas in education causes tensions for teachers given the effect of all the tough talk of standards (Ball, 2003).

There is wide acceptance that teaching is a complex task involving a high degree of professional expertise (see Sawyer, this volume). There is general agreement that good teaching is well organized, reflective and planned, is based on sound subject knowledge, is dependent on effective classroom management, and requires an understanding of children's developmental needs. Most importantly, however, good teaching inspires, stimulates, and facilitates children's creativity and imagination and uses exciting and varied approaches (Alexander, 2008).

In the United Kingdom, a government emphasis on creativity in learning has led to an expansion of artist-teacher partnerships. In these partnerships, working professional artists visit the classroom for a limited time period and work side by side with the full-time teacher. Partnerships have become a delivery model in education, which offers a forum for creative opportunities. In the United Kingdom, an emerging commitment to address the performative climate within education and children's well-being is reflected in new government initiatives such as Creative Partnerships. A £150 million initiative by the United Kingdom Department for Culture, Media and Sport (DCMS, 2004), Department of Children, Schools and Families, and the Arts Council of England, Creative Partnerships invests in relationships between creative practitioners and schools to encourage and support creativity in learning (see http://www.creative-partnerships.com).

There is a long history of collaborations between teachers and professional artists in participatory arts activities, both in schools and communities. Models of practice in partnerships between artists and teachers vary considerably. However, effective partnerships between artists and teachers in schools suggest it is in the act of creativity itself that empowerment lies. Teaching is a subtle and complex art, and successful teachers, like artists, view their work as a continuing process of reflection and learning.

These partnerships directly benefit students, but they also have the potential to indirectly benefit students by increasing teacher expertise. There is a consensus that educational partnerships are dependent on the help, trust, and openness of the individuals involved (Burnard & Swann, 2010; Craft, 2006; Galton, 2008; Jeffery, 2005). For a partnership to work well, either for students or for teacher professional development, Wenger (1998, p. 73) argued that there must be genuine collaboration, dialogue, openness, and mutual tuning. Under these conditions, a collaborative partnership potentially can develop, where teachers and artists are engaged in a dialogue and are dialogic in their teaching. For this to happen, they need to have time for thinking, to encourage and maintain ambiguity, and to share understanding concerning what they are doing and what this means within the community (Galton, 2008).

Teachers and artists co-construct a *pedagogy* when their collaboration encompasses "the act of teaching, together with the ideas, values and collective histories that inform, shape and explain that act" (Alexander, 2008: 38). To analyze how this happens, in my research I study how the core acts of teaching – namely, "task, activity, interaction, and judgment" (p. 78) – feature in the dialogue between teachers and artists.

When teachers and artists collaborate, they often have different conceptions concerning the organization of space, material, and time in the classroom. The visiting artist typically uses a more improvisational, open-ended approach, whereas the classroom teacher typically uses a more structured style. Thus, these teacher-artist partnerships provide us with an opportunity to study the teaching paradox in action: How do these dyads resolve this paradox to balance the more unpredictable, improvisational approach of the visiting artist with the more predictable, normative, and accountable style of the teacher? If this paradox can be resolved, the result would be improved teacher expertise; research tells us how important it is for teachers to alter traditional school boundaries of time and space to allow for unpredictable, rigorous, reflective, and improvisational teaching (Jeffrey, 2006).

## IMPROVISATION AND THE SPACE OF TEACHING

In music, improvisation can be thought of as "the discovery and invention of original music spontaneously, while performing it, without preconceived formulation, scoring or context" (Solomon, 1986: 224). Solomon's definition of improvisation helps advance the notion of teaching as a performative act, moving flexibly, reflexively, spontaneously, and adaptively between scripted and unscripted sections; a kind of partly improvised and partly choreographed dance in dynamic interaction with all those present.

Another dimension of improvisation often referred to in music and theater is "going with the flow" or "getting in the groove." These skilled performances are based on a high degree of tacit knowledge and practice, just as is all professional expertise (Schön, 1983). Improvised behaviors involve "ideas which leap to mind" (and to jazz players' fingers, according to Pike,

1974) and can be evidenced in the perceptual nature of responsiveness on the part of the teacher and artist to students. This resonates with the notion of Nardone (1996) who considered the lived experience of improvisation to be a coherent synthesis of the body and mind engaged in both conscious and prereflective activity. When teachers and artists work together, particularly over sustained periods, their tacit knowledge and practice can be examined, reflected on, shared, and new practices created.

Berliner (1994) offers a further understanding of the openness, uncertainty, and dialogic act of improvisation and the conditions that allows individuals to be generative, adaptive, and reciprocal. He said:

> The sense of exhilaration that characterizes the artist's experiences under such circumstances is heightened for jazz musicians as storytellers by the activity's physical, intellectual and emotional exertion and by the intensity of struggling with creative processes under the pressure of a steady beat. From the outset of each performance, improvisers enter an artificial world of time in which reactions to the unfolding events of their tales must be immediate. Furthermore, the consequences of their actions are irreversible. Amid the dynamic display of imagined fleeting images and impulses – entrancing sounds and vibrant feelings, dancing shapes and kinetic gestures, theoretical symbols and perceptive commentaries – improvisers extend the logic of previous phrases, as ever-emerging figures on the periphery of their vision encroach upon and supplant those in performance.... Few experiences are more deeply fulfilling. (1994: 216)

In this chapter, I analyze the two different roles in a creative partnership – teacher and artist – and I focus on the tension between their two different sets of tacit practices, beliefs, and professional perspectives. My goal is to understand how they resolve this tension to create a shared space for teaching that enables the emergence of improvisational forms of teaching. What takes them from teaching together, independently and side by side, to co-constructing an emergent pedagogy? I focus on two questions: When is it that artists enable teachers by working in classrooms? How are artists helping teachers improve their teaching?

When teachers and artists collaborate, their different conceptions of teaching and different paradigms of expertise must be resolved before they can construct an effective learning environment. This examination sheds light on the teaching paradox because the visiting artist represents a more creative, improvisational end of the paradox, whereas the classroom teacher represents the more constrained, scripted end. Teacher-artist partnerships have been shown to help teachers enliven and loosen up tightly scripted ways of teaching (Burnard & Maddock, 2007; Burnard & White, 2008; Jeffery, 2005).

Very often teacher identities are played out in particular professional roles where their pedagogy and values are regularly scrutinized and tested in the classroom, as behavior managers fueled/informed by an institutional dimension (often creating an inner conflict between skillfully modeling attributes of the teacher [e.g., pedagogic content knowledge]). Artists, in contrast, are stereotypically presented and seen as artists or arts practitioners, professionals involved in cultural production. The artist in education is frequently an outsider who comes into an education space and acts as a catalyst or challenger of learning and who provides ways of exploring the world which involve more sensory, immersive, and improvisatory rooted ways of working than are customary in classroom settings. The artist is often seen as precisely *not* the teacher, the "other" who is permitted to open up new contexts, frontiers, and challenges of the unfamiliar to the learners.

In this chapter, I will move beyond these divisive stereotypes of teacher and artist, and feature two examples of collaborative partnerships: each of these examples of a teacher and an artist collaboratively teaching clearly demonstrates how they create "spaces for teaching" that resolve the teaching paradox in a way that promotes conditions conducive to student creativity, such as risk taking and allowing for not knowing what might happen next. I conclude by generalizing from these specific examples to propose a set of necessary conditions that must be met to resolve the teaching paradox.

## PEDAGOGIC PARTNERSHIPS AND TEACHING FOR CREATIVITY

For many years, schools have employed visiting professional artists, in music, dance and theater, to work in educational partnerships with teachers in schools. But this practice has increased dramatically in the United Kingdom in the last decade, as a result of the publication of the report of the National Advisory Committee on Creative and Cultural Education (NACCCE 1999). In the years after this influential document was published, many subsequent government policies and advisory documents have indirectly increased the interest in artist partnerships with artists in schools. The partnerships are thought to directly impact creative learning (Creative Partnerships, 2005a), as well as to indirectly impact it by enhancing the teacher's ability to teach for creativity, even after the partnership has ended and the artist has left (Pope et al., 1999). In educational research, there is a small but growing body of research that identifies the pedagogical potential of teacher-artist partnerships (Burnard & Maddock,

2007; Burnard & Swann, 2010; Jenkins, Jeffery, & Walsh, 2008; Triantafyllaki & Burnard, 2010; Upitis, 2006). The vision and the hope are that the learning of pupils, pedagogic practices of teachers, and schools as organizations will be changed by educational partnerships and the significance they have in school improvement.

The vision and number of educational partnerships was increased dramatically in the United Kingdom as a result of the 2002 policy initiative, Creative Partnerships (2005a, 2005b). Creative Partnerships is the government's flagship creative learning program designed to develop the creativity of young people across the nation. The vision and hope of this program, set up under the auspices of the Department of Culture Media and Sport (DCMS, 2001) and the Arts Council with funding of £150 million, have brought artists who champion contemporary arts practice and creative practitioners such as architects, scientists, and multimedia developers into schools to enhance young people's learning through arts and cultural experiences. With more than 330,000 young people and more than 4,500 teacher-artist collaborations, partnerships are acknowledged to have great potential to enhance arts education and creative education in schools.

The Creative Partnerships program was established within the Arts Council England in April 2002 as a shared initiative between the Department of Culture Media and Sport and what was then called the Department for Education and Skills. Unlike the earlier "resident artist in schools" ventures in earlier decades, this flagship creative learning educational program has been rolled out to more than 1.1 million young people in 12,800 schools in 36 different areas across in the United Kingdom. Through 2010, the UK government has spent £247 million with multiple goals. One goal is to help pupils learn more creatively. A second goal is to help teachers teach more creatively; a third is to help schools become more innovative organizations. A fourth is to forge strong and sustained partnerships between schools and artists. Research on the impact of artists (more recently referred to as creative practitioners in the United Kingdom) in schools and classrooms has focused on their pedagogic practices (Galton, 2010) or on pupil perceptions of learning with artists (Burnard & Swann, 2010). This chapter provides evidence of how the teaching paradox is resolved in these collaborative pedagogic practices between teachers and artists working in partnership in schools.

In 2009, the Creative Partnerships program moved to a new national agency, Creativity, Culture & Education (CCE, 2009), which has been created to fund and manage cultural and creative programs for young people; this agency invested a further £100 million in 2009 and 2010. One of the key policy messages has been establishing "a new balance in education" through "relationships between schools and other agencies" (NACCCE, 1999: 10). The vision and hope here, in the light of these educational policy initiatives (as well as CCE, 2009; NCSL, 2002; QCA, 2005 and Schools of Creativity [Creative Partnerships Prospectus for Schools September, 2007]), are that teachers will better learn how to resolve the teaching paradox: They will be stimulated and supported by sharing the spontaneous and unpredictable nature of working in collaborative practice with artists, where the teacher makes unpremeditated, spur-of-the-moment decisions, where a considerable degree of residual decision making occurs, where the acquired skills that are normally executed as a professional repertoire of teaching strategies are linked up with those of the artists to develop a new way of resolving the teaching paradox between advance planning and the real-time practice of classroom teaching.

## PROFESSIONAL RELATIONSHIPS AND THE SPACES THAT ENABLE TEACHING FOR CREATIVITY

When artists and teachers collaborate, the full complexity of teaching is affected. Teachers and artists enter the partnership with different theories, beliefs, practices, questions, visions, and hopes. Thus the teaching paradox is played out visibly, in the social interaction between these two professionals. There is strong evidence that artists use a more improvisational approach as they engage with students and teachers (Loveless, 2008; Sefton-Green, 2008). Research suggests that artists share processes of creative thinking in classrooms through an apprenticeship model of teaching, in contrast to the instructionist style that dominates most school classrooms (Griffiths & Woolf, 2009). This is further substantiated by Pringle (2008: 14) who notes that artists view teaching "as an experiential process of conceptual enquiry that embraces inspiration, critical thinking and the building of meanings." She argues that artists teach by sharing artistic knowledge and by enabling learners to participate alongside them (Pringle, 2008: 46).

Galton (2008) studied a group of artists with a successful track record of working in schools, not only including artists from traditional disciplines but also practitioners making regular use of various forms of information and communications technology (ICT) such as digital photographers and filmmakers. As with Pringle's (2008) account, Galton found that these artists mostly felt that it was sustained dialogue with teachers (and students) and the time taken for planning that enabled them to engage in improvisational practices in the classroom. Artists define themselves as creative practitioners in terms of the artistic expertise, knowledge, and skills they possess

(Galton, 2008); they also define themselves by what pedagogical practices they use in their work in schools (Hall & Thomson, 2007; Hall, Thomson, & Russell, 2007; Jeffery, 2005).

Creative Partnerships has funded "action research" investigations (first round was 2004–05; second round was 2005–06) into these partnerships. There are some studies that explore artist-teacher partnerships in primary school contexts (Hall & Thomson, 2007; Hall, Thomson, & Russell, 2007; Maddock & Sapsed, 2008), in secondary schools (CapeUK, 2005; Cochrane, Craft, & Dillon, 2007; Galton, 2008; Jeffery, 2005), in higher education and university sectors (Cochrane, Jeffery, & Price, 2007a; Jeffery, 2005;), and in professional development programs (Jenkins, Jeffery, & Walsh, 2008; Ledgard, 2006). These primarily analyze the impact of the artists on students' experience of learning and tend to be outcomes of what artists *do* rather than what teachers learn.

While recognizing the value of the wide range of artist-led interventions in education, which can enhance students' learning (such as the long-standing tradition of theater in education), this chapter will explore the research that demonstrates the benefits, complexities, and challenges of teacher-artist partnerships and provides evidence of how artists and teachers collectively create emergent resolutions of the teaching paradox.

## IMPROVISATORY DIMENSIONS OF TEACHING FOR CREATIVITY

There is a growing body of evidence on teachers' experience of teacher-artist partnerships, its rewards, tensions, and dilemmas (Cochrane, 2008; Hall & Thomson, 2007; Jeffery, 2005; Ledgard, 2006; Upitis, 2006). In schools where the Creative Partnerships program is well established, a key issue has emerged: How do artists' perspectives on pedagogy inspire, guide, and mentor teachers? There is no lack of evidence that artists motivate students, but there is little extant research that identifies what teachers learn about teaching while working with artists. The metaphor of improvisation helps illuminate that creative learning is essentially polyphonic; it evolves not in a single line of action or thought, but in several strands and directions at once, not circumscribed by the tried and traditional, enabling risk to be borne or not, and in the face of this artists can adopt different stances and engage in different collaborative activities with teachers.

Improvisation is characterized by flexible, adaptive, responsive, and generative activity. Improvisation forms a part of the discourse of creativity, which permits an understanding of the elements that frame teaching as a performance that can move between a fixed and flexible structure, an existing or emergent framework, where choices can be made spontaneously, moving between scripted and non-scripted formulations. Teaching, like improvisation, is framed conceptually and ethically, as well as temporally and spatially. Pedagogic practices can be rigid, with impermeable borders that form barriers to students, or they can move inside and outside the safe, the known, and the predictable.

In the variability of preexisting pedagogic and artistic practices, teachers and artists engage in considerable risk taking when they work together. Improvisational teaching is always negotiating the teaching paradox: It dances between planned, scripted, deliberate, conscious episodes, and opportunistic action that ensures spontaneity by yielding to the flow; its immediacy signifies improvisational characteristics in the synchronous moment-to-moment of creating a new pedagogic practice. From teacher expertise literature (see Sawyer, this volume) we know that expert teachers have mastered the structures of teaching – a large repertoire of plans, routines, and scripts. In addition, teachers must master the practice of teaching – a range of teaching strategies that include improvisational forms.

## WHEN MIGHT "IMPROVISATION" IN TEACHING HAPPEN?

Research shows that visiting artists teach in a more improvisational manner. Can teachers learn from the emergence of these improvisational ways of teaching? Teachers cultivate and draw on a repertoire of pedagogic strategies. Artists constantly try out new ideas or adapt old ones, often taking calculated risks in the act of teaching. The difference between pedagogy and teaching, as argued by Alexander (2004) and widely accepted among others (Day & Saunders, 2006), is that teaching is an act (like improvisation) whereas pedagogy involves both *act* and *thought, belief and theory*. So, what happens when artists and teachers teach together? What happens in the fusion of their actions and thoughts, both of which are of equal interest to *who* they are and *what* they value? How do these collaborations address the teaching paradox?

Expert teachers use routines and activity structures in regulated (i.e., scripted) and improvisatory (i.e., unscripted) ways (Sawyer, this volume). Drawing on the metaphor provided by improvisational performance, like all collaborative acts and discourse, there are "entrances" and "exits" such as with actors in improvisational theater sketches where "the actors who are not actively participating in the current scene stand or sit at the back or sides of the stage; they do not want to interfere with the ongoing performance. But at the same time, they have to be close enough to the action to hear the dialogue, so they can detect when it would be appropriate to enter the performance as a new character" (Sawyer, 2001a, p. 55).

For example, one of the key features of the collaborative pedagogic act, as identified by Burnard & Swann (2010), is how "entrances" and "exits" unfold as crucial events in a temporal sequence of a teacher and artist's authoring of their lessons as played out in partnership in a classroom. As with good storytellers who make use of flashbacks and flash-forwards, introducing characters and events to engage and surprise the reader, teachers who jump into the artists' teaching frame have the possibility of using a glimpse of the end-point to act as an advance organizer or motivator for the class. As the teacher unfolds this with his or her class, over time, perhaps within and beyond the lesson, the artist and teacher reveal a shared understanding of the sequence of improvised episodes. Given any topic, it seems that individual teachers will choose different ways to introduce and different ways in which to sequence the episodes of teaching, even when they often make decisions about the order in which to cover sections of work, what to miss out, what to emphasize, and so on. For teachers, in attempting to impose order on or to engage the class in a dialogic pedagogy, a "problematic" is essential, provoking different points of view from a shared understanding of an initial situation. Teachers are often confronted with common misconceptions; their narratives, as interpreted by their students, are often responsible for introducing elements that run contrary to expectations. For artists, the plot devised and the business of working differently is reflected by their different understandings of what has gone before. This leads to the development of contextually situated problems and solutions that lead to new forms of creativity. The co-construction of new ideas, topics, and contexts can lead to significant and distinctively different pedagogic practices.

This kind of improvisatory practice does not always appear in teacher-artist partnerships. The peculiar paradox is that teachers are apparently being urged to collaborate more with artists when, in the present climate of accountability, there is less for them to collaborate on. Teachers are often pressured to teach to tests in a "hurry along" climate, and students are often pressured to "play the system" with high-stakes testing, mechanized delivery of information, and centralized accountability focused on short-term deliverables. When differences in pedagogy between teachers and artists are not resolved, the teaching paradox is realized as a clash of pedagogic cultures (Pringle, 2008; Galton, 2008). Similarly, in the work of Hall, Thomson, and Russell (2007), the issues surrounding the clash between two cultures has also identified the need to develop shared principles and values so as to underpin the collaborative pedagogic practice that one hopes will emerge.

## ILLUSTRATIONS OF STUDIES BRIDGING THE (PEDAGOGIC AND ARTISTIC) PRACTICES DIVIDE

In the following section, I draw on some transcripts from interviews with artists and teachers who utilize the improvisational dimensions in their teaching to address the teaching paradox – the tension between the creativity agenda and the accountability agenda – in different ways.

The first partnership I discuss is between Dorothy, a composer with twenty years of experience, and John, a teacher with twenty years of experience. John is the Director of Performing Arts, a music teacher, conductor, and arranger. He has great respect for Dorothy because of the results she gets with his students. I knew them both some considerable time before because he had been an enthusiast for some innovative curriculum development and she had been involved in making composition accessible and meaningful to students. This is how Dorothy described the shared space of her pedagogic practice as the *dialogic improvisation of teaching*. She said:

I'm interested in the idea of holistic creative education. I work from the understanding that there isn't a right or wrong outcome or even one answer. I want to support young people's creativity rather than drive it. I normally start with activities which open up and explore possibilities and communicate an openness to ideas in the ways we model collaborative action and a passion for the exploration of our own creative learning and teaching.... Everything evolves organically. I don't run to a detailed plan but I do hold long planning sessions with the teacher.... And, I like to spend quite a bit of time before starting a project observing the classroom practice of the teachers involved ... we conduct mutual observation. This influences how I work.... I prioritize students' ideas and work to engage students, to have them question and embark on a process of enquiry. I try to promote a kind of fluid reflective practice which is a bit like researching your own practice. I encourage risk taking and play and expect students to take responsibility for what they do. That is crucial. I get them to work in a participatory way where exchanging ideas and experiences is expected also of the teachers. I'm not there to teach but share. I do a lot of talking with the teacher during the sessions and engaging collaboratively ... it helps to share the burdens and pressures ... prior to and during the gig. I spend a lot of time after sessions talking through what was working and what wasn't working. I also have a lot of extended conversations long before and immediate after sessions and I make a big deal of shared dialogue during sessions with the teachers.... I like to explore each other's pedagogic territories ... to share the space of learning and teaching. I think learners gain a lot of understanding through this collaboration but through these exchanges and with students working along teachers. The key, for me, is that it's all about engaging in and reflecting on the making process and in reflecting on this process, encouraging both teachers and students to articulate their ideas, and play together, the space opens up, it promotes teachers' learning from the children and each other ... it opens boundaries that form bridges ... and becomes more open-ended and supportive.

As found in other studies that report artists' accounts of their own art practice and pedagogy (Pringle, 2008; Galton, 2008), this artist felt that what made the partnership work was the sustained dialogue with teachers and students that give them space and time to think and extend ideas; offering precise feedback; and extending rather than trying to change students' and teachers' ideas. Other common elements in their practice included allowing students choice and ownership of their learning, time for reflection, creating a stimulating environment, and, most importantly, modeling creative action within a genuine partnership.

Cochrane (2008) argues that when a creative partnership is working well, the teacher and the artist demonstrate mutual respect, recognizing each other's expertise and perspective; they support each other; and both speak of the powerful impact the collaborative process has on their practice.

John, the teacher, probes the reasons for the high levels of collaboration, mutual support, respect, and shared engagement; the reasons for selecting the tasks the artists ask students and teachers to undertake; and the kinds of outcomes on which he and Dorothy agree on and judge as successful. Unusually, he separates learning and the act of teaching as a transaction taking place not only between the artist and students within the classroom but between the artist and teacher. John said:

> To me, working with artists is about several things. One important thing for me is to look at and try to model their different ways of working; I've learned so much more from doing their tasks alongside the students ... rather than expecting them to come in and deliver and then go away again.... I see, in the course of lesson and across a series of lessons, how they encompass, get students to explore their own ideas before going on to decide on the tasks and activities to be undertaken and about the particular tasks which move to imaginative playful spontaneous stuff then move to create something in response, working with them in different ways to create safe spaces for risk taking. And another important thing is with the students. What I am trying to do here is to be a person who responds to ideas, just like the students; to come up with ideas and to bring our own reflections to share. But it's the giving up of control which

I struggle most with. It's like learning to teach all over again.... Standing back and just letting the students play and go about their work without jumping in and dictating further instructions of how best to approach or 'the right' way more spontaneously to do something.... The students reflect on their learning and themselves as learners. So do I, but as their teacher I bring my own practice to the surface and share it with more spontaneity with the artist. I've learned to work from the understanding that there isn't a right or wrong outcome or even one answer. I've learned more responsive ways to support young people's creativity. Just like Dorothy, I start with warm-up and release activities which open up and explore possibilities and communicate an openness to ideas. Unlike Dorothy, I do run to a detailed plan because of the continued tensions of target setting and testing but what I've learnt from Dorothy is how best to liberate myself, balance my scripted and unscripted teaching, and my students needs by minimizing the worst elements of this regime and engaging my students in regular artistic ventures where they don't have to feel fearful of "being wrong."

What emerges is that artists tend to define themselves differently and at times in opposition to teachers (Pringle, 2008). Artists often resist describing their practice as teaching. In contrast, they often describe their pedagogic practice in the language of the teaching paradox: a dialogic improvisation between the fixed plans, repertoires, and routines, yielding to high levels of real-time decision making. It is not uncommon for both teachers and artists to go through periods of uncertainty and discomfort as they negotiate this tension between different conceptions of the use of time, space, and resources in relation to how classroom and school procedures normally operate.

One artist, talking about one of the productive tensions he experienced working in a school, when interviewed at the end of an artist-led project involving ten workshops across a term, had this to say about the tensions between the two competing agendas – high-stakes testing and the importance of giving students ownership of their ideas and room for creativity:

An important thing for me is my art making demands risk taking, questioning, challenging the status quo, bending and breaking the rules, speculation, disturbance, conflict, discomfort, and shock. These principles overlay my pedagogic practice in schools. There are tensions and clearly risks attached for those engaged in the fluid nature of art-making processes. The consequence of reflection, putting in breathing spaces and still points, and reflecting critically on what, why, and how we learn and how we work in partnership with teachers and students in schools can be really tricky. The effect of encouraging students to pursue a line of think-ing may cause them to question or challenge the values and practices of their own teachers and that of the school can be seen as subversive. But I don't have a problem with this kind of subversive creativity. You have to walk a fine line and this concern shouldn't but often does lead me to comprise my professional work and educational partnerships. It's a tight-ropewalk with competing priorities that mean the inroads that I may have made can easily be lost. Sometimes you just have to invite students to find the space and take the time to sit and think about it and try and reduce the perceived risk by the offer to think and encourage thinking together about alternative ways rather than just pursue one way to go about it. It's important to recognize the role played by feelings. I'm never shy of sharing mine with the students. But this doesn't go over well with all teachers. Some just can't move away from didactic teaching and it just becomes impossible to navigate a way through or negotiate the dynamics of each others' ideology. So, they become the provider of information, or the police person.

One teacher used a deeply disciplined and scripted pedagogy; she even com-pared her own practice to "a fully orchestrated score." When she worked with an artist, she noted:

There were definite tensions. We didn't have time to build up any kind of relationship. They very loosely guided the students on a very different, quite unspecified, learning journey to me ... they used a very different kind of planning model to me and used – well – actually ... wasted time over conversations which I felt were unnecessary ... and that brought about tensions and burdens which some pupils found very challenged by. There just isn't that kind of time to sit for hours and talk. They don't seem to have any sense of how a classroom, curriculum, and its struc-tures work. There just isn't the time or curriculum opportunity to give oneself the freedom to let go and work at such an emotionally charged level as this. I watched from the sidelines rather than participated ... I don't like being put on the spot with all eyes on me and besides, I have to be on the ready to regain control and police behaviour.... I know why a few of the students get upset. It can be very destabilizing for some students.... Confidences can take a real knock when tasks are high on ambiguity and therefore perceived as very risky. I just had to help out some students by showing specifically how to do things so they could achieve the set criteria that we are all used to ... but this upset the art-ists who made it perfectly clear these differences were not going to be resolved ... there wasn't time to talk it through, to adjust to them, and I didn't feel like being very collegial anyway. They had all the talent but none of the critical elements that, for me, defines teaching like being in control and which, for me, should play out like a fully orchestrated score. In the end I didn't have the time nor energy to work it through with them.

The teaching paradox that arises in the partnership between artists and teachers can be complex and can give rise to a clash of confidence, as power relationships are forged and in some cases control relinquished to whose opinions count. Artists can hold strong views about going with the flow whereas teachers often see themselves cast in the role of didact or police-man. Pringle (2008) and Galton (2008) make similar points that artists can adopt creative and experimental pedagogic modes because generally they are free from curriculum constraints, whereas teachers are not always at liberty to do so.

In the context of the qualitative differences between artist and teacher pedagogies, Bernstein (1996) offers a framework which differentiates between pedagogies in terms of *competence* and *performance*. "Competence" pedagogies focus on the learner and what the learner has achieved, and so tend to be "active, creative and self-regulating." Performance models of pedagogy place the emphasis on clearly defined outputs so that learners are expected to acquire certain skills or to construct specific texts or products in fulfillment of the required outcome. The pedagogies of artists, who more often define themselves in terms of specialist knowledge and skills they and others perceive they possess, prioritize the development of learners' ideas and individual creativity, while encouraging them to reflect on the process and what has been achieved. The emphasis is on "competence" pedagogies that pass a greater degree of control over learning to the learner.

A "performance" model of pedagogy, Bernstein argues, "places the emphasis upon a specific output of the acquirer [learner], upon a particular text the acquirer is expected to construct and upon the specialized skills necessary to the production of this specific output, text or product" (1996: 4). In any given teaching session, performance models might include, as a core act of teaching, improvisational forms that, in-the-moment, promote learner independence and autonomy or require the teacher to spontane-ously scaffold learning so as to help learners move forward in their learning. Teachers are being pushed by two opposed agendas: They are being asked to promote creativity while at the same time meeting accountability tar-gets measured by success in standardized tests. The evidence from several studies is that there are many understandable tensions arising out of this paradox (Cochrane, 2008).

What kinds of pedagogic practices and partnerships have the potential to create better professional teacher practices? What is illuminated by these narratives of artists' and teachers' pedagogic collaborations is twofold. First, we have strong evidence that artists work adaptively with and alongside teachers and students (Galton, 2008). They work together improvisationally, as ideas are exchanged and built on dialogically (Sawyer, 2004). Second, we have strong evidence that for the teachers, working with artists involves teaching in a variety of ways. The artists tend to move between competence and performance pedagogies, splitting the focus between the learner, what the learner achieves, the teacher, and the performance of teaching. Teachers tend to favor the performance models of pedagogy, which place the emphasis on clearly defined objectives and outputs; but having seen the effects of encouraging students to pursue different lines of thinking, to question and challenge the values and practices of past lessons, and the consequences of professional reflection, most of them increasingly come to understand that creative learning is not about getting a right or wrong outcome, but is a dance that is both improvised and choreographed. As a result of the partnerships, teachers change how they approach the teaching paradox: They become more improvisational.

### BEING IMPROVISATORY WITH THE OTHER IN EDUCATIONAL PARTNERSHIPS

What matters to teachers the most is how artists deploy their specialized knowledge in practice. Shulman's (1987) construct of pedagogical content knowledge equates expertise with the deeper understanding of the structures of the subject. The teachers know how to assess progress in their students' learning. They view the artists as experts who are successful because of their superior knowledge of their subject matter honed through years of experience as performing artists. This view of artisan expertise contrasts with a more generic view of adaptive expertise, which concentrates on the ability of experts to apply their knowledge and skills to specific contexts in order to do familiar tasks in unfamiliar ways (Bransford, Brown, & Cocking, 1999). Sawyer (2004) has applied these ideas to teaching as improvisation, particularly the capacity to adapt reflexively to learning environments.

Artists often engage adaptively with specific "spaces" outside school as the means for interacting with students and their teachers. Artists often prefer to think of their role as that of a creative facilitator who offers education projects out of schools in galleries, museums, the community such as village halls and churches, and other local phenomena. Such spaces can offer the conditions necessary to support and nurture creativity in teaching and learning, and offer up new starting points, lines of inquiry, and possibilities of specific places for engaging imaginative creative activity. To engage meaningfully with the history of an environment can involve collaborations that strengthen and extend students' relationship to particular communities and places. Artists and teachers develop unique pedagogic partnerships when they mesh understandings of how children encounter place and time differently in different contexts. When artists propose such alternative spaces and demonstrate their effectiveness, the collaborating teachers learn how to create opportunities for students to learn adaptively out of the classroom setting:

> It was like the way a photographer's eye changes when, if you take up photography as a hobby, instead of looking at things as just a scene you look at it as, oh if I take a photograph of that bit and edit it like this on the computer, it could be a really good photograph. I look at things in a completely different way now. I think I now teach in a more creative way. I think I've learnt some new ways of teaching. It's like I've been given a license to explore my own artistry a bit more. I play. I'm playful. I now experiment with a revitalized sense of myself as an artist teacher and happily share my own compositions with my students. I'm more interested in the students' ideas and give them more opportunities to talk about their ideas. I think of them as artists. I understand much more about the importance of being flexible and engaging the imagination and how to generate motivation and explore ideas while still working towards an outcome. I feel a lot more confident about ways to achieve a balance between freedom and control in creativity and to navigate between being a teacher and student and shared negotiation in collaboration within the hierarchy of the school.

This teacher worked together with the artist and they adaptively supported each other. Many teachers emphasized the tensions and felt threatened by changes in routine. Yet they nonetheless spoke about the experience of being helped teach more creatively, using creative journeys as educational drivers, and developing creative skills in young people. The capacity and willingness to take risks and work with the unfamiliar created some challenges to the orthodoxies and occupational mythologies played out in artist-teacher interactions, as one teacher observed:

> There was a definite sort of tension.... They're kind of guiding the pupils on a journey... there were kind of responses that involve kind of changing another professional's approach and that brought about tensions which I could see. For example, I normally work with the desks arranged in rows. But actually I think it was a really good process to see how students could work in small groups arranged in different ways and spaces

to generate new ways of composing. They not only used space in some exciting activities; they had the students working in small groups with a new self-determined concentration, purposefully experimenting, modeling, and trying out ideas as they composed in different ways. It was a message creative space though. It felt like a combination between a science lab, an art room and a junk yard. The students were absorbed in their composing and it was not surprising really. I have rarely seen such a purposeful, buzzing and reflective climate in a group. The students were also consciously reflecting on their creative process, taking photographs and recordings of all their drafts as a record of when and in what way they felt they were being creative.

I came to a realization that they all had a gift. I realized how good they were and how much they were taking the students pieces seriously, and that they were at the top of their profession and yet remained so very, very sympathetic to all of the students, aware of what each student was risking and what made them tick. The gift was of making every idea that the students came up with live. So a simple idea that a normal teacher like me would take for granted or just say 'yes that's nice idea' they were so in tune with the kids. I've learned so much from their special engagement; it's like working in a different world now where I know that things are going on but this has become a different game. I've learned to move in different ways and to tune in to partners. I still feel the tension of accountability exerted in lots of different ways but I just love the true reciprocity of my teaching horizon being a shared horizon and so is always affected by others. That sort of connection must be good for students to see us tuning in and connecting.

What these teachers are learning is how to be more improvisational in the classroom and more collaborative with students. This involves a kind of mutual tuning in and openness to each other. Being able to *talk* about pedagogic practices, to feel that pull that one needs to be able to *listen* and tune in and to *observe* different practices, enables teachers (and artists) to experience a renewed sense of purpose and professionalism, a reduced sense of isolation, and a passion for the exploration of their teaching and learning. The business of inviting judgments on "what works" from professional artists, on how working with improvisational characteristics of practice can enrich and enliven the learning environment, *and reapplying that understanding,* is essential if teachers are to learn how to be more improvisational in the classroom (Maddock et al., 2007).

The ways that artists mutually tune in to teachers and learners provides an important clue as to how teachers can better negotiate the teaching paradox. In the same way that instruments are tuned on the basis of tension, so the success of an educational partnership depends on the tension being maintained in balance. On the one hand, as artist and teacher open themselves up to each other, they feel the pull of the other that demands respect. The point at which the partnership results in the most effective learning environment is when improvisatory acts (of collaboration) and improvisations (in classroom activities) occur. When artists and teachers attune to each other's ways of working, they create new ways to enhance creativity in education.

In sum, ways of enabling improvisational forms of creativity in pedagogic partnerships include:

1. Providing time to reflect critically on emerging pedagogic practices.
2. Allowing for a high proportion of pupil talk, much of it occurring between pupils, teachers, and artists, and reflecting on the focus of classroom discourse.
3. Modeling the use of a variety of means and media to communicate both teacher and artist's ideas to pupils.
4. Allowing time for extended planning sessions that reflect on the content to be taught being organized around a limited set of powerful ideas.
5. Modeling the ways in which the classroom ethos encourages each other along with the pupils to offer speculative answers to challenging questions without fearing failure.
6. Developing pedagogic practices that invite flexible thinking, risk taking, multivocality, professionally looking anew, and illustrating inherent freedoms that characterize improvisatory forms of creativity

Educational partnerships are essentially improvisational in nature; they model the more improvised and less formulaic and fixed approaches to teaching. Thus these experiences help teachers understand how to negotiate the teaching paradox in a different way, with a renewed focus on improvisational practice.

### REFERENCES

Alexander, R. (2004). Still no pedagogy? Principle, pragmatism and compliance in primary education. *Cambridge Journal of Education, 31*(1), 7–33.

(2008). *Essays on pedagogy.* Abingdon, Oxon: Routledge.

Ball, S. J. (2003). The teacher's soul and the terrors of performativity. *Journal of Educational Policy, 18*(2), 215–228.

Berliner, P. (1994). *Thinking in jazz: The infinite art of improvisation.* Chicago: University of Chicago.

Bernstein, B. (1996). *Pedagogy, symbolic control and identity*. New York: Rowman and Littlefield.

Bransford, J., Brown, A., & Cocking, R. (1999). Editorial introduction. *How people learn, mind, brain and school*. Joint Report to the Committees on Developments in the Science of Learning, on Learning Research and Educational Practice and the Commission on Behavioral and Social Sciences and Education, Washington DC: National Research Council.

Burnard, P. (2008). The impact of productive tensions between policy and practice on creativity in education. *UNESCO Observatory E-Journal, Multi-Disciplinary Research in the Arts*.

Burnard, P. & Maddock, M. (2007). Pupil and teacher perceptions of the nature of artist pedagogy and its impact on school change. http://www.educ.cam.ac.uk/research/projects/proj5.html

Burnard, P. & Swann, M. (2010). Pupil perceptions of learning with artists: A new order of experience? *Thinking Skills and Creativity*, 5(2), 70–83

Burnard, P. & White, J. (2008). Creativity and performativity: Counterpoints in British and Australian education. *British Educational Research Journal*, Special Issue on Creativity and Performativity in Teaching and Learning 34(5), 667–682.

CapeUK . (2005). Creative space: Collaborative approaches to science learning in schools. CapeUK.

Cochrane, P. (2008). Making space for creativity: How teachers and school leaders in England navigate mixed policy messages *Observatory E-Journal, Multi-Disciplinary Research in the Arts*, Issue 3 http://www.adp.unimelb.edu.au/unesco/ejournal/pdf/cochrane.pdf

Cochrane, P., Craft, A., & Dillon, P. (2007). King James 1 Community College creative partnerships project: Writing for radio. Durham: Creative Partnerships Durham/Sunderland (in collaboration with Exeter University).

Cochrane, P., Jeffery, G., & Price, D. (2007). *Creative partnerships and the further education sector*. London: Creative Partnerships Learning Team.

Cocker, J. (1964). *Improvising jazz*. Englewood Cliffs, NJ: Prentice-Hall.

Craft, A. (2005). *Creativity in schools: Tensions and dilemmas*. London: Routledge/Falmer.

(2006) Creativity and wisdom? *Cambridge Journal of Education*, 36(3), 336–350.

Creativity, Culture and Education (2009). Homepage. Retrieved Jan. 29, 2009 from http://www.creativitycultureeducation.org/

Creative Partnerships (2005a). *First findings policy, practice and progress: A review of creative learning 2002–2004*. London; Arts Council England.

Creative Partnerships (2005b). Creative Partnership Website. Retrieved Feb. 29, 2005 from http://www.creative-partnerships.com/about

Day, C. & Saunders, L. (2006) 'What being a teacher (really) means', *Forum 48*(3), 265–271.

DCMS (2001). Culture and Creativity: The Next Ten Years. Green Paper. London: DCMS. Accessed online September 14, 2009 at: http://www.culture.gov.uk/images/publications/Culture_creative_next10.pdf

DCMS (2004). Available online at: http://www.culture.gov.uk (accessed September 4, 2004).

Galton, M. (2008). *Creative practitioners in schools and classrooms*. London: Creative Partnerships, Arts Council England.

(2010) Going with the flow or back to normal? The impact of creative practitioners in schools and classrooms, *Research Papers in Education*, 25 (4)355–375.

Griffith, M. & Woolf, F. (2009). The Nottingham Apprenticeship Model: schools in partnership with artists and creative practitioners. *British Eductional Research Journal*, 35(4), 557–574.

Hall, C. & Thomson, P. (2007). Creative partnerships? Cultural policy and inclusive arts practice in one primary school. *British Educational Research Journal*, 33(3), 315–330.

Hall, C., Thomson, P., & Russell, L. (2007) Teaching like an artist: The pedagogic identities and practices of artists in schools. *British Journal of Sociology of Education*, 28(5), 605–619.

Jeffery, G. (2005). *The creative college: Building a successful learning culture in the arts*. Stoke-on-Trent: Trentham.

Jeffrey, B. (2006). Creative teaching and learning: Towards a common discourse and practice. *Cambridge Journal of Education*, 36(3), 399–414.

Jenkins, D., Jeffery. G., & Walsh. A. (2008). Mediated conversations at a cultural trading post: A study of the TAPP and Eastfeast PPD Programmes in support of teachers and artists. Available at http://www.creative-partnerships.com/researchandevaluation

Ledgard, A. (2006). Fair exchange: Shared professional development and reflective action. In P. Burnard and S. Hennessy (Eds.), *Reflective practices in arts education* (pp. 169–182). Dordrecht: Springer.

Loi, D. & Dillon, P. (2006). Adaptive educational environments as creative spaces. *Cambridge Journal of Education*, 36(3), 363–381.

Loveless, A. (2008) Creative learning and new technology? A provocation paper in J.Sefton-Green (Ed) *Creative learning* (pp. 61–73). London: Arts council England.

Maddock, M., Drummond, M. J., Korelek, B., & Nathan, I. (2007) Doing school differently: Creative practitioners at work. *Education 3–13*, 35(1), 47–58.

Maddock, M. & Sapsed, R. with Drummond, M. J. (2008). *Igniting a fuse: Developing the creative practice of primary educators*. Tendring: Creative Partnerships.

Nardone, P.L. (1996). The experience of improvisation in music: A phenomeno logical psychological analysis. Unpublished PhD. Dissertation, Saybrook Institute. University of Michigan, Ann Arbor: UMI.

National Advisory Committee on Creative and Cultural Education (NACCCE) (1999). *All our futures: Creativity, culture and education*. London: Department for Education and Employment.

National College of School Leadership (NCSL) (2002). Leading the creative school: A leading edge seminar, November, Nottingham.

Pike, A. (1974). A phenomenology of jazz. *Journal of Jazz Studies*, 2(1), 88–94.

Pope, M., Fuller, M., Boulter, C., Denicolo, P., & Wells, P. (1999). Partnership and collaboration in teacher education. In M. Lang, J. Olson, H. Hansen, and W. Bünder (Eds.), *Changing schools/changing practices: Perspectives on educational reform and teacher professionalism*. Louvain, Brussels: Garant.

Pringle, E. (2008). Artists' perspectives on art practice and pedagogy. In J. Sefton-Green (Ed.). *Creative learning* (pp. 41–50). England: Arts Council.

Qualifications and Curriculum Authority (2005). *Creativity: Find it, promote it : A Teacher's guide to using the video.* London: DfEE/QCA.

Sawyer, R. K. (2004). Creative teaching: Collaborative discussion as disciplined improvisation. *Educational Researcher, 23*(2), 12–20.

Schön, D. (1983). *The reflective practitioner: How professionals think in action.* New York: Basic Books.

Sefton-Green, J. (Ed.). (2008). *Creative learning.* London: Creative Partnerships, Arts Council.

Shulman, L. (1987). Knowledge and teaching: Foundations of the new reform. *Harvard Educational Review, 57*(1), 1–22.

Solomon, L. (1986). Improvisation II. *Perspectives in New Music. 24,* 224–235.

Triantafyllaki, A. & Burnard, P. (2010). Creativity and arts-based knowledge creation in diverse educational partnership practices: Lessons from two case studies in rethinking traditional spaces for learning. *UNESCO Observatory E-Journal, Multi-Disciplinary Research in the Arts, 1*(15). http://www.abp.unimelb.edu.au/unesco/ejournal/vol-one-issue-five.html .

Upitis, R. (2006). Challenges for artists and teachers working in partnership. In P. Burnard and S. Hennessy (Eds.), *Reflective practices in arts education* (pp. 55–68). Dordrecht, The Netherlands: Springer.

Wenger, E. (1998). *Communities of practice: Learning, meaning and identity.* Cambridge: Cambridge University Press.

Woods, P. & Jeffrey, B. (1996) *Teachable Moments: The Art of Creative Teaching in Primary Schools.* Buckingham: Open University Press.

# 4

## Improvising within the System: Creating New Teacher Performances in Inner-City Schools

### CARRIE LOBMAN

Teachers' lives are dominated by scripts: the overt scripts of the curriculum, the "hidden" scripts of race, class, language, and culture, and the societal scripts of how teachers and students are supposed to relate to each other. All of these, however, are informed by the meta-script that the primary job of the teacher is to help children acquire knowledge and skills – a deeply embedded cultural model of teaching and learning that has been referred to as *instructionism* (Papert, 1994), as *transmission and acquisition* (Rogoff, 1990; Sfard, 1998), or as *the banking model* (Freire, 1994). Teachers are supposed to find the best techniques for helping children learn more so that they can know more. Reform efforts that aim at addressing the current problems in education generally attempt to make such learning more efficient, equitable, or accountable through smaller classes, culturally relevant pedagogy, and a major focus on testing and assessment. By many accounts (Darling-Hammond, 2007; Kohn, 2004; Kozol, 2005; Meier & Wood, 2004; Sizer, 2004), these efforts are not succeeding.

The acquisitional understanding of learning (and its meta-script) has been criticized by many educators, who believe that it leads schools to be organized around the pursuit of a narrowly conceived set of information and skills (Egan, 1992; Eisner, 1998; Greene, 1988; Holzman, 1997, 2009). As Maxine Greene (1988) pointed out over two decades ago, "A concern for the critical and the imaginative, for the opening of new ways of 'looking at things' is wholly at odds with the technicist and behaviorist emphases we find in American schools" (p. 126). With the current focus on standardization and testing, one could argue that what Greene called "a technicist and behaviorist emphasis" has become an obsession, and that the acquisitional

In R. K. Sawyer (Ed.) (2011). *Structure and improvisation in creative teaching* (pp. 73–93). Cambridge: Cambridge University Press.

learning model is in the process of turning schools into "antiseptic environment[s]" that produce adults who are wholly unprepared to exhibit the flexibility, creativity, and collaborative skills required to thrive in today's world (Eisner, 1998, p. 85; also see Sawyer, 2004).

The history of American schools' nearly complete focus on children acquiring skills and information is intimately tied to the definition of development accepted by most American psychologists and educators in the twentieth century. Development, in this sense, is a maturational process that sets the stage for the acquiring of skills and information, and it is therefore not considered the domain of public schools. The legacy of human development as an unfolding of stages (that are independent of and that may be determinant of learning) remains to this day, as evidenced by the lack of focus on development in most public schools and a focus on designing developmentally appropriate environments and curricula in early childhood education. While there have always been scholars who have rejected this separation and have argued for attention to be paid to the whole child (Comer & Gates, 2004 Dewey, 1938; Noddings, 2005), public schools have not been heavily influenced by this position; if anything, they have become narrower in their focus, as teachers feel increased pressure to focus their efforts on the learning of skills and information.

There are, however, other ways to understand development and its relationship to learning that put development center stage for educators. Nearly a century ago, the Russian psychologist Lev Vygotsky pointed out that "learning and development are interrelated from the child's first day of life" (1978, p. 84). Learning and development are part of a dialectical emergent process where learning leads, supports, and is inseparable from overall human development. For Vygotsky, "the only 'good learning' is that which is in advance of development" (p. 89).

Many scholars have taken up Vygotsky's writings on learning and development in recent decades (see, for examples. Cole, 1998; Rogoff, 2003; Wertsch, 1985). These scholars have explored Vygotsky's claim that learning leads development by creating learning environments in which students can go beyond themselves and do what they do not yet know how to do (Cole, 1999, 2006; Holzman, 1997, 2009; Newman & Holzman, 1993; Wells, 1999). [1]

---

[1] Whereas this paper is primarily focused on the contributions of the cultural-historical tradition to developing environments where learning leads development, there are other traditions, in particular the learning sciences, that have also addressed this issue in the past few decades. For more on this, see: Bereiter & Scardamalia, 1993, Collins, 2006, Scardamalia & Bereiter, 2006.

As part of this tradition of cultural-historical psychology, Newman and Holzman (1993) have focused on Vygotsky as a dialectical methodologist (also see Newman & Holzman, 1996; Holzman, 1997, 2009, Vygotsky, 1978). Their work focuses on the dialectical, improvisational, emergent activity by which human beings create environments where people can grow – socially, emotionally, and culturally – and where in the process they become active creators and producers of their lives and learning. It is in the context of actively participating in creating environments for overall human development (not when they reach a particular stage) that young people can develop the need and desire to learn. Newman and Holzman call this approach *developmental learning*.

Given the institutional constraints of schooling, for the most part the developmental learning approach has been used in the creation of outside of school programs that support young people from inner cities to come to see themselves as learners by helping them become more cosmopolitan or citizens of the world (for more on developmental learning outside of school, see Farmer, 2008; Fulani & Kurlander, 2009; Gordon, Bowman & Mejia, 2003; Holzman, 2009). In this chapter, I describe the Developing Teachers Fellowship Program (DTFP), a modest attempt to see if learning this approach could be of use to teachers who work in traditional public school classrooms. The expectation was not that they would be able to completely ignore the demands of acquisitional learning, given that whether new or experienced, teachers do not have the power or the authority to completely throw out the school meta-script. The goal was to provide teachers with tools that they could use to play with or add to the script while still working under the constraining conditions of the current educational system.

One of the tools that the DTFP makes use of in training teachers is theatrical improvisation (improv). Improv, with its focus on continuously emergent process and ensemble activity, provides teachers with a concrete way of being playful with the scripts of schooling while including students as active participants in creating the environment in the classroom. When using improv in the classroom, the content is not disregarded; it becomes the material for the activities and performances. Students can have a more direct and creative relationship with the curriculum and as such they do not just learn the material; they develop as learners and as creators. Improv, because of its combination of rules and creativity, addresses many of the paradoxes of teaching, in particular the relationship between creativity and structure, control and freedom, and creative engagement and learning content.

This chapter addresses the question of what happens when teachers are introduced to a developmental learning methodology that allows them to play with the dominant script of the system within which they work. It begins with an elaboration of the methodology used in the DTFP and then goes on to describe the program and gives examples of how the participating teachers are making use of it in their classrooms.

## A PERFORMATORY VYGOTSKIAN METHODOLOGY

Vygotsky (1978) argued that "*human learning presupposes a specific social nature and a process by which children grow into the intellectual life of those around them*" (p. 88, emphasis in the original), and that the only "good learning" is learning that leads development (p. 89). His experimental work with children demonstrated the social nature of learning. His work reveals learning as a continuously emergent social activity that is dialectically tied to development, quite different from the standard acquisitional model of an individual learner acquiring objective knowledge.

Vygotsky is perhaps best known for introducing the term Zone of Proximal Development (ZPD), a concept that helps us understand his argument that learning leads development. There are multiple interpretations of the ZPD in the writings of Vygotsky (Cole, 1985; Daniels, Cole, & Wertsch, 2007), but many contemporary educators have defined it as the difference between a child's solitary performance and their slightly more advanced performance when assisted by a more developed adult or peer providing just enough support (Bodrova & Leong, 1996; Rogoff, 1984; Wells, 1999). Many educators and classroom teachers have now adopted the term "scaffolding" (Berger, 2009; Berk & Winsler, 1995) as a metaphor for understanding and operationalizing how teachers can take advantage of the ZPD to design learning environments.

Other educators argue that the scaffolding metaphor and the view of the ZPD as merely the distance between a child's solitary performance and his or her performance while assisted by more developed individuals is too narrow an interpretation of what Vygotsky was suggesting (Goldstein, 1999; Moll, 1992; Smagorinsky, 2007). Newman and Holzman (1993, 1997) are among this group; they expand Vygotsky's notion of the ZPD and use it to propose a concept of learning and development as a creative improvisational activity. The ZPD is the activity of people creating environments where children (and adults) can take risks, make mistakes, and support each other to do what they do not yet know how to do. Rather than being a tool for learning discrete pieces of information, "the ZPD is the ever emergent and continuously changing 'distance' between being and becoming. It is human activity that gives birth to and nurtures the ZPD and, with its creation, human learning and development" (Holzman, 2000, p. 5). From this perspective, Vygotsky's theories are useful in supporting people to create environments where children (and adults) can take risks, make mistakes, and support each other to do what they do not yet know how to do (Holzman, 2000).

From birth through infancy, toddlerhood, and preschool, children are supported to do what they do not know how to do, mostly in the form of play. Vygotsky (1978) connected the play of young children with his concept of the ZPD: "In play a child behaves beyond his average age, above his daily behavior, in play it is as though he were a head taller than himself" (p.102). Vygotsky pointed out that by virtue of the complex relationship between rules and imaginary situations, in play children are able to do what they do not yet know how to do in non-play situations. One way to understand what happens in children's pretend play is that it is by doing what they do not know how to do that children learn how to do the myriad of things they learn how to do before they arrive at school. Although Vygotsky was talking about the play of preschool children, in this chapter I expand this understanding of "performing a head taller" to older children and adults.

## Performance

One way to understand what is happening when ZPDs are created is that people are *performing* ahead of themselves. Performance has many meanings; I define it as our ability to be who we are and who we are not simultaneously. Just as with young children at play, when older children and adults perform, they do not stop being who they are, but they are also not totally constrained by who they are. Newman and Holzman (1993; Holzman, 1997, 2009) argue that our human ability to perform is too valuable a tool to only be used in the theater. From their perspective, human beings can be active creators of their development by virtue of the capacity to perform, to be simultaneously who we are and who we are not. In this understanding of performance, pretending, playing, and imagining are essential to emotional, social, moral, and cognitive development.

Most school environments do not take into account that human beings can perform as who they are and who they are becoming; rather, schools focus on seeing people as who they are or what they know (or do not know). A shift to seeing teachers and students as performers opens up space for learning, because students can be supported to go beyond who they are and what they know, and to create other ways of relating to themselves, others, and the content to be learned.

Several scholars have argued that developmental learning is the kind of learning that some children continue to do through creative or artistic experiences, often in outside of school learning environments. For example, Elliot Eisner (2005, p. 208) wrote: "The arts teach students to act and to judge in the absence of rule, to rely on feel, to pay attention to nuance, to act and appraise the consequences of one's choices and to revise and then to make other choices." Through informal learning at museums, on trips, in dance, music and art classes, and the many other environments in which they find themselves, children continue to have the experience of being able to do more than just demonstrate what they know; they can also be creators and producers of their lives and learning (Davis, 2005; Eisner, 1998). In these situations the learning that occurs is more cultural than cognitive; it is not based on what children know or do not know; rather, it is primarily about creating an environment where they can perform in new ways. By taking on multiple roles, both on and off the stage, young people come to see themselves as "capable of acting outside and beyond the expected" (Heath, 2000, p. 39). However, for many children, particularly for urban youth living in poverty, schools do not provide opportunities to engage in activities that foster the kind of creative risk taking and ensemble learning that supports overall human development (Davis, 2005; Eisner, 1998; Holzman, 2009; Karliner & Holzman, 2005; Nachmanovich, 1990). One purpose of the DTFP is to help teachers find ways to bring the performatory, developmental learning that can sometimes occur outside of school into the classroom.

## Improvisation

One tool that has been valuable in helping teachers see themselves and their students as performers is improv theater. Improv, like you might see on TV or in a comedy club, is a performance art where an ensemble collectively creates scenes or stories without a script. A number of researchers have made the connection between expert teaching and improvisation (Baker-Sennett & Matusov, 1997; Borko & Livingston, 1989; Yinger, 1980, 1987). The unifying theme of this volume is the idea that improvisation is a useful metaphor for teaching. Improvisational teaching is emergent and jointly created with students. What happens in improvisational teaching closely resembles the pretend play of young children (Lobman, 2005; Sawyer, 1997a). Indeed, teachers of improvisation speak of helping people rediscover the creative and collaborative skills they had as children (Johnstone, 1981; Nachmanovich, 1990; Spolin, 1999). In improv, as in pretend play, a group of people collectively create an emergent scene or story building off each other's ideas and suggestions.

Improvisation is a valuable tool for helping teachers create developmental learning environments, because, like many creative activities, it focuses on helping the ensemble develop and create without having to know what is being created beforehand (Lobman & Lundquist, 2007). Improvising together can help teachers and students build learning environments that are less governed by the need to be right and that support everyone to take the risks necessary to learn and develop. In addition, while improv is about emergent play, it also contains a structure. Improvisers create together using a set of rules and strategies that provide a framework for creativity (Johnstone, 1981; Sawyer, 1997b; Spolin, 1999). This combination of structure and emergent activity is critical for teachers who are working inside schools because it provides a way to address the teaching paradox – to play, yet within the constraints of the school environment.

### PROGRAM DESCRIPTION

The Developing Teachers Fellowship Program (DTFP) is a project of the East Side Institute in New York City, an independent non-profit organization that has been in the business of developing non-traditional approaches to learning since the late 1970s. Over the years, the Institute has developed its understanding and practice of developmental learning through a number of programs, including a therapeutic approach, an independent elementary school, and a close relationship with several outside of school youth development programs (for more on these programs, see Holzman, 2009). All of these programs are based on the theory of developmental learning, and the core belief that performance (simultaneously being who we are and who we are not) is what makes qualitative transformation possible. Started in 2006, the DTFP is a year-long training program for New York City area teachers who are already certified and are currently working in a public school. DTFP receives no support or payment from the schools; it is independently supported by private donations and volunteer labor.

The program consists of bi-weekly Saturday workshops and monthly on-site mentoring. The curriculum of the program includes philosophical and practical explorations of a Vygotskian inspired methodology, as well as training in theatrical improvisation. One of the goals of the program was to help the Fellows create supportive, playful learning environments with their students. However, consistent with a Vygotskian understanding of learning and development, rather than teaching them "seven steps to a supportive, playful environment," this goal was approached by inviting them to create such an environment with the directors and each other. As one of the fellows said, "A very interesting and refreshing characteristic of the program is that we are learning *about* improvisation, and we are *doing* it improvisationally. There is no separation between the content of what are learning and the process by which we are learning it." She added that this was particularly valuable because instead of leaving the workshop with a list of "how-to's," she is able to leave having had the experience of creating the learning environment with her peers. In her past experience, professional development often involved learning about a new curriculum, method or approach, but the "process of learning about it did not appear to have any relationship to what was being taught."

## Teaching Fellows

Participants were selected through a process that included a review of the applicant's resume, transcripts, and personal statement and an interview with the program directors. Fellows were purposefully selected in order to create a diverse group in terms of level of experience and grade level taught. Each of the selected participants received a $2,500 stipend upon the completion of the program.

There were eleven Fellows in the program during the 2006–2007 school year. They were a diverse group, with six of them being European-American, four African- or Caribbean-American, and one Hispanic. They worked in the full range of settings for public school teachers. While they all worked in urban schools, six of them were elementary school teachers, three worked in high schools, one in a middle school, and one was a preschool itinerant special education teacher. They ranged in experience from two to fifteen years as teachers. All of the Fellows were women. All of the Fellows worked in inner-city schools where the majority of the students were children of color who received free or reduced lunch. With the exception of two Fellows who taught at an alternative small public secondary school with a progressive curriculum, the Fellows all worked in traditional settings with standardized curriculum. With the exception of the preschool teacher, all of the Fellows were responsible for preparing their students for high-stakes tests.

## Saturday Workshops

The Saturday workshop was the core learning activity of the DTFP. The Fellows met every other week for a three-hour workshop led by the directors of the program. These sessions consisted of improvisational theater activities, philosophical dialogues, and teacher supervision, but not as discrete components of a given workshop. Rather, the workshops were improvisational and emergent. For example, while the session may have started with an improv warm-up activity, this could easily lead into a philosophical conversation about the relationship between individuals and the group, and then transform into a supervisory discussion about an incident in a Fellow's classroom. Plans for a given session emerged from the activities in the previous sessions. Moreover, these plans were continuously being reshaped as each three-hour session unfolded.

### Improv Activities

All of the Saturday workshops involved the learning and practicing of improv theater activities. Over the years, improvisers have developed a repertoire of games that are used to learn and practice improv skills. In addition to traditional improv games, the program used the activities from the book *Unscripted learning: Using improv activities across the K-8 curriculum* (Lobman & Lundquist, 2007). The activities from this book are specifically designed to be integrated with a standard public school curriculum.

Improv activities served at least four purposes: 1) building the ensemble of the Fellows in the workshop and creating a supportive learning environment; 2) teaching the skills of improvisation that are key in building the learning environment in the classroom; 3) providing teachers with improv activities that they can use in their own classrooms; and 4) drawing attention to teaching and learning as performances that can be developed.

### Philosophical Conversations

A second component of the Saturday workshops was the philosophical conversation that developed around topics such as the relationship between learning and development and the politics of teaching. Some of these conversations arose from an article or a book that the Fellows were assigned to read, whereas others emerged from the playing of an improv game or out of the conversations about practical considerations in the Fellows' classrooms. These conversations were an attempt to uncover some of the assumptions that shape teachers' and children's lives in school and out. In line with the rest of the workshops, the philosophical dialogues were often created improvisationally, with Fellows performing as each other or as the authors of the books or articles. The emphasis was as much on the process of the conversation as on the content. This helped create an environment where everyone could play or improvise with ideas and beliefs that are sometimes perceived by teachers as either too complicated or as abstractions that have no connections to their daily activity.

*Supervision*

The workshops were not organized formally as supervision of the teacher's practices, and they were not evaluative. However, in the course of learning an improv game or having a philosophical conversation, the Fellows would bring up areas of their practice they wanted to work on to get better at, or questions about how to incorporate performance into their practice. For the most part, these supervisory conversations centered on how to work with the curriculum they were using in their classrooms in a more creative manner, and how to organize their students to be more supportive of each other and of them. These conversations often led back to the creation of new performances or the creation of games.

## Monthly Mentoring

Each of the Fellows was assigned a mentor who had been trained in the Institute's performance approach to learning and teaching. The mentors visited their assigned Fellows once a month, facilitated contact among the fellows through emails and conference calls, and were available to their mentees between sessions. The mentor's job was to serve as a bridge between what the Fellows were learning in the workshops and their work in the classroom.

### CREATING NEW TEACHER PERFORMANCES
### IN THE CLASSROOM

DTFP workshops presented a set of theatrical activities (including improvisation) that can be valuable for teachers to learn and practice with their students, and also presented a theoretical framework that emphasized performance as a characteristic of all human activity (Goffman, 1959; Newman and Holzman, 1993). Whereas many of the teachers came to the program with some experience in theatrical performance, the theoretical framework was new to most of them. The following section examines some of the ways in which the Fellows were impacted by their participation in the DTFP, and it includes excerpts from the Fellows' journals that illustrate how they were making use of the program in their classrooms.

### Is Teaching a Performance?

One of the paradoxes of teaching that this volume addresses is that good teaching is creative and improvisational even when the teacher is working within a structured or standardized curriculum. This paradox leads many teachers to believe that teaching can only be creative if it breaks from the traditional teaching script. Given that many teachers do not feel free to fully make this break, they believe that they have to divide their time between teaching content and being creative. The methodology of the DTFP challenges this by introducing teachers to a new conception of performance that encourages them to relate to even the most structured activities as a form of performance.

In the course of the workshop discussions, it was discovered, not surprisingly, that the Fellows saw themselves as performing in the classroom when they did something "out of the ordinary" like speak to the students in a funny voice or put on a different costume, but that they did not see or relate to their "normal" teaching as a performance. There was their "real" teacher identity and then there was what they did when they wanted to be playful. The philosophy of the DTFP challenged this dichotomy. A goal of the program was to encourage the teachers to see themselves as performing all the time.

By beginning to see teaching as a performance, the Fellows began creating new teacher performances. For some of the Fellows this meant being able to be emotional, funny, or silly with their students. For others it meant having the option to further develop their serious, demanding, and even strict teaching performances so that these moments were more effective, creative, and more related to their students. Beth, for example, described her experience of consciously creating a more authoritative performance with her fourth-graders: "I have a hard time with authority, so I have been trying on – at my mentor's suggestion – a really over-exaggerated character of authority. Like a caricature of authority, which [the students] love and they really will behave differently for, because I play that and then they play the really super-exaggerated perfect students.... I walk around 'No smiling! No laughing! I don't want to hear that!'"

Seeing and developing performances made it possible for the Fellows to continuously create choices about how to perform instead of automatically reacting in response to what students were doing or how they were feeling in that moment. This provided their students with a model of what it might look like to develop emotionally and socially, and it gave the children an opportunity to create new performances as well. Finally, by using performance language with each other and their students, they created a new way of talking in the classroom that emphasized creativity and playfulness.

## Seeing Students as Performers

As the preceding example demonstrates, in addition to seeing themselves as performers, the Fellows also began to see their students as performers. This influenced the types of conversations they created in their classrooms.

In general, the relationship between students and teachers (particularly as children enter the middle grades) is often scripted: The roles of teacher and student are clear and the range of responses allowed to either role is quite limited. Through the program, the Fellows began to play with those roles, both in terms of how they responded to their students and in how they supported their students to respond to them and other teachers. In the following example from her fourth-grade class, Rachel used the Relationship Game – an improv activity that she learned in the workshops – to support her students to be powerful rather than victimized when teachers treated them unfairly. In the Relationship Game, two participants are given a relationship (i.e., sisters, doctor/patient, teacher/student) and a first line (i.e., You stole my wallet, I hate pistachios). The participants then perform the scene over and over again, each time starting with the same first line but improvising many different conversations in response to that line. Rachel writes:

> One particular afternoon, a student named Ariana came into class very upset with another teacher in the school. She was upset because she feels the teacher doesn't listen to her, is unfair, and doesn't let her use the restroom. The list goes on. I decided on the spot (which has been something I have been learning to do more often) to play this game with her and use the relationship of teacher-student. She chose someone to do the performance with her and we selected the first line of, "I need to go to the bathroom." Ariana performed the scene three times and every time we discussed it. The class pointed out that every time she performed it the words she used were different but the anger was the same throughout. The class suggested that the feeling in all performances was similar. Natalie, the girl who performed with her, attempted to change the tone of the performance but it was obvious that Ariana couldn't go with it.
>
> This was fascinating to discuss with the [class]. We decided collectively to ask two different people to perform the same scene. The scene was performed three times very differently which led to more discussion on the power of performance in our lives. After we played the game, Ariana was still under the impression that her teacher would not be able to respond to any new performance she came up with. The class supported Ariana to try out new performances of herself without waiting for the teacher to change.

In this example, Rachel created an environment where the class could play with some new ways of relating. She utilized a game that she had been playing in the workshops and adapted it to a situation with her students. Rachel related to her students as performers and creators of their lives rather than as people who were slaves to their reactions or victims of other people. Ariana may have felt that she was incapable of providing leadership to an authority figure, but Rachel talked to her ahead of where she was, and provided her and her classmates with an opportunity to see how they could take more responsibility for their learning.

## Classroom Creator versus Classroom Manager

Another one of the paradoxes of teaching is that in order to have a classroom where children are motivated and engaged, teachers have to give up some control. By engaging students in the active creation of the learning environment, children discover that they have the need and desire to follow directions and work together. This often goes against teachers' perception that they cannot be playful until they first maintain or manage the class. The DTFP introduced teachers to an understanding of classroom management as inseparable from being playful and improvisational.

In coming to see themselves and their students as performers, there was a shift in how the teachers in the DTFP talked about and understood classroom management. For the most part, the Fellows worked in traditional public schools and had their share of children that they found challenging. From the first day of the program, they were encouraged to talk about what was going on in their classrooms as material for an ongoing improvised play. The Fellows have embraced this methodology, and even though they did talk about difficult situations or children, they introduced these issues from the vantage point of developing their repertoire of teacher performances rather than as trying to fix the situation or to complain about the children.

For example, during a discussion about ways that the teachers felt challenged in the classroom, Heather – a second-grade teacher – asked for help in responding to a girl in her class who often had tantrums. The suggestion that came out of the workshop was that she could create a *Tantrum Theatre* where all of her students could have a chance to perform what they and others look like when they are having a tantrum. Rather than trying to get the individual child to stop or change her behavior, Heather and her students could relate to tantrums as one of the many performances that children (and adults) sometimes do, and as something that can be performed in an infinite number of ways. While the girl might still have tantrums at inopportune moments, Heather, the girl, and the rest of the class all had a different relationship to the tantrum by virtue of having created something with it. Heather said that dialogues like this one challenged her assumptions about what to do in response to children's behavior.

More importantly, the DTFP activities led the teachers to a fundamental rethinking of what "behavior" is. In this case, Heather began to interpret children's actions as *offers* (in improv, anything a performer says or does is an offer, and the ensemble creates the scene by accepting and using everyone's offers) and as performances rather than as good or bad behavior. She may still prefer certain performances to others, or find some offers useful and others a nuisance, but it has opened up the option of being creative when children are misbehaving or are not following directions.

Another example of relating to behavior as a performance occurred in Heather's class when her mentor, Gwen, was visiting. Prior to the visit, Heather had told Gwen that there was a lot of fighting in the class and that she was getting worn down. There were a few students in particular who instigated things and then the rest of the group got off-track. Heather and Gwen had decided that they were going to have the class do an improv activity of collective storytelling. Heather asked students to sit on the carpet and she reminded them of the rules of the game. The class made up a story titled "Fat Cat and Skinny Cat." Soon into the game, about a third of the class was either chatting with each other in pairs or fighting. The following excerpt from Heather's journal describes the experience:

> *Heather: Who wants to play the game? We don't have to play. It's really okay to say no. We'll find something else for those who don't want to play to do so they can support the group story telling.*
>
> Approximately a third of the class opted out of the storytelling. Gwen suggested that those who don't play listen to the new story we're going to tell, and draw a picture about it. After Gwen made that suggestion another third opted out. So there were about 7 story tellers on the carpet and about 14 kids drawing (intently and enthusiastically).
>
> The group on the rug told a new story. Midway through, Gwen asked the drawers to show everyone their pictures and none of them were about the new story we were telling. In fact they were all of Fat Cat and Skinny Cat.
>
> *Heather: Okay, we've got these great pictures to go with our story. What can we do with the story and all the pictures? Let's perform it!*
>
> Lots of hands went up to volunteer to perform. Heather picked one child, who had caused a lot of trouble earlier in the class but who was drawing intently, to play Skinny Cat. Another played Fat Cat and Gwen played the pizza man. All of the actors stood in front of the class and Heather asked the class to feed the actors their lines. Another student who had been quite disruptive was one of the most active script writers. The actors got the lines and acted them out. The class even created the words and a tune

for a finale song. Each actor sang the last verse separately as they walked down the road and exited the stage one by one.

In this instance, the children's actions made it difficult to do the collective storytelling activity in its traditional form. Rather than stopping the game or punishing the children for not behaving, in improv fashion Heather and Gwen treated their off-task actions as offers, and accepted them, then continued to create the scene/story. The first step was to make it possible for children to leave the rug and do something else without this being seen as a penalty. This is not a particularly unusual tactic; many teachers find ways for children to opt out of activities they are not ready to participate in productively. It is what happens next that demonstrates Heather and Gwen's commitment to performance. Rather than relating to the children who left the circle as non-participants in the storytelling activity, they were able to use what the children were doing at the other tables as part of the activity. The entire activity (not just the particular story) was seen as an ongoing improvised performance that everyone was participating in creating. All of the children had the experience of not only contributing to the group activity, but of actively shaping what the activity was going to be. Finally, by turning the whole thing into a written play, they were able to incorporate literacy and other skills that were important for Heather to be teaching.

## Improvising with the Traditional Curriculum

Another paradox addressed in this volume is that in order to learn the content of the curriculum, students need to be engaged creatively with the material. In the DTFP, the tools of improvisation gave teachers a way to deliver the content in a way that engaged the students in a creative activity, and this creative activity went beyond teaching content; it also helped the students come to see themselves as creators.

To help them learn to improvise within the script of the official curriculum, the Fellows took on the challenge of adapting and creating improv activities of their own that could be used to teach specific subjects and grade levels. In the following vignette, Maria described the experience of adapting another improv activity, *The Bus* (Lobman & Lundquist, 2007, p. 148), for use in her ninth-grade World History class:

> I attempted The History Bus improvisational activity in order to assess the depth of my student's understanding of the key historical figures we had studied. The class created a "bus" with eight passengers and one driver's seat in the center of the room. To begin the activity I made index cards with the

names of some of the figures we studied from September to the present. The stack of cards included the following historical figures: nomadic hunters and gatherers, Jesus Christ, Buddha, Confucius, Shi Huangdi, Akbar the Great, Martin Luther, Marie Antoinette, Louis XIV, a South Bronx monk, Medieval Knight, Machiavelli, the Pope, an Untouchable, Saladin, a Renaissance courtier, third estate citizen and various Enlightenment thinkers (Hobbes, Voltaire, Montequieu, Locke). Eight students chose a card from the deck of figures. Each of these historical "passengers" then worked with a team of 3–4 other students to review the history of this character and generate ideas on how this character might act on a bus. After 5 minutes, the "characters" lined up to wait for the bus.

To remind the students to stay in character, I made the bus driver a Renaissance courtier, a character that many students were familiar with. Despite what the historical passenger said/did to the courtier, his job was to be the consummate gentleman. As the figures entered the bus, it was interesting to see their depth of understanding, even between figures that didn't live in the same time period. For example, there was a verbal argument between Marie Antoinette and a third Estate citizen, hungry for bread; a discussion between Martin Luther and Jesus about what Jesus really intended for his followers; a disagreement between Martin Luther and the Pope; Machiavelli and Pericles; and Shi Huangdi and Voltaire.

The *History Bus* activity put a demand on Maria's students to actively engage with the content and simultaneously required them to create with each other and with Maria. Although only eight students "rode the bus," everyone contributed to the performance by working collectively to shape the characters. This meant that the students playing the characters were not put on the spot and the students who did not actively perform in the scene shared responsibility for the content. Maria was able to use improv to assess and reinforce content her students had already learned. However, unlike many traditional assessments, this activity also allowed students to continue to learn from each other.

In Maria's activity, there were the obvious benefits of history coming to life and of giving students an opportunity to see things from multiple perspectives. Another way to understand the *History Bus* activity is that the learning that was occurring was more performatory than cognitive, and that Maria's students were developing as performers and creators of their learning. Learning involves building relationships – both relationships to one's fellow learners and to the subject matter itself. However, for the most part, traditional history teaching rarely gives students a chance to actively build those relationships. Performance activities like the *History Bus* can provide a way for students to create relationships with the content of the curriculum and can help them make it their own. Maria and her students came to see the content of the curriculum as not just material to be learned, but as material for the creation of ongoing improvised performances as historians. It also demonstrated that even in a high school with a traditional curriculum and a high-stakes assessment at the end of the year, Maria was able to do something creative that supported the curriculum rather than competed with it.

Maria was pleased with the results of the History bus and other improv activities, but it did not completely eliminate her hesitance to be playful. Maria had a strong commitment to having her inner-city students succeed on the high-stakes test they had to take in June, as she believed that this was their ticket out of poverty and into the wider world. Throughout the program, even as she became more adept at integrating improv into the curriculum, she continued to express that she could not be as demanding of her students when they were playing: "They are so engaged during the improv games, they are more philosophical and grapple with the ideas, they take more responsibility for each other and the group, but I know that at a certain point I can't teach this way, I have to be the tough teacher and more of a dictator and tell them we need to get serious." This quotation gives expression to an ongoing attitude on the part of many of the teachers, namely that improvisation was ultimately less demanding than traditional schoolwork. Although the DTFP did not eliminate this attitude, it did create a context where teachers could begin to question it.

## CONCLUSION

As long as schools continue to expect teachers to use the meta-script of acquisitional learning, it is likely that they will thwart the kind of creative, continuously emergent developmental activity that characterizes truly effective learning. As teacher educators, it is critical that we find ways to help our teachers "practice becoming," to produce environments where learning and development are jointly created. We need to find approaches that can give teachers the tools they need to work creatively within a system that does not often support innovation. The improvisational training described in this chapter has provided the Fellows with a methodology that supports them in working creatively under sometimes very constraining conditions. DTFP is a program that has successfully addressed the teaching paradox.

The methodology of the DTFP is based on the understanding that learning is inseparable from development. It involves being "who you are and who you are not" – in other words, performing. This is how babies and very young children are related to before they come to school, and that is why they learn and develop so well during their preschool years. The program helped teachers learn to reshape their teaching performances, to the extent possible, into ones that support the development of their students.

Improvisation proved to be an invaluable activity in the Fellows' practice. By becoming improvisers, the Fellows have started to relate to themselves and their students as creators of an ongoing play that is related to the traditional school script but is not bound to it. Rather, in these performances, they have started to use everything, from the world history curriculum to second graders' bickering and fighting, as material from which to create the learning environment in the classroom.

The DTFP is an experimental program that trains a small number of teachers. It does not claim that it will be able to effect system-wide change. The goal of the program is to help the participating teachers bring a developmental perspective into their own classrooms and to draw attention to the possibilities for creating new approaches that support academic achievement without sacrificing creativity and playfulness. The results of this first year were promising, but there is a need for research to determine whether or not the program is having an impact on the learning environment in the schools, as well as follow-up studies to explore whether the Fellows continued these practices after the conclusion of the program, and whether those practices improved students' school experiences.

In providing teachers with new understandings of learning and teaching and with specific, practical tools consistent with these new understandings, the DTFP allowed teachers to challenge the methodology of most schools – one based on a sequential, linear understanding of learning as the acquisition and demonstration of knowledge. Rather than creating an environment where risks can be taken, and where students and teachers can do what they do not yet know how to do, schools tend to be environments where doing what one already knows how to do is valued and rewarded. One of our discoveries is that it is possible to bring development even into schools that are governed by standardization and testing. We are more convinced than ever that learning to see themselves and their students as performers is what is needed for teachers to be successful under the current constraining circumstances so many of them face.

### REFERENCES

Baker-Sennett, J. & Matusov, E. (1997). School "performances": Improvisational processes in development and education. In K. Sawyer (Ed.), *Creativity in performance* (pp. 197–212). Greenwich, CT: Ablex Publishing Company.

Berger, K. (2009). *The developing person through childhood and adolescence.* New York: Worth Publishers.

Berk, L. & Winsler, A. (1995). *Scaffolding children's learning: Vygotsky and early childhood learning.* Washington DC: National Association for the Education of Young Children.

Bodrova, E. & Leong, D. J. (1996). *Tools the mind: The Vygotskian approach to early childhood education.* Englewood Cliffs, NJ: Merrill/Prentice Hall.

Borko, H. & Livingston, C. (1989). Cognition and improvisation: Differences in mathematics instruction by expert and novice teachers. *American Educational Research Journal, 26,* 473–498.

Cole, M. (1985). The zone of proximal development: Where culture and cognition create each other. In Wertsch, J. (Ed.), *Culture, communication, and cognition: Vygotskian perspectives* (pp. 146–162). New York: Cambridge University Press.

(1998). *Cultural psychology: A once and future discipline.* Cambridge, MA: Harvard University Press.

(1999). Cultural psychology: Some general principles and a concrete example. In Y. Engeström & R. L. Punamaki (Eds.), *Perspective on activity theory* (pp. 87–106). Cambridge: Cambridge University Press.

Cole, M. & The Distributed Literacy Consortium. (Ed.). (2006). *The Fifth Dimension. An after-school program built on diversity.* New York: Russell Sage.

Comer, J. P. & Gates, H. L. (2004). *Leave no child behind: Preparing today's youth for tomorrow's world.* New Haven, CT: Yale University Press.

Daniels, H., Cole, M., & Wertsch, J. (Eds.). (2007). *The Cambridge companion to Vygotsky.* New York: Cambridge University Press.

Darling-Hammond, L. (2007). Evaluating no child left behind. Retrieved March 27, 2009 from http://www.thenation.com/doc/20070521/darling-hammond

Davis, J. (2005). *Framing education as art: The octopus has a good day.* New York: Teachers College Press.

Dewey, J. (1938). *Experience and education.* New York: Macmillan.

Egan, K. (1992). *Imagination in teaching and learning.* Chicago: University of Chicago Press.

Eisner, E. (1998). *The kind of schools we need.* Portsmouth, NH: Heinemann.

(2005). *Re-imagining schools: The selected works of Eliot Eisner.* London: Routledge.

Farmer, E. (2008). From passive objects to active subjects: Young people, performance and possibility. *Journal of the Community Development Society, 39*(2), 60–74.

Freire, P. (1994). *Pedagogy of the oppressed.* New York: Continuum Books.

Fulani, L. & Kurlander, G. (2009). *Development gap or achievement gap? Outliers and outsiders reconsider an old problem.* New York: All Stars Project.

Goffman, E. (1959). *The presentation of self in everyday life.* New York: Anchor Books.

Goldstein, L. (1999). The relational zone: The role of caring relationships in the construction of the mind. *American Educational Research Journal, 36,* 647–673.

Gordon, E., Bowman, C. & Mejia, B. (2003). *changing the script for youth development: An evaluation of the all stars talent show network and the Joseph A. Forgione development school for youth.* New York: Institute for Urban and Minority Education, Teachers College, Columbia University.

Greene, M. (1988). *The dialectics of freedom.* New York: Teachers College Press.

Heath, S. (2000). Making learning work. *Afterschool Matters, 1*(1), 33–45.

Holzman, L. (1997). *Schools for growth: Radical alternatives to current educational models.* London: Routledge.

(2000). Performative psychology: An untapped resource for educators. *Educational and Child Psychology, 17*(3), 86–103.

(2009). *Vygotsky at work and play.* London: Routledge.

Johnstone, K. (1981). *Impro: Improvisation and the theater.* New York: Routledge.

Karliner, S. & Holzman, L. (2005). *Developing a psychology that builds community and respects diversity.* Paper presented at the American Psychological Association Convention, Washington, DC.

Kohn, A. (2004). NCLB and the effort to privatize public education. In D. Meier & G. Kozol (Eds.). (2005), *The shame of the nation: The restoration of apartheid schooling in America.* New York: Three Rivers Press.

Kozol, J. (2005). *The shame of the nation: The restoration of apartheid schooling in America.* New York: Crown.

Lobman, C. (2005). Yes and: The uses of improvisation for early childhood teacher development. *Journal of Early Childhood Teacher Education, 26*(3), 305–319.

Lobman, C. & Lundquist, M . (2007). *Unscripted learning: Using improv activities across the K-8 curriculum.* New York: Teachers College Press.

Meier, D. & Wood, G. (2004). *Many children left behind: How the no child left behind act is damaging our children and our schools.* New York: Beacon Press.

Moll, L. (1992). *Vygotsky and education: Instructional implications and applications of sociohistorical psychology.* New York: Cambridge University Press.

Nachmanovitch, S. (1990). *Free play: Improvisation in life and art.* New York: Penguin/Putnam.

Newman, F. & Holzman, L. (1993). *Lev Vygotsky: Revolutionary scientist.* London: Routledge.

(1996). *Unscientific psychology: A cultural-performatory approach to understanding human life.* Westport, CT: Praeger.

(1997). *The end of knowing.* London: Routledge.

Noddings, N. (2005). What does it take to educate the whole child? *Educational Leadership, 63*(1), 8–13.

Papert, S. (1994). *The children's machine.* New York: Basic Books.

Rogoff, B. (1990). *Apprenticeship in thinking: Cognitive development in social context.* New York: Oxford University Press.

(2003). *The cultural nature of human development.* Oxford: Oxford University Press.

Rogoff, B. & Gardner, W . (1984). Guidance in cognitive development: An examination of mother-child instruction. In B. Rogoff and J. Lave (Eds.), *Everyday cognition: Its development in social context* (pp. 95–116). Cambridge, MA: Harvard University Press.

Sawyer, K. (1997a). Improvisational theater: An ethnotheory of conversational practice. In R. K. Sawyer (Ed.), *Creativity in performance* (pp. 171–193). Greenwich, CT: Ablex.

(1997b). *Pretend play as improvisation: Conversation in the preschool classroom.* New York: Lawrence Erlbaum Associates.

(2004). Creative teaching: Collaborative discussion as disciplined improvisation. *Educational Researcher, 33*(2), 12–20.

Sfard, A. (1998). On two metaphors for learning and the dangers of choosing just one. *Educational Researcher, 27*(2), 4–13.

Sizer, T. (2004). Preamble: A reminder for Americans. In D. Meier & G. Wood (Eds.), *Many children left behind: How the no child left behind act is damaging our children and our schools* (pp. xvii–xxii). New York: Beacon Press.

Smagorinsky, P. (2007). Vygotsky and the social dynamics of classrooms. *English Journal, 97*(2), 61–66.

Spolin, V. (1999). *Improvisation for the theater* (3rd ed.). Chicago: Northwestern University Press.

Vygotsky, L. (1978). *Mind in society: The development of higher psychological processes.* Cambridge, MA: Harvard University Press.

Wells, G. (1999). *Dialogic inquiry: Towards a sociocultural practice and theory of education.* Cambridge: Cambridge University Press.

Wertsch, J. (1985). *Vygotsky and the social formation of the mind.* Cambridge, MA: Harvard University Press.

Yinger, R. (1980). A study of teacher planning. *The Elementary School Journal, 80*, 107–127.

(1987). *By the seat of your pants: An inquiry into improvisation and teaching.* Paper presented at the annual meeting of the American Educational Research Association, Washington, DC.

# 5

# Teaching for Creativity with Disciplined Improvisation

RONALD A. BEGHETTO AND JAMES C. KAUFMAN

One of the biggest fears of teachers, particularly those who are just starting their career, is a classroom in chaos. Many teachers worry that inviting creativity into the classroom will result in curricular chaos (Aljughaiman & Mowrer-Reynolds, 2005; Beghetto, 2007; Westby & Dawson, 1995). At the same time, most teachers generally value student creativity (Runco, 2003) and worry that too great a focus on covering content can turn the act of teaching into little more than series of scripted monologues, delivered to a room full of passive students. These seemingly conflicting concerns and commitments result in a paradox in which teachers find themselves balancing two inverse tensions: (1) teaching requisite academic subject matter while still wanting to foster student creativity; and (2) wanting to allow for creativity yet fearing curricular chaos.

In this chapter, we address these tensions and discuss how teachers can, through disciplined improvisation, address the teaching paradox. We show how teachers can have enough structure for academic work to be productive, and at the same time allow for the improvisation necessary to encourage student creativity. We open the chapter by arguing that the teaching paradox results from the gap between the curriculum-as-planned and curriculum-as-lived. We then introduce our elaboration on the concept of disciplined improvisation and discuss how this concept can help address the teaching paradox.

## CURRICULUM-AS-PLANNED VERSUS CURRICULUM-AS-LIVED

No matter how much planning goes into teaching a particular lesson, anyone who has taught will quickly admit that there is always a gap between the

In R. K. Sawyer (Ed.) (2011). *Structure and improvisation in creative teaching* (pp. 94–109). Cambridge: Cambridge University Press.

curriculum-as-planned and the curriculum-as-lived. An understandable temptation is to attempt to regain control of the curriculum by attempting to fit the curriculum-as-lived back into the curriculum-as-planned. The problem with this strategy is that it instantiates the first tension of our teaching paradox (i.e., teaching requisite academic subject matter while still wanting to foster student creativity). Given that the curriculum-as-planned is always underdetermined, simply "sticking to the plan" will result in ignoring and sealing off the unexpected (and *potentially* creative) aspects of the curriculum-as-lived. Conversely, abandoning the lesson plan to pursue what has unexpectedly emerged in the curriculum-as-lived instantiates the second tension of the paradox (i.e., wanting to allow for creativity yet fearing curricular chaos).

We argue that when it comes to teaching for creativity, rather than trying to forcefully close or attempt to bridge this gap, it is much more fruitful to find ways to work in the "in-between" space of the gap. This space provides opportunities for newness and creative expression, as Ted Aoki (2004) has argued: "... a space of generative interplay between planned curriculum and live(d) curriculum. It is a site wherein the interplay is the creative production of newness, where newness can come into being. It is an inspirited site of being and becoming" (p. 420). This notion of working in the "in-between" space is helpful – albeit in quite an abstract way – when thinking about how to resolve the tensions underwriting our teaching paradox. But how might teachers actually dwell in this space – the space where creativity and learning of academic subject matter come into being? We argue that this can occur through planning and teaching with what has been called *disciplined improvisation* (Sawyer, 2004).

## DISCIPLINED IMPROVISATION

Sawyer (2004) initially introduced the concept of disciplined improvisation as metaphor for illustrating how teaching is a creative art.[1] Specifically, he highlighted how improvisation in teaching occurs within activity structures and routines of the classroom and involves the combination of lesson planning and actual teaching. Sawyer's discussion of the concept was primarily focused on how collaborative classroom discussions might be conceptualized as disciplined improvisation. We hope to elaborate on Sawyer's initial work by illustrating how teaching with disciplined improvisation can also

---

[1] Our use and definition of this concept is an elaboration on Sawyer's (2004) previous work and inspired by Karl Weick's concept of *Disciplined Imagination* (1989) and Weick's (1998) work on improvisational thinking in organizations.

help teachers find ways to resolve the teaching paradox we outlined at the outset of the chapter. Prior to doing so, we need to first describe our definition and elaboration of the concept of disciplined improvisation.

Although there are a variety of definitions of improvisation, we have found Paul Berliner's (1994) definition to be a useful starting point in developing our elaboration on conception of disciplined improvisation: "Improvisation involves reworking precomposed material and designs in relation to unanticipated ideas conceived, shaped, and transformed under the special conditions of performance, thereby adding unique features to every creation" (p. 241).

In elaborating on the concept of disciplined improvisation, we modified Berliner's (1994) definition as follows: "Disciplined Improvisation in teaching for creativity involves reworking the curriculum-as-planned in relation to unanticipated ideas conceived, shaped, and transformed under the special conditions of the curriculum-as-lived, thereby adding unique or fluid features to the learning of academic subject matter." In our definition, the "discipline" (of disciplined improvisation) refers to determining what aspects of the teaching and learning activity will be more or less fixed, and the "improvisation" refers to identifying what aspects will be more or less fluid. Disciplined improvisation, as Sawyer (2004) has explained, "acknowledges the need for a curriculum – there must be some structure to the classroom performance" (p. 16). "Discipline" has the added association with academic subject matter disciplines and teacher expertise, which are both necessary for helping guide teachers in determining what aspects of a learning experience can (and should) be fixed. Fixed aspects pertain to the academic subject matter that the teacher intends students to learn (often codified in content standards, curricular guides, etc.).

The improvisational component of our concept also refers to the more fluid (or unexpected) spaces in the curriculum – both the unplanned spaces between the planned and lived curriculum, and planned openings in the particular lessons that can provide opportunities for unexpected and original interpretations and expressions of academic subject matter learning. In this way, disciplined improvisation – like other forms of improvisation – is much more than just "in-the-moment" spontaneity. As Berliner (1994) has explained:

> [T]he popular definitions of improvisation that emphasize only its spontaneous, intuitive nature – characterizing it as the "making of something out of nothing" – are astonishingly incomplete. This simplistic understanding of improvisation belies the discipline and experience on which improvisers depend, and it obscures the actual practices and

processes that engage them. Improvisation depends, in fact, on thinkers having absorbed a broad base of musical knowledge, including myriad conventions that contribute to formulating ideas logically, cogently, and expressively. (p. 492)

A teacher taking a disciplined improvisation approach to teaching for creativity must, likewise, have the experience and expertise necessary to balance spontaneity with necessary academic subject matter constraints (Borko & Livingston, 1989; Sawyer, 2004). This involves not only being able to respond to unexpected moments when they arise during teaching, but also planning their lessons so that such opportunities naturally arise. In the sections that follow, we will briefly discuss the relationship between creativity and disciplined improvisation and then provide specific examples of how teachers might use disciplined improvisation both to plan and teach for creativity. In doing so, we hope to highlight how disciplined improvisation can address our two core tensions of the teaching paradox, thereby resulting in learning environments that foster creative learning.

## CREATIVITY AND DISCIPLINED IMPROVISATION

To understand how teachers might use disciplined improvisation to plan and teach for creativity, we first need to briefly define what we mean by creativity. In the field of creativity studies, there is general agreement that creativity involves a combination of originality, uniqueness, or novelty *and* meaningfulness, usefulness, or task appropriateness (Barron, 1955; Kaufman, 2009; Sternberg, Kaufman, & Pretz, 2002). Creativity – with its requisite combination of originality and task appropriateness – corresponds well with what we have already described as a disciplined improvisational approach to teaching – specifically, providing opportunities for students to express their originality (this relates to the fluid aspects of improvisation) and conforming to curricular or task constraints (this relates to the disciplined or fixed aspects of teaching and learning activities).

Importantly, what is considered original and meaningful is defined within a particular social, historical, and cultural context (Plucker, Beghetto, & Dow, 2004). Moreover, as we have described elsewhere (see Beghetto & Kaufman, 2007; Kaufman & Beghetto, 2009), there are different levels of creative expression ranging from interpretative or *mini-c* creativity (e.g., a child having an insight about how to incorporate a character from her favorite story into a song just learned), to everyday creativity or *little-c* creativity (a home cook creating a tasty fusion of leftover Thai food from a restaurant and fresh ingredients in his refrigerator), to expert or *pro-c* creativity (a mathematics professor's developing a novel solution to seemingly irresolvable mathematical problem) and finally to legendary or *Big-C* creativity (Gershwin composing music that is still enjoyed today).

In the context of the classroom, the smaller-c categories (little-c and mini-c) are clearly more appropriate – given that it takes many sustained years of intensive training to develop the domain knowledge necessary for larger-c levels of creative expression (see Ericsson, 1996). This means, for instance, a youngster's little-c idea for a science experiment can still be considered creative in the context of a particular third-grade classroom even though it may not be considered creative in other contexts. Moreover, with respect to mini-c creativity, a students' novel and personally mean-ingful insight or interpretations (which occur with great frequency while learning) are important sources of larger-c creative potential. Teachers who are aware of this mini-c potential are in a better position to use a disciplined improvisational approach to draw it out (by including fluid moments for the unexpected to emerge) and to develop it (by helping students learn the more fixed disciplinary constraints of academic subjects).

Armed with a better understanding of how creativity and disciplined improvisation are related, we now turn to a specific example of how a teacher might plan a lesson so that opportunities to improvise naturally arise.

## LESSON PLANNING WITH DISCIPLINED IMPROVISATION

In this section, we describe an example of how a teacher might use disci-plined improvisation to plan a lesson that addresses the teaching paradox of needing to teach academic content but wanting to also support student creativity. Specifically, we provide an example of how a teacher might plan a Haiku poetry lesson that simultaneously teaches students the fixed poetic form and includes the fluidity necessary to foster student creativity.

When developing such a lesson, the teacher would need to determine what aspects of the lesson will be fixed and what aspects might be more fluid. With respect to the fixed aspects, the teacher might first provide stu-dents with various model poems so students can develop an understand-ing of the relatively fixed[2] structural conventions of Haiku poetry. Students would then be given an opportunity to write their own poems (the fluid

---

[2] We say "relatively" fixed because, in fact, there are variations in Haiku form (e.g., tra-ditional Japanese form changed when it was translated into English forms). As such, structural forms can change. However, in the context of the classroom, such forms will typically be held more constant and fixed such that students can develop an understanding of the general form.

component of the lesson). In assessing students' understanding of Haiku poetry, the teacher would not simply require students to replicate a previously modeled poem; this would accomplish the goal of teaching the fixed form, but do little by way of providing opportunities for creative expression. Taken from the other extreme, a student who turned in a wildly unique poem that failed to conform to the conventions of Haiku might be considered original but still not creative in the context of this particular task (because the poem isn't a Haiku). Rather, in order for students' Haiku poems to be considered creative, the teacher would need to develop a lesson that is fluid enough for students to express their own unique contribution of content while staying within the fixed conventions of Haiku form. In this way, a judgment of whether a student's poem was creative would based on whether the content provided was original yet still adhered to the fixed form of Haiku poetry.

In the Haiku example, form was fixed and the content was made fluid. Of course, form need not always be fixed or content fluid – the opposite can also be used to promote creative learning. For instance, when this chapter's second author was in fourth grade, his teacher taught a unit on the California gold rush. Assignments had to focus on the fixed content of the gold rush, but there was ample opportunity for fluidity in the form that the content could be expressed – resulting in the creation of a miner's diary (complete with fake gold dust at the edge of the pages) that was used to demonstrate the fixed content (gold rush vocabulary) of the lesson.

As these examples illustrate, making room for fluid aspects in lessons (something many teachers do anyway) creates opportunities for originality and complements (rather than stands in opposition to) the more fixed aspects of requiring students to conform to task constraints. Planning academic learning activities in this way can help re-frame the two core tensions of the teaching paradox we are exploring in this chapter (i.e., the need to cover academic subject matter while still trying to fostering student creativity and the fear that allowing creativity into the curriculum will result in curricular chaos). Such planning incorporates subject-matter-specific constraints *and* opportunities for students to be creative within those constraints.

In summary, teachers can use a disciplined improvisational approach to plan for their lessons by considering what might need to be fixed (e.g., the content to be learned) and what can be made fluid (e.g., how students will actually represent their understanding of that content). There will always be some cases where a learning activity may be almost entirely fixed (such as teaching students how to use a Bunsen burner) and others where it will be largely fluid (brainstorming ideas for a science fair project). Moreover,

using this "fixed and fluid" heuristic in planning not only involves determining what aspects will be more or less fluid but also recognizing that
when the curriculum-as-planned meets the curriculum-as-lived, the fixed
and fluid aspects may need to be reworked in the teaching moment. Such
"in the moment" reworking includes everything from being flexible enough
to stray from a fixed lesson plan when following an unexpected but important turn in a class discussion, to reworking a fluid activity into a more
fixed lesson when a teacher discovers that students do not yet have a requisite understanding of the content. Although this is perhaps easier said
than done (Clark & Yinger, 1977), we believe that with experience and practice, the "awareness-of" the need to rework features of the curriculum-as-
planned can result in the "awareness-in-the-moment" that seems necessary
for making such improvisational moves when teaching.

### FROM PLANNED TO UNPLANNED

As we have already discussed, the disciplined improvisational heuristic of
"fixed or fluid?" can help teachers build opportunities for fluid openings in
the curriculum-as-planned (allowing more fluid spaces in the curriculum
in which students can express their originality) *and* help teachers better
navigate the unexpected moments that manifest in the curriculum-as-lived.
As we will now discuss, creating such opportunities opens up unexpected
curricular moments that require improvisational moves on the part of
teachers in order to foster students' creative potential. Although this can
occur in just about any learning activity, classroom discussions serve as a
primary site for these moments (Sawyer, 2004).

   A classroom discussion that makes room for creativity starts with the
fixed (the prepared materials or questions) and blends in the fluid (an
improvised juggling of dialogue between teacher and students). A classroom
discussion that is too improvised can descend into tangents or arguments
based on differing personal opinions. If a teacher allows the discussion to
get beyond his or her control, the conversation may end up dominated by a
few highly spirited students. The majority of the class may lose interest. Yet,
conversely, if a discussion is too scripted, students may be just as likely to
get bored and not pay attention. If nothing is left to chance and nothing is
risked, then the teacher loses the potential for creativity to emerge.

   An example of an actual teacher demonstrating disciplined improvisation to support student creativity is illustrated in Kamii's (2000) video
footage of a teacher and her second-grade students working through
double-column addition and subtraction problems. In one segment of the

videotape, the teacher writes the following (fixed or pre-planned) problem on the chalkboard:

26

-17

The teacher provides ample time for the students to think through the fixed problem on their own and then makes room for the fluid by calling students up one by one to whisper their answer to her. After several students have shared their answers, she writes the various responses on the board: 18, 11, and 9. Given that there is a "fixed" answer ("9") to this problem, the teacher could – quite understandably – have dismissed the incorrect responses and notified the class that the correct answer is "9." However, she did not take this approach. Rather, she refrained from providing evaluation at this point and simply asked students to explain how they arrived at their answer. We would argue that in this moment the teacher demonstrated "disciplined improvisation" because she reworked the conventional approach of immediately evaluating the "correctness" of a response (see Mehan, 1979) and, rather, responded in relation to unanticipated responses. This fluid move can result in not only the students arriving at the fixed answer but, importantly, developing a more robust (personally meaningful) understanding of that answer. In fact, Siegler (2006) has demonstrated that when students are prompted to explain why a wrong answer is wrong, they learn more effectively than when they focus only on the one right answer. The second-grade teacher in Kamii's (2000) video accomplishes this, in a way similar to what Sawyer (2004) has described, by facilitating "a collaborative improvisation among the students, with the goal of guiding them toward the social construction of their own knowledge" (p. 15).

The video displays several cases of students developing their own understanding. For example, the student who initially thought the answer was "18" exclaims, "I disagree with myself!" after hearing how a peer arrived at "9." Another student, Steven, is not so quick to give up on his answer of "11" and interjects, "I can prove it is 11." Again, rather than being told by his teacher that he is "incorrect," he is invited to share his explanation. Steven explains, "20 and 10 is 10 and six take away seven is one and 10 and one is 11." At this point, another student exclaims, "Disagree." The teacher then explains that Steven has a different answer and repeats his reasoning to the entire class. Multiple students now exclaim, "Disagree! – I can prove it's 9!" As other students provide their explanations, Steven, the student who originally thought the answer was "11," seems to recognize his mistaken reasoning and explains, "I disagree with myself." The teacher then double-checks with Steven, asking whether he is sure that he disagrees with his initial understanding of the problem, and he replies that "yes," he is sure.

We would argue that this teacher's move to sustain the fluid moments of students' responses (by suspending her evaluation of those responses) helps students arrive at the learning objective by allowing for a dynamic exchange of ideas that supports students in understanding the fixed answer of "9." Moreover, we argue that this can also facilitate creative expression. To make this argument, we need to quickly revisit our definitions of mini-c and little-c creativity. Recall that mini-c creativity pertains to a novel and meaningful insight (based on the interpretation or experience of some activity or interactions), and that little-c creativity pertains to unique and appropriate creative expression of the more everyday (or, in this case, classroom) kind. Given these two definitions, a student's exclamation of "I disagree with myself!" is a signifier of a potential mini-c insight (e.g., "I just had a new and meaningful insight – about this math problem!"). Of course, a student may be saying this out of the pressures of conformity with the hope that it will remove the social spotlight from them and their explanations.[3] Still, we would argue, the moment that students realize they disagree with themselves (because they have a new and meaningful insight) can be thought of as a mini-c creative moment. Although we believe such mini-c insights are important forms of creativity in their own right (see Beghetto & Kaufman, 2007), we also recognize that in the context of the classroom, it is often important to help students share and develop those mini-c insights into recognizable little-c ideas that maintain novelty while at the same time fit academic subject matter conventions (Beghetto, 2007). If we return to the example and take a closer look at students' explanations, we can see how the teacher's skillful blending of fixed and fluid provides opportunities for such little-c mathematical ideas to be shared.

The teacher, in this example, sustains fluid moments by allowing her students to share their personally meaningful explanations for how they arrived at their solutions – rather than try to move them to the more fixed or conventional strategy of borrowing to get to the solution of "9" (e.g., borrow 10 from the 20, add it to 6, that makes 16, and then take away 7). In this way, students were able to develop and express little-c explanations (explanations that were both novel and accurate). Consider one such explanation by a student named Gary. Gary explained that he arrived at "9" by first removing the six and seven from 26 and 17. He next explained,

---

[3] Although, in this example, it does not seem to be the case, particularly given the second student's willingness to present his response after already seeing other students change their minds.

"take off 10" from 20 and "that would be 10." Then, he explained, "take off 7 more" and "that would be 3." He concluded by explaining, "add the 6 back on and that would be 9." It was after the teacher repeated Gary's (clearly novel yet appropriate) method to the class that one of his peers had his own "mini-c" moment and exclaimed, "I disagree with myself!" A similar pattern occurred when another student, Chris, explained his solution, "Alright, 10 take off from 20 is 10, Alright? And then add a 6 on, it's 16, minus 7, it's 9!" It was after this solution that the student named Steven (who initially believed the answer was 11) stated: "I disagree with myself."

This classroom example illustrates how the teacher's use of disciplined improvisation can help resolve the paradox of teaching for creativity without sacrificing learning of academic subject matter. It also suggests that in order for teachers to skillfully navigate the more fluid moments of teaching without compromising on a somewhat fixed academic goal, they need to have a rather strong familiarity with the subject matter and comfort with the unexpected. Indeed, teachers need to be able to recognize and adjust when and how much feedback to provide to simultaneously support student learning and creative expression – a skill that is developed with experience and expertise (Borko & Livingston, 1989; Sawyer, 2004).

This example also illustrates that teaching with disciplined improvisation requires teachers to find ways to support students in the fluid moments of teaching such that students are willing to share their unique, unexpected, and diverse perspectives and, at the same time, challenge students to go beyond their initial conceptions – connecting their insights to the more fixed disciplinary standards and constraints. We are not suggesting that all teachers adopt the same strategy as this second-grade teacher, but rather that they take away the more general insight of how they might address the tensions of the teaching paradox by blending the challenge to teach fixed conventions with fluid opportunities for students to share their own, unique insights. A key component of teaching with disciplined improvisation involves the expertise and awareness necessary to provide students with the just right amount of encouragement and critical feedback.

Elsewhere we have described this blending of challenge and opportunity as the "goldilocks principle" (Beghetto & Kaufman, 2007). Central to the goldilocks principle is a "just right" balance between fluid encouragement and more critical feedback on how well students are learning or adhering to somewhat fixed curricular standards and conventions. If, for instance, students are given feedback based on fixed standards that are too harsh, they may come to believe that they lack ability and thereby be less willing to pursue the fluid opportunities to express their unique insights and abilities. Consider, for example, a hypothetical ninth-grade student, Regina, who has had the mini-c insight of combining what she was learning in History and Languages Arts in the form of historical, mystery stories. Unfortunately, her teachers and family were not supportive of her efforts to bring her idea to fruition; essentially, they communicated to her that she did not have what it took to be a writer. By the time that she graduated from high school, she considered herself simply not to be a creative person. She will likely stop writing mysteries even for her own enjoyment, and may only pick up a history book when it is assigned.

Conversely, if students are given feedback that is not critical enough – failing to help them become aware of domain-specific conventions and real-world standards – then the results can be potentially as devastating as receiving no support. Imagine another hypothetical student, Joshua, who is enthralled with sci-fi stories and spends much of his free time writing his own stories, but his efforts are over-praised. His parents and teachers, fearing that critical feedback would squelch his creative fervor, encourage him too strongly. His father gushes over them and tells Joshua that he should submit his stories to *Asimov's Science Fiction* magazine. His teachers provide him with nothing but empty encouragement, never telling him what is good or bad about his stories. Unfortunately, his stories are sophomoric and too reliant on what he has seen on television, with little originality or new ideas. When Joshua receives a series of form-letter rejections from *Asimov's Science Fiction*, he is shocked and discouraged. As Joshua grows older, he may continue to write science fiction, yet, unless he gets feedback on how to improve, he is ill-equipped for the real world of writing, which demands the requirements of originality and appropriateness.

Without honest and supportive feedback, students like Joshua and Regina will never learn how they might develop and expand their creativity. A key goal of teaching with disciplined improvisation, just as Goldilocks sought porridge that was neither too warm nor too cold, is to provide students with the right level of feedback to help develop their creative potential.

## TOWARD TEACHING WITH DISCIPLINED IMPROVISATION

Although we have no magic formula for teaching with disciplined improvisation, there are some basic tenets. Disciplined improvisation requires reasonable risks. Teaching is already an uncertain endeavor; good teaching requires a certain amount of performance and a dash of chutzpah. Teaching with disciplined improvisation needs a little more of both.

Indeed, the kind of teaching that seems effortless often requires the most preparation. One of us, in encouraging classroom discussions in the college class he teaches, often includes the disclaimer that he does not promote such discussions out of laziness. In fact, preparing for and orchestrating discussions requires a great deal of attentiveness and care (typically more so, in our experience, than preparing a lecture that is treated essentially as a monologue read by the professor). And there is nothing more beautiful in the classroom than an engaged group of students actively debating a concept and sharing their own opinions and personal experiences. There is also nothing more painful than the dead, dull silences from discussion topics that fall flat and have no supporting pieces in place.

Simply providing fluid opportunities in the curriculum for students to share their novel perspectives, however, will not guarantee that students will be willing to take advantage of such opportunities. Teachers need to also recognize how contextual features of the classroom – such as how student work is recognized, evaluated, and rewarded – can support or suppress students' willingness to take intellectual risks and share their ideas (Beghetto, 2005). Consequently, even when teachers attempt to create fluid opportunities in their curriculum (e.g., opportunities to write short stories on any topic they choose) they may inadvertently send motivational messages about the goals of such activities that actually suppress students' creative expression (e.g., telling students before they write that only the "best" short stories will be rewarded, by being displayed on the classroom wall, and that the "winning" authors will receive a certificate of achievement).

Teresa Amabile and her colleagues (e.g., Amabile, 1996; Collins & Amabile, 1999) have demonstrated that creative expression can be suppressed under conditions that promise rewards for creative work, stress social comparison and competition, and highlight evaluation. In a representative study in this line of inquiry, Amabile (1985) examined the effects of an intrinsic versus extrinsic motivational orientation on creative-writing graduate and undergraduate students. She asked the students to first write a poem to establish a baseline of creative writing. She then gave them a list of reasons for writing. One group received lists that stressed extrinsic motivation (i.e., "You want your writing teachers to be favorably impressed with your writing talent," "You know that many of the best jobs available require good writing skills"), whereas another group received lists that emphasized intrinsic motivation (i.e., "You enjoy the opportunity for self expression," "You like to play with words"). Amabile then had the students rank-order these reasons, and then write a second poem. The students who were given the list of intrinsic reasons to rank, as well as a control group that received no lists, showed no significant difference in the ratings of creativity. The students given the extrinsic list, however, were rated significantly lower on their second poem.

Researchers, most notably Beth Hennessey and her colleagues (Hennessey, Amabile, & Martinage, 1989; Hennessey & Zbikowski, 1993), have also conducted research on ways to help teachers protect student creativity from extrinsic motivators. This "immunization" approach involves attempting to protect students from the negative consequences of reward expectations by helping them focus on the intrinsically motivating features (i.e., the interesting, fun, and exciting aspects) of learning tasks.

Importantly, the connection between extrinsic motivators and declines in student creativity is not always present. Robert Eisenberger and his colleagues (e.g., Eisenberger & Selbst, 1994; Eisenberger & Shanock, 2003) have found, for instance, that creativity could actually be improved by a promised reward if the reward was not visible during the creative activity. Still, the takeaway point for teachers is: Be aware of the motivational messages sent during common classroom practices. Such practices can and do have impacts on students' motivation and creativity – sometimes in unintended and counterintuitive ways. Having an awareness of how motivational messages of the classroom can impact creative expression is helpful for teachers who are providing fluid moments in their curriculum, yet finding that their students are reluctant to take the risks necessary to share their own, unique perspectives.

Finally, we recognize that in the current climate of external accountability, teachers often have little say in what content will be taught and what types of assessments will be mandated. We also feel, however, that there is much that teachers can do by way of taking a disciplined improvisational approach to teaching that will not only help ensure that they are not inadvertently suppressing creativity, but also help address the teaching paradox of simultaneously teaching for academic subject matter learning and creative expression. In what follows, we highlight a few key points made throughout this chapter and offer some general suggestions that we feel can help teachers move toward a disciplined improvisational approach in their teaching:

(a) plan for and encourage students to share their mini-c insights and interpretations when learning the somewhat fixed academic subject matter by including fluid moments in lessons and activities (as was illustrated in the Haiku and second-grade math examples);

(b) take some time – "in the moment" of unexpected student responses – to briefly follow up on those ideas and comments to better understand how students are interpreting what they are learning (simply asking, "tell me more about how this relates to what we are discussing" can go a long way in drawing out students ideas in relation to the topic of discussion);

(c) let students know when their contributions are not making sense given the more fixed academic learning constraints, conventions, and standards of the particular activity or task (this pertains to the goldilocks principle in which opportunities for more fluid expression need to be counterbalanced with critical feedback that will help students also learn the subject matter requisite for creative expression);

(d) provide multiple opportunities for students to revisit their ideas in the context of the academic subject matter, and practice moving between mini-c insights and little-c expression of creativity (this might include having students "park" their ideas in a notebook or a portion of the chalkboard devoted to ideas that are not yet fully developed but can be revisited, developed, or even abandoned in light of subsequent learning and insights – "I disagree with myself");

(e) be prepared to rework fixed or fluid elements of a planned lesson in the unexpected moments of the curriculum-as-lived that suggest unanticipated fluid learning possibilities (such as the student explanations in the second-grade math example) or seem to necessitate the need for more fixed constraints (such as when a teacher discovers that students do not have requisite understanding to participate in a more fluid learning activity);

(f) provide the kind of evaluative feedback that attempts to encourage student expression and also stresses how students might improve in the context of the academic subject matter they are learning (see Black & Wiliam, 1998 for a discussion); and

(g) minimize or "immunize" the influence of extrinsic motivators by providing fluid options within a more fixed menus of learning tasks – so that students might focus on the features of a task that are interesting and personally meaningful (as was illustrated in the Haiku and Gold Rush assignment examples).

## CONCLUSION

We opened this chapter by posing the paradox of wanting to simultaneously teach for academic learning and creativity, but feeling caught between the dual tensions of fearing curricular chaos when teaching for creativity and worrying about stifling creativity when teaching for academic learning. In further elaborating on Sawyer's (2004) concept of disciplined improvisation, our goal was to describe how teachers can start to resolve these tensions. We provided a few examples of how teachers might approach the planning and teaching of their academic curricula with a disciplined improvisational approach. Although we feel there are no sure-fire recipes for navigating the uncertainties that emerge when the curriculum-as-planned meets the curriculum-as-lived, we believe that teachers can (with experience and practice) start to find ways to meaningful blend and rework fixed and fluid aspects of their curriculum to simultaneously support student learning and creative expression.

What we have aimed to do in this chapter is to propose a new way for teachers to think about how they might simultaneously encourage learning and creativity in their classroom. Although we have hoped to offer some new insights and general suggestions for doing so, ultimately it is teachers who will need to find their own specific ways for approaching their curriculum with disciplined improvisation. As always, we have great appreciation for the teachers who care enough to try.

#### REFERENCES

Aljughaiman, A., & Mowrer-Reynolds, E. (2005). Teachers' conceptions of creativity and creative students. *Journal of Creative Behavior, 39,* 17–34.

Amabile, T. M. (1985). Motivation and creativity: Effects of motivational orientation on creative writers. *Journal of Personality and Social Psychology, 48,* 393–399.

   (1996). *Creativity in context: Update to the social psychology of creativity.* Boulder, CO: Westview.

Aoki, T. T. (2004). Spinning inspirited images. In W. F. Pinar & R. L. Irwin (Eds.), *Curriculum in a new key: The collected works of Ted T. Aoki* (pp. 413–225). Mahwah, NJ: Lawrence Erlbaum Associates.

Barron, F. (1955). The disposition toward originality. *Journal of Abnormal and Social Psychology, 51,* 478–485.

Beghetto, R. A. (2005). Does assessment kill student creativity? *The Educational Forum, 69,* 254–263.

   (2007). Ideational code-switching: Walking the talk about supporting student creativity in the classroom. *Roeper Review, 29,* 265–270.

Beghetto, R. A., & Kaufman, J. C. (2007). Toward a broader conception of creativity: A case for "mini-c" creativity. *Psychology of Aesthetics, Creativity, and the Arts, 1,* 73–79.

Berliner, P. F. (1994). *Thinking in jazz: The infinite art of improvisation.* Chicago: University of Chicago Press.

Black, P., & Wiliam, D. (1998). Inside the black box: Raising standards through classroom assessment. *Phi Delta Kappan, 80,* 139–148.

Borko, H., & Livingston, C. (1989). Cognition and improvisation: Differences in mathematics instruction by expert and novice teachers. *American Educational Research Journal, 26,* 473–498.

Clark, C. M., & Yinger, R. J. (1977). Research on teacher thinking. *Curriculum Inquiry, 7,* 279–304.

Collins, M. A., & Amabile, T. M. (1999). Motivation and creativity. In R. J. Sternberg (Ed.), *Handbook of human creativity* (pp. 297–312). New York: Cambridge University Press.

Eisenberger, R., & Selbst, M. (1994). Does reward increase or decrease creativity? *Journal of Personality and Social Psychology, 66*, 1116–1127.

Eisenberger, R., & Shanock, L. (2003). Rewards, intrinsic motivation, and creativity: A case study of conceptual and methodological isolation. *Creativity Research Journal, 15*, 121–130.

Ericsson, K. A. (1996). The acquisition of expert performance: An introduction to some of the issues. In K. A. Ericsson (Ed.), *The road to excellence: The acquisition of expert performance in the arts and sciences, sports, and games* (pp. 1–50). Mahwah, NJ: Erlbaum.

Hennessey, B. A., Amabile, T. M., & Martinage, M. (1989). Immunizing children against the negative effects of reward. *Contemporary Educational Psychology, 14*, 212–227.

Hennessey, B. A. & Zbikowski, S. M. (1993). Immunizing children against the negative effects of reward: A further examination of intrinsic motivation training techniques. *Creativity Research Journal, 6*, 297–307.

Kamii, C. (2000). *Double-column addition: A teacher uses Piaget's theory* [VHS Tape]. New York: Teachers College.

Kaufman, J. C. (2009). *Creativity 101.* New York: Springer.

Kaufman, J. C. & Beghetto, R. A. (2009). Beyond big and little: The four C model of creativity. *Review of General Psychology, 13*, 1–12.

Mehan, H. ( 1979 ). *Learning lessons.* Cambridge: Harvard.

Plucker, J. A., Beghetto, R. A., & Dow, G. T. (2004). Why isn't creativity more important to educational psychologists? Potentials, pitfalls, and future directions in creativity research. *Educational Psychologist, 39*, 83–97.

Runco, M. A. (2003). Creativity, cognition, and their educational implications. In J. C. Houtz (Ed.), *The educational psychology of creativity* (pp. 25–56). Cresskill, NJ: Hampton Press.

Sawyer, R. K. (2004). Creative teaching: Collaborative discussion as disciplined improvisation. *Educational Researcher, 33*, 12–20.

Siegler, R. S. (2006). Microgenetic analyses of learning. In W. Damon & R. M. Lerner (Series Eds.) & D. Kuhn & R. S. Siegler (Vol. Eds.), *Handbook of child psychology: Volume 2: Cognition, perception, and language* (6th ed., pp. 464–510). Hoboken, NJ: Wiley.

Sternberg, R. J., Kaufman, J. C., & Pretz, J. E. (2002). *The creativity conundrum.* New York: Psychology Press.

Weick, K. E. (1989). Theory construction as disciplined improvisation. *Academy of Management Review, 14*, 516–531.

(1998). Improvisation as a mindset for organizational analysis. *Organizational Science, 9*, 543–555.

Westby, E. L. & Dawson, V. L. (1995). Creativity: Asset or burden in the classroom? *Creativity Research Journal, 8*, 1–10.

# PART 2

# THE LEARNING PARADOX

# 6

## Taking Advantage of Structure to Improvise in Instruction: Examples from Elementary School Classrooms

### FREDERICK ERICKSON

Quite early in my career I published a chapter titled "Classroom discourse as improvisation" (Erickson 1982). In it I observed that improvisation is less "free" than popular imagination would have it. Improvisation depends on structure – it works within it, taking advantage of aspects of pattern in order to create new patterns in real-time performance. For example, the improvised performance of a jazz ensemble is based in three levels of structure, each embedded within the next. First, there is the overall form of the song, the *chorus* structure of sixteen or thirty-two measures, typically in an AABA or ABAC organization of a succession of phrases – constituent units within the overall chorus. Second, within each phrase there is a sequence of chords that, taken together, form a harmonic progression that is sometimes called "changes." In addition, at the level of time duration of adjacent chords within a phrase sequence, each musician has a repertoire of *licks*, formulaic melodic contours that he has developed through years of practice, which can be inserted into improvised solos at appropriate moments. The improvisations that emerge are guided by these three levels of structure.

Research shows that expert teachers also are guided by similarly embedded levels of structure. Regarding the first two types of structure – the overall form that guides the song or the classroom and the constituent sequences of "moves" – predetermined chord sequences or oral discourse sequences – Borko and Livingston (1989) found differences in how expert and novice teachers plan in advance. Beginning teachers spent much more time on advance planning. Expert teachers spent less time, and their lesson plans

In R. K. Sawyer (Ed.) (2011). *Structure and improvisation in creative teaching* (pp. 113–132). Cambridge: Cambridge University Press.

were more amenable to improvisation – because they knew from experience that they would be improvising. To draw a musical analogy, the expert teacher's plan is a *theme* and what happens in the classroom is a *variation*. In contrast, the novice teacher's plan is a direct performance from a score. This research suggests that excellent teaching is more like improvisational music performance than like performance from a score.

Regarding the third type of structure, at the level of connected short sequences of "moves" that is analogous to the harmonic progressions that obtain between adjacent chords or to the brief melodic contours of "licks," expert teachers have developed a repertoire of practices and techniques that consist of momentary "moves" – both in classroom management and in how to teach their own content area. Expert teachers use more scripts and routines than beginning teachers (Borko & Livingston, 1989). And yet, paradoxically, expert teachers also improvise more than beginning teachers. In this chapter I focus on this version of the teaching paradox: the tension that is found in teacher expertise between plans and routines, on the one hand, and the ability to improvise within those structuring elements, on the other. My definition of improvisation, taken from improvised music, is that it is freedom within structuring constraints. Effective improvisation in the classroom is a form of *disciplined improvisation* (Sawyer, 2004) – as the teacher adapts and responds to unpredictable student actions. The expert teacher guides the class in a jointly created improvisation, aided by plans and routines that are – paradoxically – created with the intention of being improvised on.

In this chapter I provide examples from elementary classrooms that demonstrate four versions of the teaching and learning paradox:

1. The challenges of using pre-existing structures, shared by the teacher and students, to aid in guiding the improvisational flow of the classroom.
2. How a teacher can guide an improvisation, inspired by unexpected student actions, that leads to teachable moments.
3. The ways that these same structures can enable student improvisation.
4. The ways that classroom structures can act as scaffolds for improvised, creative learning.

Sawyer (2001, 2003) has identified similar tensions between structure and improvisation in theater improvisation and even in everyday conversation. Sawyer's (2001) study of improvisation in everyday discourse draws mainly on theatrical analogies – improvisatory theatrical performance, with its antecedents in the *commedia dell' arte* of Renaissance Italy. He shows by numerous examples how a pre-existing pattern is varied in its real-time enactment from one iteration of enactment to the next. Theatrical improvisation begins with condensed indications of setting, character, and plot, encapsulated in a scenario. Like the lesson plan of an expert teacher, a scenario provides only the rough outline, with details filled in by the performers on stage.

Similarly, in many musical genres, improvisation begins with a sketch-like arrangement of a few elements in combination. For example, jazz is typically improvised on the sixteen- or thirty-two-bar chorus, as I noted earlier. Many improvised musical traditions include such structures, and I refer to these structures as a theme; deviations and embellishments in performance constitute the variation. For example, one chord might be substituted for another in the harmonic sequence. Or when the melody of the theme proceeds by step (as in do, re, mi, fa), skips can be added in substitution (do-fa); or if the melody proceeds by a skip up or down between two successive notes, the interval between the two of them can be filled in by a succession of steps (DO re mi FA), or by an arabesque (e.g., do, re, do, mi, do, fa – or do, re, mi, re, mi, fa). One variation on the theme might be performed with the soprano part (the upper voice) played by a trumpet; in the next variation the soprano part might be played by a clarinet – each instrument offering different affordances and constraints in tone quality and other acoustic properties. The musical improviser makes opportunistic use of structure points in the theme in order to generate meaningful variations in its real-time performance. In other words, the structuring theme is designed to enable improvisation, not to constrain it.

If teachers stray too far from their lesson plan, students do not learn the material. Likewise in musical performance, if improvisation diverges too far from the theme, it becomes ineffective. It was a recurring criticism of J. S. Bach's organ playing during church services that he improvised so much when playing the "preludium" that introduced a hymn that the congregants could not tell what the melody of the hymn was. Highly dissonant or atonal jazz (e.g., Ornette Coleman) has likewise been criticized as too unstructured, by those listeners who prefer the clear foundational harmonies of New Orleans jazz – in which the succession of chords (the "changes") stays pretty much the same across iterations of the theme – or the simple structure of the "twelve bar blues," where the chord sequence is almost exactly the same across iterations, despite much variation in the melody line. In most improvisational genres, some features of the theme stay constant across all iterations in a performance (Sawyer, 2001). This allows other features to be varied without losing the sense of the orienting gestalt of the theme. Even in the dissonant jazz of Ornette Coleman, although the pitches he chose for his improvisations did not conform to the standard jazz conventions for melody and harmony, the timing patterns in the notes he played were nonetheless rather conventional. In Coleman's style harmony is pushed far beyond usual boundaries, but not rhythm.

In a recent book I argued that all real-time conduct of practical social action is improvisatory (Erickson 2004: 140–43, 161–74). My conception of improvisation is an attempt to address one of the core tensions in contemporary social theory – the tension between pre-existing social structures and everyday social practice. In the 1970s, the initial post-structuralist rejections of structuralism emphasized the improvisational nature of social practice (Bourdieu, de Certeau). Action theories such as Giddens (1984) likewise emphasized that structures are only found, and are reproduced, in daily practices. My focus on improvisation contributes to this line of thought by emphasizing the parallels between social action and musical performance. Social life is a performance through the ongoing course of time, and the constant forward motion of a succession of "now" moments requires the performer to do something "now" on the way to "next." I argue that all social action is improvised because all social action occurs in real time. Like a jazz band on stage, the music keeps going; at any given "now" moment *something must be done*. In each "now" moment some alternative form must be chosen (deliberately or intuitively) from a set of alternative forms that are appropriate for performance in that moment. In music the set of appropriate alternatives might be the different pitches within the same chord (e.g., in the C major chord [or "triad"] the three possible choices are c, e, and g). In talk the choice set might be alternative ways to get someone to open the window (e.g., "open the window," "please open the window," and "don't you think it's getting too warm in here?" said while looking pointedly at the window). These examples show choices within sets of alternative forms for accomplishing the same function – or a very similar one.

Sometimes a form may be chosen from outside the set of customary alternative ways of accomplishing a certain function. The result is to change the functional position that had been expected, potentially resulting in a retrospective reinterpretation of the prior sequence of actions. The conversation analysts pointed out that a question does not become a question until an answer follows it; in other words, the meaning of an action only becomes clear by the ensuing flow of actions by others (e.g., Schegloff, 1986). In the preceding musical example, if one played an e-flat instead of an e-natural in a C chord, it would no longer be a C major chord but a C minor chord – a chord in a different musical mode. In the previous window opening request example if one said, "Never mind, I'll just sit here in the heat," that would change the function of the utterance from that of a request to that of a passive-aggressive complaint. When a form is chosen outside the usual choice set for a given "now" moment then a new function is introduced at that "now" moment – a function whose occurrence had not been projected by the series of functions that had been performed in the immediately prior moments. Thus the abrupt introduction of an un-projected new function changes the overall trajectory of the action sequence, and it possibly shifts the "frame" of that action.

In classrooms, students often perform unexpected actions, resulting in a potential reinterpretation of the teacher's intended structure. Sometimes these unintended actions are purposeful challenges to teacher authority; the best way to proceed might be to simply ignore or reject that action and continue with the intended structure. Often, a better solution is the one exemplified in the first section of this paper: to use classroom structures to allow an improvised reprimand that does not disturb the ongoing flow of the lesson. On many occasions, however, those unintended actions indicate a misunderstanding, or a partially correct understanding, on the part of the student. I provide an example in the second section of this paper. In these cases an expert teacher may choose to improvise a divergence from the intended structure – creating a new structure, on the fly, that incorporates the student's unexpected action. Through disciplined improvisation the experienced teacher ultimately can improvise a way to address the student's misconception and then return to the intended structure.

## USING STRUCTURE TO GUIDE AN IMPROVISATION

In all improvisational conversation, communication occurs on two functional levels. Of course, on the most obvious level, there is the explicit content of the words spoken. In the classroom, much of the conversation between teachers and students concerns the subject matter of the lesson. However, in all improvised conversations, there is a second functional level, one that often remains implicit: the constant negotiation between participants about how the conversation will unfold. In classrooms this communication is often done explicitly, as when a teacher chides a student for talking out of turn or for an inappropriate tone of voice, but effective teachers can often do this "metacommunication" implicitly. Although this functional level is often about discipline and keeping the students on task, it can also be about how to improvisationally respond to an unexpected student misconception to create a "teachable moment."

In completely structured, scripted classrooms, this second functional level is not necessary; because all participants have memorized the script, all know at every moment what actions are acceptable, and there is no need to negotiate how the conversation will unfold. In improvised encounters, however, the interaction itself is always being negotiated (Sawyer, 2003). This second functional level has been called *contextualization cues* (see Gumperz 1992), *metapragmatics* (Silverstein, 2003), or *metacommunication* (Bateson, 1972 [1955]), and mastering it is essential to effective improvisational teaching.

Here is an example from a combined kindergarten–first grade class in which the teacher is reading aloud from a picture book on a morning just past the middle of December. She is seated on a child-sized chair on the rug at the front of the room, with all the children in the class sitting at her feet in an arrangement of concentric half circles on the rug. They are communicating primarily through speech, supported by the pictures in the book (the teacher is holding it so that the children can see the pictures as she reads). The subject matter is the words of the poem by Clement Moore, "A Visit from Saint Nicholas." One would think that improvisation would not happen in such a speech event, given that the talk that occurs in reading aloud from a text is as close as one gets in ordinary life to reading aloud from a playscript. Yet the need of the teacher both to communicate subject matter and, in the same time, to metacommunicate about the classroom's social relations resulted in the following improvisation:

T: 'Twas the **night** before **Christ**mas . .

and **all** through the **house** . .

not a **crea**ture was **stir**ring – LOUIE! –

not **even** a **mouse** . .

One might think that a literal script, such as that of a "read aloud" book, would be impervious to interruption; but Louie, a kindergartner, was being "squirrelly" as he sat on the rug. He was moving his torso, arms, and head in ways that were inappropriate. And so Ms. Wright, the teacher, inserted a "management directive" to Louie into her reading of the text of the poem. She made this insertion without either eliding or delaying the underlying "beat" in her speech – the cadence of the poetic meter that was marked by volume- and pitch-stressed syllables, which are shown in boldface type in the transcript. (N.B. The pairs of periods in the transcript indicate an approximately quarter second pause, a comma-length pause. Four periods indicate a half second or sentence terminal pause. Successive colons indicate a "sound stretch" – elongation of a vowel sound.) In inserting a management directive while reading the poem, Ms. Wright was adroitly paying attention both to subject matter and to social relations. Being a "good student" requires the ability to "read" the metacommunicative messages contained in the verbal (and nonverbal) behavior of the teacher – especially when it is implicitly communicated while he/she is simultaneously communicating subject matter information.

The next example comes from the same kindergarten–first grade classroom. It was the third day of the new school year in September, right after lunch. The kindergartners had gone home but the first graders continued their day; Ms. Wright had just begun their first mathematics lesson of the year. The lesson was about sets and set properties. This was revisiting content that had been previously taught last spring, when the children who were now first graders had still been kindergartners. Ms. Wright had placed blocks on the rug in the front of the classroom. Some were painted yellow, others were green. Some were in the shape of triangles, others were circles and rectangles. Ms. Wright had grouped one set of blocks whose members varied in shape but all were yellow – they shared the property of color. She had also grouped another set of yellow and green blocks that were all triangles – that is, the members of that set shared the property of shape. Rope rings were placed on the floor around each set. The children sat on the rug in a circle looking in at the sets of blocks in the center. They were wiggling, pointing, and talking excitedly. The discussion had proceeded to the point that Ms. Wright wanted to review what the sets on the floor showed about the concept of *set property*; this is how she began that discussion:

T: what have we decided have we decided tha::::t

As Ms. Wright began to speak the children continued to move and talk. The colons in "tha:::t" indicate that she stretched out the vowel "a". As the final "t" in the word "tha::::t" was uttered by the teacher, and during the course of the uttering of the vowel "a" in this one-syllable word, the body motions of all the children ceased and so did their speaking. It was as if a rheostat had been turned down on the children as the elongated vowel was uttered, decreasing within that half-second the verbal and kinesic activity of the children. In other words, the sound stretch "a::::::" had both accentuated the saying of the word "that" and delayed the forward movement of the teacher's speech into a new grammatical unit, stopping at the end of the previous clause with the sentence left incomplete. Her intention, which the children understood, was that this auditory and grammatical cue functioned as an implicit management directive, meaning "be quiet and sit still!" Ms. Wright frequently used stretched sounds at other times as a signal to "be quiet"; the students knew what it meant. She had other, more explicit ways to get the children to calm down: she could say "Be quiet and sit still," she could stop speaking while pursing her lips and holding up her straight index finger over the lips as a visual iconic display meaning "be quiet." Or she could say "Sh!" All teachers are bricoleurs of speaking practice, constantly improvising by choosing from among a variety of options in each particular moment.

Because the children were familiar with this implicit way of saying "quiet down," the children understood what she meant quickly and accurately. This is akin to what improvising musicians do as they adapt to one another's improvising "moves." Because the action of music and speech is so rapid in real-time performance, it is essential for participants to be able to "read" each other's implicit cues. In everyday conversation, it would be awkward and time-consuming to say everything explicitly; this is why these sorts of indexical, compressed, implicit expression are common in all social interaction (for further discussion of this indexicality and indirection, along slightly different lines, see Silverstein 2003 and Gumperz 1992).

One paradox for teachers is that these two functional levels are often in tension. It is difficult to communicate subject matter and at the same time implicitly negotiate the unfolding improvised flow of the classroom. A second paradox for teachers is that implicit metacommunications are easier for students to misunderstand. The collective improvisation of implicit metacommunicative meaning is not always successful, as illustrated by the next transcript, which occurred a few moments after the previous example. Earlier in the lesson the teacher had held up two yellow triangles and asked the children what was the same and what was different about them. Answering in chorus, the children said that the blocks were the same color and the same shape. "What is different?" Ms. Wright then said. The children hesitated. "S:::" said Miss Wright. "Size!" said the children together, again answering in chorus.

Two minutes later, the teacher said, "What have we decided have we decided tha::::t . ." She then held up a block from the triangles set, and pointing to that set, said "**these** blocks all have the property of . ." "Shape," the children replied in chorus. "So they go in this set even though they have different colors," Ms. Wright said. Then she pointed to the other set and started to say, "These blocks all have the same/" As she spoke, one of the children, Ricky, who was directly in front of her, started to speak and rock back and forth as he did so. Ms. Wright improvised a management directive before she completed the clause. She said "These blocks all have the same . **sh** (to Ricky)." Immediately the rest of the children said, in choral response,

"**SHAPE!**" Apparently the children thought that the "sh" directed to Ricky was a hint, just like two minutes earlier when she had said "S:::" to help them get the answer "Size."

## GUIDING IMPROVISATION FOR TEACHABLE MOMENTS

There is no obvious solution to the tension between explicit and implicit metacommunication. Explicit statements about the unfolding course of the class are often the most effective ways to accomplish discipline and keep students on task; but they take time and interrupt the flow of content delivery, so an implicit metacommunication is sometimes the more effective strategy.

However, it is not always the case that a student's unexpected action is a disciplinary challenge. In many cases, a student's unexpected answer indicates a misconception or a useful exploration of a related concept. A teacher who is unable to improvise might choose to ignore these events, to treat them as disciplinary challenges. An experienced teacher, however, is capable of responding to these "teaching moments" and diverging from the prepared structure.

Here is an example from Deborah Ball's third-grade math class (Green, 2010). She started the day by calling on Sean, who says, "I was just thinking about six. I'm just thinking, it can be an odd number, too." Ball listened and allowed him to keep talking, as he became more excited. "Cause there could be two, four, six, and two – three twos, that's make six!"

Ball simply said, "Uh-huh."

Sean continued, "And two threes. It could be an odd and an even number. Both!"

Ball looked out at the class. "Other people's comments?" she asked.

This discussion was not a part of Ball's lesson plan for the day. Yet with her improvisational guidance, by the end of the class, a girl from Nigeria had proposed a precise definition of even and odd. The class also coined a name for a new type of number, a number that is the product of an odd number and two (like two times three equals six): They called them "Sean numbers."

In cases where the unexpected action can potentially lead to a useful, if unplanned, lesson discussion, effective teachers often turn to implicit metacommunicative strategies. In cases like Ball's class above, the teacher was not delivering content knowledge – she was guiding an improvisational discussion among students. In other words, she was working at the second functional level, the metacommunicative level. Improvisational teaching often results in a shift in focus, from delivery of content knowledge – the first functional level of improvisational conversation – to the second functional level, the one of guiding and channeling the student's improvisational contributions.

## STUDENT IMPROVISATION USING STRUCTURES

The cadential timing of stressed syllables in talk that was apparent in the reading aloud of the poem, in the earlier example of "Twas the night before Christmas," also happens in ordinary talk, and among other things, that regular pattern of rhythm functions to indicate where appropriate moments for turn exchange are located in the temporal stream of real-time performance of talk. In the earlier example, we saw the teacher taking advantage of a pre-existing structure to more effectively metacommunicate. But of course, students also know these structures, and they occasionally use them creatively to accomplish their own goals. This next example shows a student improvisation within a structure by Carlos, one of the children in an inner-city bilingual first-grade classroom in which all the students were Spanish-dominant.[1]

Early in the school year the students were being introduced to Arabic numerals and to the Spanish words designating each number from one to ten. The numerals were displayed in a series of large cards, one card for each numeral, that were attached above the chalkboard at the front of the classroom. The series of cards covered the width of the chalkboard; thus each numeral was large enough to be read by all the students in the class.

The teacher asked Carlos to stand before the chalkboard, holding a pointer, and to point up at each numbered card in succession as the teacher said the "name" of each numeral. There was a cadence-like timing to her speech, with a stressed syllable coming on next "beat" preceded by the word "numero", thus: "numero **uno**.... numero **dos**.... numero **cinco** ....". Then, she paused and Carlos shifted the pointer to the next card.

After completing all ten numbers, the teacher said, "Muy bien, Carlito," and asked him to go to his seat so that another child could take a turn. Carlos shook his head in annoyance and sat down reluctantly; he apparently wished to remain at the board. As the next child began to answer by pointing to each number card at the appropriate moment, Carlos picked up

---

[1] This example was discussed in my early paper on classroom discourse as improvisation (Erickson 1982). It also appears in a recent chapter on the musicality of classroom talk (Erickson 2008), and the discussion presented here is adapted from that which appeared in that chapter.

two pencils on his desk and started to use them as drumsticks, "drumming" when the teacher paused for the next student to move the pointer. This was minimally disruptive, and the teacher ignored it.

Carlos was able to continue acting in a manner that did not result in approbation from the teacher by taking advantage of the predictability of the emergent structure provided by the teacher-student interaction sequence. Students' knowledge of conventional classroom discourse structures, and the timing entailed in their performance, enables them to improvise, bending rules – even breaking them. One cannot steal some other student's turn at talk during classroom conversation without understanding the order of the discourse sequence one is disrupting (see the discussion in Erickson 2004: 53–71). In the case of the improvisation by Carlos, he did not actually steal the other child's turns; rather he hitched rides on them by performing his drum strokes in the same moment as the other student was performing an answer by pointing.

## STRUCTURES AS SCAFFOLDS FOR STUDENT IMPROVISATION

As a last set of examples, let us consider an innovative approach to the teaching of science that has been developed at the special elementary school housed on the campus of the University of California, Los Angeles – the University Laboratory School (ULS). For the past eight years I have been engaged with early-grades teachers there in producing a multimedia Web site that shows the backstage of how this pedagogical approach teaches the physics of matter, energy, and motion for deep conceptual understanding by children aged five through seven.[2] In these examples, I argue that the curriculum is effective because the teachers provide their students with the structures within which effective learning improvisations can occur. These improvisational structures are what many education researchers call *scaffolds* – guiding formats that aid students in moving from novice to expert performance (Wood, Bruner, & Ross, 1976).

The science curriculum was piloted by two kindergarten–first grade teachers in adjoining classrooms. Their basic teaching approach is to concentrate on a few key concepts, making sure that students understand them thoroughly and that all students in the class understand each of the "big ideas"

---

[2] The Web site project, titled the "Classroom Ecosystem Explorer," has been supported by a grant from the National Science Foundation, Project #0554615. Instructions for access to the Web site can be found on my own faculty Web site, whose URL is http://www.gseis.ucla.edu/faculty/members/erickson. See also the description of this pedagogy in Jurow and Creighton 2005.

that are being presented, before instruction moves on to the next big idea. Student understanding is fostered by providing multiple firsthand experiences with a key concept, rotating across various sensory modalities for such experience – visual, auditory, kinesthetic, tactile (cf. Edwards, Gandini, & Forman. 1998 on the approach taken by the school at Reggio Emilia). For example, to introduce the basic principles of dynamics in physics, they have children roll a marble down a grooved inclined plane and then vary the angle of the plane to see the consequences of that variation for changes in the speed of the rolling marble. That provides the child with a firsthand visual and kinesthetic experience. Second- and thirdhand experiences are also provided – for example, looking at a drawing of an inclined plane, having the teacher demonstrate the marble rolling (for the child, a secondhand visual experience) while also explaining what is happening to the marble and providing vocabulary for such explanation (for the child, a secondhand auditory experience). Or the child might see a picture of an inclined plane in a book, accompanied by written text (a thirdhand visual experience).

In this teaching approach, multiple semiotic (symbolic) media are used to communicate subject matter content – for example, analytic drawing, writing, and speaking. A diversity of semiotic means of representing understanding are also built into sets of tasks for the students to complete; they are designed so that the same key idea is communicated by differing semiotic means. For example, early in the school year a key idea was that matter can change in state – from solid to liquid to gas. The underlying molecular mechanics of a state change cannot be directly observed (as heat is added to a substance, its molecules move with increasing velocity and amplitude), so in this class this concept was approached metaphorically. When the molecules in a solid increase in kinetic energy past a tipping point, the solid becomes a liquid, and after further heat is added to the liquid, at a tipping point it becomes a gas. Children can melt an ice cube and then boil the water and see the steam, but that is a secondhand experience – one cannot see the motion of molecules directly. Metaphorically, as heat is added, a substance's molecules "dance," and they dance with ever-greater animation with further increases of heat. That can be experience firsthand (metaphorically) kinesthetically by children, by dancing as a molecule to which more and more heat is being added. Then, after firsthand and secondhand instruction experiences that communicate the relationships between molecular motion and the state of a substance as solid, liquid, or gas, the children are asked to represent their understanding of these basic ideas, creating representations using a variety of semiotic media. For example, children can be asked to model the relative motion of molecules, using found objects stuck into

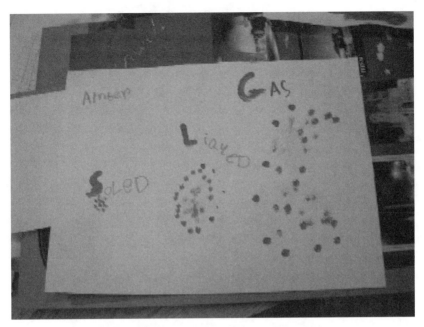

FIGURE 6.1. Amber's molecules diagram.

clay. They can be asked to explain their model verbally. They can be asked to write about the motion of molecules. They can be asked to make an analytic drawing of the relative motion of molecules across the three states of matter. And, revisiting a firsthand experience by which they initially learned ideas about molecule motion, they can be asked to dance as a molecule of matter in a gas, then as that same molecule in a liquid, and as that molecule in a solid.

They can also be asked to represent their understanding in drawing and by modeling in clay and found objects. Figure 6.1 is a photograph of Amber's analytic drawing of the three sets of molecules – her two-dimensional representation shows the differences in amplitude across three states of matter, but it cannot in addition show velocity.

Figures 6.2, 6.3, and 6.4 show the representations with wire and clay that were made by Eli, a kindergartner. The first photo shows the motion of molecules in a solid, the second shows that motion in a liquid, and the third shows that motion in a gas.

Eli's written text accompanying these creations follows:

SoLids are cloSe TogeTher

my soLid is very cLose

FIGURE 6.2. Eli's clay model – solid.

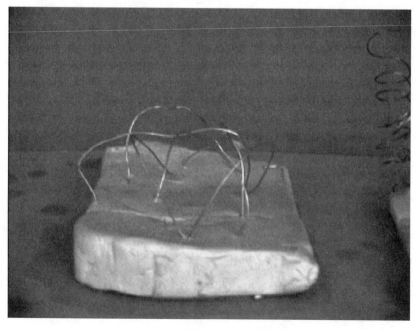

FIGURE 6.3. Eli's clay model – liquid.

FIGURE 6.4. Eli's clay model – gas.

Together. my liqui is
is aLiTTl Bit and ah LiTTL Bit
Fare apart. my gas is very sprd
apart

I argue that the teachers' goal in providing multiple learning experiences and multiple opportunities for students to represent what they have learned is to provide structures that will scaffold the students in an improvisatory practice. Alternating between various sensory and semiotic ways of experiencing new ideas is analogous to the theme and variation genre of musical improvisation discussed earlier in this chapter – each child is improvising with external representations of their developing understanding, and this process of articulation and reflection contributes to deeper understanding (Sawyer, 2006).

Later in the school year the curriculum shifted to energy and motion, and the students learned about simple machines. They and the teachers decided on a culminating project – to build a classroom-sized roller coaster by which messages could be sent between the two adjoining classrooms. The project would be demonstrated to the parents on the last day of school.

To complete this project, the students had to use their understanding of the distinction between potential and kinetic energy. As the roller coaster car goes up an incline, it gains potential energy and loses kinetic energy; as it comes down on the other side of the incline, it gains kinetic energy and loses potential energy. Potential energy is maximized at the top of the incline, and kinetic energy is maximized at the bottom of the decline.

Together, the teachers and students improvised variations in ways of experiencing firsthand the difference between potential and kinetic energy. The children first experienced the difference between kinetic and potential energy kinesthetically, by moving back and forth on the playground swings (the pendulum action of the swing alternates between kinetic and potential energy). Some weeks later, the classes took a field trip to the LegoLand theme park and rode the roller coaster there. Also a group of sixth graders visited the pair of kindergarten–first grade classes and demonstrated the operation of a three-foot-high roller coaster that they had built and studied. This demonstration provided a secondhand experience for the early-grades students.

Thirdhand experiences came from looking at diagrams of pendulums and roller coasters and reading about them. The students drew pictures of the playground swings, showing their operation, and they wrote about their pictures.

Finally, the students built a roller coaster on the outside wall of their adjoining classrooms. Their idea was to use a hollow rolling ball and put the folded written message inside the ball. In the process of construction they had to "de-bug" various aspects of the operation of the system so that the ball, once it had been pulled to the first peak by a pulley system, would then travel down the first incline and up the second incline, reaching the top and then coming down the final incline. On the day before the parents were to visit, students were preparing to place labels on the roller coaster showing the places in the system at which kinetic and potential energy were maximized. As they did this it became apparent to the teachers that some of the students still did not understand kinetic and potential energy – they held the misconception that as speed increased, energy was gained, and as speed decreased, energy was lost.

To address this misconception, the teachers chose to reteach the basic idea back in their respective classrooms. In one of the classrooms the teacher improvised a new instructional procedure as a way to manifest the instruction "theme" – the difference between kinetic energy and potential energy, and to identify the places in a roller coaster system where each kind of energy was maximized. She drew a schematic diagram of a roller coaster on the whiteboard. (N.B. this was not a copy of the actual roller coasters the students had constructed – rather it was a more general model of a roller coaster. Thus she was improvising a new way to display the crucial physics concepts that were entailed in the instructional theme.) First, she explained to her class that energy was not lost in the change between the kinetic form and the potential form – it was merely converted. Then, asking a child to come forward to the board, the teacher held the child's hand and, with an ink stick, traced the trajectory of an imaginary car onto the whiteboard diagram of the roller coaster. As the ink stick went up the initial incline to its peak the teacher said, with increasing volume:

"potential, potential, potential, **potential, maximum potential!**"

As the ink stick descended the downward slope to its bottom the teacher said, with increasing volume:

"kinetic, kinetic, kinetic, **kinetic, maximum kinetic!**"

In class discussion a few moments later, one of the students improvised on the general model, proposing an analogy between what the model showed and previous kinesthetic experiences the students had had as they engaged the key ideas in the instructional theme in various sensory modes. He said, "Is this like when we run up and down the hill?" The teacher thought for a moment about this proposed analogy. Then, in an improvised reaction to the student's improvised suggestion of an analogy with running on the hill the teacher said, "Yes, it's sort of like that … let's go to the hill!" (There is a hill on the university campus a few blocks from where the laboratory school is located.) She and the children left the classroom and walked over to the hill. Then the entire class ran up the hill, shouting "potential, potential, potential!" and they turned around at the top and ran back down the hill, shouting "kinetic, kinetic, kinetic!"

The curricular "theme" on this last day of teaching about the physics of energy and motion was the distinction between kinetic and potential energy. When the teachers realized that it was necessary to reteach the key concepts in that theme, they improvised at the level of phrases, riffs, and licks to take advantage of this teachable moment. The teacher's whiteboard drawing was an improvised way of communicating yet again the distinction between potential and kinetic energy, and the notion that energy is not "lost" but rather is converted from one form to the other. Uttering "potential, potential, potential …" louder and louder while drawing on the board was an improvised way to highlight the big idea using speech, sound, and visuals. Next, the student's insight that there was an analogy between what the animated diagram showed and what happened in running up and down "the hill" was an improvised cognitive connection – demonstrating the student's ability to transfer the concept from the classroom to a real-world setting. Finally, the teacher's decision to take the class to the hill so the children could enact that insight kinesthetically was yet another improvisation, the last of a series of variations on a foundational theme.

## CONCLUSION

In this chapter I use the term "improvisation" to refer to social action that is guided by existing structures, but that still provides opportunities for choice for participants. I have identified four versions of the teaching paradox, each based on this tension between structure and improvisation. The structures of the classroom are not simply constraining; they also enable many improvisational actions, for both teachers and students, as my examples demonstrate. Improvisation in managing student deportment was apparent in the talk of Ms. Wright. Improvisation was also apparent in the teaching of the physics of matter, energy, and motion, as alternations in sensory modalities and media of articulation were planned for and executed in curriculum and instruction by the early-grades teachers at the UCLA lab school. These theme-and-variation repetitions in experience and representation are analogous to improvised variations on the same musical theme, and are also analogous to the replaying of theater scenes on the basis of kernels of plot, character, and situation, as in *commedia dell' arte*.

Good teachers improvise as they talk to their students – they do not simply read from a script or follow the teacher's manual exactly. They interrupt the ongoing lesson to issue a management directive – as Ms. Wright did when reading aloud a picture book. They look for teachable moments and take opportunistic advantage of them – as the lab school teachers did when they decided to reteach the notion of potential/kinetic energy. Students are improvising too – not only in their speech, but also cognitively, as they work to make sense of what teachers are saying implicitly as well as explicitly. As Sawyer (2003) has argued, constructivist learning is a form of creative improvisation.

Further, as my examples demonstrate, classroom improvisations can only work when the students and the teacher share the same understanding of the pre-existing structures that guide the improvisation. When Ms. Wright said "have we decided tha:::::t" her students knew how to interpret her sound stretch as meaning "sit still and be quiet!" They were experts in de-coding their teacher's improvised indexicality in her speaking, just as

Ms. Wright was expert in de-coding her children's indexicality in speaking (and just as Eli's teacher was expert in de-coding the improvised indexicality of his modeling "dancing molecules" with clay and wire, and in a written text using invented spelling). All the partners in interaction need to be adept at encoding indexicality in their own verbal and nonverbal expressions and in de-coding the indexicality in the expressions of others – just as improvising musicians do – in order to coordinate their mutual actions together in *interaction*.

In all classrooms in which students are given opportunities for participation, active learning, and collaborative learning, students must improvise to learn effectively, and teachers must be masters at facilitating that improvisation. In all such classrooms, teacher and student improvisation is guided by shared, pre-existing structures. This is the teaching and learning paradox – finding the right balance between structure and improvisation. At one extreme, teachers might attempt to stamp out improvisation and replace it with elaborately scripted teaching and learning. This would be a mistake, because then students would have no opportunity to actively construct their own learning; it also would be a mistake, because teachers would lose the opportunity to pursue unexpected teachable moments. At the other extreme, teachers might allow anything to happen in their classroom in a naïve belief that students should be in complete control of their own learning. Yet, my examples have shown that structure is not opposed to creative learning, but rather often can enable creative learning. Our goal should be to foster pedagogical improvisation and to encourage teachers and students to improvise more and more skillfully in their interaction together.

### REFERENCES

Bateson, G. (1972). A theory of play and fantasy. In G. Bateson (Ed.), *Steps to an ecology of mind* (pp. 177–193). New York: Chandler. (Reprinted from American Psychiatric Association Research Reports, 1955, II, 39–51)

Borko, H. & Livingston, C. (1989). Cognition and improvisation: Differences in mathematics instruction by expert and novice teachers. *American Educational Research Journal*, 26(4), 473–498.

Edwards, C., Gandini, L., & Forman, G. (1998). *The hundred languages of children: The Reggio Emilia approach – advanced reflections*. Westport, CT: Ablex.

Erickson, F. (1982). Classroom discourse as improvisation: Relationships between academic task structure and social participation structure. In L. C. Wilkinson (Ed.), *Communicating in the classroom* (pp. 155–181). New York: Academic Press.

(2004). *Talk and social theory: Ecologies of speaking and listening in everyday life*. Cambridge: Polity Press.

(2008). Musicality in talk and listening: A key element in classroom discourse as an environment for learning. In S. Malloch and C. Trevarthen (Eds.), *Communicative musicality: Exploring the basis of human companionship* (pp. 449–463). Oxford: Oxford University Press.

Giddens, A. (1984). *The constitution of society: Outline of the theory of structuration.* Berkeley: University of California Press.

Green, E. (2010). Building a better teacher. *New York Times* (March 2).

Gumperz, J. (1992). Contextualization and understanding. In A. Duranti and C. Goodwin (Eds.), *Rethinking context: Language as an interactive phenomenon* (pp. 229–252). Cambridge: Cambridge University Press.

Jurow, A. S. & Creighton, L. (2005). Improvisational science discourse: Teaching science in two K-1 classrooms. *Linguistics and Education, 16*(3), 253–362.

Sawyer, R. K. (2001). *Creating conversations: Improvisation in everyday discourse.* Cresskill, NJ: Hampton Press.

(2003). Emergence in creativity and development. In R. K. Sawyer, V. John-Steiner, S. Moran, R. Sternberg, D. H. Feldman, M. Csikszentmihalyi and J. Nakamura (Eds.), *Creativity and development* (pp. 12–60). New York: Oxford.

(2004). Creative teaching: Collaborative discussion as disciplined improvisation. *Educational Researcher, 33*(2), 12–20.

(2006). The new science of learning. In R. K. Sawyer (Ed.), *Cambridge handbook of the learning sciences* (pp. 1–16). New York: Cambridge.

Schegloff, E. A. (1986). The routine as achievement. *Human Studies, 9,* 111–151.

Silverstein, M. (2003). Indexical order and the dialectics of sociolinguistic life. *Language and Communication, 23*(3–4): 193–229.

Wood, D., Bruner, J., & Ross, G. (1976). The role of tutoring in problem solving. *Journal of Child Psychology and Psychiatry, 17,* 89–100.

# 7

# Breaking through the Communicative Cocoon: Improvisation in Secondary School Foreign Language Classrooms

JÜRGEN KURTZ

Language is not just a tool for communication. It is also a resource for creative thought, a framework for understanding the world, a key to new knowledge and human history, and a source of pleasure and inspiration.
(Kern 2008: 367)

In this chapter, I provide specific examples of how I have used guided improvisation in English as a Foreign Language (EFL) classrooms in Germany. Very few attempts have been made to examine the potential of improvisation for learning and teaching foreign languages in schools. I demonstrate that improvisation provides a unique way to balance the teaching paradox: Improvisation is not only related to directionality, competence, performance, and design, but to spontaneity, intuition, and chance as well. Thus, it contrasts with the traditional view of teaching as transmission of knowledge and skills, that is, of delivering a prescribed curriculum, attending to a particular methodology, following a specific procedure, actuating a lesson plan, and interacting in pre-arranged ways. This traditional view avoids the teaching paradox altogether, but at the cost of removing all student creativity. Moreover, because improvisation encompasses attunement to a situational context, involving "an opaque stock of past experience" (Ciborra 1999: 79) as well as spontaneous decision making and problem solving, openness and unpredictability, it also contrasts with current educational trends that place tremendous emphasis on standardization, predictable improvement, outcome-orientation, and testing.

In R. K. Sawyer (Ed.) (2011). *Structure and improvisation in creative teaching* (pp. 133–161). Cambridge: Cambridge University Press.

As Sawyer explains in the Introduction to this volume, improvisation – whether in jazz, theater, or the classroom – is never completely free; it always occurs in the presence of structures, rules, and frameworks. It is exactly this mix of structural and operational dependence and independence, of planning and emergence, conformity and novelty, intention and attention, that makes improvisation of fundamental importance to enhancing foreign language instruction in actual everyday practice. As Ciborra (2002: 50) argues, "the power of bricolage, improvisation, and hacking is that these activities are highly situated, they exploit, in full, the local context and resources at hand, while often pre-planned ways of operating appear to be derooted, and less effective, because they do not fit the contingencies of the moment." Examining how improvisation can be incorporated into foreign language instruction is therefore of great interest, especially because of its potential to provide a new way to address the teaching and learning paradox, to move beyond a style of foreign language instruction which is rather artificial and monotonous in many schools around the globe at present, especially at the secondary level of foreign language education.

My examples of improvised learner discourse were gathered as part of an ongoing research project aiming at illuminating the potential of improvisation to enhance learners' target language oral proficiency.[1] The project originated from the observation that while improvisation is ubiquitous in everyday life (see Hodgson & Richards 1966), there is usually very little room for learners in German EFL classrooms to participate actively in partially self-determined and self-regulated target language exchanges as they unfold, using language more freely, improvising whenever necessary and appropriate (see Legutke 1993, Kurtz 2001).

Based on this observation, in 1996–1997, I carried out a pilot study in Dortmund, Germany's sixth largest city, in three secondary schools: a secondary school for grades 5–13 (with comprehensive intake), a middle school (grades 5–10), and a selective junior and senior high school leading to university entrance. The objective was to explore how beginning, intermediate, and upper-intermediate learners reacted to and coped with communicative activities and tasks specifically designed to induce spontaneous, largely unprepared interaction in the target language (for a compact overview of the key theoretical tenets of communicative language

---

[1] For detailed descriptions of the project, see Kurtz 2001, 2006a, 2006b, 2008; for an evaluative review, see Thaler 2009; a DVD-Video/ROM documentation of exemplary classroom practice is included in Siebold 2004a. I would like to thank Claire Kramsch, Leo van Lier, Keith Sawyer, and Virginia Teichmann for their helpful comments on earlier drafts of this chapter.

teaching, see Richards, 2005). The central discovery evolving from this pilot study was that increasing the improvisational demands on learners by confronting them with progressively less predictable communicative settings contributes to the gradual transformation and expansion of learners' participatory repertoires in the target language and culture (the pilot study is documented in Kurtz, 1997a, 1997b, 1998).

Prior to starting this study, I was a secondary school EFL teacher in different schools in Dortmund, Germany, over a period of eight years. In 1997–1999, I was granted a research fellowship at the University of Dortmund, which allowed me to focus full time on this project. Because I did not have any further support in terms of human and financial resources, I decided to carry out the main study in the same three schools in Dortmund, including a total of 546 beginning, intermediate, and upper-intermediate learners aged eleven to seventeen, and six male and female teachers aged twenty-six to fifty-four (1998–1999). While observing classrooms, analyzing video recorded lessons, interviewing teachers and learners, and discussing video sequences of improvised learner discourse with university students in their teaching practice, it became increasingly clear that active engagement in goal-directed communicative activity, situated and meaningful language use, playfulness, creativity, and improvisation play an important role in improving learners' willingness to speak, and that they (largely positively) affect learners' readiness to engage in more autonomous and more extended interaction (for a detailed description of the holistic and iterative design of the study, as well as the multi-perspective action-research methodology employed, see Kurtz, 2001, 61–103, 2006b).

The data gathered in the course of this main study showed that when provided with meaningful communicative activities and a more open and flexible infrastructure for target language interaction and collaborative language learning in a relaxed classroom atmosphere, learners spoke more freely, and they were inclined to take more communicative risks. Furthermore, they articulated themselves differently than in traditional classroom exchanges, which are relatively scripted and largely dominated by the teacher (see Kurtz, 2001: 197–239).

Over the past years, follow-up research on improvised speaking (see Siebold, 2004a, 2004b, 2006; Liu, 2006; Rossa, 2007; Beecroft, 2008) has provided further evidence that when given the opportunity to express themselves more freely in class, many EFL learners become what Swann and Maybin (2007: 491) have recently referred to as "creative designers of meaning" who "recreate, refashion, and recontextualize linguistic and cultural resources in the act of communication" (on the role of creativity in everyday conversation, see Sawyer, 2001; Carter, 2004). There is a body of research suggesting that this is of critical importance for more profound learning to take place (in combination with many other factors, of course, see, for instance, Swain, 2000, 2005).

Starting with an inside view of the EFL classroom, summing up what is currently criticized as traditional classroom interaction in the international research literature, this chapter moves on to present two exemplary improvisational activities designed to prompt extemporaneous learner-learner interaction in the target language. Commented transcripts are added to illustrate important effects and side effects. This is followed by a brief discussion of how the activities and the underlying theoretical approach are related to the current theoretical discussion on foreign and second language learning and teaching. At the end of the chapter, an outside view of the EFL classroom is adopted, raising some important questions concerning foreign language instruction (including improvisation) under the current regime of competence-, standards-, and outcome-orientation.

## TRADITIONAL LANGUAGE INSTRUCTION IN EFL CLASSROOMS: TEACHER-DRIVEN DISCOURSE

Teachers orchestrate classroom interaction in many different ways around the globe. Consequently, it is difficult to generalize about the current status and the nature of classroom discourse at the secondary school level. There is nevertheless a converging body of evidence indicating that in many foreign or second language classrooms worldwide, learners are exposed to a surprisingly similar environment of instruction, which is suggestive of a "communicative cocoon" spun by teachers to foster and scaffold culture-sensitive target language learning in systematic ways. The discursive design of the cocoon is relatively simple and inflexible. It is typically based on brief sequences of exchanges between the teacher and individual learners. In the research literature, this omnipresent, cocoon-like architecture of classroom interaction has long been identified and referred to as IRF discourse, because it consists of three highly conventionalized and routinized communicative units: teacher initiation (I), learner response (R), and teacher follow-up or feedback (F; see, for instance, Sinclair & Coulthard, 1975; Sinclair & Brazil, 1982, Coulthard, 1992).

According to McCarthy and Slade (2007), IRF discourse is the most frequently occurring format of interaction in today's foreign language classrooms. "Along with teacher monologues and activities of various kinds," it is the "stock-in-trade in language teaching, especially where large groups of learners are involved, and especially when curricular pressures militate against more imaginative communication in the classroom" (McCarthy & Slade, 2007: 863). Lin (2008: 67–80) comes to a very similar conclusion when she writes that IRF dialogue is the foreign language teacher's main tool to drive a lesson forward, usually in combination with the text-book and related teaching materials. The DESI-study (*Deutsch Englisch Schülerleistungen International*), a Germany-wide empirical assessment study of ninth-graders' achievements in German and in English (see Beck & Klieme, 2003; Klieme & Beck, 2007; Klieme et al., 2008), adds further weight to these observations, indicating that classroom discourse in German secondary school EFL classrooms is usually composed of and largely con-fined to teacher-dominated exchanges of the three-part IRF type.

## The Problem with Traditional Instruction

Looking at classroom interaction in institutionalized settings more than ten years ago, Mercer (1995: 4) states that "some of the most creative thinking takes place when people are talking together." However, as he continues, in traditional IRF-based environments of instruction, "opportunities for learn-ers to make any kind of active contribution" are "severely limited" (Mercer, 1995: 19). The teacher usually "controls the flow of the discourse" by using "direct/cued elicitations, confirmations, rejections, elaborations, reformu-lations, literal recaps, reconstructive recaps, 'We'-statements" (1995: 34). In consequence, learners often simply fill the discursive slots provided, so that "the course of the event is determined more by the teacher's understand-ing of the topic than by the gaps in students' understanding of it" (1995: 6). Furthermore, "while the 'right' answers of some pupils are informative for the rest of the class, in routines like this the number of pupils who can contribute is only a tiny proportion of the whole" (1995: 6).

Over the last two decades, further research on classroom interaction has accumulated indicating (a) that IRF discourse is symptomatic of an asym-metrical classroom culture that is still "fixated on grammatical form" to a large extent (see Thornbury, 2002: 98); (b) that IRF-based instruction tends to pertain to the norms of written language and sentence grammar, rather than the specific communicative "syntax of action" (Drew & Heritage, 1992: 15) and "grammar of speech" (Brazil, 1995) outside the classroom; and (c) that opportunities for learners to exercise communicative initia-tive and control are severely restricted by the IRF format of interaction (see van Lier, 2001: 90–96). IRF discourse is thus the epitome of pre-planned instruction – of recurrent, highly routinized and ritualized, in many parts relatively stiff and pedantically controlled interaction in secondary school foreign language classrooms. This is not to say, however, that IRF discourse is inappropriate or ineffective. Rather, it is a pedagogical compromise that is, to a certain extent, necessary and unavoidable because of the dual status of the target language as the central learning objective and, at the same time, the main medium of communication and instruction in institutionalized settings. Seedhouse (1996: 23) argues that classroom discourse should be seen, ultimately, "as an institutionalized variety of discourse produced by a speech community convened for the institutional purpose of learning English, working within particular speech exchange systems suited to that purpose." As such, however, it often leaves learners with too little room to break through the communicative cocoon of widely scripted and form-focused interaction in everyday practice. Cocooned away from the complexity and limited predictability of language use outside of the classroom, large numbers of language learners fail to develop into interculturally sensitive and communicatively competent speakers of the specific target language.

Moving Beyond IRF: Improvisation in Foreign Language Classrooms

In a number of publications on learning and teaching English as a foreign language, including some introductory books, improvisation is considered to be important and necessary in shaping more flexible, less IRF-dependent environments of instruction that are better suited to enlarge learners' participatory repertoires in the target language and culture. For instance, Davies and Pearse (2000: 82–84) state that in order to "develop the ability to participate effectively in interactions outside the classroom," learners need to be accustomed to "combining listening and speaking in real time," because "in natural listening-speaking situations the listeners must be able to handle [...] shifts of topic and unpredictable language in listening, and then they must be able to improvise their responses." Bygate (2001: 18) underlines the role of improvisation in fostering oral proficiency as well, emphasizing that "improvised speech needs practice, but around some content familiarity."

Statements like these, although undoubtedly convincing, are little more than common sense. Teachers need more specifics: They need a clear orientation as to what improvisation is or what it amounts to in the classroom, and they need concrete guidance on how to facilitate improvisation in everyday foreign language instruction and learning. Unfortunately, vague mentions of improvisation are more typical than specific advice. An equally vague reference to improvisation can, for instance, already be found in Brumfit (1991: 186) who points out in the historical context of the emerging communicative approach to foreign language learning and teaching in the 1970s:

> Not to allow the learner *some* freedom to use the newly developed skills in unpredictable directions will be to frustrate the very abilities which will be necessary for the most effective response to the predicted needs. Language uses which do not require improvisation are really demanding language-like behaviour rather than true linguistic behaviour, for improvisation is a characteristic of any human interaction.

Recently, however, van Lier (2007: 53–54) has developed a more elaborate theoretical framework, focusing on the significance of planned and unplanned (improvised) lesson sequences in foreign language teaching and learning in particular:

> Lessons and tasks are planned, but they can never be planned so carefully that every moment goes according to plan. This means that there is always – and should always be – an element of improvisation. At the same time, there are parts of lessons that are predictable routines, or rituals, recognizable episodes that recur from lesson to lesson, week to week. But there are also episodes in which new and unexpected things happen, surprising or unexpected occurrences that may lead to exploration and innovation. These two parameters, planning-improvisation on the one hand, and routine-novelty on the other, intersect in several ways, and create different flavors of lessons. The dynamism (and tension) between the planned and predictable and the improvised and unpredictable is essential in the development of true AB [action-based] pedagogy, and I would argue, in all pedagogy.

This view of foreign language classroom instruction largely converges with Sawyer's (2004a: 13–14) more general educational considerations:

> Effective classroom discussion is improvisational, because the flow of the class is unpredictable and emerges from the actions of all participants, both teachers and students. Several studies have shown that as teachers become more experienced, they improvise more [...]. Creative teaching is *disciplined* improvisation because it always occurs within broad structures and frameworks. Expert teachers use routines and activity structures more than novice teachers; but they are able to invoke and apply these routines in a creative, improvisational fashion. In improvisational teaching, learning is a shared social activity, and is collectively managed by all participants, not only the teacher. [...] In improvising, the teacher creates a dialogue with the students, giving them freedom to creatively construct their own knowledge, while providing the elements of structure that effectively scaffold that co-constructive process. (See also Sawyer 2001, 2004b.)

Taken together, both of these statements indicate that conceiving of classroom instruction and interaction in terms of a dynamic interplay of routine
and novelty, planning and improvisation, predictability and unpredictability
(see also Stern, 1992: 199), appears to be highly important for successful
learning and teaching. And yet, these suggestions are still too abstract to
provide foreign language teachers with the necessary know-how and skills
needed to redesign instruction appropriately.

### EXAMPLES OF IMPROVISATIONAL CLASSROOM TASKS AND ACTIVITIES

The research project, "Improvised Speaking in the EFL Classroom," was
launched to remedy the overly vague and general ways that "improvisation"
has appeared in the literature, by expanding the notion into specific practices that teachers can use. The following two exemplary tasks and activities are designed to consist of scripted and unscripted, predictable and
largely unpredictable communicative sequences: (a) a scripted opening
part or lead-in intended to break the ice and to reduce speaking inhibitions
among learners; (b) an unscripted middle part leaving enough space for a
wide range of spontaneous ideas and interpretations, topics, and improvised learner-learner exchanges; and (c) a scripted final part with which
the improvised dialogue can be brought to an end once the participants feel
that they cannot or do not want to go any further. The last part is intended
as a "communicative emergency exit" that is usually missing in traditional
role-plays and simulations, causing a number of negative side effects in
terms of motivation in actual classroom practice.

From the teacher's perspective, parts (a) and (c) – that is, the scripted
communicative frame which establishes an "implicitly understood, shared
contextual framework" (Verriour 1993: 52) – can and should be prepared in
advance, whereas part (b), the improvisational part in the middle, is unpredictable and emerges on the spot in the classroom. Every improvisational
enactment needs to be followed by teacher-guided or teacher-supported
whole-class reflection (conducted in the target language as well). Here, the
focus is not primarily on communicative problems and linguistic deficits,
but on communicative success and on expanding the learners' participatory repertoire in the target language. Explicit error treatment should,
of course, not be neglected, but it needs to be integrated in a way that
is not threatening to the learners' willingness to speak English. This then
serves as a basis for subsequent enactments and reflections, arranged in an
iterative manner.

In this way, both of the exemplary tasks and activities demonstrated in the following two examples seek to bring together two basic facets of authentic, natural everyday communication in the EFL classroom: a) the predictability of socio-communicative scripts and behavioral patterns (unwritten scripts, socio-functional routines, or event schemata), and b) the unpredictability of spontaneous ideas and topical shifts within a given socio-communicative framework.

## The Improvisation *Bus Stop*

Inspired by the central theme of the movie *Forrest Gump*, that is, "life is like a box of chocolates – you never know what you're going to get," the improvisation *Bus Stop* (for a more detailed description, see Kurtz, 2001: 135–143 and Siebold, 2004a: 114–125, which also includes classroom video recordings) offers EFL learners a flexible communicative framework that consists of a brief introductory sequence, an incentive to talk spontaneously (i.e., an integrated task: improvising a dialogue based on different cues), and, in contrast to traditional role-plays, a communicative emergency exit allowing them to end the conversation at any time without losing face. This is the basic format or "procedural architecture" of classroom "talk-in-interaction" (see Schegloff, 2007: 22), in this case designed for beginning EFL learners toward the end of their first year (L = learner):

L1: Hello.
L2: Hello, I'm [name].
L1: Pleased to meet you, [name]. I'm [name].
L2: Are you waiting for the bus?
L1: Yes. How about some sweets?
L2: Thank you.

$L_2$ accepts the offer and draws a piece of paper from a box. He/she finds one of the following exemplary cues to continue with:

- I'm on the way to school, you know. I'm in the 5th grade. ...
- I'm on the way to the supermarket, you know. I'd like to buy...
- Hey! Look at that boy over there. What is he doing?
- Listen! Can you hear that? It's coming from that old bag over there. What's in it?
- Excuse me, is this [...] yours? ...
- Excuse me, why are you smiling?
- I'm on the way to the pet shop. This is my cat "Fluffy". It ...
- I'm on the way to the disco. My hobby is dancing. What's your hobby?

Communicative emergency exit:

> L1/2:  Oh, here comes my bus. I have to go. Nice talking to you. Bye.
> L1/2:  Good bye.

*Documentation and Brief Analysis of an Exemplary Exchange*
When beginning learners of English as a foreign language are confronted with
a communicative improvisation task such as *Bus Stop*, how do they manage to
keep the exchange going? How do they spontaneously negotiate meaning and
coordinate turn taking when speaking without a script? How do they help
each other when target language vocabulary or grammar problems occur?
How frequent and important are code switching and code mixing?

The following transcript documents a brief dialogue between two eleven-
year-old German fifth grade students (after about nine months of learning
English in a comprehensive school in Germany) (L = learner; T = teacher;
… = pause; ? = intonation suggesting a question):

> T:  All right .. Benjamin .. throw the dice now
> L1:  It's .. twelve /twölf/
> T:  So .. who has got number twelve … Dilek? … O.K. .. Once again Benny
> L1:  Sixteen
> T:  Kerstin? … Very good. … Dilek and Kerstin .. go to .. em .. the bus stop
> and sit down please … [+++ *applause* +++]
> T:  Are you ready? Let's count …
> [Whole class] THREE .. TWO .. ONE .. ACTION …
> L12:  Hello
> L16:  Hello .. my name is .. Kerstin
> L12:  Pleased to meet you .. em .. Kerstin .. I'm Dilek
> L16:  Are you waiting /ai/ for the bus?
> L12:  Yes .. how about some sweets?
> L16:  Thank you.… [*cue:*] I'm on the way to the supermarket, you know
> … I'd like to buy … [*begin impro:*] … mmh … apples .. [4 sec] .. apples ..
> bananas .. chocolate
> L12:  Bananas and chocolate? … for you?
> L16:  No .. that is for my little … brother
> L12:  I'm driving to .. the pet shop
> L16:  Pet shop? What is this?
> L12:  It's for dogs, cats … and animals .. [5 sec] .. It's in Selby Road [*reference
> to EFL textbook used*]
> L16:  What's your hobby? .. [2 sec] .. hobbies?
> L12:  My hobbies? .. [5 sec].. Yes .. em .. swimming
> L16:  Swimming? Is .. er … swimming difficult?

L12: Sorry no idea ... [*end impro*] ... Oh .. here comes my bus .. I .. go .. nice talking to you .. bye ..

L16: Good bye

T: O.K. very good ... let's stop here .. that was very good indeed .. thank you Dilek and Kerstin .. well done

+++ [*applause*] +++

The transcript indicates that even at a very early stage of their target language development, secondary schoolchildren are able to communicate effectively. In the exemplary sequence above, they do not simply get a message across individually, but spontaneously co-construct a target language exchange all on their own, using a number of more or less convincing strategies such as variation of intonation (rising/falling), of meaning (general/specific), of change of topic, and so on. In essence, they negotiate meaning in many creative ways (more complex exchanges are documented on video in Siebold, 2004a).

The learners' target language repertoire is limited, of course. Nevertheless, subsequent instruction should not be reduced to the correction of target language pronunciation, vocabulary, and grammar errors. The focus of teaching should be placed on dialogically enriching and carefully expanding the tiny little interactive threads that the transcript shows, for instance: "$L_{16}$: Pet shop? What is this? – $L_{12}$: It's for dogs, cats, and animals".

## The Improvisation *Surprise Encounter*

*Surprise Encounter* is an improvisational activity designed for intermediate and upper-intermediate learners. The procedural infrastructure for interaction is similar to *Bus Stop*, but the communicative framework provided (see also Murphy, 1995) is much more open and flexible. The basic communicative task learners are faced with is to pass along surprising (good or bad, pleasant or unpleasant) news to somebody they know. Delivering unexpected facts or news in an appropriate way is particularly difficult for EFL learners, because they usually lack knowledge of culture-specific politeness conventions such as "be conventionally indirect" (Brown & Levinson, 1978: 132), and they do not have the necessary repertoire of pragmatically adequate routine formulae or "gambits" (Edmondson & House, 1981) that are usually employed in this context by native speakers of English. Being unaware of culture-specific social conventions can lead to serious misinterpretations and misunderstanding. As Bardovi-Harlig et al. (1991: 4) point out:

> Speakers who do not use pragmatically appropriate language run the risk of appearing uncooperative at the least, or, more seriously, rude or

insulting. This is particularly true of advanced learners whose high linguistic proficiency leads other speakers to expect concomitantly high pragmatic competence. This is not to say, however, that classroom activities designed to increase pragmatic awareness are appropriate only for advanced learners; such activities can and should take place at lower levels as well.

Situational appropriateness thus needs to be addressed before the improvisation *Surprise Encounter* can begin. Learners need to be made aware by the teacher that "a lot of misunderstanding between people comes from *how* they say something, not *what* they say" (Keller & Warner, 1988: 35). In this context, teachers should introduce a small set of suitable gambits which, according to Edmondson and House (1981: 69) function as "discourse lubricants" in everyday conversation. For instance:

| Opening gambits be used to introduce pleasant/good news or facts: | Opening gambits that can be used to introduce unpleasant/bad news or facts: |
| --- | --- |
| • You're going to like this. ... <br> • Have I got news for you! ... <br> • You'll never guess what's happened.... | • Well, you're not going to like/to believe this, but ... <br> • Well, I'm afraid I have bad news for you. ... <br> • Well, I don't know how to tell you/to put this, but ... |

The communicative framework of *Surprise Encounter*, in this case designed for ninth grade intermediate EFL learners, looks like this (see also Keller & Warner, 1988):

Opening part:

L1: Hi, [name]. How are you?
L2: [Name]! What a surprise! I didn't expect to see you here today.
L1: Well, after last night I just had to come.
L2: Why?

Middle part ($L_1$ delivers the piece of news). Here are a few examples illustrating what learners came up with in the past:

- You'll never guess what's happened. We won't have to walk home from the disco again.
- Have I got news for you! The police have found your stolen bike.
- Well, you're not going to like this, but my name is not Yvonne and I'm not single.

- Well, I'm afraid I have bad news for you. You remember the girl we met here yesterday? She had an accident on her way home.

Final part or "communicative emergency exit," with four different sequences to choose from, depending on the direction the dialogue takes:

a) For L1 to finish the improvisation with in case of good/pleasant news:

L1: Anyway, I thought you'd want to know.
L2: Oh, absolutely. Thanks a lot.
L1: Well, I'm afraid I have to go now.
L2: Okay, see you then.
L1: Bye.

b) For L1 to finish with in case of bad/unpleasant news:

L1: Well, I can see you want to be left alone. I think I'd better go now.
L2: Okay, thanks for letting me know.
L1: See you, then. Take care.
L2: Bye.

c) For L2 to finish with in case of good/pleasant news:

L2: Well, I've got to tell my [mum and dad] about it.
L1: Okay, bye.
L2: Bye-bye.

d) For L2 to finish with in case of bad/unpleasant news:

L2: Well, thanks for letting me know anyway. I think I'd better go [home] now.
L1: Okay, take care. See you tomorrow.
L2: Yes, bye.

Everything else (the situational setting, the kind of news to be passed on, etc.) has to be made up and negotiated by the learners, in part spontaneously, as they go along. Brainstorming for ideas in advance of each improvisational activity can help reduce communicative pressure considerably.

### Documentation and Brief Analysis of an Exemplary Exchange

The following transcript documents a dialogue between two fifteen-year-old German ninth grade students (after about four and a half years of learning English in a grammar school in Germany) (L = learner; T = teacher; ... = pause; ? = intonation suggesting a question; capital letters signal special emphasis; German-English translations in brackets; learner names have been changed):

T: O.K., let me throw the dice again now ... [3 sec] ... Oops ... That was an accident ... em ... I can't see it from here ... Yvonne ... can you help?

L13: Yes ... em ... fifteen

T: Right ... Who has got fifteen? ... Mario? Good ... Let's give Mario a nice round of applause ... Come on everybody ... Clap your hands! ... [10 sec] ... Yvonne ... Why don't YOU throw the dice now?

L13: *ICH? ... muss ich wirklich Herr X?* [Me? Do I really have to, Herr X?]

T: Where's the problem? Come on ... go ahead

L13: *Na gut ...* [5 sec] ... *SIX* [O.K. then, ...]

T: Who has got six? ... [5 sec] ... Dennis? Fine ... now we can begin ...

CLASS: +++ *applause* +++

T: Oh yes ... sorry ... em ... right ... let's ... em ... let's clap our hands for Dennis ... [10 sec] ... Mario and Dennis ... are you ready? ... O.K. ... quiet please ... [5 sec] ... go ahead

L6: *Ähm ... einen Moment noch ... wir müssen eben klarmachen wer anfängt* [One moment, please. We need to check out who is going to begin] ... [15 sec] ... We are ready ... We meet us in a youth club

T: O.K. you two ... Go ahead ... and the others ... listen please!

L15: Hi Dennis ... How are you?

L6: MARIO ... WHAT A SURPRISE ... ähm ... I didn't expect to see you here today

L15: Well, after last night I just had to come

L6: Why? [*begin impro*]

L15: Well I don't know ... mhm ... how I can tell you this ... ähm ... Meike was in the Sound Garden [a local discotheque] yesterday

L6: Meike?

L15: Yes ... Meike ... you remember? Your girl-friend

L6: *Ich hab doch gar keine Freundin* [But I do not have a girl-friend!]

CLASS: +++ *laughter* +++

L15: *Egal ... jetzt aber ...* and her name is Meike [So what? Now you have a girl-friend and her name is Meike]Class: +++ *laughter* +++

L6: O.K. O.K. ... [5 sec] ... Meike ... öhm ... my new girl-friend ... [8 sec] ... alone ... mhm ... Was she alone in the Sound Garden?

L15: At first [smiling]

L6: And later?

L15: Later she wasn't alone [+++ whole class laughing +++]

L6: What did you saw? What was she doing? ... Tell me

L15: Äh ... well ... em ... I saw her ... äh ... with Christian ... äh ... and he kissed her

L6: He? [pointing at a classmate]

L15: Yes ... he

L6: So YOU kiss MY girl-friend?

CLASS: +++ *laughter* +++

L3: *Nee ... ich war's nicht ... wirklich nicht* [No, it was not me, believe me!] [*end impro*]

L15: Well ... I can see you want to be left alone ... I think I better go now

L6: Ok ... thanks for letting me know

L15: See you then ... take care

L6: Bye

The transcript illustrates how difficult improvising is for EFL learners not used to speaking freely, even after four years of (traditional, largely IRF-based) target language instruction. As the improvised middle part following the memorized scripted opening sequence shows, there is definitely no lack of imagination, commitment, and fun, but the learners' limited ability to access what they already know (or should know after about four years of learning English in terms of grammar, lexis, etc.) noticeably restricts the interaction. The transcript indicates how highly important it is to give learners more room for unprepared interaction in unpredictable contexts and for articulating themselves in the target language more freely and spontaneously.

*Documentation and Brief Analysis of a Whole-Class Follow-Up Discussion*
To briefly illustrate how the improvised dialogue above was used to initiate a whole-class reflective discussion, an additional transcript is provided (for obvious reasons it is only possible to present the opening sequence of this discussion here):

T: Now before we listen to Mario and Dennis again ... before we listen ... em ... to the recording let me first ask you what you think about their ... eh ... conversation ... [5 sec] ... Let's collect ... yes ... let's collect your first impressions ... [10 sec] ... Yes Simone?

S1: I think it was very funny

T: Oh really? Can you explain why?

L1: Because Dennis play so cool ... äh ... when he was angry about Christian ... äh ... after Christian had kissed his girl-friend Meike

T: Mmh ... O.K. ... What about the others? What do YOU think of the conversation?

L13: Dennis was good ... but Mario not

T: Mario wasn't? Can you tell us why?

L13: Because Mario is the best friend of Dennis ... em ... so he ... äh ... I think he ... he must not tell Dennis about Christian and Meike

T: You mean he shouldn't have told him?

L13: Yes ... it's not fair. He is NOT a reporter

CLASS: +++ noise +++

T: O.K. O.K. ... Calm down please ... We can't go on if you all speak at the same time ... Isa ... you wanted to say something?

L7: Yes ... *hör doch mal auf Tim ... ich will was sagen* [Stop that, Tim! I want so say something]

T: TIM ... come on

L7: I think Mario and Dennis are good friends ... and good friends have no ... *Geheimnisse?*

T: Secrets

L7: Yes ... and Mario wouldn't be ... *ehrlich?*

T: Honest

L7: Mario ... he ... he wouldn't be ... *wie noch mal?*

T: Honest

L7: He wouldn't be honest if he doesn't tell his best friend

T: So you think that friends should always be honest to each other?

L7: Yes

T: All right ... in Isa's opinion honesty ... *Ehrlichkeit* ... is very important ... You should always be honest to your friends ... Do you all agree? ... No? ... Who doesn't?

This third transcript shows that in a follow-up discussion, learners are free to say and to comment on whatever they want, as long as it relates to the improvised exchange. Because the focus is on the content of the exchange initially, message-oriented communication is still dominant and, consequently, error treatment by the teacher is carried out in an indirect way. This does not mean that in such reflective whole-group discussions there is no place for (immediate) error treatment and for brief, integrated teacher-led instruction on specific, especially on problematic, language forms. Optimal learning requires message-oriented and form-oriented instruction to be balanced out carefully (see Butzkamm, 2004). Mixing up both should be avoided, however (see Doff & Klippel, 2007: 198–204).

To promote more complex and fluent speaking, learners also need to be given additional input (lexical input in particular, as becomes visible when $L_7$ tries to express her personal view in the class discussion). Apart from this, learners should be provided with some conversational follow-up gambits that are necessary and useful for more lively, pragmatically adequate conversational exchanges, for instance:

| *Follow-up gambits that can be used as conversational "links" by the bearer of the news (Keller & Warner, 1988, 35)* | *Follow-up gambits that can be used as "uptakers" by the recipient of the news (Edmondson & House, 1981, 71–74)* |
|---|---|
| • *Really?...* <br> • *You don't say ...* <br> • *Oh dear ...* <br> • *Good heavens ...* <br> • *Great ...* <br> • *Terrific ...* <br> • *Damn ...* | • *To start with ...* <br> • *It may sound strange, but ...* <br> • *To tell you the truth ...* <br> • *To be honest ...* <br> • *Frankly, ...* <br> • *Actually, ...* <br> • *Believe it or not ...* |

## PLACING IMPROVISED SPEAKING IN A WIDER THEORETICAL CONTEXT

As the previous examples show, improvisations aim at encouraging learners to make the most of their limited target language resources in task-driven communicative contexts that are partially unpredictable (for a brief discussion of the concept of task, see Skehan, 2003; for a more detailed account, see, for instance, R. Ellis, 2004). Designed along Piepho's (2003: 108) SMART principles (S = significant, M = meaningful, A = achievable, R = relevant, T = time-related), the focus is on spontaneous, collaborative target language interaction and learning-while-doing in communicative classroom scenarios devoid of threat and anxiety. Particular attention is given to what learners say, how they initiate exchanges and keep them going, how they respond to their classmates and cooperate with them in largely unprepared communication. This is taken as the basis for further message-oriented and form-oriented instruction, arranged in a cyclical way.

Target language production (or output) and target language comprehension (or input) interact in many interdependent ways in foreign/second language learning and teaching. Elaborating on the potential role of learner-produced output, Swain (2000: 99) points out that:

> ... the importance of output could be that output pushes learners to process language more deeply – with more mental effort – than does input. With output, the learner is in control. In speaking or writing, learners can "stretch" their interlanguage to meet communicative goals. To produce, learners need to do something. They need to create linguistic form and meaning, and in so doing, discover what they can or cannot

do. Output may stimulate learners to move from semantic, open-ended, strategic processing prevalent in comprehension to the complete grammatical processing needed for accurate production. Students' meaningful production of language output would thus seem to have a potentially significant role in language development.

During an improvisation, learners notice "that they do not know how to express precisely the meaning they wish to convey at *the very moment of attempting to produce it* – they notice, so to speak, a 'hole' in their interlanguage" (Swain, 2000: 100). They also recognize that they frequently cannot bridge these "gaps in their linguistic knowledge" (Swain, 2000: 101) entirely on their own, and that interacting (sharing, negotiating, etc.) is the key to success. In line with Swain (2000: 104) and even more so with sociocultural (or ecological) approaches to second and foreign learning use and learning (see, for instance, Kramsch, 2000; Lantolf, 2000; van Lier, 2000; for more recent accounts, see Kramsch, 2002; Lantolf & Thorne, 2006; van Lier, 2004), improvised speaking in EFL classrooms can thus be conceived of as a closely interrelated cognitive and social activity.

However, in contrast to Swain's conception of collaborative dialogue – which she defines as "linguistic problem-solving through social interaction" (2000: 104), thus largely excluding the affective dimension of foreign language learning – improvised speaking is a more holistic phenomenon that is strongly affected by parameters such as motivation to speak and speaking anxiety. Linguistic problem solving through interaction is certainly an important part of improvised speaking, but memorization, imagination, pleasure, and play are equally central.

In order for improvised speaking to occur, the overall psychosocial context of target language learning in institutional contexts needs to be taken into consideration. Improvisations such as *Bus Stop* and *Surprise Encounter* were developed with this in mind, offering learners a) meaningful and challenging communicative frames roughly tuned to their competences and abilities; b) communicative tasks that are linguistically within their reach and thematically interesting (tasks as incentives), allowing for playful and experimental language use; and c) an error-tolerant instructional environment, distinguishing clearly between opportunities for communicative action and opportunities for communicative reflection (including systematic error treatment and language practice).

In line with Sawyer (2004a: 13), improvised speaking in EFL classrooms can thus be conceived of as an instance of "disciplined improvisation" that is always related to a given event structure and a communicative framework.

In the past, very little research has been undertaken to specify these structures and frameworks for foreign or second language instruction in secondary schools (as examples see: Glasser, 1971; Phillips, 1993). This research project cumulatively indicates that in order to trigger improvised target language interaction and spontaneous language use in systematic ways, learners need to be confronted with adequate scenarios on the one hand (see Di Pietro, 1987; Piepho, 2003, 2005), while on the other hand, they are provided with a carefully planned procedural infrastructure for classroom talk-in-interaction (see Schegloff, 2007) that can serve as a communicative anchor (or scaffold) to which they can tie their attempts to speak freely (see Kurtz, 2001: 121–133). Structures and frameworks that are too vague can easily overburden EFL learners and significantly reduce their willingness to engage in such activities and take any further communicative risks.

How does this conceptualization of improvisation in EFL classrooms relate to current research on foreign and second language learning? First of all, and contrary to cognitively oriented second language acquisition research grounded in the computation-representation-paradigm, target language learning is modeled as a holistic process that can only with difficulty be reduced to the intrapersonal mental processes involved in using and acquiring a foreign or second language (for a fundamental critique of the cognitive approach, see Firth & Wagner, 1997, 2007). The emphasis is placed rather on the interpersonal dynamics of collaborative, learner-learner and teacher-learner classroom discourse, and on the fluidity of co-constructed and emergent foreign language and intercultural development and growth in institutionalized "communities of practice" (Wenger, 1998). The *I* and the *We* (Elias, 1987), the self and the other, the *taking in* and the *taking part*, are thus seen as being intertwined in many ways. Dewey (1897) made a similar point more than a hundred years ago:

> I believe that the only true education comes through the stimulation of the child's powers by the demands of the social situations in which he finds himself [...]. I believe that this educational process has two sides – one psychological and one sociological; and that neither can be subordinated to the other nor neglected without evil results following [...]. I believe that the psychological and social sides are organically related and that education cannot be regarded as a compromise between the two, or a superimposition of one upon the other [...]. In sum, I believe that the individual who is to be educated is a social individual and that society is an organic union of individuals. If we eliminate the social from the child we are left only with an abstraction; if we eliminate the individual factor from society, we are left only with an inert and lifeless mass.

More specifically, foreign language learning is conceived of here as a complex transformative process (on learning as "transformation of participation" see Rogoff, 1998) that is mediated through language use (see Lantolf, 2000), that emerges over time (on language emergence see N. Ellis & Larsen-Freeman, 2006), and that cannot be regulated entirely (see Bleyhl, 2004). The instructional strategy adopted in this study is to confront learners with communicative tasks and activities that are partially unpredictable, thus stimulating improvised language use. This study shows that improvised language use is associated with significant changes in learner participation in the classroom. On the whole, learners participate more actively, more creatively, and more autonomously than in traditional IRF-based learning environments. This is of considerable importance to the gradual expansion of their participatory repertoires in the target language and culture. Butzkamm and Caldwell (2009: 161–162) come to a similar conclusion. They point out:

> Whereas abortive attempts at free communication can be destructive in so far as they undermine the pupils' confidence in handling the language, time must be regularly given for unplanned and unpredictable communication. Dialogues are composed with ample time for consideration and revision, which robs them of the spontaneity characteristic of most spoken language. We can catch some of this spontaneity by taking a further step and invite the pupils to improvise role-plays, thus taking them from the shelter of the cove into the open sea. Learners use their newly developed skills in unpredictable directions and develop the ability to think on their feet. Improvised play helps to make minds more flexible and inspire confidence in coping with unanticipated situations.

## POTENTIAL BARRIERS TO IMPROVISATION IN SECONDARY EFL CLASSROOMS

Transformative learning and development can neither be captured adequately in terms of a focus on individuals' possessions of concepts and skills (Rogoff, 1998), nor can its progress and "outcome" be measured in a linear and all-embracing way. Recent developments in education politics, governance, and administration seem to largely run counter to this. They cannot be ignored, of course, because they set the conditions under which foreign languages are taught in secondary schools. This is why they are problematized in the following.

Secondary school foreign language education is currently passing through a period of transition and change, turbulence and uncertainty. Faced with the pressing challenges and the growing demands of globalization, countries all around the world have rushed to embark on large-scale reform projects aimed at improving the quality and outcome of foreign language learning and teaching in systematic, more calculable, and predictable ways. Inspired by the notion of education as an investment in human capital, a plethora of more or less intrusive and consequential reform initiatives have been developed and implemented over recent years. At the core, these include the introduction of national standards, outcome-oriented (core) curricula, and obligatory nationwide performance tests, as well as comparative quality assessment and assurance frameworks, embracing new school inspection and stronger accountability strategies. However, as Breen (2007: 1071–1072) points out critically, "such measures have been put in place on the basis of two unproven assumptions: that whatever teachers achieved before is no longer adequate and that the bureaucratic surveillance of teachers' work will improve their students' performance."

It still remains to be seen if the continuing global trend to elevate intensive monitoring and meticulous evaluation of learning outcomes to the status of an educational imperative will turn out to be beneficial for foreign language instruction. Rather than fostering a spirit of enthusiasm, inspiration, and creativity among frontline educators, the new standards-driven and evidence-based reforms may instead contribute to creating a climate of regimentation and conformity, which is likely to obstruct substantial change, innovation, and progress in foreign language learning and teaching.

Improving foreign language education in everyday classroom practice is a classic example of the teaching paradox; it is complex and subject to the interplay of a wide variety of interacting influence factors. By importing and adapting reform strategies and measures that are largely based on values, goals, and concepts that (arguably) have been proven successful in business, commerce, finance, and industry, this complexity may appear to be manageable. However, the price to be paid for injecting market pressure into secondary school education, for turning foreign language classrooms into arenas of competition for the best test results, for coating instruction with more and more layers of assessment, for reducing educational "quality" to a limited number of measurable performance indicators, and for conceiving of output or outcome as the linchpin of quality development, may be hefty and unacceptable. In many countries, concerns are continuing to grow that standards- and test-driven compliance pressures on teachers are likely to rise, and that, in consequence, foreign language classroom instruction may increasingly and largely be condensed, redesigned, and repackaged toward improving isolated skills performance in standardized tests (see, for instance, Bausch et al., 2005; Böttcher et al., 2008; Doff, Hüllen, & Klippel, 2008).

In view of the growing need for more creative and flexible, meaning-ful and language-rich, culture-sensitive and individually-tailored instruc-tional practices designed to simultaneously achieve a variety of educational as well as "functional" foreign language learning goals, it would definitely be a step backward if the ongoing marketization of education led to a wide-spread "teaching to the test" type of orientation among teachers, or if it led to a test-directed monoculture of classroom interaction and instruction in secondary school foreign language classrooms aimed above all at ensuring high passing rates and test scores in the annual assessment marathon.

It would also run counter to recent developments in international research on foreign and second language learning and teaching. As an accumulating body of scholarship shows, traditional input-interaction-output theories of instruction have come under critique for being too narrow, in particular for portraying the learner primarily as a mental being and a largely indepen-dent self, thus failing to adequately account for the social and cultural nature of acquisition and/or learning and, ultimately, for the learner as a social being and a fundamentally interdependent self (see Firth & Wagner, 1997; Zuengler & Miller, 2006). In her review of Block's *The Social Turn in Second Language Acquisition* (2003), Byrnes (2005: 434) emphasizes the growing cri-tique of the up-to-now dominant, largely cognitively oriented line of research in the following, albeit in parts polemically exaggerated, way when she states that: "Not only is learner background disregarded (e.g., second and third lan-guage learning), but incorrect assumptions are also being made about the nature and efficacy of naturalistic learning, and learners themselves reduced to cognizing automatons who obey universals of cognition in a fashion unim-peded by the social context within which they live and use their language."

Viewed from a less polemic perspective, it is as yet too early to speak of a major paradigm shift in researching second language acquisition and/or foreign language education (see also Kurtz, 2003). Nevertheless, there is cur-rently a strong trend toward more holistic, transdisciplinary approaches to theory construction and research emphasizing the interpersonal dynamism and the emergent and transformative character of co-constructed learning and development in complex psychosocial environments (including the project "improvised speaking"). In this theoretical framework, learners are conceived of "as part of a larger social matrix, affiliated with diverse communities and interacting in dynamic ways with members of these communities" (Cummins & Davison, 2007: 615). Consequently, learning is conceptualized as occurring "within communities of practice rather than reflecting an accomplishment of isolated individuals" (Cummins & Davison, 2007: 615). The overall theoretical focus is on "how learning and development occur as a process of transformation of participation in socio-cultural activity" (Rogoff, 1998: 687), rather than on the individual acquisition and possession of competencies, concepts, and skills.

It is evident that the ongoing colonization of education by global market ideologies and business management practices – and the corresponding accentuation of regulative control – is very difficult, if not impossible, to bring in line with these developments in research. Forcing learners to demonstrate (annual) progress in standardized and often discrete-point-only performance tests might be desirable from an educational governance perspective – one that is founded on the questionable idea of linear improvement, immediate payoff, and the pressing need to hold down costs – but it is hardly compatible with the psychosocial ecology and the long-term character of foreign language and intercultural development and growth in secondary schools. As van Lier (2007: 52) underlines in this context: "[The] idea of education as emergent expertise of course flies in the face of much of the standards-accountability-testing mechanisms that school systems tend to favor. In those scenarios, everything should be predictable (and testable, of course) to the highest degree possible. If not, the power and control [...] that policy makers want would be weakened and jeopardized."

Policy drivers and secondary school administrators are well advised not to base reform strategies on seemingly plausible yet premature equations between test scores and foreign language teaching and learning quality. Simplistic cause-and-effect considerations such as, for instance, "if you can't measure it, you can't control it and if you can't control it, you can't improve it" are grossly inadequate in addressing the manifold challenges of improving the overall process and outcome of learning and teaching in foreign language classrooms. In the worst case, they could contribute to pathologizing education as a whole, as intellectual and personal development in the widest sense; and, more specifically, they could contribute to suffocating creative thought and interaction in everyday classroom practice. (see also Kurtz, 2005)

Focusing on target setting, measurable gains in learners' test performance, or increased external evaluation and accountability (only or predominantly), will not provide sufficient orientation and support for teachers in their quest for enhancing instruction. The quality of foreign language education in everyday classroom practice can only be raised substantially if the psychosocial complexity of learning and teaching is taken into consideration more thoroughly, both holistically and in detail, culminating at best in the formulation of opportunity-to-learn standards based on culture- and context-sensitive examples of good practice (with regard to improvised speaking in EFL classrooms, see the videos included in Siebold,

2004a), which can serve as exemplary "vicarious experiences" that allow for "naturalistic generalizations" (Stake, 1995: 63–68, 85–88). In scientific arenas the necessity to complement externally set standards by suitable and continuous pre-service as well as in-service support is widely acknowledged (see, for instance, Lankes, 2008; O'Day, 2008), but in education politics this has as yet not been given the attention and priority it deserves.

CONCLUDING REMARKS

The "cultivation of the speaking skill," as Rivers (1968/81: 94) put it forty years ago, takes time and patience. Next to and in combination with intercultural learning in institutional contexts, it is probably the most difficult challenge foreign language teachers are faced with in the Internet Age. Although Rivers (1968/81: 246) wrote about this important aspect of learning back in 1968, it is by no means anachronistic or inconsistent with foreign language education in the twenty-first century:

> The flowering of natural language use will come in its own time; it cannot be forced. When students begin to interact naturally, if only for a few minutes, we must be quick to recognize the change and let the natural interaction take over until its energy is spent. Being able to withdraw and leave students space and room to take over and learn through their own activity is the mark of the real teacher.

However, qualitative research on improvised speaking carried out over the past decade in more – and more varied – instructional contexts indicates that foreign language teachers can and should do a lot more to encourage learners to speak freely. Carefully designed improvisational activities can help teachers negotiate the teaching and learning paradox; they can help foster more extended, flexible, and creative target language production and learner participation beyond incidental spontaneous classroom speaking, if integrated into (well-balanced, form- and meaning-focused) classroom practice as early as possible and, above all, on a regular basis. The potential gains, not in terms of part-skill measurable outcome, but in more holistic, long-term effect and efficiency, should not be underestimated.

REFERENCES

Bardovi-Harlig, Kathleen; Hartford, Beverly A. S.; Mahan-Taylor, Rebecca; Morgan, Mary J. & Reynolds, Dudley W. (1991). "Developing pragmatic awareness: closing the conversation." *English Language Teaching Journal*, 45 (1), 4–15.

Bausch, Karl-Richard; Burwitz-Melzer, Eva; Königs, Frank G. & Krumm, Hans-Jürgen (Eds.) (2005). *Bildungsstandards auf dem Prüfstand. Arbeitspapiere der 25. Frühjahrskonferenz zur Erforschung des Fremdsprachenunterrichts.* Tübingen: Narr.

Beck, Bärbel, & Klieme, Eckhard (2003). DESI – Eine Längsschnittstudie zur Untersuchung des Sprachunterrichts in deutschen Schulen. *Empirische Pädagogik*, 17 (3), 380–395.

Beecroft, Raphaëlle (2008). *Dichte Kommunikation. Improvisationstheater in der translationsorientierten Fremdsprachendidaktik.* Unpublished master's thesis, University of Mainz, Germany.

Bleyhl, Werner (2004). Das Menschenbild als Basis für eine Didaktik des Fremdsprachenunterrichts. *Zeitschrift für Fremdsprachenforschung*, 15(2), 207–235.

Block, David (2003). *The Social Turn in Second Language Acquisition.* Washington, DC: Georgetown University Press.

Böttcher, Wolfgang; Bos, Wilfried; Döbert, Hans & Holtappels Heinz Günter (Eds.) (2008). *Bildungsmonitoring und Bildungscontrolling in nationaler und internationaler Perspektive.* Münster: Waxmann.

Brazil, David (1995). *A Grammar of Speech.* Oxford: Oxford University Press.

Breen, Michael P. (2007). Appropriating uncertainty. In: Cummins, Jim & Davison, Chris (Eds.) (2007). *International Handbook of English Language Teaching.* New York: Springer, 1067–1084.

Brown, Penelope & Levinson, Stephen C. (1978). *Politeness. Some Universals in Language Usage.* Cambridge: Cambridge University Press.

Brumfit, Christopher (1991). "Communicative" language teaching: An educational perspective. In: Brumfit, Christopher & Johnson, Keith (Eds.) (1991). *The Communicative Approach to Language Teaching.* Oxford: Oxford University Press, 183–191 (1st impr 1979).

Butzkamm, Wolfgang (2004). *Lust zum Lehren, Lust zum Lernen. Eine neue Methodik für den Fremdsprachenunterricht.* Tübingen: Francke.

Butzkamm, Wolfgang, & Caldwell, John A.W. (2009). *The Bilingual Reform. A Paradigm Shift in Foreign Language Teaching.* Tübingen: Narr.

Bygate, Martin (2001). Speaking. In: Carter, Ronald & Nunan, David (Eds.) (2001). *The Cambridge Guide to Teaching English to Speakers of Other Languages.* Cambridge: Cambridge University Press, 14–20.

Byrnes, Heidi (2005). The social turn in second language acquisition (review). *The Canadian Modern Language Review / La revue canadienne des langues vivantes*, 61 (3), 433–436.

Carter, Ronald (2004). *Language and Creativity. The Art of Common Talk.* London: Routledge.

Ciborra, Claudio (1999). Notes on improvisation and time in organizations. *Accounting, Management and Information Technologies*, 9 (2), 77–94.

(2002). *The Labyrinths of Information. Challenging the Wisdom of Systems.* Oxford: Oxford University Press.

Coulthard, Malcolm (Ed.) (1992). *Advances in Spoken Discourse Analysis.* London: Routledge.

Cummins, Jim & Davison, Chris (Eds.) (2007). The learner and the learning environment: Creating new communities. In: Cummins, Jim & Davison, Chris (2007). *International Handbook of English Language Teaching. Volume 2.* New York: Springer, 615–623.

Davies, Paul & Pearse, Eric (2000). *Success in English Teaching*. Oxford: Oxford University Press.

Dewey, John (1897). My pedagogic creed. *School Journal*, 54 (3) 77–80. Online: http://dewey.pragmatism.org/creed.htm

Di Pietro, Robert J. (1987). *Strategic Interaction. Learning Languages through Scenarios*. Cambridge: Cambridge University Press.

Doff, Sabine & Klippel, Friederike (2007). *Englischdidaktik. Praxishandbuch für die Sekundarstufe I und II*. Berlin: Cornelsen.

Doff, Sabine, Hüllen, Werner & Klippel, Friederike (2008). *Visions of Languages in Education*. München: Langenscheidt-ELT.

Drew, Paul & Heritage, John (Eds.) (1992). *Talk at Work: Interaction in Institutionalized Settings*. Cambridge: Cambridge University Press.

Edmondson, Willis & House, Juliane (1981). *Let's talk, and talk about it: a pedagogic interactional grammar of English*. München: Urban & Schwarzenberg.

Elias, Norbert (1987). *Die Gesellschaft der Individuen*. Frankfurt am Main: Suhrkamp.

Ellis, Nick & Larsen-Freeman, Diane (2006). Language emergence: Implications for applied linguistics – introduction to the special issue. *Applied Linguistics*, 27 (4), 558–589.

Ellis, Rod (2004). *Task-Based Language Learning and Teaching*. Oxford: Oxford University Press.

Firth, Alan & Wagner, Johannes (1997). On discourse, communication, and (some) fundamental concepts in SLA research. *The Modern Language Journal*, 81(3), 285–300.

(2007). Second/foreign language learning as a social accomplishment: elaborations on a reconceptualized SLA. *The Modern Language Journal*, 91, 800–819.

Glasser, Barbara (1971). Improvisational drama in an urban junior high. In: McClosky, Mildred G. (Ed.), *Teaching Strategies and Classroom Realities*. Englewood Cliffs, NJ: Prentice Hall, 181–187.

Hodgson, John & Richards, Ernest (1966). *Improvisation*. London: Methuen.

Keller, Eric & Warner, Sylvia T. (1988). *Conversation gambits. Real English conversation practices*. Hove: Language Teaching Publications.

Kern, Richard (2008). Making connections through texts in language teaching. *Language Teaching: Surveys and Studies*, 41 (3), 367–387.

Klieme, Eckhard & Beck, Bärbel (2007). *Sprachliche Kompetenzen – Konzepte und Messung. DESI-Studie (Deutsch-Englisch-Schülerleistungen-International)*. Weinheim: Beltz.

Klieme, Eckhard; Helmke, Andreas; Lehmann, Rainer H.; Nold, Günter; Rolff, Hans-Günter; Schröder, Konrad; Thomé, Günther & Willenberg, Heiner (Eds.) (2008). *Unterricht und Kompetenzerwerb in Deutsch und Englisch. Ergebnisse der DESI-Studie*. Weinheim: Beltz.

Kramsch, Claire (2000). Social discursive constructions of self in L2 learning. In: Lantolf, James P. (Ed.) (2000). *Sociocultural Theory and Second Language Learning*. Oxford: Oxford University Press, 133–135.

(2002). *Language Acquisition and Language Socialization. Ecological Perspectives*. London: Continuum.

Kurtz, Jürgen (1997a). Improvisation als Übung zum freien Sprechen. *Englisch*, 3, 87–97.

(1997b). Auf dem Wege zum selbständigen Sprechhandeln im 5. Schuljahr: Die Improvisation "The Chase". *Englisch*, 4, 121–127.

(1998). Kooperatives Sprechhandeln im Englischunterricht: Die Improvisation "Once Upon a Time". *Englisch*, 2, 41–49.

(2001). *Improvisierendes Sprechen im Fremdsprachenunterricht. Eine Untersuchung zur Entwicklung spontansprachlicher Handlungskompetenz in der Zielsprache.* Tübingen: Narr.

(2003). Menschenbilder in der Theorie und Praxis des Fremdsprachenunterrichts: Konturen, Funktionen und Konsequenzen für das Lehren und Lernen. *Zeitschrift für Fremdsprachenforschung*, 14 (1), 149–167.

(2005). Bildungsstandards als Instrumente der Qualitätsentwicklung im Fremdsprachenunterricht: *Towards a checklist approach to foreign language learning and teaching?* In: Bausch, Karl-Richard; Burwitz-Melzer; Eva; Königs, Frank G. & Krumm, Hans-Jürgen (Eds.), *Bildungsstandards auf dem Prüfstand. Arbeitspapiere der 25. Frühjahrskonferenz zur Erforschung des Fremdsprachenunterrichts.* Tübingen: Narr, 159–167.

(2006a). Improvised speaking in the EFL classroom: Aufgaben als Elemente einer unterrichtlichen Figurationstheorie fremdsprachlichen Lehrens und Lernens. In: Bausch, Karl-Richard; Burwitz-Melzer, Eva; Königs, Frank G. & Krumm, Hans-Jürgen (Eds.), *Aufgabenorientierung als Aufgabe. Arbeitspapiere zur 26. Frühjahrstagung zur Erforschung des Fremdsprachenunterrichts.* Tübingen: Narr, 130–139.

(2006b). Fremdsprachendidaktische Forschung als hermeneutisch-empirische Unterrichtsforschung (ein Auslaufmodell?). *Fremdsprachen und Hochschule*, 75, 23–41.

(2008). Szenische Improvisationen – theoretische Grundlagen und unterrichtliche Realisierungsmöglichkeiten. In: Ahrens, Rüdiger; Eisenmann, Maria & Merkl, Matthias (Eds.), *Moderne Dramendidaktik für den Englischunterricht.* Heidelberg: Winter, 409–424.

Lankes, Eva-Maria (Ed.) (2008). *Pädagogische Professionalität als Gegenstand empirischer Forschung.* Münster. Waxmann.

Lantolf, James P. (2000). Introducing sociocultural theory. In: Lantolf, James P. (Ed.). *Sociocultural Theory and Second Language Learning.* Oxford: Oxford University Press, 1–26.

Lantolf, James P. & Thorne, Steven L. (2006). *Sociocultural Theory and the Genesis of Second Language Development.* Oxford: Oxford University Press.

Legutke, Michael (1993). Room to talk. Experiential learning in the foreign language classroom. *Die Neueren Sprachen*, 92 (4), 306–331.

Lier, Leo van (2000). From input to affordance: Acquisition theory and the truth(s) about relativity. In: Lantolf, James P. (Ed.). *Sociocultural Theory and Second Language Learning.* Oxford: Oxford University Press, 219–243.

(2001). Constraints and resources in classroom talk: issues of equality and symmetry. In: Candlin, Christopher & Mercer, Neil (Eds.), *English Language Teaching in Its Social Context.* London: Routledge, 90–107.

(2004). *The Ecology and Semiotics of Language Learning. A Sociocultural Perspective.* Dordrecht: Kluwer Academic.

(2007). Action-based teaching, autonomy and identity. *Innovation in Language Learning and Teaching,* 1 (1), 46–65. Online: http://www.multilingual-matters. net/illt/001/illt0010046.htm

Lin, Angel (2008). Using ethnography in the analysis of pedagogical practice. Perspectives from activity theory. In: Bhatia, Vijay K.; Flowerdew, John & Jones, Rodney H. (Eds.), *Advances in Discourse Studies.* London and New York: Routledge, 63–80.

Liu, Wen-Chung (2006). Memorization and improvisation. A comparison of two strategies in the oral acquisition of English as a second language. Online: http:// dlibrary.acu.edu.au/digitaltheses/public/adt-acuvp124.../02whole.pdf

McCarthy, Michael & Slade, Diana (2007). Extending our understanding of spoken discourse. In: Cummins, Jim & Davison, Chris (Eds.), *International Handbook of English Language Teaching.* Volume 2. New York: Springer, 859–873.

Mercer, Neil (1995). *The Guided Construction of Knowledge. Talk amongst Teachers and Learners.* Clevedon: Multilingual Matters.

Murphy, Richard A. (1995). *From Practice to Performance. A Manual of Teacher Training Workshop Activities.* Vol. 1. Washington, DC: United States Information Agency.

O'Day, Jennifer (2008). Standards-based reform: Promises, pitfalls, and potential lessons from the U.S. In: Böttcher, Wolfgang; Bos, Wilfried; Döbert, Hans & Holtappels, Heinz Günter (Eds.), *Bildungsmonitoring und Bildungscontrolling in nationaler und internationaler Perspektive.* Münster: Waxmann, 107–157.

Piepho, Hans-Eberhard (2003). *Lernaktivierung im Fremdsprachenunterricht. Szenarien in Theorie und Praxis.* Hannover: Schroedel.

(2005). Szenarien. In: Müller-Hartmann, Andreas & Schocker-v. Ditfurth, Marita (Eds.), *Aufgabenorientierung im Fremdsprachenunterricht. Task-Based Language Learning and Teaching. Festschrift für Michael K. Legutke.* Tübingen: Narr, 119–124.

Phillips, Elayne (1993). Improvisation in drama as a means to effective communication. In: Oller, John W. Jr. (Ed.). *Methods That Work. Ideas for Literacy and Language Teachers.* Boston: Heinle & Heinle, 143–152.

Richards, Jack C. (2005). *Communicative Language Teaching Today.* Online: http:// www.professorjackrichards.com/pdfs/communicative-language-teaching-today-v2.pdf

Rivers, Wilga M. (1981). *Teaching Foreign-Language Skills.* Chicago: Chicago University Press (first edition 1968).

Rogoff, Barbara (1998). Cognition as a collaborative process. In: Damon, William (Ed.) (1998). *Handbook of Child Psychology.* 5th edition. Vol. 2: Cognition, Perception, and Language. New York: John Wiley & Sons, 679–744.

Rossa, Henning (2007). *Improvisationen als interaktive Lernarrangements: Anwendung eines Konzepts zur Förderung spontansprachlicher Handlungskompetenz in der Zielsprache Englisch dargestellt auf der Grundlage eigener Unterrichtserfahrungen in einem Grundkurs der Jahrgangsstufe 11 des Gymnasiums.* Online: http://www.standardsicherung.schulministerium.nrw. de/cms/upload/Sprachenwerkstatt/improvisationen_rossa_2007.pdf

Sawyer, R. Keith (2001). *Creating Conversations. Improvisation in Everyday Discourse.* Cresskill, NJ: Hampton.

(2004a). Creative teaching: Collaborative discussion as disciplined improvisation. *Educational Researcher,* 2, 12–20.

(2004b). Improvised lessons: Collaborative discussion in the constructivist classroom. *Teaching Education,* 2, 189–201.

Schegloff, Emanual A. (2007). *Sequence Organization in Interaction. A Primer in Conversation Analysis. Volume 1.* Cambridge: Cambridge University Press.

Seedhouse, Paul (1996). Classroom interaction: Possibilities and impossibilities. *English Language Teaching Journal,* 50(1), 16–24.

Siebold, Jörg (Ed.) (2004a). *Let's Talk: Lehrtechniken. Vom gebundenen zum freien Sprechen.* Berlin: Cornelsen [including DVD-Video].

Siebold, Jörg (2004b). Interaktion und Sprachproduktion in improvisierten Schülergesprächen. In: Deringer, Ludwig (Ed.). *Innovative Fremdsprachendidaktik. Kolloquium zu Ehren von Wolfgang Butzkamm.* Aachen British and American Studies. Frankfurt am Main: Lang, 149–166.

(2006). Unter der Lupe: Improvisierte Gespräche in einer 6. Realschulklasse. *Praxis Fremdsprachenunterricht,* 4, 27–32.

Sinclair, J. McH. & Coulthard, Malcolm (1975). *Towards an Analysis of Discourse. The English Used by Teachers and Pupils.* Oxford: Oxford University Press.

Sinclair J. McH. & Brazil, David (1982). *Teacher Talk.* Oxford: Oxford University Press.

Skehan, Peter (2003). Task-based instruction. *Language Teaching,* 36, 1–14.

Stake, Robert E. (1995). *The Art of Case Study Research.* Thousand Oaks, CA: Sage.

Stern, H.H. (1992). *Issues and Options in Language Teaching.* Oxford: University Press.

Swain, Merrill (2000). The output hypothesis and beyond: Mediating acquisition through collaborative dialogue. In: Lantolf, James P. (Ed.). *Sociocultural Theory and Second Language Learning.* Oxford: Oxford University Press, 97–114.

(2005). The output hypothesis: Theory and research. In: Hinkel, Eli (Ed.). *Handbook on Research in Second Language Teaching and Learning.* Mahwah, NJ: Lawrence Erlbaum Associates, 471–484.

Swann, Joan & Maybin, Janet (2007). Introduction: Language creativity in everyday contexts. *Applied Linguistics,* 28 (4), 491–496.

Thaler, Engelbert (2009). *Offene Lernarrangements im Englischunterricht.* München: Langenscheidt-ELT.

Thornbury, Scott (2002). Training in instructional conversation. In: Trappes-Lomax, Hugh & Ferguson, Gibson (Eds.), *Language in Language Teacher Education.* Amsterdam: John Benjamins.

Verriour, Patrick (1993). Drama in the teaching and learning of a first language. In: Schewe, Manfred & Shaw, Peter (Eds.), *Towards Drama as a Method in the Foreign Language Classroom.* Frankfurt am Main: Lang, 43–57.

Wenger, Etienne (1998). *Communities of Practice: Learning, Meaning, and Identity.* Cambridge: Cambridge University Press.

Zuengler, Jane & Miller, Elizabeth R. (2006). Cognitive and sociocultural perspectives: Two parallel SLA worlds? *TESOL Quarterly,* 1, 35–58.

# 8

# Improvising with Adult English Language Learners

ANTHONY PERONE

## INTRODUCTION

My interests in improvisational theater (improv) and language learning and teaching go almost hand in hand and first surfaced during my undergraduate teaching experiences (Perone, 1994). Since then, I have been learning about and performing improv and integrating my improv experiences with my experiences as an adult educator. As a result, I have considered the rules and activities of improv to be a mechanism and an instructional tool for fruitful and developmental learning environments.

In this chapter, I describe my experiences using improv activities in formal learning environments with adult English language learners. For my purposes, improv is "a form of unscripted performance that uses audience suggestions to initiate and/or shape games, scenes, or plays created spontaneously and cooperatively according to agreed-upon rules or structures" (Seham, 2001, p. xvii). In what follows, I first describe several rules of improv that are shared by the professional improv acting community. Then, the bulk of my chapter explores three conflicts that are versions of what Sawyer (this volume) calls *the learning paradox* – the unavoidable tension, found in all constructivist learning environments, between the necessity of providing a range of options for creativity and improvisation on the part of the learner, while guiding that learning with the appropriate level of supporting structure. The three conflicts are: *a priori* scripts versus emergent scripts, experts/novices and confidence/embarrassment, and the individual versus the group. Afterward, I describe six improv games that are well known among professional improvisers (e.g., Halpern, Close, and

In R. K. Sawyer (Ed.) (2011). *Structure and improvisation in creative teaching* (pp. 162–183). Cambridge: Cambridge University Press.

Johnson, 1994; Johnstone, 1981, 1999; Spolin, 1963) and illustrate how I used them to support the language learning and development of the members of the learning environment. Based on these illustrations, I argue that improv activities are effective at negotiating the learning paradox; they yield opportunities for newer and richer models of instruction and interaction among the members of the learning environment. I conclude that the use of appropriately structured improvisation in the classroom can lead to revolutionary alternatives to current educational models.

## ESSENTIAL RULES OF IMPROV

There are a host of improv games and forms that are practiced throughout the world (Kozlowski, 2002; Libera, 2004; Napier, 2004; Sawyer, 2003a). Despite this variety, there is a set of rules that all improvisers agree on in order to yield more effective improvisational performances. This set of rules is a grassroots theory known as an ethnotheory. According to Lutz (1987, pp. 291–292), an ethnotheory is an explicit and abstract body of knowledge, as well as a set of everyday practices. In this section, I focus on a subset of these rules that I consider relevant to the inclusion of improv activities within formal language learning environments.

### "Yes, and"

The essential rule and overarching approach of improv is "yes, and" (Halpern, Close & Johnson 1994). This rule has two parts to it. First, agree to the verbal, aural, and/or physical activity immediately done by another improviser ("yes"). Second, provide a verbal, aural, and/or physical response that reacts to, supports, and extends it ("and"). For example, with two improvisers on stage at the start of an improvised scene, one may say, "It is so hot today." Improvisers refer to the introduction of new information as an *offer*; in this example, this improviser is offering a scene in which the weather is hot. This person's improv partner should agree to the offer (explicitly or tacitly) and react to, support, and extend it. For example, the second improviser may reply, "Yes, (as s/he gasps for air) "I think I am going to melt off all these pounds I gained this winter!" The "yes, and" rule is essential so that the dialogue continues; when adhered to, it is also an improviser's promise to support another's offer and a declaration that offers are always welcomed and will be implemented in the game, scene, or play in some manner and to some extent (Lobman & Lundquist, 2007; Sawyer, 2001b, 2003a, 2003b).

Essential Warnings: Do Not Negate or Play Write

Many rules of improv are admonitions about what not to do, such as
"do not negate" and "do not play write" (Sawyer, 1997, 2001b, 2003a, b).
Taken in turn, negation is the converse of the "yes, and" rule; negating is denying a person's offer rather than accepting it, that is, implying
"no" rather than "yes." To continue with my previous example, the second improviser denies the initial offer "It is so hot today," by responding,
for example, "It's not hot today!" Improvisers may also deny a location
(e.g., by saying "We're not in Mexico," immediately after another improviser offers the line of dialogue "I am so happy we're together on vacation
here in Mexico.") or a relationship or status (e.g., by saying, "I'm not the
President," immediately after another improviser addresses him/her as
such). Negating stalls the development of the improvisation and challenges the building of trust and support among the improvisers (Halpern,
Close, & Johnson 1994).

*Playwriting* occurs when one improviser directs the emergent activity
at the expense of the other improviser(s); playwriting should be avoided,
because no one has advance knowledge of or sole responsibility for the
game, scene, or play. For example, the person who offers the opening line,
"It is so hot today," offers only that line of dialogue; all anyone is aware of
so far is that the weather is hot. No improviser should make assumptions
about, for instance, the scene's location or the relationship between the
people in the scene (e.g., "This scene takes place at the beach and we are
movie stars"). The importance of "yes, and" emerges and is best applied
when improvisers are listening and reacting naturally and spontaneously
to offers rather than fitting, defining, or confounding offers to their own
expectations or self-imposed direction (Sawyer, 2001b).

To continue with the previous example, the "yes, and" offered by the
second improviser (i.e., "I think I am going to melt off all these pounds I
gained this winter!") continues to develop the activity, and together the two
improvisers make meaning. The second improviser reacts to and supports
the first offer, and in their improvised activity, their conversation becomes
a co-construction rather than one person's exclusive creation (Gergen, 1994
as cited in Holzman, 1997). Continued turns will develop the interaction
(e.g., its location, narrative, and the relationship between the speakers)
while concomitantly developing the trust and support between the improvisers that is needed to do so. In summary, key questions about these rules
(and their possible answers in parentheses) are:

- Who creates an improvised dialogue? (All involved.)
- How is an improvised dialogue created? (By listening and reacting naturally, following the rule of "yes, and" and by not negating.)
- When is an improvised dialogue created? (Not completely beforehand as that would not be improvised. As well, improvisers should not exclusively assume the narrative of the dialogue or predict what another improviser will say or do; those approaches fall under *playwriting*.)
- Why are these rules important? (They establish the groundwork for collaborative, emergent activity that advances the agenda, i.e., the game, scene, or play that the improvisers create.)

These rules, however, do not only apply to the games, scenes, or plays created by improvisers on a theater stage. They are also possible rules of engagement for creating language and meaning together in a multitude of contexts including, but not limited to, formal learning environments. Others (e.g., Holzman, 2009; Lobman & Lundquist, 2007) discuss the extension of improv rules and activities to formal learning environments, and their work provides support for my inclusion of improv activities in formal language learning environments for adults. Yet including improv activities in formal language learning environments is not without its conflicts. In the next section, I consider three interrelated conflicts that may emerge.

## CONFLICT 1: *A PRIORI* SCRIPTS VERSUS EMERGENT SCRIPTS

One significant conflict relates to scripts. By "scripts," I mean shared cultural understandings such as previously established linguistic forms, cultural knowledge, and motifs/clichés that are considered essential to human social encounters. Scripts have been framed as important cultural learning tools that support socialization into and awareness of community practices (Göncü, 1993; Nelson, 1981; Sawyer, 2001a; Schank & Abelson, 1977).

There are many instructional materials available to language teachers that support the use of role play in the language learning environment (Maley & Duff, 1982; Stern, 1993; Wessels, 1987), but such materials tend to be in the form of *a priori* scripts (i.e., printed dialogues) given to the learners, rather than allowing emergent contextualized scripts to be created by them (Kurtz, this volume). These already created dialogues tend to be read or performed out of textbooks or other published resources (e.g., Bercovitz & Porter, 1995; Jenkins & Sabbagh, 2001), or learners are given the opportunity to prepare them in writing in advance (either alone or with other students) and then perform them from memory or by reading them.

For example, learners may be asked to read, prepare in advance, and/or memorize dialogues such as how to interact with a sales clerk at a store. Let us consider a brief example of a script (i.e., a dialogue that one might find in an English language learning textbook). Below is a possible sales transaction between a sales clerk and a customer in a clothing department store in the western world.

| | |
|---|---|
| Sales clerk | Did you find everything OK? |
| Customer | Yes (handing sales clerk clothing for purchase) |
| Sales clerk | (Scanning and then placing clothes in a bag). Your total is $54.56. Will that be cash, check, or credit? |
| Customer | Cash (handing sales clerk cash) |
| Sales clerk | Thank you. Here is your change, your receipt, and your items. Have a great day! |
| Customer | Goodbye. |

Dialogues such as this one often appear to adult English language learners as fixed – that *this* is how one shops in English and that *these* are the grammatical structures used to pay for merchandise. Language learners often assume that meaning is in the printed dialogue, in the vocabulary words, or derived from grammar rules (Holzman, 1997), and language learners often assume that these dialogues apply similarly across contexts: The dialogue is a ready-made that must be honored, and as such they may be unable, unwilling, or unlikely to question, vary, or improvise on it (Goodman & Goodman, 1990; Lantolf & Thorne, 2006).

Additionally, the attribution of roles in the dialogue appears to be established in advance (i.e., that there is a sales clerk and a customer, and who will read/perform each role). Language learners are likely to be more attentive to or prefer to practice the language of the role they assume they might play in a similar dialogue if/when performed outside of the learning environment, e.g., as the customer interacting with a sales clerk. Their attention to the offers of their partner in the dialogue (e.g., a member of the new language community such as a sales clerk) is merely instrumental, and the learner's focus is to comprehend these utterances and respond accordingly and correctly. As a result of these perceptions, the assignations of meaning and roles of the dialogue, even if created by the learner as an instructional activity, are perceived as something apart from the learners who practice or create it – it is of "the real world" of the new language community and must be respected as such.

Reliance on *a priori* scripts is also supported in teacher professional resources and materials where the already existing "real world" is considered the most authentic (re)source for such dialogues. For instance, Oller (1993, p. 63) advises language teachers to "[use] materials that are grounded in real experience in the first place. We don't have to invent the world. God already did that." Oller's advice is to provide authentic materials (e.g., *realia* or "real-life" dialogues) that will enhance language instruction and contextualize new language use within its communities, but he also seems to suggest that the real world exists apart from the people who live and communicate in it – regardless of religious affiliation, the assumption is that God (i.e., some "other," possibly extrapolated to mean "the native speakers of the language community") creates these scripts, their meanings and functions, and the roles we are assigned in them.

Improvisers might take issue with much of this discussion of *a priori* scripts as it applies to their work. Although improvisers certainly rely on existing tools such as language and other existing cultural phenomena (e.g., the script of a sales transaction), their scripts in improv performances do not previously exist, are not prepared in advance, and are not necessarily wholly representative of the existing scripts of one or more language communities. The rules of "yes, and" and "do not play write" support emergent, collaborative interactions and the directions or goals of these interactions are not assumed to precisely mirror those already familiar to either the improvisers or their audience. Instead, improvisers spontaneously make their own scripts and invent their worlds in their dialogues rather than merely imitate existing dialogues and conceptions of the world. In an improvised performance of a sales transaction, the improvisers together use "yes, and" statements to create a dialogue between a sales clerk and customer. The possibilities for the relationship or location of this dialogue are infinite. Either improviser, regardless of his/her experiences, could be the sales clerk or the customer. The improvisers could realize, during the co-construction of the dialogue, that the sales clerk and customer are long-lost twins. The store where this transaction takes place could be on the Moon. Whereas any of these possibilities might be odd in the everyday, *a priori* script of "sales transaction," any of these (and others) may be an acceptable emergent script in improv. Whereas *a priori* scripts are fixed, emergent ones are essentially infinite because they occur in a possible, improvised play space where the rules of engagement and assignations and functions of roles *emerge* in context rather than in an actual, *a priori* space where rules of engagement and assignations and functions of roles exist in advance and are adhered to and applied to a context.

In summary, essential questions that may emerge from this conflict are: When are scripts created and to what extent are they expected to conform to cultural knowledge and community expectations?

## CONFLICT 2: EXPERTS/NOVICES AND CONFIDENCE/EMBARRASSMENT

In the context of formal language learning, it is likely that these scripts are presumed to emanate from those to whom "more" is attributed: for instance, more experience, more knowledge, more power, and more voice (hooks, 1994). There is a perceived "expert knower" of the scripts, and frequently this expert is perceived as the teacher. Therefore, learners perceive the scripts to be modeled by the teacher, as a representative of the larger language community that learners seek to enter, and perceive the offers and performances of the scripts of the teacher as standard and perceive their own (and their classmates') as a derivative of this standard. This perception tends to engender feelings of doubt and embarrassment on the part of the language learner about communicating (primarily verbally) in the new language, as opposed to certainty and confidence to do so.

This perception is rooted in theory within the field of language teaching and learning. Stevick (1980) points out that one of the major factors hindering language learning (particularly for adults) is fear or apprehension about performing in it. This fear is the cornerstone of The Affective Filter Hypothesis of new language acquisition (Krashen, 1981, 1982). Krashen's Affective Filter Hypothesis posits that learners of a new language vary with respect to the strength of their affective "filters" – a clever image of a barrier to language learning due to learners' lack of confident use of the new language. Krashen argues that the filter is lowered when learners are part of an anxiety-free environment where they confidently express themselves in whatever way possible.

Krashen's Affective Filter Hypothesis is particularly germane to language learners who are older. Adults have heightened rational thinking, self-reflection, self-awareness, and an overarching concern for epistemology (of the information kind, i.e., knowing vocabulary words or grammar rules) that negatively impact new language expression and exploration (Colarusso, 1993; Newman & Holzman, 1997; Vandenberg, 1983). This focus on correctness, accumulating vocabulary words, and perfecting use of grammatical rules is exacerbated by two factors: prior schooling experiences that place attention on accuracy; and experiences with "expert" members of the new language community who often appear judgmental of adult language learners' foreign accents, different pronunciations, and/or imperfect oral and written expression when considered against standard language use (Cook, 2000).

Trained improvisers, however, perform confidently and operate under the assumption that they and their improv partners are experts. Issues of accuracy and error are not relevant. The concern for or labeling of error assumes that there is an expectation or standard; in improv, the only expectations are collaboration and agreement to create and make meaning emergently (S. Messing, personal communication, April 13, 2008). What is created in improv and how collaboratively it is done so is much more interesting and important than how correct or rooted in the familiar it is.

In summary, an essential question that emerges from this conflict is: how can we support confident use of tools such as language without an overabundant concern for how (well) such use maps to the standard or expected use of the tool?

### CONFLICT 3: THE INDIVIDUAL VERSUS THE GROUP

While language has been conceptualized as a social phenomenon (e.g., Vygotsky, 1978, 1986), our focus on language learning is primarily attentive to individual concerns and development. This establishes the third conflict: the nearly exclusive focus on (the development of) the individual language learner rather than on the creation and development of the group (or ensemble) of language learners. This focus may be rooted in American teachers' – and also frequently their learners' – sense of independence rather than interdependence, and competition rather than collaboration (cf., Rogoff, 2003).

Teachers meet individual needs and consider how well individual students are doing by observing, assessing, and comparing individual progress. The notion of "group" mainly suits teachers' desires to adopt a "one-size-fits-all" approach to lesson planning, instruction, and assessment. In language learning classrooms, the diversity of the learners is recognized, but mainly is considered in such areas as "home country" or "native language(s)." The diversity of new language experiences and needs is frequently not recognized, because tracking and grouping practices in formal learning environments in the United States are usually based on a single characteristic, for instance, age (e.g., "first graders ages 6–8"), knowledge base (e.g., "Level 6 – advanced"), or content area (e.g., "English for business purposes"). It is uncommon, but certainly possible, for teachers to go beyond such single characteristics to create an ensemble of learners who present their individual experiences, styles of learning, needs, and goals as *offers* to be shared, built on, and developed together.

The focus on the individual is problematic not only for teachers, but also for language learners. Frequently, language learners enter a language learning environment to improve their own skills and attain their own goals; they frequently do not consider their classmates as resources and opportunities for mutual goal attainment and development (McCargar, 1993; Nunan, 1992; Parrish, 2004). Classmates might be perceived as having "inaccurate" new language skills and at best distract the individual learner from progressing and at worst supply incorrect offers that impede the individual learner's standard use of the language.

In contrast to language learning environments, a focus on the individual is generally not part of the practices of improv. Within the improv community, individual improvisers do, of course, make up an improv game, scene, play, or ensemble; however, improvisers consider the communication and development of their games, scenes, and plays to be connected to and impacted by each other and, if applicable, their audience members. Improvising assumes that creating a unique script in a unique context is collaborative, and that the presentation and meaning of offers is a mutually informing and mutually informed activity. While this approach is evidenced in the rules of improv, professionals in the improv community, in their writing, also emphasize the group. For instance, the improv director, Paul Sills (quoted in Sweet, 1978, pp.18–19) stated, "That's what this work [improv] is about: the finding of the self in a free space created through mutuality ... [i]t's not what I know and what you know; it's something that happens between us that's a discovery ... you can't make this discovery alone. There is always the other."

In summary, essential questions raised out of the third conflict are: How can we consider the group as the unit of development in formal learning environments when learning is nearly always considered on an individual basis? How can we recognize individual discovery and growth as stemming from collaboration with other learners rather than impeded by or in competition with them?

## THE ADULT LANGUAGE LEARNERS AND OUR LEARNING ENVIRONMENT

For this chapter, I center my instructional anecdotes and examples of improv activities around my most recent teaching experience as a lead English teacher of a teaching team of two to four assistant teachers. We served within a family literacy-focused language program for adult immigrants. The program was open enrollment and had a flexible attendance policy. What we offered, with respect to content, was informed by broad topics that are often a part of family literacy programs (e.g., language practice around the family, school, and health); however, particular topics or needs within these broader topics were informed by the day-to-day needs of and feedback from the group.

The learners were both very similar and very different from each other. The adult learners almost exclusively came from Spanish-speaking countries in North, Central, and South America. Learners were predominately women but differed considerably with respect to English language use in and out of the formal learning environment, frequency of class attendance, psychological openness to learning and using English, and age. The adult learners almost always had limited formal learning experiences in their home countries and frequently expressed little or no comfort or proficiency in using spoken and written English in the United States. They differed widely in their English language experiences; for instance, some learners might have recently arrived to the United States and had no experience with English, whereas others had lived in the United States for years, spoke conversationally, but could not write in English. Many of the adults in this program entered with an individualistic perspective on their role as learner and expected instruction and feedback from the teachers to advance their individual language goals. They also tended to perceive the teachers as "experts of the scripts"; they looked often only to the teachers to offer them correct American English wording or pronunciation.

Based on the program model and our learners, my assistant teachers and I recognized the importance of creating a space where all members of the learning environment felt connected to one another as an ensemble and felt comfortable expressing themselves. Feeling connected and comfortable might inspire offers that we could use to create and develop together both *a priori* and emergent scripts.

In the following, I describe six improv activities that we performed in our class: Names and Motions/Names and Sounds; Zip Zap Zop; The Ball; Word Cards; Soup; and Gibberish.

## Names and Motions/Names and Sounds

We often started our class with an improv activity called Names and Motions. For this activity, we all stood and formed a circle. Each person took a turn saying his/her name and then spontaneously doing a physical motion (e.g., saying "Tony" and then jumping twice in place). The others in the circle together listened, watched, and subsequently, as a group, repeated the person's name and copied the person's motion as precisely as possible.

Repeating each person's name and motion together and honoring the manner in which it was offered was a collaborative "yes" to each person's offer. Furthermore, each person's turn to say his/her name and make a motion served as an "and" to previous offers.

We then extended this exercise by passing our own name and motion to one particular person who then copied them and passed his/her own name and motion to another person; this pattern of passing, copying, and passing continued randomly. I also at times invited the group members to state their name in a different voice (e.g., higher or lower in pitch) or perform their motion at a different speed (e.g., faster or slower). Names and Motions in all its variations was also replaced at times with an equivalent called Names and Sounds, where a sound made (e.g., "beep beep") replaced the physical motion of Names and Motions.

Names and Motions and Names and Sounds were welcomed by the adult learners insofar as they enjoyed when an assistant teacher or I modeled the activity; they usually laughed as if we were performing something comical for them. When many adult learners took their first turn at the game, they were often ostensibly uneasy. The adult learners were, at times or for the first few times, hesitant saying their names or making their motions or sounds because they were likely concerned about being watched and judged by their teachers and the other adult learners. Nevertheless, we aimed to create a judgment-free environment, and so the assistant teachers and I welcomed and encouraged all offers (e.g., quiet, simple, or unfamiliar) and politely discouraged the adult learners from friendly teasing or negative evaluation of anyone's motion or sound.

Many of the adult learners felt more comfortable expressing themselves over time and they teased or judged others' offers in this activity less often. Laughter was still present, but I interpreted the laughter over time differently. As we were creating and sustaining a supportive ensemble, we laughed more so *with* each other rather than *at* each other. We laughed based on the trust and the support we were creating with and for each other. From engaging in Names and Motions and Names and Sounds, we created, over time, a group whose individual/collective "filter" was lowered and whose mutual support for offers was strong, respected, and built on throughout our time learning together.

After a large group activity such as Names and Motions or Names and Sounds, we often offered learning topics (e.g., learning family vocabulary words, practicing personal information, or reviewing cardinal numbers), announced the teacher who would facilitate a particular topic, and the place in the classroom where a topic's activities would take place. After those announcements, the adult learners assembled to one or more learning spaces. These learning spaces were invitations for the learners to explore English that was potentially interesting and important. The learning spaces activity was unfamiliar to both learners and teachers; my assistant teachers and I were more accustomed to the script of "directing learners," and the adult learners were expecting to be directed to what to learn (Kurtz, this volume; Sullivan, 2001). All of us were also more accustomed to one lesson plan created for the entire class. Nevertheless, my assistant teachers and I recognized the diversity of peoples' interests and needs and offered different learning spaces to honor such diversity. Whatever learning spaces the adult learners opted for on a particular day created multilevel groupings with respect to English language use. These multilevel groupings were not addressed with a wholly teacher-centered, didactic approach (Bell, 2004). Instead, my co-teachers and I frequently offered improv activities that were modified to suit language practice among all members of these smaller groups.

### Zip, Zap, Zop and The Ball

One of the improv activities we practiced in these smaller groups was Zip, Zap, Zop. The name of the activity represents the order of three sounds that are repeatedly passed from one person to another. One person begins by saying "Zip" while extending one hand to simulate passing to the person to whom s/he wants to pass the sound. The person who receives "Zip" then is responsible for passing "Zap" to another person in the circle who in turn says "Zop" and passes it to a different person. Play continues similarly and starts again with "Zip."

At times, we played Zip, Zap, Zop. However, this activity was also transformed to meet the needs and interests of the adult learners. For group members in a learning space practicing family vocabulary words, we renamed the activity to suit whatever vocabulary words we wished to practice verbally. For example, the sounds Zip, Zap, Zop could now be replaced with the words "mother," "father," "daughter" and passed as previously described. Other members of this group who were comfortable with family vocabulary words were invited to transform and play another Zip, Zap, Zop where now the words that replaced Zip, Zap, and Zop formed a sentence that included family vocabulary words (e.g., "I" "have" "a" "daughter."). Still others who were comfortable with these family words or sentence formations may have played another Zip, Zap, Zop with less common family words, longer sentences, or questions/answers about personal information (e.g., "How" "old" "is" "your" "grandson?" "He" "is" "7."). We maintained the repetitive passing from the first to the last word of the sentence or question just like we had passed the original sounds Zip, Zap, and Zop.

Another improv activity we played was The Ball. To play The Ball, a group stands and forms a circle. An imaginary ball is used but its features (e.g., size and color) are created and agreed on by the group. Much like the movement of Names and Motions and Zip, Zap, Zop, The Ball activity is an opportunity to spontaneously pass words or sounds to each other. To warm up to the activity, we often used our names or sounds made from our mouth. The person who has the ball mimes tossing it to another person and says his/her own name or makes a sound. The receiver catches not only the ball but also repeats the name or sound of the giver. This receiver then tosses the ball and gives his/her own name or his/her own sound to another person. Play continues in a similar fashion.

After warming up, we transformed this activity to meet the needs and interests of the adult learners. For group members practicing family vocabulary words, the movement of the game was similar but instead of passing names or sounds, we passed family vocabulary words (e.g., mother, father, daughter ...). Another group of learners playing The Ball in another learning space may have passed cardinal numbers (e.g., 1, 2, 3 ...). The categories were not fixed; at some point anyone in the circle could spontaneously change the category from family vocabulary words to, for example, letters of the alphabet or symptoms and illnesses. This possibility for category change increased the awareness of the ensemble's *a priori* scripts (what category of words we started with and what words were in any particular category) and emergent scripts (the spontaneous change from one category to another).

For Zip, Zap, Zop or The Ball, my assistants and I welcomed the adult learners' offers of vocabulary words, sentences, or questions. Should an adult learner offer an example for practice for Zip, Zap, Zop, (e.g., "I have a daughter"), we celebrated this suggestion by together saying "Yes." The adult learners laughed when an assistant teacher or I replied, "Thank you, Teacher," when an adult learner offered a sentence or question for us to practice. The meaning I make of this laughter is similar to the laughter in activities such as Names and Motions; we all were creating new ways of performing and, in this instance, the adult learners began to perceive themselves and others (perhaps in new ways or for the first time) as both the teachers and learners (i.e., creators) of this environment.

If anyone was concerned with the accuracy or meaning of the offer, or requested translation, my assistants and I often initially remained quiet; we encouraged our adult learners to support and assist with each others' questions and ideas (Goodman & Goodman, 1990). We frequently reminded our adult learners that "We all have English," and that together the group could create language with which to play Zip, Zap, Zop or The Ball. This collective response to each others' offers and needs made the responsibility of learning a collective and relational task.

## Word Cards and Soup

Word Cards and Soup are variations of the improv game One Word Story (Halpern Close & Johnson 1994; Johnstone, 1999). In One Word Story, an ensemble of improvisers extemporaneously and collaboratively tells a novel story where each ensemble member, in turn, offers only one word at a time. For example, Improviser 1 may begin with "Once," Improviser 2 continues with "upon," Improviser 3 follows with "a," and Improviser 4 says, "time," with play continuing as such until the group has created a story to its satisfaction.

We transformed One Word Story to the sentence level (Word Cards) and word level (Soup). For Word Cards, our adult learners were offered a large number of index cards, some of which had only one word on it and many more that were blank. Having both types of cards reflected the *a priori* and emergent scripts we might create as an ensemble. All index cards were strewn all over the table or floor. As we might be practicing how to communicate information about our families, a particular card may have had a word on it such as "daughter." To introduce the activity, the teacher introduced a sentence/question orally (e.g., "I have a daughter"). Together, learners had to quickly find (and/or create) the word cards to form that sentence or question. The total number of words in the sentence or question was represented in individual index cards where each card had only one word written on it and was held by only one person. Each person stood with his/her card shoulder to shoulder with others to create visually the sentence/question offered. In this example, four adults might stand next to each other, such that the sentence "I have a daughter" appeared from left to right and where each adult holds only one index card. Play continued similarly, but after a few examples, an assistant teacher or I invited the adult learners to offer orally the sentences or questions for the group to create. We welcomed their suggestions and thanked learners for their offers.

We also attempted to create emergent scripts via this activity. For example, I might have taken a card with the word "I" on it, stood up, and gestured an invitation to any other person to stand up, one at a time and with a different index card, to help me complete a sentence. It was my not sole creation: I did not suggest what the next word should be, ask anyone to guess what word I wanted to be next, or select someone to help me.

I was not playwriting; I was open to what we could come up with and, after extending my offer of the first word card, I was inviting the group to create it with me. At first the adult learners were unsure what card to bring up or if it was the "correct" card. Eventually one adult learner might take or create a card with the word "have" and stand next to me such that we formed two words: "I" and "have." Another person might follow with another card with the word "a" written on it. One person at a time continued offering a word to complete the sentence until we were satisfied; in this case, we may have created the sentence, "I have a daughter." Once this sentence was completed to our satisfaction, I stepped away with my "I" card and returned with a new card such as "He." Play continued in a similar fashion for a few rounds until I (or another teacher) no longer was the first person up but an adult learner made the first offer of a new sentence or question.

In Word Cards, a form of negation appeared at times among the adult learners when working with *a priori* or emergent scripts. Using my previous example, once the word "I" was offered, at times one or more adult learners scolded another adult learner for adding another word that was perceived to be inaccurate, tantamount to negation. This notion of inaccuracy primarily took a grammatical perspective (such as when "I" was followed by "has"). With respect to grammatical concerns, I modeled a communicative competence (Savignon, 1983) and meaning-making approach to our emergent, ensemble-created scripts of sentences and questions. The focus was on making meaning of our collaboratively made sentences and questions rather than on strict acceptance of and adherence to external grammatical rules such as subject/verb agreement or singular/plural nouns.

Playwriting also emerged in Word Cards. Often, one adult learner forced another to select or write a particular word card, or perceived another adult learner's word card choice as unexpected. For example, the emerging sentence "I" "have" could have been met with self-driven enthusiasm on the part of one adult learner who yelled out and directed the rest of the members of the activity to form a sentence such as "I have a daughter." With supportive side coaching (Lobman & Lundquist, 2007), we encouraged everyone to create the sentence or question one card at a time and not to have any of us drive what we were creating in advance and at the expense of our creating it emergently. Over time, fewer instances of playwriting occurred, and those more familiar with the activities' variations shared insights with and otherwise supported newer members of the group as we performed the activity.

For Soup, each letter of the twenty-six-letter English alphabet was printed separately on an index card to create a set of twenty-six alphabet cards. Multiple sets of alphabet cards were available. These sets of index cards were then strewn all over the floor (or a table) and mixed much like an "alphabet soup." Similar to the movement of Word Cards, a teacher began with *a priori* scripts by orally stating a vocabulary word (e.g., "daughter") whereby we searched for the letters to create that word, but with each person only finding, holding, and standing up with one card. After a few examples offered by a teacher, we encouraged our adult learners in the group to offer a word in advance that the group could form together. As noted in previous examples, we welcomed their suggestions and thanked learners for their offers.

We also attempted to make words emergently. For example, the first person may select, hold, and stand with a card that had the letter "d" on it. While some adult learners tried to guess the word, I reminded them that there were many possibilities. Playwriting was once again a concern because at times, one person pushed others to form the word she had decided should be the final word. In one instance, after the letter "d" was chosen, one of the learners insisted on creating the word "daughter." This insistence blocked creating other possibilities to create together the words "dog" or "desk," for example. A friendly side-coaching reminder was to honor and build emergently from each other's offers. Over time, fewer instances of playwriting occurred and those more familiar with the activities' variations shared insights with and otherwise supported newer members of the group to perform the activity. Issues of correct spelling were similarly addressed as were issues of grammatical accuracy in the Word Card activity.

Playing Zip, Zap, Zop, The Ball, Word Cards, and Soup kept in mind the three conflicts introduced at the outset of the chapter. First, by attending to meaning over accuracy, we stressed the confidence to explore and express rather than the fear of making errors. Our approach to these activities illustrated that we welcomed the suggestions of group members, not only of the teacher, to play with *a priori* scripts and create emergent scripts that served our collective language learning and development needs. In the particular case of Word Cards or Soup, by having each word coming only from one person to complete a word, sentence, or question, we were also continuously reminded that these scripts, however *a priori* or emergent they might be, were the responsibility and creation of the group.

## Gibberish

Gibberish is the name of an improv activity where improvisers utter nonsensical sounds where the meaning is conveyed only by pitch, tone, or gesture (Spolin, 1963). For example, one person could utter, "gereee vop stog" and another could respond, "fee foo biko boo." Gibberish was especially helpful when we were overly focused on grammatical accuracy, judged the accent of one or more learners in the class, or deliberated too much on what word to say or write during an improv activity. Gibberish is fraught with possibility to make meaning together, build the ensemble spirit, and avoid playwriting. At times, we modified the above games – Zip, Zap, Zop or The Ball, the words we created in Soup, and our written transformations in Word Cards – and played them using Gibberish. By using Gibberish, the language and the meaning we made were concurrently and emergently created by the group.

In our learning environment, Gibberish sometimes created consternation because it was uncomfortable not to work with an already existing language. However, the Gibberish activity, when situated as a part of our overall language practices with(in) these improv activities, aided in creating a sense of playfulness and confidence with our language expression. We developed performances of our shared, rather than individual, development and learning and realized that we can successfully and emergently create language (and meaning) in context and in concert with others by relying on language made up together. In doing so, we assumed no predetermined standard or definition of accuracy and instead, with more practice, assumed our collective expert status of creators of language and makers of meaning.

## THE NEXT OFFER: IMPROV ACROSS LEARNING ENVIRONMENTS

Although my discussion of improv rules and activities was considered within a particular context of adult language learning and teaching, these experiences have relevance to other learning environments as well. In this final section of the chapter, I return to the three conflicts I introduced earlier (*a priori* scripts versus emergent scripts, experts/novices and confidence/embarrassment, and the individual versus the group) and reflect on how improv activities informed, re-formed, and transformed our formal language learning environment. I then briefly consider these activities' relevance for learning environments across age groups and content levels. As this is a descriptive chapter, I will relate mainly my own reflections to drive discussion, but as much as possible, I will base my reflections on the interactions and discussions with my assistant teachers and our adult learners.

With respect to the conflict of *a priori* scripts versus emergent scripts, engaging in improv activities reminded us that *a priori* scripts were helpful in providing a framework for language rules such as syntax. For Zip, Zap, Zop, it was pleasant for us to work with an existing sentence and repetitively pass its words around the circle. However, an exclusive focus on the already established scripts limits the agency of those learning about the nature and presence of scripts; by merely embracing and utilizing *a priori* scripts, and not creating emergent ones, my learners would have disengaged themselves from language learning, perceived their activity primarily as acquisitional, and would have not embraced its meaning-making and developmental nature. By emergently making our own words or sentences in Soup or Word Cards, respectively, or communicating in Gibberish in any of these activities, we all shared together the concomitant joy and frustration of sometimes not knowing what we were creating and in effect designing the script while performing it. In doing so, we learned that language and its rules are neither exclusively predictable nor rigidly binding. We also learned that we make meaning with our language, not merely receive meaning from external sources.

The challenge for learning environments across the lifespan and across content areas is to avoid exclusive allegiance to activities whose rules and content are established apart from and without the contributions of those making sense of them. Such a challenge calls out for more playful interactions in formal learning environments where people are creating possibilities together; where people are not exclusively held accountable to standard use that is imparted on or expected from them.

With respect to the conflict of experts/novices and confidence/embarrassment, inviting learners to construct emergent scripts in Word Cards, Soup, or Gibberish, for instance, the attribution of scripts to those who have more experience or power in the new language dissipated and now included the learners as agentive producers of scripts. The label of "novice" and the embarrassing feeling associated with such a label did not necessarily transform into a false sense of expertise or sudden "native speaker"-like communication, but our perceptions of ourselves as contributors with valuable and accepted contributions lessened the stigma and presence of "novices" and increased self-efficacy to teach what we knew, share our experiences, and recognize our roles as the teachers and learners of each other. The challenge across learning environments then is to embrace the power and potential of all members of the group, and – while not providing a false sense of security in the content area – to recognize that expertise is a relative, developmental, and gradual process that emerges out of activity that is afforded by a welcoming and collaborative community of learners.

Creating a community of learners brings about discussion of the conflict of the individual versus the group. Our improv activities abandoned the predominant notion of individual development and favorably helped form and sustain an ensemble whose individual members took on new perceptions of themselves as mutually developing, mutually informing learners and teachers. By engaging, for example, in activities such as Names and Motions, Zip, Zap, Zop, or Soup, we recognized the value of an individual (and not only the teacher) making an offer, the empowerment felt when that offer was recognized and integrated into the group's practices, and the co-related trust that came out of such recognition and integration. In doing so, we learned that offers, while perhaps initiated by an individual, were really the responsibility of all members of the emerging and developing ensemble to honor and extend. In our doing so, notions of the competitive and of the teacher-driven gave way to notions of the collaborative and of our roles as the teachers and learners of each other.

The challenge for learning environments across the lifespan and across content areas is to re-form individualistic and top-down perspectives into ones that honor sharing and building off of personal experiences, strengths, and needs. For example, within the field of language learning for adults, the Learners' Lives as Curriculum (LLC) approach to curriculum and instruction draws upon learners' experiences and narratives to drive classroom activity. LLC is a model in which learner experience and learner-generated texts are integral to teaching and learning (Weinstein, 1999). It strives for contextualized learning and sincerely considers the backgrounds and experiences of the learning community. It is important to remember that learner experiences may come from previously shared experiences with others (i.e., they are never purely "individual") and are now transformed into new, shared experiences with the members of the co-created learning environment. With an environment that constitutes and is supportive of everyone's contributions, learning (regardless of content area and across cognitive, social-emotional, and language domains) now begins to be construed as an active, shared, liberating, and inclusive process.

Based on my conversations with my assistant teachers and our adult learners, these improv activities created a supportive learning environment where all of us could enjoy teaching and learning together, learn about and from each other, and confidently express ourselves. Improv gave us a chance to consolidate conceptual schemes, syntactic structures, and our newer sense(s) of self with (the support and development of) other people. Improv also contributed to our enhanced and more nuanced senses of self as members of multiple language/cultural communities who are agents of our learning and teaching together and who can spontaneously create playful spaces of inclusion for us and for/with others.

Based on these insights and observations, I suggest that formal learning and teaching environments incorporate improv. Improv activity at once addresses, confronts, and celebrates conflicts in conceptual, linguistic, and psychosocial ways, and re-frames them as possibilities for learning, teaching, and development. As such, I invite us to consider improv as essential to language education and to other content areas across the human lifespan. Additional empirical and practical work across other learning environments is needed to support and develop this claim. However, any additional work or alternative instructional approach begs us to confront our commonly held assumptions, experiences, and predilections as to what teaching/learning environments are (as frequently models based on transmission of cognitive-focused information by an individual teacher and its acquisition by an individual learner) and unite them with what else learning and teaching environments may become (Moll, 1990). This chapter has been an illustration of how we might create and recreate ourselves and our learning environments and how, in doing so, we recognize the presence and value of conflicts and alternative models to effect newer and richer possibilities for learning and development.

## ACKNOWLEDGMENTS

I would like to acknowledge Nate Baumgart, Francisco José Benavides, Artin Göncü, Carrie Lobman, and R. Keith Sawyer for their feedback on previous versions of this manuscript.

## REFERENCES

Bell, J. (2004). *Teaching multilevel classes in ESL*. Toronto, Ontario: Pippin Publishing Corporation and Dominie Press.

Bercovitz, L. S. & Porter, C. (1995). *Parents as educational partners: A school-related curriculum for language minority parents*. Des Plaines, IL: Adult Learning Resource Center.

Colarusso, C. A. (1993). Play in adulthood. *Psychoanalytic Study of the Child, 48*, 225–246.

Cook, G. (2000). *Language play, language learning*. Oxford: Oxford University Press.

Göncü, A. (1993). Development of intersubjectivity in social pretend play of preschoolers. *Human Development, 36*, 185–198.

Goodman, Y. M. & Goodman, K. S. (1990). Vygotsky in a whole-language perspective. In Luis C. Moll (Ed.), *Vygotsky and education: Instructional implications and applications of sociohistorical psychology* (pp. 223–250). New York: Cambridge University Press.

Halpern, C., Close, D., & Johnson, K. (1994). *Truth in comedy: The manual of improvisation.* Colorado Springs, CO: Meriwether Publishing.

Holzman, L. (1997). *Schools for growth: Radical alternatives to current educational models.* Mahwah, NJ: Lawrence Erlbaum Associates.

(2009). *Vygotsky at work and play.* New York: Routledge.

hooks, b. (1994). *Teaching to transgress: Education as the practice of freedom.* New York: Routledge.

Jenkins, R. & Sabbagh, S. L. (2001). *Stand out: Standards-based English.* New York: Heinle ELT.

Johnstone, K. (1981). *Impro: Improvisation and the theater.* New York: Routledge.

(1999). *Impro for storytellers.* New York: Routledge.

Kozlowski, R. (2002). *The art of Chicago improv: Short cuts to long-form improvisation.* Portsmouth, NH: Heinemann.

Krashen, S. D. (1981). *Second language acquisition and second language learning.* Oxford: Pergamon.

(1982). *Principles and practice in second language acquisition.* Oxford: Pergamon.

Lantolf, J. P. & Thorne, S. L. (2006). *Sociocultural theory and the genesis of second language development.* New York: Oxford University Press.

Libera, A. (2004). *The Second City almanac of improvisation.* Evanston, IL: Northwestern University Press.

Lobman, C. & Lundquist, M. (2007). *Unscripted learning: Using improv activities across the K-8 curriculum.* New York: Teachers College Press.

Lutz, C. A. (1987). Goals, events, and understanding in Ifaluk emotion theory. In D. Holland & N. Quinn (Eds.), *Cultural models in language and thought* (pp. 290–312). New York: Cambridge University Press.

Maley, A. & Duff, A. (1982). *Drama techniques in language learning.* New York: Cambridge University Press.

McCargar, D. F. (1993). Teacher and student role expectations: Cross-cultural differences and implications. *Modern Language Journal, 77,* 192–207.

Moll, L. C. (1990). Introduction. In Luis C. Moll (Ed.), *Vygotsky and education: Instructional implications and applications of sociohistorical psychology* (pp. 1–27). New York: Cambridge University Press.

Napier, M. (2004). *Improvise: Scene from the inside out.* Portsmouth, NH: Heinemann.

Nelson, K. (1981). Social cognition in a script framework. In J. H. Flavell and L. Ross (Eds.), *Social cognitive development: Frontiers and possible futures* (pp. 97–118). New York: Cambridge University Press.

Newman, F. & Holzman, L. (1997). *The end of knowing: A new developmental way of learning.* New York: Routledge.

Nunan, D. (Ed.) (1992). *Collaborative language learning and teaching.* New York: Cambridge University Press.

Oller, J. W., Jr. (1993). *Methods that work: Ideas for literacy and language teachers* (2nd ed.). Boston: Heinle and Heinle Publishers.

Parrish, B. (2004). *Teaching adult ESL.* New York: McGraw-Hill.

Perone, A. (1994). Autonomy, awareness, and action: Learning and teaching languages through drama. Unpublished undergraduate honors thesis.

Rogoff, B. (2003). *The cultural nature of human development.* New York: Oxford University Press.

Savignon, S. J. (1983). *Communicative competence: Theory and classroom practice.* Reading, MA: Addison-Wesley.

Sawyer, R. K. (1997). Improvisational theater: An ethnotheory of conversational practice. In R. K. Sawyer (Ed.), *Creativity in performance* (pp. 171–193). Greenwich, CT: Ablex.

(2001a). *Creating conversations: Improvisation in everyday discourse.* Cresskill, NJ: Hampton Press.

(2001b). The improvisational performance of everyday life. *Journal of Mundane Behavior* 2(2), 149–162.

(2003a). *Improvised dialogues: Emergence and creativity in conversation.* Westport, CT: Ablex Publishing.

(2003b). *Group creativity: Music, theater, collaboration.* Mahwah, NJ: Erlbaum.

Schank, R. C. & Abelson, R. P. (1977). Scripts, plans, and knowledge. In P. N. Johnson-Laird & P.C. Wason (Eds.), *Thinking: Readings in cognitive science* (pp. 421–432). New York: Cambridge University Press.

Seham, A. E. (2001). *Whose improv is it anyway? Beyond second city.* Jackson: University Press of Mississippi.

Spolin, V. (1963). *Improvisation for the theater.* Evanston, IL: Northwestern University Press.

Stern, S. L. (1993). Why drama works: A psycholinguistic perspective. In J. W. Oller, Jr. (Ed.), *Methods that work: Ideas for literacy and language teachers* (pp. 70–83) (2nd ed.). Boston: Heinle and Heinle Publishers, Inc.

Stevick, E. W. (1980). *Teaching languages: A way and ways.* Rowley, MA: Newbury House Press.

Sullivan, P. N. (2001). Playfulness as mediation in communicative language teaching in a Vietnamese classroom. In J. P. Lantolf (Ed.), *Sociocultural theory and second language learning* (pp. 115–131). New York: Oxford University Press.

Sweet, J. (1978). *Something wonderful right away: An oral history of The Second City and The Compass Players.* New York: Limelight Editions.

Vandenberg, B. (1983). The psychological view of play; or why does Alice have such long legs? Paper presented at the Association for the Anthropological Study of Play, February, Baton Rouge, LA.

Vygotsky, L. S. (1978). *Mind in society.* Cambridge, MA: Harvard University Press.

(1986). *Thought and language* (A. Kozulin, Ed.). Cambridge, MA: MIT Press.

Weinstein, G. (1999). *Learners' lives as curriculum: Six journeys to immigrant literacy.* McHenry, IL: Delta Systems, Inc.

Wessels, C. (1987). *Drama.* Oxford: Oxford University Press.

# 9

# Productive Improvisation and Collective Creativity: Lessons from the Dance Studio

## JANICE E. FOURNIER

In an era emphasizing accountability, standards, and coverage of the curriculum on a timetable, integrating improvisational activities in the classroom can be risky. By its nature, improvisation invites surprises and can quickly head in unexpected directions. Not knowing where such activities will lead, how can teachers ensure that they will be productive – that they will in fact help accomplish an instructional goal? This is the crux of the teaching paradox. Teachers who are expected to follow a standardized curriculum may be reluctant to experiment with activities that deviate from the book, with good reason. The skills needed to teach according to a prescribed format differ markedly from the skills needed to teach by attending to what arises in learners themselves. The latter requires joining with students in a fundamentally creative process – teachers who invite input from students must then find ways to take up their ideas and use them to chart a new, flexible path toward instructional goals. In this chapter, I draw on research from dance – specifically, how choreographers and dancers compose a dance together – to illustrate how a collective creative process can indeed be effective pedagogy. The improvisational strategies choreographers employ to ensure mutual understanding of material and independent mastery in performance can also be used in the classroom to help effectively address the learning paradox.

The arts, and dance in particular, are underrepresented in educational research. Yet choreography possesses multiple features that make it unique as a cognitive activity and therefore rich with potential for expanding our understandings of how people learn. In recent years, researchers from anthropology and sociology have expanded notions of cognition by looking at people "knowing" in a range of non-traditional contexts: engaged in

In R. K. Sawyer (Ed.) (2011). *Structure and improvisation in creative teaching* (pp. 184–206). Cambridge: Cambridge University Press.

daily tasks (Lave, 1988), at work (Goodwin, 1993; Hutchins, 1995; Scribner, 1997), and practicing a craft (Keller & Keller, 1996). Central to these studies is the notion of cognition as a *system of activity*: These studies examine how social and environmental structures, use of particular tools, and the spatial and temporal arrangement of people, objects, and events contribute to the achievement of tasks and development of understanding, both individually and collectively. In this chapter, I draw on a similar ethnographic study designed to examine cognition in the dance studio (Fournier, 2003). This study was conducted to address gaps in what we know about how people learn by engaging in a creative activity, and in particular how they engage in a creative process together. Like other studies on learning in non-traditional settings, this study of learning in the dance studio suggests new ways to view learning in the classroom. I link dance and learning by considering choreography as a case of collective, creative work and learning through improvisation.

Contemporary dance performances are typically composed by a choreographer working collaboratively with an ensemble of dancers. The reality is quite different from popular images of choreography, which suggest that a choreographer comes to the dance studio with all the movements worked out ahead of time; the choreographer teaches the movements, and the dancers learn and perform them. These images promote a limited understanding of what choreography is and of dancers' role in the process. In my research on composing in dance, I rarely observed choreographers using "direct instruction" to teach specific steps or movements (Fournier, 2003). Instead, I found that choreographers and dancers create and learn dances through a collaborative, reciprocal relationship and sustained creative investigation.[1]

Choreography is more than movement; composing a dance also involves making choices about the arrangements of dancers in space and time, the qualities (e.g. staccato; languid) with which the movement will be performed, and how sound, lighting, and costumes will be used (if at all) as components of the dance. While inspiration for a dance may come from many sources, *performers* are necessary to enact a dance, and as a result they become integral elements of the creative process. Many elements of

---

[1] Participants in this study were professional choreographers and dancers in contemporary dance. They requested that their real names be used. All were engaged in making performances that might be described as post-modern art works. The studio practices of choreographers creating ballets or dance intended as entertainment as part of a musical or MTV video may differ from what I have described here. However, choreographers of all types of dance actively use their dancers to greater and lesser degrees in their creative process, and they all depend on dancers to embody their work so that they might view and revise it; in this way, all choreography is a distributed activity and collective accomplishment.

a dance can and do change because of who dancers are or what they do in rehearsal; the particular physical attributes of dancers or their individual personalities, for example, may influence the movement a choreographer generates, or a choreographer may prefer dancers' spontaneous solutions (or even their "mistakes") over the movement he or she originally intended. Many choreographers intentionally make active use of their dancers to generate movement phrases or scores (organizational structures) for the dance (Fournier, 2003; John-Steiner, 1985).

Of course, the work of a choreographer and a classroom teacher are not the same. But they do share several characteristics. Choreographers, like teachers, are designers of learning experiences. They are also responsible for facilitating remarkable feats of learning within a set time frame. Unlike teachers, however, choreographers can rarely specify ahead of time the exact outcome they are seeking in their work, and they have no curriculum guide or tested sequence of lessons that will ensure a path toward achievement. Instead, choreographers must call on their own knowledge and skills, as well as the knowledge and skills of their dancers, to build a dance. Through carefully structured rehearsal activities designed to maximize contributions from all, choreographers move the group from an initial concept for a dance to final performance. Improvisation is a fundamental tool in this process, supported by the collaborative relationship between choreographer and dancers.

In this chapter, I use the example of choreography to show how improvisation functions in a sustained creative process and how it can support both individual and collective learning. I also show how choreographers use improvisation for different purposes over a series of rehearsals, and how classroom teachers can and do use improvisational activities for similar purposes. As a group of individuals engaged in collective creative work, choreographers and dancers form a unique type of learning community. To close, I discuss how the particular roles and interactions of choreographer and dancers function to support productive, creative group work, and what this model might imply for teachers and students in the classroom.

## IMPROVISATION, THE CREATIVE PROCESS, AND LEARNING

Improvisation is commonly defined as the act of creating without preparation and without following a set text or score. In dance improvisation, dancers simultaneously originate and perform movement without preplanning or censorship (Chaplin, 1976). Contemporary dancers often engage in improvisation in the studio, as part of a regular warm-up routine or as part of rehearsals during the making of a dance. In this sense, improvisation may be thought of as a practice, a regular part of dancers' work, or as an episode of this practice contained in a specific time period. In dance, whole performances may be improvised, or choreographers may use improvisational exercises in rehearsal to generate movement material that might eventually be incorporated into a choreographed piece.

Improvisation might also be thought of more broadly as a fundamental component of a sustained creative process, and even as a core component of everyday intelligent behavior. Here, improvisation might be conceived as a particular disposition or intellectual capacity that is essential to productive creative work. In this sense, it is an ability to remain open to new possibilities as they arise, an inclination to actively seek and to exploit the potential for unexpected events to inform the direction of the work. Eisner (2002) borrowed the term "flexible purposing" from Dewey (1938) to describe this improvisational aspect of intelligence. Especially in the arts, where the aims of a project might not be well defined at the start, flexible purposing describes an ability to change direction, to revise and refine one's aims when better options emerge in the course of one's work. Eisner points out that "flexible purposing" conflicts with what we believe to be rational. As Eisner explains, the standard view of rationality holds that "ends are supposed to be well defined, firmly held, and used to formulate means, which are theoretically related to achievement of those ends" (2002, p. 78). Teacher education programs are largely structured according to this standard view of rationality: They emphasize training in how to create rational lesson plans, but they rarely provide equivalent training in pedagogical improvisation – how to handle the inevitable unexpected events in the classroom that, though not included in the plan, have great potential to engage students in meaningful learning (see DeZutter, this volume).

In the arts, the practice of improvisation, when mindfully engaged as the practice of flexible purposing, always results in learning. With no predetermined steps to follow, choreographers and other artists learn by simply engaging with their material and remaining sensitive and responsive to the work as it evolves. They may begin with a goal for a piece, act on this goal, reflect on the results and see new possibilities, and begin the cycle again (Flower & Hayes, 1994; Swados, 1988). Through a generative and iterative process, they continually refine and clarify the meaning and intention in their work (Keller & Keller, 1996; Schön, 1990). The encounter with the work is unstructured and unpredictable, like a conversation; this is why many artists describe their work as "speaking" to them. For example, painter Ben Shahn has described the creative process as "a conversation back and forth" between the painter and the painting, in which the artist is acutely sensitive and responsive to the colors, light, textures and relationships that arise before him on the canvas (1957, p. 57).

Choreography, too, is a creative act; composing in dance requires both experiencing and viewing movement choices in order to discern what belongs in a piece and how it should be arranged in time and space (Arnheim, 1974). Choreographers who work alone, creating their own solo performances, often use studio mirrors and a camcorder to understand how movement might be perceived from a viewer's perspective. They are both painter and painting, conversing with themselves about the evolving work, often recording ideas and thoughts in notebook entries (Fournier, 2003; John-Steiner, 1985).

More often, however, choreography is a creative act undertaken by multiple individuals. In this case, it is a *distributed activity*, a task accomplished not by an individual alone, but by multiple individuals acting together (Perkins, 1993; Salomon, 1993). In dance, the same conversational process that occurs between painter and canvas happens literally between choreographer and dancers over multiple rehearsals. Choreographers depend on dancers to be both record and recorders of movement, playing back what created so that it can be edited and refined. Dancers contribute to the evolving composition in a variety of ways – generating movement ideas, raising questions or providing observations, and performing their own interpretations of movement. Choreographers and dancers both remain open and responsive to possibilities for the work that arise in the course of rehearsal, though the choreographer remains the arbiter of creative decisions. Together, the *group* develops and "learns" the dance – what the dance is about and how to perform it.

Even though a "distributed creative process" is not how we typically characterize learning that takes place in classrooms (exceptions are Rogoff, 1990; Scardamalia & Bereiter, 2006), the specific activities and goals of the dance studio are common to many learning environments. In the process of mastering their material, choreographers and dancers, like teachers and students, engage together in solving problems, conducting investigations, sharing interpretations, establishing mutual understandings, and reflecting on what they have learned. For choreographers, improvisation is a fundamental tool for achieving these goals, and a tool that teachers can use for the same purposes.

## PRODUCTIVE IMPROVISATION OVER AN ARC OF LEARNING

In this section, I use choreography to highlight both the promise and process of improvisation as a pedagogical tool. In the pages that follow, I describe three broad purposes for improvisation used at different times over a course of making a dance: the first is improvisation to generate ideas; the second, improvisation to explore material; and the third, improvisation as it is used in live performance. These uses roughly correspond to the beginning, middle, and end points on an arc of learning, one that may be as applicable in the classroom as it is in the dance studio. For each purpose, I provide examples of how improvisation functions in the dance studio to move both choreographers and dancers forward in their work of composing. I follow with examples from the classroom to show where and how improvisation may serve the same purposes in schools, and support teachers and students in learning from one another. By describing in detail what choreographers and teachers do in these settings to accomplish their goals, I hope to expand our conceptions of what constitutes "productive improvisation" and to envision new possibilities for creative collaboration in the classroom.

## Improvisation to Generate Ideas

In the first stage of rehearsal, choreographers use improvisation to generate movement material – movement that will be used to create the dance. In dance, generating material involves translating ideas into movement images, or exploring movement to see what the movement itself connotes or evokes. Solo performers who choreograph their own work can translate their thoughts directly into movement with a fair amount of ease. In contrast, choreographers who work with an ensemble face a complex challenge: how to involve multiple individuals in the process of realizing ideas and images that reside in the choreographer's mind alone. As I mentioned earlier, it is rare for choreographers of contemporary dance to come into the studio ready to instruct their dancers in a prepared sequence of moves. More common is for choreographers to actively include their dancers in the task of generating ideas and movement. This strategy quickly and efficiently generates a wide range of material from which the choreographer can draw. It also allows the choreographer to see what ideas individuals bring to the project and what the group can do collectively.

To set the stage for collaborative learning, choreographers may begin at the very start of a rehearsal process with improvisational activities designed to orient all performers toward a common understanding of the composing task. In effect, these activities serve to say, "Here is the project we are embarking on, and what ideas might you add?" A choreographer may begin by giving dancers an improvisational exercise structured around a particular problem or theme ("How many different ways can you spiral?").

Or she may engage dancers in explorations of a specific image, idea, or sensory experience. The exercises convey what the choreographer has in mind for the dance – a subject or line of investigation – and invite dancers to think within the same framework as the choreographer, not merely to learn movements as instructed.

These exercises are bodily versions of verbal brainstorming activities – they share the goal of generating as many ideas as possible in a short period of time, with the understanding that only a few of these ideas will eventually be used. In the early stages of developing a piece titled "Attracted to Accidents," for example, choreographer KT engaged her dancers in brainstorming on the theme of accidents and their allure. Ideas generated during the verbal discussion (accidents happen fast, some activities are risky, there's always the onlooker) led to improvised movement that was eventually set and used in a choreographed piece:[2] The group produced fast, chaotic, and dangerous leaps and falls intended to evoke anxiety in viewers. Days later, the group decided they needed to break up the fast-paced rhythm of the dance. As the choreographer explained, "We started talking about that moment of animated suspension you have before an accident, and how that's always shown in movies in slow motion, or how cartoon characters always have a stop in mid-air before they fall. People always describe those moments as a stillness, or time slowing, you know. And we loved the idea of developing movement like that."

KT immediately challenged the group to create the illusion of someone falling slowly from a great height. Her response to what the group generated is an example of Dewey's "flexible purposing." For KT, the work of choreography requires her to be opportunistic, to seize on good ideas wherever they appear and turn them into collective activities that move the group toward its goal: to generate movement for the foundation of the dance.

In other cases, the orienting activity might be more abstract. Crispin is a choreographer who often uses improvisation as a *prompt* to generate movement from her dancers. She uses physical movement to communicate the qualities she wants to see in her dancers, without specifying exactly how those qualities should be embodied. Crispin explains her technique – "thrown movement" – as follows:

> I basically do a very short improvisation in the middle or in front of a group, and [the dancers] try to do it, they get whatever they can

---

[2] Dancers commonly speak of "set movement" or of choreographers "setting a dance on dancers." When a dance is set, it exists (to various degrees) as a specified sequence of movements that can be repeatedly reconstructed in performance. At the beginning stages of making a dance, movement sequences might be tentatively set and open to revision many times over. Choreographic decisions become more firm over a series of rehearsals.

remember, grab something and rehearse it. I don't want the dancers to look the same, but I want them to come from the same intention.... I am looking for people to, for instance, drop levels in a certain way or puncture the air in a certain way. I'll get something very different from one person to another. But when you put them together, there's some kind of shared information.

Crispin gives her dancers directions to compose a movement phrase, but the information she wants them to include in that phrase is articulated in movement rather than in words. Again, the activity effectively orients all performers around a common goal – in Crispin's words, the movements "come from the same intention" – but it also elicits individual understandings or experiences of the material. The activity forces dancers to improvise by making a substitution out of materials that are available at hand – in this case, to develop a movement phrase based on what the dancers remember from their own personal experience.

### Improvisation to Generate Ideas in the Classroom

Improvisational activities similar to these can be valuable in classrooms, although the material generated is typically expressed verbally rather than bodily. A wide variety of improvisational activities can be used at the start of a unit to orient both teacher and students and create a framework for the learning that will follow. For example, open-ended questions and improvised discussions (Sawyer, 2004) allow a teacher not only to introduce students to a new topic, but also to understand where they are coming from in their current thinking. Watson and Konicek (1990) tell the story of Deb O'Brien, a fourth-grade teacher in Massachusetts, who began a science unit one winter by asking students, "What is heat?" As she discovered, seemingly simple questions have the power to elicit students' naïve theories and misconceptions; students answered O'Brien by saying that heat came from the sun, their bodies, and also sweaters, hats, and rugs. O'Brien followed the activity not with facts to refute their beliefs, but by asking the students to test them. As with KT and her dancers, O'Brien took the ideas offered and used them to propose a communal activity. As students designed experiments to see just how hot sweaters and hats could get, they also made progress on O'Brien's goal of teaching students how to conduct scientific investigations.

The right prompt can also elicit students' creative ideas or relevant experiences. Tom Holt, a college history professor, sought to find the right question to effectively engage a particular group of students in understanding the African-American experience during Reconstruction (Holt, 1990). Rather than beginning with the question of what freedom meant to former slaves, Holt first asked his students, "What does freedom mean to you?" encouraging them to define the word in terms of their personal experience. The range of answers he received revealed that students thought primarily in terms of negative freedom – freedom *from* constraints – rather than positive freedom, the freedom to possess resources for self-realization (18). Their answers helped Holt determine the right jumping-off point for a discussion on Reconstruction.

It may be more difficult to imagine a parallel for Crispin's "thrown movement" activity in the classroom. Such improvisational activities, however, are not so different from any classroom activity that requires students to observe closely in order to figure out how to participate. In language classes, for instance, in which students are immersed in a foreign tongue, students pick up and piece together what they are able (Kurtz, this volume; Perone, this volume). Pronunciation, vocabulary, and sentence structure may not be identical to that of the instructor, but what each student produces in interaction with the instructor conveys his or her current understanding. The emphasis in these activities is not on "getting it exact," but on getting the *gist* – on making meaning and seeing what one can do with the materials at hand. By listening closely, a teacher can use the information he gathers from these activities to plan the most logical next step for his students' development.

### Improvisation to Explore Material and Deepen Understanding

Shortly after generating material for a dance, choreographers work with dancers to explore the material further. As one dancer explained, this is the point in the rehearsal process to "mess with the material" to better understand its meaning, its potential qualities and connotations, and its place within the dance. Choreographers and dancers may experiment with different ways to execute the movement, changing the speed or quality with which it is performed, or the arrangement of dancers in space. This is the essence of creative inquiry – purposely exploring options to see which offer the most promise.

In contrast to the improvisational exercises I described earlier, which are designed to quickly generate ideas, the goal of these successive explorations is a deeper and more refined understanding of material. In dance, this means attending closely to how the movement feels to perform as well as what it looks like from the perspective of the viewer. Both choreographer and dancers attend to these perceptions, often using the studio mirrors to help them reflect visually on their work. In this stage, choreographers join their dancers in practicing movement phrases, attending to what they perceive as they perform. In discussions following each practice run, the performers share their individual observations with one another, negotiating their understanding of the movement and clarifying aesthetic choices. These cycles of activity and consolidation define the nature of rehearsal: "Practice" is not mindless repetition, but goal-directed inquiry.

To demonstrate how a group learns through successive iterations of movement, I offer the example of a choreographer and two of her dancers working on a section of a dance they referred to simply as the "women's trio." Movement for this section was generated during an earlier rehearsal at which the dancers experimented with ways of getting to and from the floor without using their arms. In this particular rehearsal, KT's goal was to decide how the arms should be used to complement the movement in the legs. The plan was merely to practice the sequence to see what ideas emerged.

The choreographer and her dancers repeated the trio – a sequence that took just over a minute to perform – five times over the course of twenty minutes. The focus of each iteration was determined by dancers' discoveries in the run immediately preceding it. The first time through, for instance, KT proposed that the group practice the sequence essentially "without arms," crossing them over their chests. Finding this option much too difficult, the group then focused on how they used their arms naturally, and then in a third repetition, how they might intentionally "sculpt" the arm movement. The dancers talked about their experience at the end of each performance.

During these discussions, individual dancers returned to specific parts of the sequence they had noticed while performing. Insights about the qualities of the movement ("the hands are kind of loose, it makes them seem immobilized") and questions about how to execute the movement ("I'm using my left hand there on the floor, are you?") were publicly shared, evaluated, and negotiated by the group. Dancers often tried the movement again, effectively "trying out" another's perspective on the problem. Through this reflective process, the dancers deepened their collective understanding about the potential connotations of the movement as well as how to best perform it. Consolidating these discoveries at the end of each round of practice, KT chose a focus for the next round that would encourage the dancers to make even finer observations about the movement or their performance.

By closely analyzing their performance, the dancers accomplished their goal of clarifying when and how they would use their arms. Through their talk and action, the dancers established mutual understandings of the details in the movement and at the same time marked these details in their bodies. Notably, the choreographer did not articulate what had been decided for the arms before asking her dancers to perform the sequence again; she assumed these decisions had been learned through the process of close attention, individual execution, and discussion. The example also illustrates how discussions and negotiations of meaning based on individual observations can result in powerful understandings of material.

The path of these discussions is not predictable. While KT had in mind a goal for the day – to choreograph arm movement for the women's trio – she did not decide ahead of time the focus of each run or to practice the sequence five times. Rather, KT structured an activity for the group that would allow them to explore successive proposals, beginning with "What happens if we perform the sequence with our arms crossed?" By consolidating the discoveries from each trial, KT defined where the group should focus attention in the next iteration. With each practice run, KT narrowed the focus of exploration, and the group observed finer details in the material. One dancer's observation about the "immobilized" hands, for example, gave rise to further explorations in the fourth and fifth practice runs of other moments in the dance where the hands had similar qualities. The observations shared by her dancers allowed KT to make necessary choreographic decisions, and they also solidified in the group a strong, collective grasp of the details, nuances, and distinctions in the movement – why it is *this* here and, importantly, *not that*. Such sophisticated understandings are rarely constructed by individuals working alone, or by learners following a predetermined sequence of problems that do not emerge from their own observations. The understanding KT and her dancers construct through practice and reflection on that practice is a group accomplishment.

## Improvisation to Explore Material in the Classroom

In her research on community-based arts education programs, Shirley Brice-Heath (1999) noted a difference between the kind of discourse adults and children practiced in these settings and the kind of discourse commonly heard in school classrooms. In the arts programs, Heath found, discourse was marked by the language of possibility: "What if we try ...?" What about ...?" "Here's something that might work ..." "I have another idea ..." In these settings, as in KT's dance studio, a rehearsal was more than scheduled time to run through a performance; it also offered participants sustained practice in imagining different scenarios, explaining their ideas, arguing for a particular approach or solution, and critically evaluating choices. Such talk, while abundant in arts organizations, need not be confined there. The same improvised explorations and discourse of possibility can be practiced in the classroom as well, with important implications for collective learning in any subject (Craft, 2002; Cremin, Burnard, & Craft, 2006).

Magdalena Lampert (1990), for example, has documented her success in teaching students in a fifth-grade mathematics class to participate in mathematical discourse. Students do not merely find the answers to math problems, but construct mathematical knowledge by practicing ways of knowing central to the discipline. In contrast to a knowledge-telling classroom in which the teacher indicates which answers are right or wrong, Lampert's students are taught to think and speak in terms of possibilities – "conjectures" in the language of mathematics – that can be argued and revised, proven and refuted. Students arrive at the solution to a mathematical problem through an emergent, discursive process.

Like choreographers in the dance studio, Lampert engages her students in a series of focused explorations following an initial activity designed to orient them to the new topic. As Lampert explains,

> At the beginning of a unit ... the problem we started with was chosen for its potential to expose a wide range of students' thinking about a bit of mathematics, to make explicit and public what they could do and understand. Later problems were chosen based on an assessment of the results of the first and subsequent discussions of a topic, moving the agenda along into new but related mathematical territory. (1990, p. 39)

Lampert's selection and sequencing of problems are deliberate, but the pace at which the lessons unfold is determined by students' investigative process. In a unit on exponents, for example, Lampert's students spent three days investigating patterns in a table of squares from $1^2$ to $100^2$. Lampert had students consolidate their observations in a number of statements about these patterns before moving on. The new problem – "What is the last digit in $5^4$? $6^4$? $7^4$?" – required students to consider how to operate with exponents. Although easy enough to answer using a calculator, Lampert challenged the students to see if they could prove their assertions true without doing the multiplication. In effect, she set the parameters for a focused exploration of the properties of exponents. Students had to improvise, thinking creatively about how to extend and apply their discoveries about squared numbers to a new realm.

As in the dance studio, the public discussion of the students' individual ideas and assertions contributes to deeper, shared understanding of mathematics as well as mathematical practice. When students make an assertion, they are not merely stating an opinion; rather, they explain their own reasoning process and often analyze the thinking of others. All members of the learning community consider the legitimacy of an individual's conjecture by comparing it to what they have (so far) observed to be true ("… it's odd number times odd number and that's always an odd number."). They draw attention to apparent contradictions ("It can't be 9, 1, 9, 1, because $7^3$ ends in a 3") or evidence that would suggest a pattern. Like KT's dancers, they share these observations with the group, and the group evaluates them, revising their thinking as they go. The collective thinking produced by the class is a group concern; Lampert teaches her students to consider the legitimacy of each conjecture and why it might make sense to the person who offered it, even if it is proven wrong. The discussion, allowed to emerge from students' perceptions, ensures that students begin to make distinctions in their understanding (i.e., $5^4 = 5^2 \times 5^2$, not $5^2 \times 2$) and develop a more robust theory of how exponents operate.

Engaging students in true inquiry – where the answer is not known or cannot be ratified by an outside authority – cultivates students' own creative and improvisational thinking skills. By carefully structuring focused explorations of material, teachers can create openings where learners' contributions (at whatever stage of development) are encouraged, acknowledged, and actively supported. Replicating the practices of professional discourse communities in the classroom is one way to help students learn the skills of inquiry as well as how to learn from each other. Whereas dancers in the studio have had years of practice reflecting on and sharing perceptions in movement, students in classrooms may not know how to construct knowledge by considering one another's ideas and strategies. Teachers may need to instruct students in disciplinary-specific language and structures for participating in meaningful discussions about ideas. Many recent studies (e.g., Cornelius & Herrenkohl, 2004; Engle & Conant, 2002) have focused on how specific "structures of participation" can best support learning in different communities of practice. Lampert spends time teaching her students the intellectual skills and discourse of the mathematics community so that she can have productive, improvisational discussions. As Lampert has observed, productive improvisation and collective learning will not happen if students are silent, if they criticize one another's ideas, or if they lack the words to explain what thinking processes or observations led them to their conclusion.

However, productive improvisation requires more than just the mastery of effective participant structures. Effective teaching through improvisation also requires harvesting – selecting from among the many student contributions those that are most ripe for further exploration, or consolidating contributions in a manner that clearly connects one step to the next. Harvesting requires holding two perspectives in mind – the individual learners' perspective and a global perspective on the learning community that Hutchins (1995) calls the "design" perspective. In the dance studio, choreographers function as designers as they keep in mind a global view of the dance as a whole, projecting forward and casting back over rehearsals in order to shape and develop movement material into a unified composition. The changes they implement in the learning environment are intentional and supervisory: making choices about the options that will be explored, planning a path of action, all in light of the emerging dance and the aesthetic intention. Remaining aware of the learner's perspective happens naturally as choreographers literally step in and out of the evolving composition by temporarily taking on the roles of different dancers in order to make appropriate compositional choices.

Like choreographers, teachers must have ways of participating alongside their learners, remaining aware of their progress, while also holding in mind the final performance they expect students to achieve. Harvesting requires evaluating what students produce in light of this final goal – not evaluating contributions for whether they are right or wrong, but the degree to which they hold potential to move the group along toward that goal. To harvest well, teachers must be sensitive to the flow of events and to the points of student engagement, and be able to adjust activities or design new ones appropriate for the situation. In pedagogical improvisation, the sequence and nature of curriculum activities grow out of the links teachers forge between their more expert knowledge in a field and students' current thinking (Eisner, 2002). These links might take place in the middle of a discussion, such as when Lampert steps in to restate a student's argument or ask for clarification of a claim, knowing that the point holds a powerful distinction that is important for all to understand. Or they might happen days later, when a teacher recalls or re-presents to students the products of an earlier discussion and uses these to introduce a focused lesson. In Holt's history classroom, students' initial ideas about freedom were repurposed in a later activity in which students were asked to analyze historical documents for evidence of the slaves' views of freedom. The improvised discussion that followed drew attention to the multiple meanings and nuances in the word.

Performing Live: "Everyday Improvisation" and Dance

Toward the end of the rehearsal process in dance, an important transition
occurs – from generating, exploring, and developing movement material to
reviewing, consolidating, and refining what has been created. This results in
an important shift in the relationship between choreographer, dancers, and
the dance. Over the course of the rehearsal period, dancers gradually take
on more and more of the dance. As the choreographer organizes the dance
into its final form, dancers shift from practicing and developing movement
to *inhabiting* the movement and imbuing it with meaning; they must make
the movement their own. This later stage is a creative and generative stage
for dancers; as one dancer commented, "Getting to a place where you can
run it from start to finish is where the piece really starts to grow."

For dancers, this final step involves creating intention for the movement
they have been assigned and developing a meaningful relationship between
their specific role in the dance and the dance as a whole. In essence, the process is an extension of the collective interpretation that took place in earlier
phases of rehearsal. As choreographer and dancers analyzed and shared their
observations about movement during practice, they constructed common
understandings about the properties of the movement, its potential connotations, and how to perform it so that it best aligned with the intentions of the
dance. A choreographer's decisions about the arrangement of movement –
who will dance what parts, at what point in time, in what spatial arrangement – also inform dancers' understandings of the dance and its particular
dynamics from start to finish. These earlier distributed activities now feed
individual activities; dancers borrow from these earlier group conversations
(both verbal and non-verbal) to construct a "personal subtext" for the movement they perform and an interpretation of their part in the whole.

This final stage in creating a dance is, I argue, the final challenge of any
learning arc – to make sense of disparate parts or experiences, to develop a
cohesive theory or narrative, something that holds together with an inner
consistency. This is the work of dancers at the end: to take what they have
learned and "own" it, to draw the relationship between parts and whole from
their individual perspectives and in this way consolidate their understandings of the dance. This work is internal, but it is not isolated. In the dance
studio, dancers and choreographer engage in "reciprocal creative development" (Blom & Chaplin, 1982); the activities they engage in together feed
their individual creative choices and vice versa, in what Salomon (1993) has
depicted as an ongoing spiral of learning through interaction and individual work. Individually, the dancers embody and extend the choreographer's

intention for the dance. The strength of the internal worlds they create plays a critical role in bringing the performance to life.

The point at which the dance goes live before an audience is the true test of what the group has learned –about the movement in the dance and how to execute it; about the subject of the dance and its significance; about how to work with one another moment to moment. All rehearsal activities prior to opening night are structured with the goal of the final performance in mind. In this last stage of polishing the dance, a large part of the choreographer's role is letting dancers go, allowing them to self-correct, providing only small edits and corrections. The group may move from the dance studio to the stage for dress rehearsals with music, costumes, and lights, but until an audience is present to respond to the work, all is still preparation.

Many dancers report that it is in interaction with an audience that they finally fully experience the dance. Sheri, a choreographer and performer, explained that being live on stage has a special intensity:

> Having an audience changes everything. You're actually expressing something to somebody, to many somebodies hopefully. And so the full dynamic of it as an art form, as a mode of expression, is in full play. And so it can happen that I'll be on stage, and I'll think, "Now I understand why I take so long here, I can even take longer. I can feel the audience's attention on it." … You can always visualize how you want things but to actually see it, and to have the feedback of the audience coming back at you, the dance just lifts off.

There is excitement in going live, and an opportunity to understand the true meaning of a work as it unfolds before a responsive audience. An ensemble may have practiced a dance a thousand times, but performing live means small improvisations – holding something a moment longer because of the audience's attention, pausing for laughs, spontaneously improvising when a fellow performer missed a cue, continuing forward as if no mistake had occurred. It may seem contradictory to speak about "improvising" on stage, when the work is presented as a fixed composition, but here is where evidence of mastery is greatest, and the rewards are deeply felt. Being able to improvise when the conditions call for it demonstrates in the performer a refined sensibility, knowing just what to do when.

## "Live" Performance in the Classroom

Authentic performance assessments (Wiggins, 1989; Wolf et al., 1991) and culminating projects associated with project-based learning (Krajcik & Blumenfeld, 2006) can replicate the experience dancers have when they "go live" with a performance. Such tasks require students to apply their new skills and knowledge in a real-world context, with all the attending unknowns and uncertainties. In Holt's history classroom, midterms and finals are occasions for students to *perform as historians*. As he explains,

> I was much less interested in recognition knowledge than in what they could *do* as historians. On their take-home midterm examination, for example, I gave my students three labor contracts from different periods and asked them to act as curators preparing an annotation of the documents to accompany a display in a museum. Students were evaluated on how much information they could extract from the documents and on their skill in elaborating the historical context concisely and accurately. On their in-class final, I gave students much shorter excerpts from a variety of documents and asked them to draw on their knowledge of the relevant history *and* a close reading of the text to reconstruct the larger narrative of which the document was a part. (p. 29)

Like dancers, students in these activities are asked to perform all that they have learned over the course of previous rehearsals, applying knowledge and skill to give shape and meaning to raw material. Such activities fulfill Bruner's (1960) call for providing students with authentic opportunities for learning that are "different in degree but like in kind" to those of professionals in the same discipline.

Projects that involve an authentic audience offer even more opportunities for the improvisational exercise of expert knowledge, because students can then respond to the emergent qualities of an unscripted interaction. For example, Holt might ask his students to take their new knowledge one step further and create a living history museum – answering questions for visitors from the perspective of historical figures and mindset of the period. Unable to anticipate just what questions visitors might ask, students would be required to make the history their own in order to improvise a truthful and accurate response. Projects such as these ask students to bring themselves to the work; when students "own" their work, they take on the identity of one who knows, and they imbue their performance with meaning and significance (Heath, 1999).

Many activities can function both as a unit project and an authentic assessment of students' learning. Proposals for a new playground that must be brought before the school board, maps and materials intended to orient new students to the school, a campaign to increase recycling efforts at the county level – all are projects that require a significant synthesis of knowledge. They also require presentation to individuals who may be unfamiliar with the rehearsal scenarios of the classroom. Responses from this audience provide students with authentic feedback on their work as well as the opportunity to improvise in the moment. If one persuasive strategy for the new playground is not working, the students will need to try another. If the new students at school have limited English language skills, the authors of the orientation materials will quickly learn if their maps and symbols are sufficient.

Dancers know at the very start of a rehearsal process that a final performance will happen; they look forward to sharing what they have learned with people beyond the studio or practice environment. Working together, choreographer and dancers create both a performance and *performers*, people who are able to bring to life all that was learned in rehearsal. A culminating project at the end of a curriculum unit, like a dance performance, can provide continued, important opportunities for learning through improvisation – opportunities that are perhaps too rare in schools. Often told they are being prepared for the "real world," students nevertheless are rarely placed in situations that require exercising their new skills in unplanned scenarios, or where they might receive immediate feedback on their competency through direct consequences.

Authentic performances that require interaction with people in the real world change the dynamics in the classroom, because students are performing for an audience other than the teacher. Like the choreographer, the teacher becomes another participant in the learning community, eager to see how the authentic audience will respond.

If they have practiced enough, students are able to improvise – to act in response to emergent conditions in ways that are appropriate, and to make do with what is available. They understand the overall structure, operations, or intention; they understand the whole. After all, a curriculum ultimately has little meaning except as preparation for a real-world activity, and the real world – especially in the current age – is unpredictable, requiring improvisational skill.

## A SHARED CREATIVE ENDEAVOR

The collective learning that occurs when choreographers and dancers develop a piece is very different from the learning that occurs in a traditional instructionist classroom – here, individual achievement is often considered more important than what a group can accomplish together, teaching is not conceived of as a "design problem," and there is little emphasis on fostering a climate of creative reciprocity. Teachers are generally viewed as having the responsibility to impart to students specific knowledge and skills, and students generally learn from a curriculum they took no part in shaping. In contrast, dancers and choreographer join in a shared, creative enterprise; they are *in something together*, even if that "something" may not be fully formulated at the start. This is the work of shared knowledge building, and it requires trust in the effectiveness of the evolutionary process itself and in learners' ability to contribute to advancements in thinking (Zhang et al., 2009). Choreographers, on some level, trust the particular expertise of their dancers, trust that their dancers will bring new insights to the collective endeavor, and trust that the work will evolve in relation to what is produced. In choreography rehearsals, the system as a whole learns. This is not the model of learning most teachers are encouraged to use as the basis for their lessons.

But what if it were? What would be the effect of conceiving of education as a collaborative endeavor in which students and teachers are "intellectual partners" in a creative process? Beyond the kind of improvisational activities I have described in this chapter, some exceptional teachers and schools have adopted the values of collaboration and creative reciprocity as a foundation of their work; they provide examples of what teaching as an artful practice might entail.

This vision of collective learning is not so different from the vision advanced by contemporary learning sciences; in communities committed to the "knowledge building" advocated by Scardamalia and Bereiter (2006), for example, researchers and teachers together investigate pedagogical practices that can best support students in taking collective responsibility for advancing the knowledge of the group (also see Zhang et al., 2009). A teacher's role here is to re-create with their students the evolutionary cognitive and social processes that characterize professional learning communities and drive innovation within a field (Bereiter, 2002).

Other examples underscore a sustained commitment to teaching based on emergent events and social interactions. Kindergarten teacher Vivian Paley (e.g., 1986) simply and carefully observes her students and takes notes, using their words and actions as material to shape their next educational experience. And teachers in the pre-primary schools of Reggio Emilia, Italy (Edwards, Gandini, & Forman, 1998), are taught from the start of their professional training how to construct a curriculum that emerges from students' interests and ideas. Working together, Reggio teachers collaboratively document and reflect on student learning and on how it might be developed through group activities. In the Reggio schools, children, colleagues, and the community are viewed by teachers as an ongoing source of professional inspiration and development.

In each of these settings, the work of education is design work; and here I mean "design" in terms of Hutchins's (1995) perspective mentioned earlier: Teachers take on the *design function* in a classroom by holding in mind a global view of the learning community, projecting forward and casting back in relation to a goal, creatively developing and shaping what emerges into a unified whole.[3] Design combines flexible purposing with creative decision making. Like artists conversing with their unfolding work, teachers attend to the learning context defined by their interactions with students and let this context "speak" to them. Using their professional judgment, teachers exploit unanticipated opportunities for meaningful learning as they emerge, following paths they could not have foreseen, pursuing goals that may not have been part of their original plan. The achievements in these classrooms are accomplished by practicing an inherently qualitative and relational intelligence, a sensitivity to the "rightness" of a particular choice in timing, structure, or direction for a specific audience or goal. The capacity to improvise is part of the artistry of teaching, and it is a significant cognitive skill – one that differs fundamentally from the ability to follow prescribed steps toward a predetermined goal.

## CONCLUSION

Although I believe that the practice of choreography can shed light on the practice of teaching, needless to say, the work of choreographers and classroom teachers is not the same. Although both may be challenged to produce learning on a set timeline (teachers with students over a term, choreographers with dancers over a rehearsal period), the goals of their work differ: Whereas the job of teachers is often conceived as imparting a set body of knowledge, the job of choreographers is to continually create *new* knowledge, new works of art. Such a charge – along with the fact that dances are composed with dancers – necessitates a fundamentally improvisational and social orientation to the work of facilitating learning. Choreographers must rely on their knowledge and skills in the creative process to establish mutual understandings and realize a final performance. Dancers and their ideas, their unexpected interactions, and even their errors are part of

---

[3] Readers may be familiar with other uses of the term "design" in relation to teaching. Teachers conducting action research investigate a research question through a particular *study design* (e.g., single-case design, quasi-experimental design). The terms *design research* and *design experiments* are also used in the learning sciences community to describe deliberately structured educational interventions. These interventions are intended to identify what works practically to support specific forms of learning as well as to develop and refine educational theory (Cobb et al., 2003). I am using the term to draw a parallel between the work of teachers and the work of artists/designers engaged in a creative process.

the raw material from which to craft an artwork. Although improvisational practices may be unfamiliar to many classroom teachers, choreography offers valuable lessons on how this approach to pedagogy can be used effectively to advance the thinking and knowledge of all members of a learning community.

These practices need not be confined to the dance studio. I have provided examples from Holt, O'Brien, and Lampert that demonstrate how improvisational practices can be successfully integrated with multiple subjects and at any level. In doing so, however, a teacher's work shifts from imparting knowledge to co-constructing knowledge with students – work that requires a different set of skills (Scardamalia & Bereiter, 2006). Curriculum is not abandoned in these examples, but is used as a resource; familiarity with the big ideas and fundamental questions in a domain can help teachers organize and frame students' suggestions or naïve theories and facilitate productive discourse around them – discourse that ultimately teaches students how to engage in the collective advancement of knowledge (Zhang et al., 2009).

Improvisation encompasses more than spontaneous creativity in the arts. It can also refer to a disposition or cognitive skill that is fundamental to creative work and to learning – an ability to be flexible in one's goals, and to be open to the potential in unexpected events to change the course of one's work. For choreographers, such "flexible purposing" characterizes both their individual decision making and their interactions with dancers. Working together, choreographers and dancers accomplish the tasks of both *composing* a dance and *learning* a dance; the aesthetic intention for a dance evolves along with an understanding of how to best realize that intention in performance. A similar process happens in classrooms where co-construction of knowledge and/or the curriculum is the aim. For classroom teachers, learning objectives may take the place of an aesthetic intention. Held in mind flexibly, multiple pathways to achieving those objectives (or newly defined ones) may arise in the course of interacting with students and attending to how their contributions change the evolving problem space. In essence, this is creating the curriculum as one goes, and using improvisation as a form of pedagogy.

## REFERENCES

Arnheim, R. (1974). *Art and visual perception: A psychology of the creative eye.* Berkeley: University of California Press.

Bereiter, C. (2002). *Education and mind in the knowledge age.* Mahwah, NJ: Erlbaum.

Blom, L. A. & Chaplin, L. T. (1982). *The intimate act of choreography.* Pittsburgh, PA: University of Pittsburgh Press.

Bruner, J. (1960). *The process of education*. Cambridge, MA: Harvard University Press.

Chaplin, L. T. (1976). Teaching dance improvisation creatively. *Journal of Physical Education and Recreation*, April.

Cobb, P., Confrey, J., diSessa, A., Lehrer, R., & Schauble, L. (2003). Design experiments in educational research. *Educational Researcher, 32*(1), 9–13.

Cornelius, L. & Herrenkohl, L. (2004). Power in the classroom: How the classroom environment shapes relationships with each other and with concepts. *Cognition and Instruction, 22*(4), 467–498.

Craft, A. (2002). *Creativity and early years education: A lifewide foundation*. New York: Continuum.

Cremin, T., Burnard, P., & Craft, A. (2006). Pedagogy and possibility thinking in the early years. *Thinking Skills and Creativity, 1*, 108–119.

Dewey, J. (1938). *Experience & education*. New York: Collier Books.

Edwards, C., Gandini, L., & Forman, G. (Eds.) (1998). *The hundred languages of children: The Reggio Emilia approach – advanced reflections* (2nd ed.). Greenwich, CT: Ablex Publishing.

Eisner, E. W. (2002). *The arts and the creation of mind*. New Haven, CT: Yale University Press.

Engle, R. A. & Conant, F. R. (2002). Guiding principles for fostering productive disciplinary engagement: Explaining an emergent argument in a community of learners classroom. *Cognition and Instruction, 20*, 399–484.

Flower, L. & Hayes, J. R. (1994). A cognitive process theory of writing. In R. B. Ruddell, M. R. Ruddell, & H. Singer (Eds.), *Theoretical models and processes of reading* (4th ed.). Newark, DE: International Reading Association, 928–950.

Fournier, J. E. (2003). *Composing in dance: Thinking with minds and bodies*. Unpublished doctoral dissertation, University of Washington, Seattle.

Goodwin, C. (1993). The blackness of black: Color categories as situated practice. *Discourse tools and reasoning: Situated cognition and technologically supported environments*. November. Lucca, Italy.

Heath, S. B. (1999). Imaginative actuality: Learning in the arts during nonschool hours. In E. B. Fiske (Ed.), *Champions of change: The impact of the arts on learning*. Washington, DC: The Arts Education Partnership, 19–34.

Holt, T. (1990). *Thinking historically: Narrative, imagination, and understanding*. New York: College Entrance Examination Board.

Hutchins, E. (1995). *Cognition in the wild*. Cambridge, MA: MIT Press.

John-Steiner, V. (1985). *Notebooks of the mind: Explorations of thinking*. Albuquerque: University of New Mexico Press.

Keller, C. H. & Keller, J. D. (1996). Thinking and acting with iron. In S. Chaiklin and J. Lave (Eds.), *Understanding practice: Perspectives on activity and context*. Cambridge: Cambridge University Press, pp. 125–143.

Krajcik, J. S., & Blumenfeld, P. (2006). Project based learning. In R. K. Sawyer (Ed.), *Cambridge handbook of the learning sciences* (pp. 317–333). New York: Cambridge University Press.

Lampert, M. (1990). When the problem is not the question and the solution is not the answer: Mathematical knowing and teaching. *American Educational Research Journal, 27*(1), 29–63.

Lave, J. (1988). *Cognition in practice: Mind, mathematics, and culture in everyday life.* Cambridge: Cambridge University Press.

Paley, V. G. (1986). On listening to what the children say. *Harvard Educational Review, 56*(2), 122–131.

Perkins, D. N. (1993). Person-plus: A distributed view of thinking and learning. In G. Salomon (Ed.), *Distributed cognitions: Psychological and cognitive implications.* Cambridge: Cambridge University Press.

Rogoff, B. (1990). *Apprenticeship in thinking: Cognitive development in social context.* New York: Oxford University Press.

Salomon, G. (1993). No distribution without individuals' cognition: A dynamic interactional view. In G. Salomon (Ed.), *Distributed cognitions: Psychological and educational implications.* Cambridge: Cambridge University Press, 111–138.

Sawyer, R. K. (2004). Creative teaching: Collaborative discussion as disciplined improvisation. *Educational Researcher, 33*(2), 12–20.

Scardamalia, M. & Bereiter, C. (2006). Knowledge building. In R. K. Sawyer (Ed.), *Cambridge handbook of the learning sciences* (pp. 97–115). New York: Cambridge University Press.

Scribner, S. (1997). Mind in action: A functional approach to thinking. In E. Tobach, R. J. Falmagne, M. B. Parlee, L. M. Martin, & A. S. Kapelman (Eds.), *Mind and social practice: Selected writings of Sylvia Scribner.* Cambridge: Cambridge University Press.

Schön, D. A. (1990). The design process. In V. A. Howard (Ed.), *Varieties of thinking.* New York: Routledge.

Shahn, B. (1957). *The shape of content.* New York: Vintage Books.

Swados, E. (1988). *Listening out loud: Becoming a composer.* New York: Harper & Row.

Watson, G. & Konicek, R. (1990). Teaching for conceptual change: Confronting children's experience. *Phi Delta Kappan, 71*(9), 680–685

Wiggins, G. (1989). A true test: Toward more authentic and equitable assessment. *The Phi Delta Kappan, 70*(9), 703–713.

Wolf, D., Bixby, J., Glenn, J., and Gardner, H. (1991). To use their minds well: Investigating new forms of student assessment. *Review of Research in Education, 17,* 31–74.

Zhang, J., Scardamalia, M., Reeve, R., & Messina, R. (2009). Designs for collective cognitive responsibility in knowledge-building communities. *Journal of the Learning Sciences, 18*(1), 7–44.

# PART 3

# THE CURRICULUM PARADOX

# 10

# How "Scripted" Materials Might Support Improvisational Teaching: Insights from the Implementation of a Reading Comprehension Curriculum

ANNETTE SASSI

Scripted teaching and improvisational teaching seem to be diametrically opposed. Improvisational teaching emphasizes that teaching and learning emerge in the moment and that teachers need to engage with their students and the ideas that they have. It draws attention to how the enacted curriculum grows out of what students' learning needs are at a given time. In what is commonly referred to as *scripted teaching*, teachers are provided with materials that consist of explicit step-by-step directions and word-for-word scripts. There would seem to be an unbridgeable gap between improvisational teaching and scripted teaching. Yet, as Sawyer (2004a) aptly points out, teaching – even teaching that is explicitly designed to capture improvisational elements – cannot happen without some type of structure and framework. Constructing that just-right degree of structure is a delicate balancing act, which can be especially challenging for the teacher trying to establish a collaborative classroom.

In this chapter, I focus on two of the paradoxes that Sawyer identified in his introduction: the *teaching paradox*, or the tension between crafting the "well-managed" classroom and sliding toward the "chaotic" classroom; and the *curriculum paradox*, or the tension between meeting curriculum goals and responding to students' ideas and curiosities. Regarding the teaching paradox, teachers need to establish productive classroom routines in order for students to work together effectively. For example, students need to learn effective norms of collaborative discourse such as turn taking or asking follow-up questions to ensure productive group discussions. They need

In R. K. Sawyer (Ed.) (2011). *Structure and improvisation in creative teaching* (pp. 209–235). Cambridge: Cambridge University Press.

to learn appropriate social norms that respect the sharing of ideas. When students are expected to work together in small groups, teachers need to help them learn strategies to stay focused and on task.

Regarding the curriculum paradox, teachers have a responsibility to honor their commitments to teaching subject matter, and not to improvise so much that they give in to the whims of the moment. Pendlebury (1995), in examining the qualities of wise teaching practice, cautions against what she calls the "perceptively spontaneous teacher" who habitually "pushes aside disciplined work in favor of new, exciting, or immediately absorbing activities, and affairs" (p. 56). Such a teacher might jettison plans for revisiting multiplication strategies because a student brought in a new book, or might allow students to discuss whether or not a thumb is a finger for a whole lesson that was initially intended to explore making groups of five. Pendlebury argues that such a teacher would not be honoring her commitment to either her students or the subject matter. If some students are struggling to understand the meaning of multiplication, sidestepping the issue is irresponsible teaching. Ball (1993), writing about her mathematics teaching, articulates this tension between responsiveness to students' immediate ideas and responsibility to the discipline: "How do I value their interests and also connect them to ideas and traditions growing out of centuries of mathematical exploration and invention?" (p. 375)

Effective teachers know that they have to construct a disciplined classroom that allows students to learn subject matter content in systematic and developmentally appropriate ways. Improvisation should not devolve into chaotic, unfocused, or substantively weak classroom practice. However, effective teachers also recognize that creating a too rigid classroom does not encourage independent thinking and creativity. Negotiating the balance between structure and flexibility is the essence of the teaching paradox, and there is no single resolution; the paradox must be continuously addressed – both practically and conceptually. This is especially the case for novice teachers and teachers learning how to teach for understanding.[1]

This chapter takes a closer look at the role of what might be considered "scripted" curriculum materials. I show that these materials have the potential to support creative, responsive, yet responsible teaching. This chapter begins with a brief discussion of the ways in which scholars and education researchers currently think about the role of published materials in

---

[1] Such teaching is also referred to as "constructivist" teaching, where the emphasis is on students' construction of their own knowledge. Throughout this paper, I refer to this kind of teaching as "teaching for understanding" because it captures the interrelationship between the work of students and the pedagogical roles of teachers.

classrooms committed to teaching for understanding. Teaching for understanding is an image of educational practice "where students and teachers acquire knowledge collaboratively, where orthodoxies of pedagogy and 'facts' are continually challenged in classroom discourse, and where conceptual (versus rote) understanding of subject matter is the goal" (McLaughlin & Talbert, 1993, p. 1). Then, using data collected as part of an evaluation of a reading comprehension curriculum pilot implementation (Neufeld & Sassi, 2004), I consider how certain types of more innovative scripted materials may be used to support such teaching, particularly for teachers just learning this approach to teaching and learning. In discussing the use of scripted materials, the chapter focuses on published materials that are themselves designed to support teaching for understanding. Such materials are built on constructivist or inquiry-based principles and incorporate multiple opportunities for collaborative learning. Unlike more directive and prescriptive teaching materials, the materials I examine here are more readily integrated with collaborative approaches to learning and teaching. In closing, I discuss how teachers using these materials can cultivate an improvisational stance that honors the requirements and responsibilities of teaching disciplinary content.

## DESIGNING CURRICULUM MATERIALS THAT CAN SUPPORT CLASSROOM IMPROVISATION

Often when people describe a curriculum as scripted, they have in mind curricula that are based on traditional or didactic pedagogical assumptions about learning and teaching. These curricula are often referred to as *direct teaching* or *direct instruction*. Such materials emphasize repetition, drill-and-practice, and teacher-directed activities over collaborative, inquiry, and self-directed learning. Teacher-student interaction often follows a discourse pattern that consists of the following three turns: (1) teacher initiation (e.g., a question with a pre-determined answer); (2) student response; and (3) teacher evaluation of the student's response. Direct teaching, by design, requires no improvisation; it limits teachers' creativity and minimizes active student engagement, and contemporary researchers and teachers generally agree that such materials often limit opportunities for children to learn in deep and lasting ways.

Educators and researchers interested in teaching for understanding have considered how curriculum materials can be designed to further both student and teacher learning. These researchers are not calling for eliminating published materials in classrooms but rather for rethinking how materials can be designed to be effective teaching tools for teachers (Ball & Cohen 1996; Brown & Edelson, 2003; Remillard, 2000). They recognize that teachers and students can benefit from well-designed materials that support creative investigations, encourage collaborative discourse, and allow in-depth study of relevant content.

In considering how materials can serve as tools to help teachers not only teach but also learn how to be better teachers, Ball and Cohen (1996) laid out some possible considerations for redesigning curriculum. For example, they suggest that teachers' guides can better help teachers learn to listen and interpret what students say and to anticipate better what students might do or say in response to instructional activities. This might be accomplished through such things as providing examples of student work or dialogues that might occur in the classroom. Materials could also support teachers' learning the content more deeply by including discussions of alternative answers or representations and the connections among them. It also could include, as they note, "small forays into the content itself" (p. 7). Ball and Cohen also suggest that developers could make more transparent their reasoning for designing lessons in particular ways and offer the strengths and weaknesses of alternative designs.[2] Finally, they suggest that materials could be more specific about how to design lessons that address the development of content and community across the school year.

Ball and Cohen's position certainly supports some degree of scripting in published materials. Scripting, as I use the term in this chapter, is similar to but distinct from the direct instruction types of curricular structures that Sawyer describes in the introduction. Routines may be considered learned patterns of interaction that teachers call on when teaching, but they are not content-specific. And, while an activity is a planned classroom project that integrates routines with content-specific material, it does not necessarily require teachers to follow specific word-for-word instructions. Curricular materials that entail a degree of scripting may in fact be activities and may make use of numerous classroom routines. What distinguishes them is the degree of specificity in instructions, the amount of word-for-word prompts such as questions and responses, and the level of pedagogical decisions already incorporated into the design of the materials.

There are many current and emerging curricula, across different subject areas, that incorporate scripted elements. Examples include *Investigations in Data, Number, and Space* (Pearson Education/Scott Foresman) and

---

[2] In her paper, "With an Eye on the Mathematical Horizon: Dilemmas of Teaching Elementary School Mathematics" (1993), Ball does just this when she lays out the strengths and weaknesses of using different models to teach negative numbers.

*Mathscapes: Seeing and Thinking Mathematically* in mathematics, *Foundations Science: A Comprehensive High School Curriculum* (Education Development Center (forthcoming) in science, and *Making Meaning* (which is examined further in this chapter) in literacy. Although these curricula differ in the degree to which they are scripted, they share certain commonalities: They lay out day-by-day investigations into subject-matter ideas and concepts; provide teachers with specific questions to prompt discussions; build in time for student inquiry, group work, and dialogue; and may offer sidebar "dialogue boxes" that illustrate potential dialogues that could occur in the classroom. In most of these curricula, teachers are encouraged to use the materials in an established sequence because that sequence is built on research about how children develop and build on ideas.

While researchers and curriculum developers have been developing materials intended to foster collaborative classroom practices that support teaching for understanding, questions remain about how teachers should actually integrate these materials into their classrooms. Should they use them as written, following each lesson plan on a day-by-day basis? Should they view the materials more as guidelines, adapting when needed? And, given that one key goal of these more innovative materials is indeed to support collaborative learning, is there room for improvising with them? Where is the improvisation in classrooms that use such curricula? Consider the perspective of two different pairs of researchers who have been considering such questions.

Brown and Edelson (2003) argue that a teachers' interaction with curriculum is always improvisational. In reporting on a study about the implementation of an inquiry-based science unit, they argue that teaching might better be viewed as a design activity and suggest that curriculum materials "play an important role in affording and constraining teachers' actions" (p. 1) (for a discussion of affordances and constraints, see Wertsch, 1998). Their study is based on the premise that teachers will notice and use different aspects of the curriculum as they customize them to work within their unique school and classroom contexts. Depending on their needs, teachers will follow the curriculum as written (which they refer to as "offloading"), modify it to fit a particular situation (adaptation), or improvise by using a "seed" idea from the materials. They consider improvising to occur when teachers follow their own instructional paths. Central to their view, however, is the idea that teachers inevitably interact with materials in dynamic ways and that some degree of modification and improvisation is likely to occur even when teachers implement the curriculum as written – what the authors in this volume refer to as the curriculum paradox. The issue

I explore here is the degree to which the materials can be designed to encourage *specific kinds* of improvisational responses rather than just the inevitable adjustments that occur as part of day-to-day interactions.

Slavin and Madden's (Slavin & Madden, 2001, Slavin, Madden, & Datnow, 2007) experience with implementing their comprehensive reading program for elementary schools, *Success for All (SFA)*, illustrates the ongoing challenge of finding appropriate balance between program fidelity and flexibility when implementing highly structured instructional programs. SFA offers reading curriculum materials aligned with instructional methods, cross-grade groupings, parent involvement, one-to-one tutoring, and extensive professional development in reading instructional methods. In a paper summarizing the role research played in the evolution of the program (Slavin, Madden, & Datnow, 2007), the authors note that SFA has been misperceived as "completely scripted." They acknowledge that early in the program's history, there was a greater emphasis on "doing the program," but that, as schools became more experienced with the program, SFA came to recognize the importance of allowing school-based adaptations aimed at improving student outcomes and meeting an individual school's goals. They call this new approach "goal focused implementation" in contrast to the initial "fidelity focused" stance. This shift to "goal focused" implementation acknowledged that schools and teachers would still need a certain degree of autonomy and discretion in making the program work within their schools. The emphasis now is not so much on implementing the program precisely as written but on understanding and accepting the rationale behind activities when making adaptations and modifications.

### What It Means to Improvise When Teaching

Researchers, curriculum developers, and teachers agree that some degree of improvising will occur with any program. As Slavin and Madden's experience with SFA indicate, too much control can run the risk of undermining student learning. For instructional programs to be successful, teachers need to exercise some discretion in their classroom. What it means to improvise when teaching, then, is partly a definitional issue: How much variation in an executed lesson would have to take place before one would consider it to be "improvisational"? I propose three levels of improvisational teaching, where the most interactive level is the one I focus on in this chapter.

At the broadest level – the level of design – one might refer to the process of curriculum development as improvisation when teachers design their own lessons, activities, or investigations. As noted earlier, this is what Brown and Edelson (2003) call improvisation. In this case, teachers have not relied on a specific set of published materials but have developed their own lessons, perhaps by drawing components from a particular curriculum, integrating different pieces from several curricula, or inventing their own activities.

At a second level, improvisational teaching can also refer to actions in the classroom that vary from what the teacher had planned in advance – for example, when a teacher who is following a particular lesson plan shifts direction in response to what students might say or do. Many teachers have had to rethink a lesson in the moment. Perhaps they sensed that students had not fully grasped an idea or a student raised a point that warranted attention. In such situations, a teacher may end up crafting an entirely different lesson on the spot. For example, Ball (1993) has written about how she decided to follow one student's unexpected assertion that six could be either odd or even. She describes the unplanned exploration that resulted because she chose to open this assertion to classroom discussion.

Third, improvisation can occur in the context of a planned lesson. It is this level of improvisation that is most influenced by the materials that teachers use. In this chapter, I focus not on the improvisation that occurs when teachers design their own curriculum or when they follow an unplanned direction, but rather on the improvisation that can occur within the context of a planned lesson. Specifically, the chapter focuses on teachers' abilities to respond to students in the classroom and to actively engage students in learning. Listening to students, understanding what they are grappling with, and making wise teaching moves in response to what is happening in the classroom are hallmarks of improvisational teaching (Pendlebury, 1995; Sassi, 2002). Improvisation occurs in the spaces between planned moments. In considering improvisational elements of teaching within the constraints of implementing a scripted lesson, we can more readily open up the consideration of the role of scripted or highly structured materials in supporting a teacher's capacity to listen and interpret what is happening in the classroom, and in facilitating dialogue among students.

## MAKING MEANING – INTEGRATING A SCRIPTED CURRICULUM INTO A COLLABORATIVE LEARNING CONTEXT

In the spring of 2004, the Boston Public Schools and the Boston Plan for Excellence asked us to evaluate a reading comprehension curriculum being piloted in selected elementary schools. The curriculum, *Making Meaning: Strategies That Build Comprehension and Community*, was created and is published by the Developmental Studies Center (DSC, 2004) and was first made available to schools in 2003. It is designed to serve as the reading comprehension component of a school's reading program and to be effectively integrated with other reading programs including both more traditional basal programs and more collaborative or student-centered approaches such as Reader's Workshop.

## Background: Supplementing the Workshop Approach

The Boston Public Schools decided to pilot *Making Meaning* to see how it might work as a supplement to Reader's Workshop (see Calkins, 2001), the reading approach they had adopted several years before. To understand why *Making Meaning* seemed like a good supplement to Reader's Workshop, it is helpful to describe briefly what Reader's Workshop is. Importantly, it is not a curriculum but an approach to structuring literacy instruction intended to foster student engagement and independent learning.

Workshop has a four-part structure: 1) a "mini-lesson" during which the teacher presents or models a teaching objective such as a reading comprehension strategy, idea, or skill; 2) independent reading time, during which students read on their own, applying the concept presented in the mini-lesson; 3) guided reading, small group conferences, or small book clubs, which the teacher facilitates during independent reading time; and 4) whole group sharing, when the teacher facilitates discussions in which students share how they applied the concept from the mini-lesson in their own independent reading and the teacher summarizes key learning objectives of the day.

The Workshop's approach aligns well with the notion of teaching for understanding as well as with Sawyer's (2004a) notion of disciplined improvisation. It provides an overall structure and framework within which teachers can design lessons geared toward the needs of the students in the class. When implemented well, Workshop allows teachers to create many opportunities for students to develop their own understanding and for teachers to incorporate many perspectives into the classroom dialogue. Yet, one of the challenges teachers face in implementing Reader's Workshop well is that it is indeed only a framework for organizing teaching. Teachers are responsible for designing their own mini-lessons and finding their own resources – indeed, filling in the framework with relevant content. Boston Public Schools became interested in the *Making Meaning* curriculum because Boston teachers, together with their literacy coaches and principals, realized that they lacked strong curriculum and associated resources to use within the Workshop framework. Even though many teachers had worked with their coaches to develop reading strategy-focused units of study, there was general agreement that developing high-quality units takes a great deal of time, teachers do not have the material resources at hand to support the units of study, and not all or even most teachers have the literacy backgrounds necessary to develop curriculum units that are well aligned to the strategies they need to teach and to the Citywide Learning Standards. Those teachers who have the requisite literacy backgrounds to find the resources reported that they did not have the time to create their entire reading curriculum (Neufeld & Sassi, 2004). *Making Meaning* was seen potentially to fill a need, particularly in providing substantive content for the mini-lesson component of Workshop.

## The Design of *Making Meaning*

*Making Meaning* is aimed at students in grades K-8. It provides a developmental set of reading comprehension lessons that build on two interrelated strands: comprehension and community. Both strands of the program are essential to the program's explicit assumptions about the influences on children's ability to learn. As the developers note, "children's ability to learn reading comprehension is inextricably linked to their ability to work together and to bring democratic values like responsibility, respect, fairness, caring, and helpfulness to bear on their own behavior and interactions" (p. xii). The dual focus harmonizes well with the requirements and instructional processes associated with Workshop instruction.

The *Making Meaning* curriculum can be considered scripted in three ways: 1) It is developmental; 2) It incorporates a standardized lesson format; 3) Each lesson entails step-by-step teaching instructions, including teacher questions and other prompts.

### Developmental Structure

*Making Meaning* is designed to begin at the start of each school year. Each grade level has eight units of two to six weeks each that systematically build on each other. Based on research on how students develop the ability to comprehend texts (e.g., Pearson et al., 1992; Pressley, 2002), it teaches nine reading comprehension strategies over the course of nine grades (K-8). These are: (1) retelling; (2) using schema/making connections; (3) visualizing; (4) wondering/questioning; (5) making inferences; (6) determining important ideas; (7) understanding text structure; (8) summarizing; and (9) synthesizing. Basic strategies such as retelling and visualizing are taught in the primary grades and the remaining strategies are introduced systematically over the subsequent years.

For each grade, teachers receive a set of twenty to thirty children's trade books to use as read-alouds. These books cover different genres, including fiction, non-fiction, poetry, historical fiction, biography, and realistic fiction. The reading comprehension strategies are taught through the use of these multiple genres. For example, students will have the opportunity to explore making inferences in a range of genres such as poetry, fiction, or historical fiction.

In addition, *Making Meaning* entails a systematic approach to developing social values, social skills, and community. As with the reading comprehension strategies, the social skills – such as learning and using classroom procedures, speaking clearly, taking turns, appreciating and respecting one another's ideas – are introduced when developmentally appropriate from kindergarten through eighth grade. For example, kindergarten and first grade focus on skills such as learning and using classroom procedures and taking turns, while the later grades pay attention to complex skills like asking clarifying questions, reaching agreement, and giving and receiving feedback.

The curriculum utilizes five *cooperative structures* to provide a context in which students can practice and learn both the social skills and the reading comprehension strategies. These include: (1) turn to your partner; (2) think, pair, share; (3) think, pair, write; (4) heads together; and (5) group brainstorming. Again, these are introduced systematically over the course of the years.

*Standardized Lesson Format*
Secondly, the curriculum has a scripted quality in that each week's set of lessons has a similar format. The first lesson of the week begins with a read-aloud, followed by a whole group discussion. It may introduce the reading comprehension strategy that is the focus for the rest of the week. Lessons on the remaining days of the week focus on the particular reading comprehension strategy and provide students opportunities to practice the strategy within the framework of specific cooperative structures. The read-aloud text, chosen specifically to match the particular reading comprehension strategy, is used throughout the whole week. Teachers who were interviewed said that they valued having these kinds of routines and said that they thought that their students valued having them as well.

*Step-by-step Teaching Instructions and Discussion Questions*
Thirdly, the Teachers' Guide provides specific instructions for teaching each lesson in the unit. Each lesson begins with a description of the read-aloud

text and how to introduce it. It describes which cooperative structure to use for the lesson, and lays out the questions to ask throughout the lesson. Some questions are posed as directives; for example, "Ask: What seems most important to understand and remember in the part I just read?" Other questions are posed as suggestions; for example, "Facilitate a discussion among the students using questions such as: Do you agree or disagree with what [name of student] shared? Why?" The Teachers' Guide defines vocabulary words that might be important to highlight, especially for students learning English as a second language.

These three qualities of the program – its developmental design, standardized lesson format, and step-by step instructions with specific teacher questions and prompts – give each lesson a scripted quality. How might such a program be compatible with – and indeed enhance – instructional programs committed to supporting teaching for understanding? The next section examines how one teacher new to teaching for understanding used *Making Meaning* as the mini-lesson component of Reader's Workshop. After considering the example in some detail, the section considers the potential – and possible pitfalls – of using a program like *Making Meaning* to fostering creative engagement between teacher and students.

## Using *Making Meaning* in the Classroom

Improvising while using materials that prescribe a scope and sequence may look different from improvising that occurs when teachers develop their own instructional materials. And, indeed, one key purpose of using a script is to provide a guide that can take away some of the burden of creating one's lessons from scratch. However, in watching teachers use *Making Meaning*, I could see how such instructional programs can have the potential to help teachers engage with their students in disciplined improvisation. We can consider three features of the *Making Meaning* lessons that might support such disciplined improvisation: 1) the structure of the lesson moves between scripted and non-scripted dialogue; 2) each scripted portion holds improvisational potential; and 3) the scripted portions provide intellectual boundaries to guide the dialogue and provide a mechanism for teacher and students to stay focused on the core intellectual ideas of the lesson. Each is considered in the context of a lesson segment that follows.[3]

---

[3] The study focused on fourth and fifth grade teachers because they face the challenge of developing reading comprehension skills in students who may not have yet mastered them. At the same time, students in these grades are expected to use their reading skills to gain new knowledge in a range of curriculum areas.

The lesson segment was taught by a teacher who was somewhat familiar and comfortable with the workshop approach. She was at a school in which the literacy coach took a very active and involved role during the initial implementation of *Making Meaning*.[4] This segment is selected to highlight how the components of a *Making Meaning* lesson are executed in an actual class by a teacher learning to use the material. Using this example, I can then point to ways in which materials like these might support teachers as they develop the capacity to improvise in the classroom. The lesson is from the third day of the first week of a unit entitled "Exploring Important Ideas and Summarizing." The Teachers' Guide describes the unit as follows:

> During this unit, the students make inferences to understand text. They also think about important and supporting ideas in a text and use important ideas to summarize. Socially, they develop the group skill of giving reasons for their opinions, discussing them respectfully, and reaching agreement. They also develop the group skill of supporting one another's independent work and giving feedback in a caring way. As they practice these skills, they continue to relate the value of respect to their behavior. (Grade 5 Teachers' Guide, p. 282)

The read-aloud book for the week was *Letting Swift River Go*, by Jane Yolen. The book, in the genre of historical fiction, tells the story of the creation of the Quabbin Reservoir in western Massachusetts through the narrative of a woman, Sally Jane, who recalls her childhood in the river valley and the events leading up to the flooding of the valley. The book ends with Sally Jane recounting being with her father in a boat on the new reservoir. As her father remembered where all of the buildings and roads were, her mother called from the shore to let the past go.

On the first day of the lesson, the teacher read the whole story and discussed it with the class. Students were introduced to the skill of giving reasons for their opinions and practiced that within the structure of a whole group discussion. Days 2 and 3 were guided strategy practice lessons, with the focus on determining important and supporting ideas. On Day 2, the teacher read the first half of the story again, stopping at three points to have the students reflect on what they thought was the most important part. The cooperative structure they had used was called "think-pair-write," in which they first thought on their own what the important part was, talked with their partners, and then wrote their thought in their

---

[4] The study had both men and women, but all participants are referred to as "she" to ensure anonymity.

notebooks. What follows is a narrative description of the third lesson in this sequence of four lessons:

> The teacher instructed the students to come to the rug with their partners, a pencil, and their reader response notebooks. She had an LCD projector which projected a slide onto a screen at the front of the room that said, "Letting Swift River Go: Think, Pair, Write to think about what is important in the story." Following the instructions in the Teacher's Guide, she briefly recounted what they had done on Monday and Tuesday: She asked the group, "What were some of the important things we found out yesterday?"[5]
>
> One student said, "Boston needed more water so they were going to drown the town." Another student said, "They were going to have to move the graves and trees to get ready for the area to be flooded." Reiterating the important idea suggested in the Teacher's Guide from the previous day, the teacher said, "So, those were some of the important things. And we also said in the beginning that the world felt like a safe place for Sally Jane." She continued describing the plan for the day: "I'm going to read the rest of the story aloud and we're going to stop reading three times. I'll 'think-share-write' what is important the first time. The next two stops you will 'think-pair-write.'" She continued reading the story and stopped at the point suggested by the Teachers' Guide. She asked, "What was important in this part of the story?" and answered the question herself by saying, "I think that one of the important things was that all of the families were getting ready to leave the valley and another thing was that Sally Jane was losing her friends." She wrote that on the chart at the front of the rug. The students copied what she wrote in their notebooks.[6]
>
> The teacher continued reading the story and stopped at the point when the dam to create the reservoir was being built. She said, "Think for a second, what was the most important thing? Then I want you to share it with your partner. Don't write it down yet.[7] The teacher sat with two girls. She and one girl exchanged comments and the teacher told the class that the girl had said to her that the people in the story were building a dam. At this point, the teacher reread the passage in order for them "to see if you think that's the most important part and if your partner gave you any good ideas. After another minute or so, she said, "Okay,

---

[5] This question is very close to the question in the Teachers' Guide, which reads, "What are some of the important ideas we identified in the first part of Letting Swift River Go?

[6] The Teachers' Guide offers the following suggestion of what to say: "What seems most important to understand and remember in this part of the story is that the families in the valley had to move away and Sally Jane was separated from her friends."

[7] The question in the Teachers' Guide at this stopping point is, "What is most important to understand and remember in the part I just read?"

now write down what you think is important." The students took some
time to write in their notebooks.

The teacher then asked someone to share. A girl spoke and the teacher
repeated what the student said, "It didn't seem like their town any more."
The teacher asked her why she thought that it didn't seem like their town.
She replied and the teacher repeated her response for the whole group
to hear, "So, she's giving me some things from the text to support that.
There were no bushes or buildings." Another student said that it took
seven years to flood the town.[8]

The teacher then read to the end of the story and asked, "What did you
think?" One boy whom the teacher looked at just shrugged his shoul-
ders and the teacher moved on to having the students work with their
partners. She sat down with two students, one of whom was the girl she
first sat with, and said to them, "Tell me in one or two sentences, what
happened first. And then what happened. So, that's what you need to
be able to do, you need to be able to say it in one or two sentences." The
teacher then brought this point to the attention of the whole class: "I was
just talking with [the girl]. You need to be able to say it in one or two
sentences." She read the ending of the book again.

When she finished reading, she said, "I want you to write down, 'what I
think is important.'" One boy was not writing and the teacher had a conversation with him and he picked up his booklet. After students had a chance
to write, the teacher asked the boy to share what he wrote but he refused.
She asked the boy's partner to share and he said that the girl in the story
had to forget about the town. The teacher asked the group, "What strategy
did he just use?" One student responded that he made an inference and the
teacher said, "Nice." Another student shared what she wrote: "Her dad was
showing her in the water where it [the town] used to be."

Another student said that "she used to play with her friends but now she
doesn't any more." The teacher asked her, "Was this in this section or the
section before?" When no student responded, the teacher said, "That was
an important part of the section before." The teacher concluded the content part of the lesson by saying, "Remember that thinking about what is
important in a story helps you to identify what you need to understand
the story." She then moved on to a brief debriefing of the social skills
component of the lesson.

In this example, the teacher quite faithfully implemented the lesson as
written in the Teachers' Guide. She asked the questions provided, used

---

[8] The questions in the Teachers' Guide for this portion of the discussion are: "Why does
that idea seem important?" and "What other ideas seemed most important as you
listened to the passage? Why?"

the cooperative structure think-pair-write (as directed) to have students talk with partners, and followed each think-pair-write with a brief whole group sharing. From an improvisational standpoint, there may not seem to be much happening. The teacher was new to using the materials and, given that I observed for the purposes of an evaluation, it is possible that the teacher consciously tried to implement the lesson as closely as possible to how it was written. But, we can look more carefully to see how teachers might use such materials to move into more improvisational and responsive teaching. I consider the three features noted earlier: 1) moving between script and open-ended dialogue; 2) tapping into the improvisational potential of the guiding questions; and 3) staying focused on the key ideas.

### Moving between Script and Open-Ended Dialogue

First, although *Making Meaning* is scripted in its presentation, it does not provide teachers with sentence-by-sentence lesson plans and the discussions questions are not all designed to elicit one right answer. Rather, they are designed to stimulate some degree of open-ended discussion. Indeed, if the materials were to try to create such complete lesson plans, it would not be congruent with the ideas that underpin its own curriculum or Workshop instruction more broadly construed. What *Making Meaning* provides is a carefully designed framework with which teachers can lead lessons that enable students to learn a set of specific reading comprehension strategies. Each scripted portion sets the students up to work independently or with each other and, ideally, explore the reading comprehension strategy for themselves. Through the cooperative structures, the curriculum provides a framework that allows students to work without direct instruction from the teacher. During the times that students work on their own, the teacher has the opportunity to walk around, sit with students, assess what ideas they are working with and perhaps grappling with, and make some tentative decisions about how she might follow up in the whole group discussion. As one principal aptly noted, for example, "They give you a few questions to start off, but that curriculum could never script the entire conversation and anticipate where the students go wrong. And it's so much dependent upon the teacher, then, to follow where the students have gone astray in their thinking, and provide the right scaffolding to bring them back."

In describing the place where the script leaves off, the principal focused on following where the students "go wrong," and in fact, we see the teaching doing that in the earlier example. The questions set the discussion in motion, leaving it the responsibility of the teacher to work with what the students offer. In the example, the teacher was sitting with two students during their "think, pair, write" time, listening to what they were discussing and gauging how she needed to respond.[9] At one point, after talking with the two girls and effectively reviewing with them how to summarize a passage, she said to them, "You need to be able to say it in one or two sentences" and then made the same point to the whole class. She told us in an interview afterwards that: "... I stopped and said, I think there's some confusion about what the idea is. Let's see if you can listen again and tell me what that was all about in one or two sentences. And then we went back and did it again, and that was a little more successful."

However, it is not only that the teacher needs to anticipate where the students can go wrong; the teacher must also anticipate the full range of ideas that they might have. This point brings us to the second feature of *Making Meaning* that can allow it to support classroom improvisation: Each scripted portion holds improvisational potential that teachers can learn to identify and utilize.

### Improvisational Potential Designed into Scripted Portions

In *Making Meaning*, the teacher's questions and other directives hold the potential for being starting points for a more substantive discussion. For example, the materials systematically instruct teachers to ask for evidence from the text, as in the previous example where the teacher asked the student why she thought that the town did not seem like the residents' town any longer. While the teacher was likely not experienced enough with the materials to take the discussion further, it was evident that the children had a range of opinions and ideas: It did not seem like the residents' town any longer; the town no longer looked like their town because it was lacking trees and bushes; the girl in the story would have to forget about her town. These kinds of responses hold the potential for more open-ended dialogue. A teacher more experienced with the curriculum might then be able to parlay such responses into a deeper discussion about identifying important ideas of a story.

### Staying Focused on Core Ideas

The third feature of a *Making Meaning* lesson that can allow it to support disciplined improvisation is that it keeps the focus on a particular component skill of reading comprehension. In the previously described lesson, the teacher was able to employ both the questions and the cooperative structure

---

[9] It is useful to note here that not all teachers that I observed actually sat with students or walked around the room while the students were engaged in pair or individual work. This teacher was making a very conscious effort to join a pair as they worked through the question.

of think-pair-share to keep the students focused on identifying important ideas in the text while giving them some room to explore this concept on their own, with their partner, and with the whole class.

This feature may not seem like it would necessarily support improvisation but it can help by providing intellectual channels that maintain attention to the core intellectual ideas. Rather than view scripts as constraining, I suggest that certain types of scripted materials, especially those designed to create collaborative learning opportunities, may offer teachers valuable guides for channeling discussions and ensuring that they stay within the intellectual focus of the curriculum. Indeed, some of the teachers I spoke with found this quality of the materials appealing. One teacher, who had been using materials by Pinnell and Fountas (e.g., Pinnell & Fountas, 2002) to design Workshop lessons, noted, "... that was like a kid with ADHD, because the book is two inches thick and it has limitless material. But, you look through it and it's like where do I begin?"

Before having access to *Making Meaning*, some teachers – especially those with limited familiarity with the Workshop approach – found it challenging and time-consuming to find appropriate materials on their own, were not sure how they could use different genres to teach different reading comprehension strategies, and were not clear how to lead mini-lessons or conference with students during independent reading. As one coach remarked, "I just think that they didn't have a vision for: What should these mini-lessons cover? What's the content supposed to be? And, what am I supposed to go around and talk to the kids about when I confer with them?"

For these teachers, *Making Meaning* offered content and lesson structure as well as intellectual anchors that they could return to throughout the lesson.[10] The lessons in *Making Meaning*, especially because they are based on read-aloud texts that have been chosen to illustrate a particular reading comprehension strategy, help teachers avoid going off on unproductive tangents. For example, in describing a lesson in which the teacher asked students to make connections from their own experience to make inferences, a coach noted:

> When teachers teach making connections, and kids say, "I have a cousin in Jamaica," they say, "Oh great, you made a connection." But it's not really a meaningful connection.... [In contrast], I observed a teacher teaching a making inferences lesson about [a poem called] *My Man Blue* (Grimes, 2002). They had the piece of text up on the overhead, and the

---

[10] A teacher who was not from the district and not part of this study commented that such materials might be thought of as flow charts in which there are different decision points where the teacher must exercise judgment and discretion.

kids had a copy and they were marking it up. There was a discussion that followed around: this is the piece of text, this is the inference that I made. What I heard the teacher doing in that lesson was not just taking the answer and moving on, but actually saying, "So, how does that evidence – how does that lead you to that inference?" Because everyone had that same piece of text, she could monitor it more closely.

## CULTIVATING AN IMPROVISATIONAL STANCE – COMBINING MAKING MEANING WITH PROFESSIONAL DEVELOPMENT THAT SUPPORTS IMPROVISATIONAL RESPONSIVENESS IN CLASSROOMS

### Limits to Improvising with Scripted Materials

Even though we can identify points in scripted materials such as *Making Meaning* that can support improvisation, it is not a given that teachers will know how to take full advantage of them. Although such materials can be designed to support a substantively rich discussion around specific content, the teachers who were observed were still not at the point to realize this potential. As one principal remarked:

> I do think that whenever you implement something new that has this much of a script, the teachers are focusing so much on learning the script and they're not listening to the students. They're thinking about their next question because it's written there. Whereas, if you're doing more responsive teaching without a script, you have to listen to the kids to know what to ask next. I think this is the case with any new curriculum like Making Meaning. Their first time through it, they kind of walk through the motions.... I think the curriculum structures enough opportunities for students to really, authentically respond, and the teachers really liked seeing that. They couldn't help but respond to them.

Similarly, one coach noted that:

> I think with any program like that, one of the things I've talked with teachers over and over again in the CCL[11] cycles is that you can't just follow this blindly. You've got to have a sense of what your kids are doing

---

[11] CCL stands for Collaborative Coaching and Learning, which is an approach to professional development in which disciplined-based coaches are assigned to schools. A literacy CCL cycle in Boston generally involves weekly meetings for about four to six weeks during which the teachers meet, observe demonstration lessons (taught either by one of them or by the coach), and discuss issues around a particular topic. See Neufeld and Roper (2002, 2003) for a report of the implementation of Collaborative Coaching in Boston's public schools.

and thinking and saying. And if something comes up, you can't just go on to the next question. And I think this is hard, because some people are loving Making Meaning because it gives them a very ready plan. They don't feel like they have to prepare as much. But, to do it well you do have to prepare as much, and pre-read the lessons and try to understand.

These comments return us once again to a key benefit of improvisational teaching: being able to listen to students and understand what they are saying.

### The Role of Professional Support in Effectively Using Scripted Materials

Drawing from improvisational theater, Sawyer (2004a; 2004b) has addressed how teachers might benefit from learning strategies that foster effective improvisational classroom discourse. For example, he suggests that teachers might benefit from learning strategies adapted from improvisational theater. But, as he and others also recognize, thoughtful improvisation requires deep and flexible content knowledge and an ability to link that knowledge with instructional practices in the classroom. The question that I raise here is: how might teachers' professional development integrate the learning of improvisational responsiveness – that is, being able to employ a repertoire of responsive and collaborative instructional strategies in the context of teaching – with deepening their understanding of specific disciplinary content and how students come to learn it? To address this question, we can look at a brief segment from another *Making Meaning* lesson that was observed. The literacy coach working at the school also observed the lesson, providing both the teacher's and the coach's perspective on the lesson.

Like the lesson explored earlier, this lesson was from a unit called Exploring Important Ideas and Summarizing and focused specifically on finding important ideas in the text. The class was reading *A Picture Book of Rosa Parks* and the lesson observed was from Day 2 of the unit. The following excerpt is from the middle section of the lesson. Prior to it, the teacher had read a paragraph from the book and had modeled selecting the most important idea from it. The segment below begins with the teacher reading the next section of the text:

The teacher asked the students to read along as she read the next paragraph from the book:

"At the next stop, some white passengers go on, and because the bus was crowded, moved to the middle section, where Rosa was sitting. The driver told the four African American passengers in Rosa's row to get up. Three of them did, but not Rosa Parks. She had paid the same fare as the white passengers. She knew it was the law in Montgomery that she give up her seat, but she also knew the law was unfair. James Blake called the police, and Rosa Parks was arrested."

The teacher reminded the students to talk with each other and select the most important sentence in the paragraph. After a few minutes, the teacher brought the students back together and asked a question from the Teacher's guide: "What is the paragraph about?" The following dialogue ensued:

GIRLA: Rosa Parks
TEACHER: What about her?
GIRLA: She didn't want to sit in the back.
TEACHER: Can someone say more?
GIRLB: She didn't think it was fair because she paid the same fare.
TEACHER: What's the most important information this paragraph gives you?
GIRLB: (Indecipherable answer)
TEACHER: Can you think about what is *most* important?
GIRLB: She knew the law required her to give up her seat.
TEACHER: Okay. Someone else?
BOYA: It's important to know she was arrested.
TEACHER: So, she knew the law, she knew it was unfair, and she was arrested.
GIRLC: Three of them did but not Rosa Parks.
GIRLD: reads the first sentence of the paragraph
TEACHER: (after listening to the two girls): Which part is important?
GIRLD: That white passengers got on.

At this point, the teacher seemed puzzled about what to say next. She had been offered multiple options for the most important sentences but there was no resolution. The Teacher's Guide only suggests that the teacher make notes in the margins on an overhead displaying the paragraph being discussed, which the teacher did. After encouraging students to make their own selections, she called on another girl to read her choice, which was "She knew it was the law." For the first time, the teacher asked, "Why is that sentence important." The girl responded, "Because even though she knew it was the law and she would be arrested, she didn't get up." The teacher turned to a boy and asked him to restate the girl's response, which he did.

Again, we can see in this example that the teacher was able to use the *Making Meaning* framework to have students move between working with each other and sharing together as a whole class. The question they discussed – what is the most important idea in this paragraph? – was open to interpretation, and the teacher solicited ideas from several students. Yet, the teacher was still tentative about how and when to respond to what students offered. In talking with us afterward, she reflected on how she might do the lesson differently:

> Today, if time was available, I would have said, "Why don't you all open your books, read a chapter, and try to summarize, or read a paragraph, a couple of sentences, and summarize what that says for me." And, I would go to some of the students – there were five, six students I would have targeted right away. "Why don't you read this paragraph, then tell me in your own words what it means." The independent reading part is key. And then what would happen is, over a couple of days, if I noticed a group of four or five students who were having trouble with the skill, during independent reading time, I might take four kids together as a group, sit on the rug together, sit on the table together, and work on that skill as a group again.

This teacher was beginning to consider how she might work with the unstructured time: how she might listen differently to students, how she could identify students who were struggling with the concept, how she could create a small working group. She was beginning to reflect on how she could modify – or improvise – within the structure provided by *Making Meaning* to address particular needs of particular students.

The coach also shared her thoughts about how she might have debriefed this lesson with the teacher. We can see in her response a greater attention to the ideas underlying summarizing and less attention to adjusting the cooperative structures:

> I would have talked to [the teacher] afterwards about how it's good to hear what the students' thoughts are but it's also important they move to get deeper into why they were giving that as their suggestion, and to try to bring that out. Is it because it's the first sentence of the paragraph, the last sentence of the paragraph? Some of it seemed like it was the thing they knew best about Rosa Parks. And then also for us to look through the text and say, "What do the two of us think is the most important?" I think what we would maybe have talked about was how, the next day, she could have brought back some of the things for kids to look further in the text for, like, is this just an idea that is mentioned once and disappears, or is this one of those ideas that carries you through the text for a very long time, and therefore really helps you understand something about Rosa Parks better?

This coach focused on how she might help the teacher work in a more improvisational way with students' responses in order to probe more deeply into why they thought what they did. This would involve not only helping the teacher deepen her repertoire of responses – such as asking students to give their reasoning – but also deepen her own skill at identifying important segments of text. This coach's reflection highlights a critical part of learning to respond improvisationally: doing it effectively requires deep content knowledge.

When first using *Making Meaning*, teachers stayed pretty close to the script and did not readily follow up with students. As previously noted, teachers appeared reticent to move from asking the initial questions to asking follow-up questions during whole group discussions. They were not quite sure of their own role in shaping students' independent work. In this sense, they did not yet realize the improvisational potential in the materials.

In thinking about the role of scripted materials and what skills teachers need to use them effectively, consider briefly the metaphor of musical improvisation. In many musical traditions that use improvisational elements – including not only jazz but also a myriad of folk traditions that include Klezmer, Irish traditional music, and other genres – the tunes can be written down using conventional musical notation. This is akin to a scripted curriculum. Yet, playing the tunes well *within the tradition* requires knowing what to do with the notes and what to do between the notes – adding ornaments, moving from one note to the next, and so forth – to achieve the sound and style of the tradition.

In a similar way, using materials that are scripted requires knowing the disciplinary domain – and how children learn it – deeply and flexibly enough to know what to do and where one can move in the moments that are not scripted. Using the example of making inferences, as described in the initial evaluation report, it seemed evident that some teachers who themselves could draw inferences from text were nonetheless unclear about how to help children develop this reading strategy. They were unable to make the process transparent and, as far as one could tell, the Teachers' Guide was not a large help in this regard. In short, teachers may have had difficulty asking students the "next question" following a response not solely because they lacked improvisational instructional skills. More likely, they were not sure what to make of the students' responses; they may not have understood what the students' incomplete answer implied about what they understood, nor understood how to lead them to the next level of understanding. For teachers to gain such skill, their use of materials like *Making Meaning* needs to be accompanied by on-site professional development/coaching support tied to specific content and how children learn it. (See Neufeld & Donaldson, in press, for a more in-depth analysis of coaching for instructional improvement.)

This support was evident in one school in the study. The literacy coach and the principal realized that implementing the materials well was not a matter of just reading through them to understand their logic and flow. They realized that it involved making sure teachers understood both the content and the pedagogy that underlay the script and understood how the curriculum fit into their particular classrooms. As the coach noted:

> The principal and I wanted this to be done through CCL so teachers weren't just handed these curriculum guides without talk around them. The guide is helpful to some extent, but we've all probably seen how any script can be done just as poorly as anything else, even though it's right there in front of you. So, the hope with introducing it through CCL was that, with my coaching, with us collaborating together, with teachers watching me teach it, being in their rooms to help them, we could make some decisions about [how to use it]. Do we need to ask this question that the script is telling us to ask, or should we make some adjustments?

In this school, the CCL cycle was used in concert with the curriculum to deepen teachers' knowledge of how to teach reading, not to teach them directly how to use the program. To this end, the CCL cycle that accompanied teachers' use of the first unit in the curriculum included attention to multiple aspects of Workshop instruction, as the coach notes:

> We had all of the components of CCL. We met for six hours of inquiry – one hour each week of the six weeks. And we did readings around the principles and basics of Workshop that Making Meaning was bringing out. We read about independent reading, we read about conferring, we read about student talk in classrooms, we read about asking questions – those types of things. Because those were what we were working on, for example, with the "turning and talking" in Making Meaning, or with the unit on exploring expository text.

In this statement, the coach acknowledged that critical to implementing *Making Meaning* – or any curriculum – well is understanding what one is listening for when listening to student talk, being able to ask follow-up questions, and being able to make judgments in the moment.

In thinking about professional development that can help teachers be responsive in the classroom, we need to think about how to integrate instruction about general teaching strategies with deepening their understanding of content. For example, the teacher whose lesson is profiled earlier described how she planned her lesson: "Well, I read the book that we were going to teach, and then I read the teacher's guide, and followed the steps, kind of role played the whole thing in my mind, and I used some post-its in the book to help guide me through it."

One direction in supporting teachers would be to capitalize on the idea of role playing. Yet, it is critical that role playing moves from memorizing stock responses to playing out possible scenarios – that is, as teachers "role play" lessons in their minds or with others – they are given opportunities to practice anticipating what is not written down. Coaches or other colleagues might help here, for instance, by having teachers consider different scenarios and practice the different ways in which they could respond to students. Here, the skills of improvising that Sawyer (2004a; 2004b) and others speak of would be integrated with deepening understanding of the content and of how students learn that content. The evaluation of the *Making Meaning* curriculum highlighted how critical it is to provide teachers with high-quality resources that support their learning of approaches to teaching. Yet, these kinds of materials also run the risk of being used unreflectively or by rote. It is therefore critical that their implementation be accompanied by high-quality professional support that links responsive teaching with subject matter knowledge and how students learn it.

## CONCLUSION: LINKING STRUCTURE WITH IMPROVISATION

Finding the balance between structure and flexibility in teaching is an ongoing challenge for teachers. It entails the continual negotiation of several paradoxical aspects of high quality instruction. Teachers need to establish effective classroom routines while keeping the learning environment engaging and open to surprises. They need to respond to students' needs and interests while continually keeping their eyes on desired learning outcomes.

It is particularly challenging when teaching for understanding is at the heart of high-quality instruction. Teaching for understanding, as I use the term, is an image of educational practice "where students and teachers acquire knowledge collaboratively, where orthodoxies of pedagogy and 'facts' are continually challenged in classroom discourse, and where conceptual (versus rote) understanding of subject matter is the goal" (McLaughlin & Talbert, 1993, p. 1). This type of teaching requires teachers to understand their subject matter deeply and to have command over pedagogical strategies that enable students to actively engage in their own learning, and to actively make meaning of academic content. Engaging students in this kind of learning requires disciplined improvisation in the context of clear curricular goals.

How can teachers acquire and use improvisation effectively given that most teachers have had scant opportunity to learn such strategies?

I have argued that carefully developed curricula and related materials that are intended for use in collaborative classrooms, accompanied by teacher guides that offer appropriate teaching scripts, can support teachers' efforts to teach for understanding. I have also argued that such instructional materials can support disciplined improvisation. They can provide teachers with a strong basis from which to respond to students' efforts to make meaning without going off on tangents or losing the thread of their instructional goals.

The scripted materials described in this chapter have the potential to play a valuable role in providing a framework for teachers as they implement teaching for understanding in their classrooms. They can function as guides that help teachers identify critical openings into which they can enter a more improvisational space. They can provide structured questions that can serve as valuable prompts to elicit student thinking with which the teacher can further craft the discussion. They are not "teacher proof" – teachers require expertise to use them well and they require coaching support to encourage their understanding of both the content and pedagogy embodied in the curriculum. Although it may seem like a contradiction, I have argued that high-quality scripted materials, used well, can be supports for achieving the goals of teaching for understanding, a pedagogy that has proven difficult to implement well but one that holds promise for high-quality student learning.

### ACKNOWLEDGMENTS

I would like to thank Barbara Neufeld for all of her contributions in the development of this chapter. It was gratifying to work with her on the initial evaluation of the *Making Meaning* implementation. Subsequently, her critical reading and thoughtful editorial comments on the several drafts of the chapter proved most helpful. I would also like to thank Keith Sawyer for his careful reading of the chapter and his numerous substantive and editorial comments, all of which made this chapter much stronger.

### REFERENCES

Ball, D. L. (1993). With an Eye on the Mathematical Horizon: Dilemmas of Teaching Elementary School Mathematics. *The Elementary School Journal*, 94(4): 373–397.

Ball, D. and Cohen D. (1996). Reform by the Book: What Is – or Might Be – the Role of Curriculum Materials in Teacher Learning and Instructional Reform? *Educational Researcher*, 25(9): 6–8, 14.

Brown, M. and Edelson, D. (2003). Teaching as Design. *The Center for Learning Technologies in Urban Schools: LeTUs Report Series.*

Calkins, L. (2001). *The Art of Teaching Reading.* New York: Addison-Wesley Longman.

Developmental Studies Center (2004). *Making Meaning: Strategies That Build Comprehension and Community.* Oakland, CA: Developmental Studies Center.

Education Development Center (forthcoming). *Foundations Science: A Comprehensive High School Curriculum.* Newton, MA: Education Development Center.

Grimes, Nikki (2002). *My Man Blue.* London: Puffin Books.

McLaughlin, M. W. and Talbert, J. E. (1993). Introduction: New Visions of Teaching. In D. K. Cohen, M. W. McLaughlin, and J. E. Talbert (Eds.), *Teaching for Understanding: Challenges for Policy and Practice.* San Francisco: Jossey-Bass.

Neufeld, B. and Donaldson, M. (in press). Coaching for Instructional Improvement: Conditions and Strategies That Matter. To appear in B. Kelly and D. F. Perkins (Eds.), *The Cambridge Handbook of Implementation Science for Educational Psychology.* Cambridge: Cambridge University Press.

Neufeld, B. and Roper, D. (2002). *Off to a Good Start: Collaborative Coaching and Leaning in the Effective Practice Schools.* Cambridge, MA: Education Matters.

(2003). *Year II of Collaborative Coaching and Learning in the Effective Practice Schools: Expanding the Work.* Cambridge, MA: Education Matters.

Neufeld, B. and Sassi, A. (2004). *Getting Our Feet Wet: Using Making Meaning for the First Time.* Cambridge, MA: Education Matters.

Pearson, P. D, Dole, J. A., Duffy, G. G., and Roehler, L. R. (1992). Developing Expertise in Reading Comprehension: What Should Be Taught and How Should It Be Taught? In J. Farstup and S. J. Samuels (Eds.), *What Research Has to Say to the Teacher of Reading.* Newark, DE: International Reading Association.

Pearson Education/Scott Foresman *Investigations in Number, Data, and Space.*

Pendlebury, S. (1995). Reason and Story in Wise Practice. In H. McEwan and K. Egan (Eds.), *Narrative in Teaching, Learning, and Research.* New York: Teachers College Press.

Pinnell, G. S. and Fountas I. C. (2002). *Leveled Books for Readers, Grade 3–6.* Portsmouth, NH: Heinemann.

Pressley, M. (2002). *Beginning Reading Instruction: The Rest of the Story from Research.* Washington, DC: National Education Association.

Remillard, J. T. (2000). Can Curriculum Materials Support Teachers' Learning? Two Fourth-Grade Teachers' Use of a New Mathematics Text. *The Elementary School Journal, 100* (4), 331–350.

Sassi, A. (2002). Cultivating Perception: Helping Teachers to Attend the Salient Features of Their Mathematics Classroom. Center for the Development of Teaching Paper Series, Education Development Center, Newton, MA.

Sawyer, R. K. (2004a). Creative Teaching: Collaborative Discussion as Disciplined Improvisation. *Educational Researcher, 33*(2): 12–20.

(2004b). Improvised Lessons: Collaborative Discussions in the Classroom. *Teacher Education, 15*(2): 189–201.

Slavin, R. E. and Madden, N. A. (2001). *Success for All: Research and Reform in Elementary Education*. Mahwah, NJ: Erlbaum.

Slavin, R. E., Madden, N. A., and Datnow, A. (2007) Research In, Research Out: The Role of Research in the Development and Scale-Up of Success for All. In S. H. Furhman, D. K. Cohen, and F. Mosher (Eds.), *The State of Education Policy Research*. Mahwah, NJ: Lawrence Erlbaum Associates.

Wertsch, J. V. (1998). *Mind as Action*. New York: Oxford University Press.

# 11

# Disciplined Improvisation to Extend Young Children's Scientific Thinking

## A. SUSAN JUROW AND LAURA CREIGHTON MCFADDEN

Science is more than special terminology and techniques; it is also about wonder, questioning, and discovering patterns in the natural world. In this chapter, we describe the ways that two K-1 teachers, Ms. Rosenthal and Ms. Rivera, designed their science instruction to inspire their students to feel the sense of wonder and curiosity that drives scientists, with the hope that this would help them understand the discipline and practices of science. They did this by creating a constructivist-oriented learning environment that encouraged students to explore objects, situations, and concepts deeply, for extended periods of time, and from multiple perspectives. Children made personal observations of these experiences through writing in journals, drawing pictures to compare what they thought might happen in a science experiment (i.e., their hypotheses) with what actually happened, and through talk that their teachers carefully documented and often displayed on the walls of the classroom.

In constructivist classrooms, the goal is to help students develop their own understanding so that they can use and apply knowledge in diverse contexts and draw connections among multiple representations of a given concept. True constructivist teaching always faces the teaching paradox because it is not "discovery learning," an unstructured, learner-centered environment where students are left to themselves; it requires that teachers develop a structured environment – the term educators often use is *scaffold* – within which students are guided as they construct their own knowledge (Mayer, 2004). In this sense, these classrooms are neither teacher-centered nor student-centered, but are a bit of both; they are partially organized by teachers, in that teachers create and present the scaffold; and their flow is

In R. K. Sawyer (Ed.) (2011). *Structure and improvisation in creative teaching* (pp. 236–251). Cambridge: Cambridge University Press.

partially determined by the students, in that children work within the scaffold to construct their own knowledge.

As in many constructivist classrooms, Ms. Rivera and Ms. Rosenthal faced a curriculum paradox centered on helping children express and explore their own thinking while also helping them connect these ideas to accepted disciplinary practices. We observed that one way that they managed this tension was through the use of *disciplined improvisation* as a resource for scaffolding the children's thinking (Sawyer, 2004). Disciplined improvisation is a type of instructional interaction that is improvisational in that neither the teacher nor the students know what the specific flow or outcome of the exchange will be. It is disciplined because teachers build on students' ideas in order to connect them to disciplinary concerns, concepts, and discursive practices.

By listening carefully and by seriously considering children's contributions, teachers can use these contributions as a foundation to construct the beginnings of scientific understanding. When teachers use student questions and observations to make connections, they are of necessity improvising – but improvising in an artful way that balances the tension between what is coming from the student and the science practices to which they are trying to connect students' ideas. Unlike scientists, young children are not yet proficient in scientific discourse. Their ideas may be unorganized or underdeveloped; but "if the educational goal is to help students understand not only scientific outcomes and the concepts that support them but also *how* one knows and *why* one believes, then students need to talk about evidence, models and theories" (Michaels, Shouse, & Schweingruber, 2007, p. 93). Disciplined improvisation provides students the opportunity to experience authentic science – science as dynamic, creative, and open to debate and discussion. In the following, we present two cases that show how Ms. Rosenthal and Ms. Rivera used disciplined improvisation to negotiate the paradox of allowing children to explain and articulate their own thinking while also engaging them in the accepted practices of science as introduced in their curriculum.

## CONCEPTUAL FRAMEWORK

Improvisation among students and teachers is ubiquitous in classrooms (Erickson, 1982). When a student makes a comment during a whole-class discussion, tells a joke, shares an emotional story about their family's difficulties during circle time, or jumps up to act out how a seed turns into a flower, the teacher needs to make a decision regarding how to respond to the child's contribution. There are endless ways in which a teacher could respond, including ignoring what she might perceive as a distraction, briefly acknowledging what was said and then moving on to her next point in the lesson, or exploring the new issue raised by the student and using it to stimulate further discussion or a future activity. How a teacher chooses to respond depends on the content of the contribution and her view of its potential meaning, her sense of the child's social and emotional well-being, the amount of time she has to spend on the topic, and her plans for the day's lesson (cf. Lampert, Rittenhouse, & Grumbaugh, 1996). And, as Borko and Livingston (1989) found, experienced teachers' responses to the unexpected were based on their understanding of the structure of the curriculum and disciplinary concerns.

Although effective teachers often improvise to more effectively manage the classroom, this is not our concern here. Rather, our focus here (and in the other chapters of this volume) is on how improvisation can be used to help students learn subject matter more effectively. As educators interested in discipline-based learning, we are concerned with those moments of improvised action between teacher and student(s) where the content of the exchange is connected to or can be linked to the central issues and practices of the discipline of science. Yet we believe that the practices we describe here carry important messages for all teachers, not only science teachers.

Improvisational science dialogues between teachers and students can be significant moments for learning science because science fundamentally involves exploring questions and ideas, but without a set pathway to a particular answer. Scientific exploration does not, however, take place without guidelines. Participating effectively in the discipline of science includes learning to use its substantive content (e.g., definitions) as well as the discursive practices that sustain scientific thinking and activity (e.g., providing evidence for claims) (Lemke, 1990). For students to learn science, teachers must, as Hicks (1995/1996, p. 59) writes, "... set the stage ... by providing the discursive 'slots' that enable novice learners to participate in disciplinary practices." We call it "disciplined improvisation" when teachers create these "slots" by strategically utilizing student contributions to provide opportunities for learners to reflect on, participate in, and extend their scientific understanding.

## APPROACH TO TEACHING SCIENCE

Ms. Rivera and Ms. Rosenthal viewed science as a dynamic field with systematic ways of investigating and organizing the world; and they viewed science as open to new discoveries and approaches to understanding. Science instruction, as it was enacted in these teachers' classrooms, included teaching students to think flexibly with the ideas and practices of science, with the goal of helping them learn how to engage in the foundational practices of the discipline. In their classrooms, five- to seven-year-olds spent extended periods of time exploring scientific concepts through talking about and questioning ideas, creating physical representations of those ideas in multiple forms of media (e.g., paper-and-pencil drawings, clay sculptures), and by engaging in long-term projects that allowed them to work concretely and creatively with scientific concepts (Edwards, Gandini, & Forman, 1993; National Research Council, 1996). By enabling children to engage in authentic scientific practice, the teachers created a space in which the children's questions and interests came into contact with foundational ideas of science. The teachers invited the children into the wonder and messiness of science in action (cf. Latour, 1987) by presenting the complexities and practices of inquiry-based science.

Ms. Rivera and Ms. Rosenthal's approach to science instruction is aligned with current research on science education (e.g., Forman & Sink, 2006; National Research Council, 2000). According to the National Science Council report, which synthesized research on K-8 science learning to develop a new framework for what it means to be proficient in science, students should: know, use, and interpret scientific explanations of the natural world; generate and evaluate scientific evidence and explanations; understand the nature and development of scientific knowledge; and participate productively in scientific practices and discourse (Duschl, Schweingruber, & Shouse, 2007, p. 36). Even young children like the five- to seven-year-olds in Ms. Rosenthal's and Ms. Rivera's classrooms can participate in a version of authentic scientific practice (Michaels, Shouse, & Schweingruber, 2007). However, when working with young children, it is imperative that teachers really hear their ideas in order to refine and extend them in line with the accepted practices of the discipline. To manage the curricular paradox between allowing children to explore their own thinking and linking these contributions to disciplinary concerns thus requires teachers to put listening at the center of their instructional practice (Schultz, 2003). As we show in the following, listening well enabled the teachers we studied to engage in disciplined improvisation that both honored children's ideas and brought them closer to the practices of science.

## RESEARCH CONTEXT

### School

This study took place at an elementary laboratory school located at a research university in one of the western United States. As part of the school's charge, the student population was recruited to be ethnically, linguistically, and socioeconomically diverse. To accommodate the school's second-language learners, a bilingual (Spanish-English) strand ran through the school from its pre-K to fifth-grade classes.

## Teachers

At the time of this study, Ms. Rivera and Ms. Rosenthal had taught as a team for five years at the K-1 level. Ms. Rivera taught students in a bilingual Spanish-English classroom and right next door, Ms. Rosenthal taught students in a monolingual English classroom.

## Data Sources

The analysis presented in this article is based on data collected as part of a larger ethnographic study documenting how teachers teach long-term science projects. The information sources for the study include digital recordings of classroom interactions, field notes based on classroom observations, interviews with the two teachers, and documents and artifacts created by students.

## TWO CASES OF DISCIPLINED IMPROVISATION

In this section, we describe how the teachers improvised with their students to help them learn and do science. As we demonstrate, the improvisation in which the teachers and students participated was shaped by their curricular goals for science. That is, while the teachers encouraged students to make their own connections with the scientific concepts under study, they were always attuned to how the children's understandings related to or could be made to relate to the discipline and practices of science.

Each case illustrates how Ms. Rosenthal and Ms. Rivera managed the tension between connecting young children's ideas to science and staying true to the children's ideas and insights. Rather than directly telling students how to talk or think like scientists, the teachers built on the children's natural language, ideas, and experiences in order to teach them to value and engage in scientific ways of understanding the world.

### Case 1: Offering Students Disciplinary Tools to Refine Their Thinking

A central aspect of learning to do science is learning how to "talk science" (Lemke, 1990). Learning to talk science refers not only to knowing and meaningfully using specialized terms, but also to understanding the norms of scientific discourse such as asking questions, constructing explanations, and engaging in scientific argument and debate. This is certainly not all it takes to do science, but the language of science is an important entry point into doing science, because the specialized terms and how they are used convey both the substantive content of science and the value system that underlies a scientific worldview (Gallas, 1995). K-1 students begin to learn how to talk science, for example, by explicitly stating their own views about the topic under study, considering the reasoning used to support their views, and differentiating what they think from why they think it (Duschl, Schweingruber, & Shouse, 2007). From a constructivist perspective, the teacher needs to provide students with opportunities to observe and interact with phenomena that will enable students to notice and then have a reason to articulate ideas related to science. Because young children may not attend or know how to attend to the particular phenomena or set of relations that teachers want them to notice, especially when an activity is purposefully designed to encourage exploration, one can expect many unplanned-for observations. The teacher in such a case thus has many opportunities for improvisation. A main challenge in classrooms like Ms. Rosenthal's and Ms. Rivera's is how to improvise with students so that they are led to express their unique ideas and insights in appropriately scientific language. In the following case, Ms. Rosenthal engaged in disciplined science improvisation with the children in order to apprentice them into the discursive practices of science.

### Background
The lesson was structured around curricular goals for science instruction that were set by national and local standards, but the enactment of the lesson was flexible so that Ms. Rosenthal could respond creatively to students' insights and observations. One of the goals for physical science instruction at the primary level is for students to be able to identify the properties of objects and materials. As stated in the National Science Education Standards (National Research Council, 1996, p. 126), "(y)oung children begin their study of matter by examining and qualitatively describing objects and their behavior." These concrete experiences along with subsequent reflections on what students have observed provide the foundation for learning more abstract scientific ideas in the upper grades.

The following scene took place in November toward the beginning of the children's investigation of different forms of matter. Small groups of children rotated through two table centers where they could touch, look at,

pour, mix, and otherwise manipulate solids (at a "solids table") and liquids
(at a "liquids table"). Ms. Rosenthal organized the activity so that the children could have firsthand experiences with solids and liquids, which would
then support their descriptions of their characteristic properties and their
differences. In the exchange, a group of five children were at the liquids table
that included a set of common liquids that their teacher carefully selected to
provoke the children's thinking about what liquids look like, how they feel,
and how they interact with each other. The liquids she selected included:
water, shampoo, molasses, and oil.

*Activity*
At the table, the children enthusiastically poured the various liquids in and
out of clear cups. In between giggles and tastes of molasses, they helped
each other mix fluids together and watched what would happen to various combinations. When Ms. Rosenthal checked in with the children after
a few minutes of exploration, she asked them to consider "the differences
between your experiences" with the solids and liquids.[1]

| 54 | Bradley: | Liquids always separates. |
|----|----------|---------------------------|
| 55 | Ms. Rosenthal: | Liquids can separate? [How do they separate? |
| 56 | Bradley: | (nods head in agreement) |
| 57 | Ricardo: | No, you cannot separate. |
| 58 | Bradley: | Unless you like mix them together with something. No, you can mix them together with your own hands but if you just pour them together they separate. |
| 59 | Ms. Rosenthal: | If you pull- how can you separate? Where are they separating? |
| 60 | Bradley: | You know (moves loosely cupped hands together and then apart)? It looks like they're not, but they are like in different categories really close together. |

In response to Ms. Rosenthal's question about how solids and liquids are
different from each other, Bradley (line 54) asserted that "liquids always
separate(s)." Ms. Rosenthal was surprised by Bradley's observation asking, "Liquids can separate?" Rather than telling Bradley that liquids do
not *always* separate, Ms. Rosenthal asked Bradley what he meant by the

---

[1] The transcription conventions we use include the following: emphatic speech is shown
with uppercase letters, action descriptions are shown in parentheses, overlapping speech
is marked with matching brackets across speaking turns, a dash indicates an interruption,
and stre::tched enunciation is indicated with repeated colons.

word "separate." Bradley then explained how it is possible to "mix" liquids together using your hands but if you just poured the liquids on top of each other they would remain in "different categories."

At this point in the exchange, the teacher did not know how to proceed. She knew that while some liquids (like oil and water) do in fact separate, others (like molasses and water) do not. How should she respond to Bradley's claim that liquids *always* separate? This is a moment with which many teachers are familiar. A student says something that is factually incomplete, and a teacher needs to juggle multiple concerns, including attention to this particular student's understanding, the collective understanding or potential misunderstanding of the group, and concern for validating the student's thinking so as to encourage their future willingness to share their unique perspectives. In addition to these issues, Ms. Rosenthal needed to consider how Bradley's comment might be explored in relation to engaging the children in the foundational discursive practices of science.

In her next move, the teacher decided to step to the side in order to put the students' ideas at the center of the discussion. She recognized this as an opportunity to demonstrate a practice that is central to science: the practice of making generalizations from multiple observations, and then testing those generalizations with additional observations. Bradley not only stated an observation, but a generalization that was testable and therefore could be revised by re-examining the data at hand. In turn 70, she posed a physical challenge to the children intended to engage them in the scientific practice of providing evidence for claims (in this case, Bradley's claim about liquids):

| 70 | Ms. Rosenthal: | Are you ready for my question? (students continue mixing liquids) Actually, I'm going to ask you to do something for me. I'm going to ask you now, in this other cup that you have, separate your liquids, please. Separate the molasses, separate the oil, and separate the shampoo for me. |
|----|----------------|---|

Rather than asking the students a "next question," the teacher changed her mind (starting her request with "actually," which indicates a shift in her thinking) and asked the students to separate the various liquids they had just combined with each other. In line with Engle & Conant's (2002) view of disciplinary engagement, by proposing this activity, Ms. Rosenthal positioned the children with the authority to participate in science. She then left the children to work on their own. When she returned a few minutes later, she asked them if they were able to separate the liquids:

| 90 | Ms. Rosenthal: | Can you separate the liquids? |
|----|----------------|-------------------------------|
| 91 | Some students: | NO. |
| 92 | Ms. Rosenthal: | Could you separate the solids? |
| 93 | Some students: | YES. |
| 94 | Ms. Rosenthal: | (pauses and holds out both hands palms up) |
| 95 | Ella: | AH HA! THAT'S THE DIFFERENCE! (points at Ms. Rosenthal) You can't- you can't separate liquids, but you could separate solids. |

At lines 90 and 92, Ms. Rosenthal asked questions that led the children to identify a difference they observed between liquids and solids: You cannot separate liquids, but you can separate solids. Bradley, however, was undeterred in expressing his view. Rather than agreeing with Ella (and Ms. Rosenthal), he further specified his claim:

| 102 | Bradley: | If you have certain kinds of liquids you- they don't like mix together (waves hands back and forth) |
|-----|----------|--------|
| 103 | Ms. Rosenthal: | Like what Bradley? |
| 104 | Roshi: | Soap |
| 105 | Bradley: | Like (reaches for a bottle of oil) |
| 106 | Ms. Rosenthal: | Which liquids did you find out that don't mix easily? Like what? What is that? (points to the bottle of oil) |
| 107 | Bradley: | I don't know (laughs). |
| 108 | Ms. Rosenthal: | What is this? (reaches for the almost empty bottle of oil) What was this? (holds up the bottle) |
| | | ... |
| 116 | Ella: | Oi::l |
| 117 | Ms. Rosenthal: | It's oil! |
| 118 | Bradley: | That's what I was trying to get. |
| 119 | Ms. Rosenthal: | Oil and water do not mix easily. |
| 120 | Bradley: | I know. That's what I was trying to s- |
| 121 | Ms. Rosenthal: | So you are saying that some liquids you can separate but others you can't? Is that what you're saying? |
| 122 | Bradley: | (nods head affirmatively) |

*Summary*
By the end of this exchange, Bradley stated with much greater precision what he had initially noticed from his exploration at the liquids table. What began (line 54) as a sweeping generalization about what liquids "always" do became a more qualified claim about the behavior of "certain" kinds of liquids such as oil and water (lines 119–122).

Ms. Rosenthal's decisions regarding what to say and do in this episode were informed by her knowledge of the national and school science standards, the process of doing science, and her belief that children should actively construct their own understandings. By challenging the students to separate the liquids, Ms. Rosenthal emphasized that scientific claims need to be tested in light of all available evidence. Specifically, through the collection of additional data (i.e., trying to separate other liquids that they had combined), the students proved that Bradley's claim was not generalizable to all liquids, nor was some of the children's belief that "you can't separate liquids." Scientists would not classify an object as a solid or liquid based on whether or not you can separate them, but this is a reasonable observation for the children to make based on their experiences. Later in the exchange, when Bradley stated that "certain kinds of liquids don't mix together," Ms. Rosenthal saw another opportunity to help him make his claim more scientific. She assisted him in tying this more qualified observation to specific data. Rather than accepting Bradley's vague statement about "*certain* kinds of liquids," she led him to identify the actual liquids that he found did not mix together easily (i.e., oil and water).

In this case, Ms. Rosenthal effectively managed the curricular paradox between allowing a student to explain and appreciate his own ideas and connecting them to the discipline. Her questions about Bradley's ideas and her directives to him and the other students to investigate their materials offered a scientific lens for Bradley to explain (and perhaps better understand) his ideas. The teacher did not simply tell Bradley that his idea was incorrect; she engaged in disciplined improvisation to create a space for him to consider his ideas more thoroughly and scientifically. Although she did not know exactly where he was going with his thinking, she listened carefully to Bradley's ideas and used his thinking to lead her teaching. Her exchange with him also helped orient him toward the value of scientific discourse practices including careful observation, provision of evidential backing for claims, analysis of claims made from observations, and the use of precise language to make scientific claims.

## Case 2: Developing Lessons to Amplify Children's Emergent Disciplinary Insights

This case details how Ms. Rivera used disciplined improvisation to clarify the disciplinary content of one child's personal insight to help the whole class deepen their understanding of scientific concepts. In it, Ms. Rivera manages the tension between allowing children to explore their own thinking and helping them make their thinking more scientific by designing a science lesson that drew its inspiration directly from the child's contribution but explicitly highlighted the science in it. In this way, Ms. Rivera made the science in the child's original contribution more readily available to him and the class.

### Background

This case comes out of Ms. Rivera and Ms. Rosenthal's joint work on a long-term project focused on physical science, in particular the study of force and motion. The culmination of the project involved building a roller coaster that the children planned on using to send messages between their adjacent classrooms. In the context of the roller coaster design and construction, the students explored the concepts of kinetic and potential energy.

On the final day of the project, it was revealed that some students equated gaining and losing speed with gaining and losing energy. This is incorrect, because as a ball rolls up an incline and slows down, its kinetic energy is reduced yet it gains potential energy. This led the teachers to ask a class parent/physics professor who served as a consultant on the project for advice on how to talk with the children about these ideas. In response, he referred to the law of conservation of energy, which states that you never lose energy, but rather it is transformed from one form to the other. As he explained:

| 1 | Professor: | You're at the top of the hill and you're rolling down the road, right? As you roll off the hill, you lose your potential energy, but you... |
|---|---|---|
| 2 | Ms. Rivera: | Gained your kinetic energy. |
| 3 | Professor: | (simultaneously)...gained your kinetic energy. And this always – they never, you still have the same amount of energy – it's just in two different forms. |

Through this conversation, the teachers realized that although they had been talking with the students about different forms of energy, they had not explicitly discussed the notion of the *transformation* of energy, which may have contributed to the students' confusion. This realization served as the impetus for Ms. Rivera to revise her plans for class. What follows is an analysis of the day's science discussion and activity.

*Activity*

Immediately after the conversation with the professor, Ms. Rivera drew a diagram of a roller coaster on the board and asked a student to the front of the room to use his finger to act as a car moving along the roller coaster track. Guiding the student's finger along the diagram of the roller coaster, the students identified where potential and kinetic energy could be found along the track of the roller coaster. As they did so, the teacher highlighted the highest and lowest points on the roller coaster's track, indicating where there is maximum and minimum potential and kinetic energy. Following her lead, the children sang in chorus with her as she directed the students' attention to relevant points on the roller coaster diagram.

As the children transitioned from this discussion to another topic, Manuel offhandedly noted that what they had been talking about in terms of the transformation of energy on the roller coaster was "just like" when he and his classmates run on the grassy hill near the school. Manuel's brief observation was powerful in that it connected the abstract notions of kinetic and potential energy to his lived experience. His comment suggested that he was in the process of developing a more general understanding of these concepts by moving them from one context (roller coasters) to another (running on a hill). Though it was the end of the day and the final day of work on the project, Ms. Rivera heard the possibility in the student's observation for deepening the class's collective understanding of the transformation of energy. She re-voiced Manuel's observation to the class and suggested that they could all try to appreciate how running on the hill was "just like" a car's movement along a roller coaster by actually going to the hill to consider it for themselves. With this move, Ms. Rivera problematized the connection between the two different activities and gave the students the opportunity to investigate the similarities for themselves.

Upon arriving at the hill, Ms. Rivera improvised an activity that originated in Manuel's observation, but that linked it more closely to her curricular goal of helping students appreciate the law of the conservation of energy. To provide a disciplinary framework for the students' actions at the hill that could highlight the similarities between a car riding along a roller coaster track and a person running up and down a hill, Ms. Rivera asked the students to link the science concepts and formal academic language they were learning in class with their kinesthetic experience of running up and down the hill. Under her orchestration, the children ran up the hill shouting "potential energy" and at its top they shouted "maximum potential" to indicate the point of maximum potential energy. On their way down the hill, they shouted "kinetic energy" and at the bottom of the hill they shouted "maximum kinetic" to indicate the point of maximum kinetic energy. The children ran up and down the hill over and again joyfully expending their energy, labeling their physical experiences with scientific terms, and feeling the transformation of energy in their bodies.

## Summary

In this case, Ms. Rivera heard in a student's unanticipated observation an opportunity to make a strategic link between often disconnected kinds of scientific experiences in classrooms – linguistic and graphical representations with the kinesthetic embodiment of scientific concepts. By making this connection, she validated and clarified the child's insight by turning it into the basis for a more extensive science activity. We are not arguing, nor would Ms. Rivera, that through this activity the five- to seven-year-olds understood the law of conservation of energy, nor that they firmly grasped the concepts of potential or kinetic energy; rather, as is appropriate for young elementary school children, they were introduced to these concepts and to a way of thinking about science as both a way of knowing and inquiring.

Ms. Rivera's action was a form of disciplined improvisation in that her response to Manuel was created in the moment, but it was deeply informed by her views of scientific thinking and acting. In particular, she presented science as involving the use of specialized terms as well as the creative integration of language, graphical representations, and embodied action (Nemirovsky & Borba, 2004; Ochs, Gonzales, & Jacoby, 1996). Her lesson thus introduced the students to an authentic and developmentally appropriate method for gaining scientific insights: using one's body to understand and interrogate scientific concepts (Papert, 1980).

By turning a child's insight into an impromptu science lesson, Ms. Rivera managed the tension between hearing and exploring children's ideas and connecting them to science. The lesson drew its inspiration directly from the connection Manuel made between his personal experience and the science he was learning, but the lesson extended Manuel's connection in important ways. First, Ms. Rivera created an activity that allowed all the children the opportunity to make a personal connection between foundational ideas about physics and their embodied experience. Second, she made the science that was implicit in Manuel's observation more explicit by asking all of the students to name – and thus support reflection on – the component parts that make up their physical experience of running up and down the hill using scientific terminology. Using disciplined improvisation, Ms. Rivera was able to clarify and amplify one child's thinking in order to create greater opportunities for the whole class's science learning. Her improvised lesson enabled her to effectively manage the tension between allowing a child to articulate and appreciate his own thinking while also making its connection to science more clear.

## CONCLUSION

In improvisational teaching, both children and teachers are active contributors to the unfolding lesson. However, the way in which they participate is asymmetrical; children bring their ideas and questions to the interaction while teachers provide direction and guidance for the children's further investigations and activities. Managing the curricular paradox between allowing children the space to articulate and explore their own ideas and leading them into valued disciplinary practices is an essential challenge for constructivist teachers. Without guidance, children are unlikely to discover disciplinary concepts on their own. Yet without opportunities for developing their own ideas, children's thinking about the discipline is likely to be fragile or limited in scope. Disciplined improvisation is a valuable resource for managing this teaching paradox because it allows teachers to listen to children's ideas in order to refine and extend their disciplinary significance.

Based on our observations of Ms. Rivera's and Ms. Rosenthal's classrooms, improvisational teaching thrives when teachers create opportunities for children to make and share their observations, design activities that capitalize on children's insights, and then treat these contributions as ideas to think with rather than evaluate. As we showed in the two cases, the teachers listened to what their students were saying and used their ideas to develop productive paths for their disciplinary learning. Specifically, the teachers used disciplined improvisation to offer students disciplinary tools to refine their own thinking and to develop lessons that extended children's emergent disciplinary insights. Through these improvised interactions, children were able to participate in productive disciplinary learning that was well aligned with constructivist approaches to knowing and teaching.

The analysis we presented in this chapter underscores the need for an expanded conception of teacher expertise along the lines that Sawyer (Chapter 1) recommends. To teach disciplinary content effectively, teachers must be able to recognize the potential in students' ideas and build on these to further disciplinary ways of knowing. This is not an easy task, but by studying examples of effective disciplined improvisation, we can begin to identify a repertoire of practices that enable teachers to do so with creativity and skill.

REFERENCES

Borko, H. & Livingston, C. (1989). Cognition and improvisation: Differences in mathematics instruction by expert and novice teachers. *American Educational Research Journal, 26*(4), 473–498.

Duschl, R. A., Schweingruber, H. A., & Shouse, A. W. (Eds.) (2007). *Taking science to school: Learning and teaching science in grades K–8.* Washington, DC: National Academies Press.

Edwards, C., Gandini, L., & Forman, G. (Eds.) (1993). *The hundred languages of children: The Reggio Emilia approach to early childhood education.* Norwood, NJ: Ablex.

Engle, R. A. & Conant, F. C. (2002). Guiding principles for fostering productive disciplinary engagement: Explaining an emergent argument in a community of learners classroom. *Cognition and Instruction, 20*(4), 399–483.

Erickson, F. (1982). Classroom discourse as improvisation: Relationships between academic task structure and social participation structure in lessons. In L. C. Wilkinson (Ed.), *Communicating in the classroom* (pp. 153–181). New York: Academic Press.

Forman, E. A. & Sink, W. (2006). Sociocultural approaches to learning science in classrooms. Commissioned paper for the National Academies Committee, "Science Learning Study, K-8."

Gallas, K. (1995). *Talking their way into science: Hearing children's questions and theories, responding with curricula.* New York: Teachers College.

Hicks, D. (1995/1996). Discourse, learning, and teaching. *Review of Research in Education, 21,* 49–95.

Lampert, M., Rittenhouse, P., & Grumbaugh, C. (1996). Agreeing to disagree: Developing sociable mathematical discourse. In D. R. Olson & N. Torrance (Eds.), *The handbook of education and human development: New models of learning, teaching, and schooling* (pp. 731–764). Cambridge, MA: Blackwell.

Latour, B. (1987). *Science in action: How to follow scientists and engineers through society.* Cambridge, MA: Harvard University.

Lemke, J. L. (1990). *Talking science: Language, learning, and values.* Norwood, NJ: Ablex.

Mayer, R. (2004). Should there be a three-strikes rule against pure discovery learning? The case for guided methods of instruction. *American Psychologist, 59*(1), 14–19.

Michaels, S., Shouse, A., & Schweingruber, H. (2007). *Ready, set, science!: Putting research to work in K-8 science classrooms.* Washington, DC: National Academy Press.

National Research Council. (1996). *National science education standards.* Washington, DC: National Academy Press.

National Research Council. (2000). *Inquiry and the National Science Education Standards.* Washington, DC: National Academy Press.

Nemirovsky, R. & Borba, M., (Eds.) (2004). *Body activity and imagination in mathematics learning.* Dordrecht: Kluwer [Special issue of Educational Studies in Mathematics].

Ochs, E., Gonzales, P., Jacoby, S. (1996). "When I come down I'm in the domain state": Grammar and graphic representation in the interpretive activity of physicists. In E. Ochs, E. A. Schegloff, S. Thompson (Eds.), *Interaction and Grammar* (pp. 328–369). Cambridge: Cambridge University Press.

Papert, S. (1980). *Mindstorms: Children, computers, and powerful ideas.* New York: Basic Books.

Sawyer, R. K. (2004). Creative teaching: Collaborative discussion as disciplined improvisation. *Educational Researcher, 33*(2), 12–20.

Schultz, K. (2003). *Listening: A framework for teaching across differences.* New York: Teachers College Press.

# 12

# Improvisational Understanding in the Mathematics Classroom

## LYNDON C. MARTIN AND JO TOWERS

In many mathematics classrooms, students learn largely by memorization; they memorize procedures, such as how to multiply two fractions, and they are then assessed by being presented with similar problems, which they can solve if they have memorized the procedure. The problem with this approach is that all too often, students fail to acquire any deeper understanding of mathematical ideas and concepts – for example, what does a fraction represent? How is it similar to a decimal, a ratio, or a percentage? What does it *mean* to multiply two fractions? Almost all experts in mathematics education agree that understanding mathematical ideas and concepts is a critical and desirable component of the mathematics classroom, yet teachers continue to struggle with meaningful ways to teach for mathematical understanding. Almost all teachers agree that understanding involves more than procedural knowledge and that it includes the ability to reason with and to make sense of what is learned, but the translation of this into concrete teaching strategies that can be implemented in the classroom remains a challenge.

In the last two decades, teacher education programs have emphasized constructivist and collaborative methods of teaching, fueled by learning sciences research that has demonstrated that these result in deeper understanding and better retention (Darling-Hammond & Bransford, 2005). These efforts have been particularly strong in mathematics education; in the United States, for example, the National Council of Teachers of Mathematics has been a strong advocate of these research-based methods (e.g., NCTM, 2000). Yet in spite of these efforts, traditional modes of teaching, which emphasize prediction, measurement, and control in the

In R. K. Sawyer (Ed.) (2011). *Structure and improvisation in creative teaching* (pp. 252–278). Cambridge: Cambridge University Press.

classroom, still dominate K-12 education in North America. In the area of mathematics instruction, research conducted in the United States by Jacobs, Hiebert, Givvin, Hollingsworth, Garnier, and Wearne (2006) and others (e.g., Hiebert & Stigler, 2000) has shown that current teaching approaches are more like the kind of traditional teaching reported for most of the past century (Cuban, 1993) than reflective of the research-based teaching methods being advocated by schools of education and by national organizations like the NCTM. This is especially true when the current context of educational policy imperatives for efficiency, standardization, and accountability – particularly involving "high stakes" testing – exist as a powerful alternative vision of school reform in many countries (e.g., No Child Left Behind Assessments in the United States; Statutory Assessment Tests in the United Kingdom; Education Quality and Accountability Office Assessments in Ontario, Canada; National Center Test for University Admissions in Japan).

Teachers, then, must navigate a teaching paradox: the tension between calls for teaching that aim to press efficiently toward individual student competence as measured by tightly defined, standardized assessments, and calls for teaching that occasion deep and powerful understandings of mathematical concepts – the kind of classrooms in which students have opportunities to construct their own knowledge through a creative process of inquiry. In the introduction to this book, Sawyer refers to this as the *curriculum paradox* – the need for teachers to conform to administrative structures while providing the student with room for the creative action required for learning. One of the reasons that teachers experience this as a tension is because different kinds of teacher expertise are called on in order for a teacher to be recognized as competent in these two alternative visions, and often these forms of expertise are in conflict with one another.

Building on the research summarized in Sawyer's introduction, we agree that teacher expertise involves both the possession of a body of knowledge and the capacity to apply this body of knowledge in practice, in a creative and responsive way as the situation demands. For example, mathematics-teaching expertise involves being able to recognize and respond to the kinds of mathematical understandings learners are building. As Matusov (1998) notes, "skillful mastery of joint activity cannot be dissected and reduced to the individual situation-free skills of its participants because, in a joint activity, the participants often become contextual motivators and dynamic environment for each other's actions" (p. 332). This kind of "skillful mastery," which we think of as improvisational practice, may be invisible if what the observer is looking for is clear objectives communicated to learners, good

time management, regular formal assessments, and specific learning outcomes for each lesson – more scripted and structured practices that are
often mandated at the national level (e.g., Department for Children, Family
and Schools, 2006; No Child Left Behind Act, 2001).

In spite of these pressures, and even though most teachers continue
to teach in a traditional fashion, an increasing number of teachers are
responding to the research findings, moving beyond traditional forms
of teaching and developing the kind of expertise we describe earlier. As
Hiebert, Carpenter, Fennema et al. (1997) note, "most teachers would say
that they want their students to understand mathematics, and in fact, that
they teach for understanding" (p. 3). Unfortunately, however, the research
literature presents many versions of classroom practice under the guise of
"constructivist teaching" or "collaborative learning," and it is not always
clear precisely which aspects of practice facilitate *understanding* in these
classrooms. We believe that the improvisation metaphor can help us clarify
which practices lead to mathematical understanding. In this chapter, we
explore the teaching paradox by seeking to identify more precisely the kind
of classroom practices and teacher actions that can encourage the growth
of collective mathematical understanding and that therefore illuminate the
kind of teacher expertise we value. In order to render visible, and to understand, these practices, we invoke the lens of improvisation as we explore the
phenomenon of collective mathematical understanding.

## MATHEMATICAL UNDERSTANDING AS AN
## IMPROVISATIONAL PROCESS

In our research, we are interested in the kinds of shared or collective mathematical actions we may see when a group of learners, of any size, work together
on a piece of mathematics. We see mathematical understanding not as a static
state to be achieved, but as a dynamical process, emerging through responsive collaboration, interaction, and purposeful discussion between learners
as well as between learners and teachers. This shared, collective process we
characterize as being improvisational in nature and form. This characteriza-
tion offers both a means to describe growing understanding and a powerful
way to think about potential teaching strategies for encouraging it.

Improvisation is broadly defined as a process "of spontaneous action,
interaction and communication" (Gordon-Calvert, 2001, p. 87). It is a
collaborative practice of acting, interacting, and reacting, of making and
creating, in the moment, and in response to the stimulus of one's context and
environment. Ruhleder and Stoltzfus (2000), in talking of the improvisational

process, draw attention to "people's ability to integrate multiple, spontaneously unfolding contributions into a coherent whole" suggesting that many of our everyday actions are improvisational in nature (p. 186). In some sense, all human action is improvisational (Erickson, 2004; Sawyer, 2001). Pressing (1984) writes that:

> To the extent that we are unpredictable, we improvise. Everything else is repeating ourselves or following orders. Improvisation is thus central to the formation of new ideas in all areas of human endeavour. Its importance experientially rests with its magical and self-liberating qualities. Its importance scientifically is that it presents us with the clearest, least-edited version of how we think, encoded in behavior. (p. 345)

We suggest that by using the lens of improvisation, it is possible to observe and account for acts of mathematical understanding that are not simply located in the minds or actions of any one individual, but instead that emerge from the *interplay* of the ideas of individuals, as these become woven together in shared action, as in an improvisational performance. Our perspective on the growth of collective mathematical understanding is compatible with Stahl's (2006) view: "A group meaning is constructed by the interactions of the individual members, not by the individuals on their own. It is an emergent property of the discourse and interaction. It is not necessarily reducible to opinions or understandings of individuals" (p. 349). We thus see the growth of collective mathematical understanding as a dynamical, creative, ever-changing interactive process where shared understandings exist and emerge in the discourse of a group working together. We use the word "shared" not to suggest that understandings "happen to overlap and their intersection is shared" nor that "some individuals communicate what they already knew to the others," but rather to indicate that understandings emerge and are "interactively achieved in discourse and may not be attributable as originating from any particular individual" (Stahl, 2006, p. 349; see also Matusov, 1998; Sawyer, 1997b).

Scholars who study improvisation in jazz and in theatre have argued that these same characteristics are essential and defining features of improvisation. Berliner (1997) claims that "the study of one musician's creative process cannot capture the essence of jazz, because more than any other performance genre, a jazz performance is a collective, emergent phenomenon" (p. 10). He also offers a metaphor for group improvisation as being like a conversation in which jazz is the language, and, as with any conversation, demands "finely honed skills of listening" (p. 37). Sawyer (2000), in considering acts of collaborative emergence in improv theatre, suggests that "in an ensemble improvisation, we can't identify the creativity of the performance with any single performer; the performance is collaboratively created," and that although each individual is contributing something creative, these contributions only make sense "in terms of the way they are heard, absorbed, and elaborated on by the other musicians" (p. 182). The performance is something that emerges from the actions of all the players, and does not exist prior to its start (and indeed, does not exist once it is finished – there is no product of an improvisational performance).

We contend that the same can be true of a group of individuals working together mathematically, and that through this working there can be observed a mathematical performance that is both emergent and creative and exists only in the moment as the group members collaborate. In the following, we identify three main elements of improvisational actions as being observable in (and vital for) the growth of mathematical understanding: the presence of multiple potential pathways, the emergence of collectively created structures, and the interactional norms that guide the improvisation. After describing these three characteristics, we provide several examples of how a teacher of mathematics might enact these in the classroom. The ideas we are advancing here are based on data from many observational studies of mathematical understanding we have conducted over a number of years and are informed by theories we have developed to help us explain those data. (See Kieren, 2001, p. 225 for a discussion of our collective "research-in-process").

## Potential Pathways

Sawyer (2001), in theorizing on the nature of improvised theatre and verbal performance, offers a number of key features of collective emergence. Of particular importance is the notion of "potential," of the unpredictability of pathways of actions that a group may follow in the performance. Although an improvisational theatrical performance may appear to be something that is planned and tightly scripted (partly due to the natural appearance of the emerging dialogue), it is actually the case that at any point in the performance, there are many different paths the performance might follow. As Sawyer (2001) notes, "an improvisational transcript indicates many plausible, dramatically coherent utterances that the actors could have performed at each turn. A combinatorial explosion quickly results in hundreds of potential performances" (p. 183). At the start of any scene, the potential is unlimited; it is here that the widest range of choices are open to the actors, and "the determination of who will begin the scene is itself emergent from the split-second decisions of all actors" (p. 183).

## Collective Structure and Striking a Groove

Of course, it is the actions of those participating in the improvisation that determine both the nature of the potential that is created and also how the potential is then developed into a coherent performance. For there to exist the opportunity for a range of possible pathways, it is vital that each participant follows what Sawyer (2001) calls the "Second Rule of Improv: Don't Write the Script in Your Head" (p. 17). This rule refers to the importance of participants being willing to allow the structure and script to develop from collective actions, and not to anticipate, plan, and guess what the responses of the other participants might be as the improvisation develops. Sawyer (2003) comments that a desire to anticipate "also prevents the beginner from listening closely to the partner's response and responding to it" (p. 56). The notion of listening as a means for occasioning collective action is one discussed extensively by Davis (1996) who talks of responsive, attentive listening as "hermeneutic," being evident in "the negotiated and participatory manner" of the interactions observed (p. 113). Clearly, such a form of listening is also necessary and compatible with the one required to generate "potential" within an improvisational framework, and indeed we would suggest that hermeneutic listening can be usefully characterized as improvisational.

In contrast to, though also as a consequence of, the potential initially created in an improvisation, Sawyer (2000) suggests that, quite early in a scene, a "collectively created structure" will emerge, which "now constrains the actors for the rest of the scene" (p. 183). To remain coherent, subsequent actions must fit with this structure, yet of course will still add to it. Thus we have a complex interplay between individual actions and the collective structure as these co-emerge together. Berliner (1994, 1997), in talking about improvisational jazz, refers to the development of this collective structure as "striking a groove." More specifically, and in the musical context, striking a groove involves "the negotiation of a shared sense of the beat," and is a subtle and fundamental process to allow the performance to develop to its fullest.

The "groove" is the underlying element of the structure that allows the improvisation to proceed in a coherent and productive way, and it is the responsibility of all the players to collectively maintain the groove. This involves avoiding major changes in tempo while still allowing subtle fluctuations in response to the developing structural features of the piece. Sawyer (2003) also describes the process of the emergence of a collaborative structure in terms of the more general phenomenon of "interactional synchrony." Drawing on the work of Condon and Ogston (1971), interactional synchrony refers to the coordination of the rhythm and timing in the behavior of two or more people, and thus the resulting improvisational activity can only be "conceived of as a jointly accomplished co-actional process" (Sawyer, 2003, p. 38). He further develops the notion to talk of "group flow," where "everything seems to come naturally" (p. 44). Of course, this is not to suggest that interactional synchrony or group flow always occurs in any group collaboration; indeed, Berliner (1994) talks of it in terms of "magical moments" (p. 388), suggesting that group flow can be both momentary and transitory. However, Berliner also notes that "the highest points of improvisation occur when group members strike a groove together" (p. 388), speaking to the importance and power of such instances of collective emergent activity, moments that cannot be attributed to the contribution of any one individual.

## Etiquette and the Group Mind

A number of conventions govern the ways in which an improvisational performance develops and group flow emerges (Becker, 2000; Berliner, 1994; Sawyer, 2003). Becker (2000) calls these conventions the "etiquette" of improvisation; they include, for example, the requirement that everyone pay attention to the other players and be willing to alter what they are doing "in response to tiny cues that suggest a new direction that might be interesting to take" (p. 172). Becker (2000) notes the subtlety of the etiquette operating here, as every performer understands

> that at every moment everyone (or almost everyone) involved in the improvisation is offering suggestions as to what might be done next. As people listen closely to one another, some of those suggestions begin to converge and others, less congruent with the developing direction, fall by the wayside. The players thus develop a collective direction that characteristically ... feels larger than any of them, as though it had a life of its own. (p. 172)

The importance of "listening to the group mind" is one described by Sawyer (2001) as "The Third Rule of Improv" and again refers to the vital role of listening in improvisation. Sawyer (2001) comments that people who have never improvised "watch the soloist and ignore the rest of the band; they don't realize how much conversation goes on between the musicians. The ability to listen is the hardest skill for a musician to learn, and I can always tell which jazz musicians are novices, because they play without listening.

The unique, defining feature of jazz improvisation is the importance of group interaction" (p. 19).

One implication of "listening to the group mind" is that when one person does something that is obviously better (in the view of the group) then "everyone else drops their own ideas and immediately joins in working on that better idea" (Becker, 2000, p. 175). Of course this requires some understanding of what "better" might look like and of how to recognize it. Interestingly, Becker also suggests that in collaborative improvisations, as people follow and build on the leads of others, they "may also collectively change their notion of what is good as the work progresses," (p. 175) leading to a creative production or performance that could not have been predicted prior to the activity.

## EXAMPLES OF MATHEMATICAL UNDERSTANDING AS IMPROVISATION

Here, we illustrate our thinking through considering some extracts of our video data. The first extract features elementary school children from Canada; the second, high school pupils from England. We deliberately present both extracts in their entirety, and have refrained from the usual practice of breaking the transcript and of commenting on or annotating smaller pieces of it. This is consistent with our claim that the episodes can be seen and understood as emergent, improvisational performances, which are best "listened to" in their entirety.

In both extracts, the groups of students do not "solve" the problem that was presented to them. In fact, the first group generates an incorrect answer (though they do later generate a correct solution). However, our focus here is not the correctness of their mathematics, but is rather the improvisational character of their mathematical actions and co-actions, and how this is contributing to a growing understanding of the concept, albeit one that will require more work. This is consistent with our claim that mathematical understanding is best conceived of as an emergent process rather than as a state to be achieved.

### Extract 1

The first data extract we offer features three Canadian Grade Six students starting work on a problem in an interview setting with the second author. The students have been presented with the problem of calculating the area of a parallelogram, a figure with which they have not worked before. Prior to this task-based interview, the students had worked on developing strategies for calculating the area of squares, rectangles, and triangles, but not parallelograms. The interview was conducted in the last week of the school year. The three students had been selected by their teacher as "high-ability" students who had not worked together in class during the school year. The teacher had recommended them because he was interested to see what they might be able to accomplish when challenged with new mathematics. (Note, in our transcripts we use ... to indicate a momentary pause in speech).

| | | |
|---|---|---|
| 1 | Interviewer: | Okay. So what I have here is a little bit of a different shape for you. (She passes over a piece of paper on which is drawn a parallelogram with no dimensions provided) |
| 2 | Natalie: | Parallelogram, I think? |
| 3 | Interviewer: | Mmmmm! It's a parallelogram. Well done. I wonder if you could figure out for me how to find out the area of that parallelogram. I have rulers here if you need a ruler. |
| 4 | Natalie: | Can try it ... measure ... sides. (She begins to measure one of the shorter sides). |
| 5 | Stanley: | Ten. |
| 6 | Natalie: | Mm hm. And that's ten right? (She points to the opposite side). They're both ten. And then the top one is longer, and that is ... |
| 7 | Thomas: | ... it's eighteen. |
| 8 | Natalie: | Yep. So that's ten ... and eighteen. (She writes the numbers on the sides). Ok, so we could ... |
| 9 | Thomas: | ... multiply ... |
| 10 | Natalie: | ... the area, yeah ten by eighteen ... and then see what we get. |
| 11 | Thomas: | It would be this ... |
| 12 | Natalie: | yep (pause) and then if we wanted to do ... so that would be the area then? |
| 13 | Stanley: | But look at the shape. |
| 14 | Natalie: | I know that's what I'm saying that can't be right cause that – that's a little bit ... |
| 15 | Stanley: | Okay. Wait, I know .... draw a straight line, here and here, you get triangles, and squares. (He adds lines to the parallelogram, see Figure 12.1) |
| 16 | Thomas: | Oh I know ... |
| 17 | Stanley: | Now these triangles ... I think ... |
| 18 | Thomas: | is half? |
| 19 | Natalie | These triangles will make up that square though. So then if we just measure that .... |
| 20 | Stanley: | and times by two. |

| 21 | Natalie: | Yeah. Because these two, these triangles make that square, right? (They have concluded (wrongly) that the two outer right-angled triangles are equivalent in area to the inner rectangle). |
|---|---|---|
| 22 | Thomas: | That'll work. |
| 23 | Stanley: | I think … |
| 24 | Natalie: | So if we … what is … this it's still, it's not eighteen though, anymore. Because we're cutting it … it will be twelve. (*She measures the sides of the rectangle that has been created*). |
| 25 | Thomas: | and then ten |
| 26 | Natalie: | and this side is … no it wouldn't be ten. (She is referring to the width of the rectangle, i.e., the perpendicular height of the parallelogram). |
| 27 | Thomas: | Like, eight? |
| 28 | Natalie: | this side is eight, yep. So … |
| 29 | Stanley: | and then 12 times 8 … is … |
| 30 | Thomas: | … is … ninety … |
| 31 | Stanley: | Yeah, ninety-six. (This is the area of the inner rectangle). |
| 32 | Thomas: | … six |
| 33 | Natalie: | So ninety-six times … |
| 34 | Stanley: | So ninety-six times two, so uh ninety-s …. |
| 35 | Thomas: | a hundred … I mean no, not a hundred … yeah a hundred – eighty-uh … three? |
| 36 | Stanley: | *ninety-* three … |
| 37 | Natalie: | ninety-six. One ninety-six. |
| 38 | Stanley: | Okay. |
| 39 | Natalie: | How does that work? Two times six is twelve. One ninety … two. |
| 40 | Thomas: | So it's one ninety-two. |
| 41 | Stanley: | Yeah, one ninety-two … |
| 42 | Natalie: | … is the area of that. So it's the area of the whole … |

In this extract, the students are engaged in developing a collective understanding of how to measure the area of a parallelogram, and although this is emerging from the contributions of individuals, we see a single understanding emerging – that to find the area of a parallelogram, one doubles the area of its internal rectangle. Although these students are working in an interview scenario, they pay little attention to the presence of the interviewer. Instead they focus on solving the problem posed. The devotion to the problem they display is striking; the students were so engrossed in the collective problem solving that they failed to notice the bell ringing to signal the end of the session, despite this being the last day of the school year.

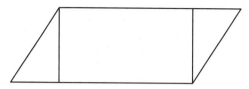

FIGURE 12.1. The annotated parallelogram.

Extract 2

The second extract features two students (Rachel and Kerry) from a Year Ten (equivalent to North American Grade Nine) middle-ability class in a British school. This session consisted of a single ninety-minute classroom lesson that had as its focus the finding of the area of any segment of any circle. The lesson was planned to be a problem-solving session. The students were introduced to the problem by the teacher asking the whole group to imagine a cake, drawn as a circle on the board, and then to think about finding the surface area of the "top" of any size of slice (sector) of the cake (see Figure 12.2).

The teacher did not specify a particular size of sector or size of circle, and the question as set was to be able to work out the area of any sized slice of cake. Rachel and Kerry collaborated to solve this initial problem by choosing as their "slice" a quarter of a circle of radius six units. Later in the lesson, the teacher gathered the class together again and moved the investigation one step further, asking the students to find the area of the segment of the circle (i.e., the area of the remaining part of the sector if the triangular shaded part is removed [see Figure 12.3]). A likely way to proceed here would be to find the area of the triangle – using trigonometry – and then subtract this from the previously calculated area of the sector. The answer would be the area of the segment of the circle. Kerry and Rachel return to their initial example of a quarter of the circle and develop a method for finding the segment, which involves calculating half of the area of a square of side 6 (the radius of their circle) and subtracting this from the area of the sector (see Figure 12.4).

Again, they have a method that is specific to a particular sector of the circle, and their method is problematized by the teacher when she next visits their table. Rachel and Kerry now begin to expand their method, first trying another specific example (a sector angle of thirty degrees). They solve this problem by recognizing that thirty degrees is a third of ninety degrees and assuming that they can therefore divide their previous answer (for a quarter of a circle) by three. This is incorrect, because the

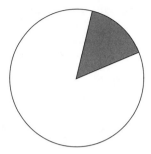

FIGURE 12.2. The "cake," showing the sector.

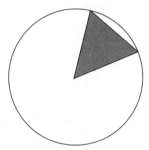

FIGURE 12.3. The "cake," showing the sector and segment.

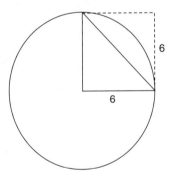

FIGURE 12.4. The circle with the drawn square.

area of the segment of a thirty-degree sector is not equal to that produced by calculating one-third of the area of a segment of a ninety-degree sector. Though they believe their method is correct, they are troubled by its specificity and call the teacher over to explain that they have a method that works for thirty degrees because it is a "fraction" of ninety degrees, but that it would not work for "something like twenty-two [degrees]" (see Figure 12.5).

| | | |
|---|---|---|
| 43 | Kerry: | We just keep referring to this (*the right angle*) and saying like divide that by three and |
| 44 | Rachel: | No but that won't work if you've got something like twenty-two |
| 45 | Kerry: | No that won't work if you've got something like twenty-two. So we don't know! |
| 46 | Teacher: | Ah. So you could do that because it was |
| 47 | Kerry: | Because we know the right angle |
| 48 | Teacher: | a fraction of this |
| 49 | Kerry: | Yeah, but if it was say eighteen or something we wouldn't know. |
| 50 | Teacher: | OK. Tell me what you think you are doing here to find that shape (*the segment for the sector angle of thirty degrees*). What are you really doing? |
| 51 | Student off camera: | We're trying to find out the area of the triangle. |
| 52 | Teacher: | Right. |
| 53 | Kerry: | That's what we've been trying to do but we can't do it. |
| 54 | Teacher: | Alright. What do you ... Pop out that triangle (*for the sector angle of thirty degrees*) and draw it for me there. And write on everything you know about that triangle. |
| 55 | Kerry: | (*drawing*) ... it's six. That's six centimeters ... It's thirty degree angle is thirty and that's six ... |
| 56 | Teacher: | Good. So we know quite a bit about the triangle. How can we find the area of a triangle? What of those pieces of information do we know? Do we know the base? (*She points to the triangle the students have drawn and of which they are trying to find the area; see* Figure 12.5). |
| 57 | Rachel: | Yep ... |
| 58 | Kerry: | No ... |
| 59 | Rachel: | Yes ... six |
| 60 | Kerry: | No, it's not six ... |
| 61 | Rachel: | Why's it not six? |
| 62 | Kerry: | Because the radius is six, that's coming across there. |
| 63 | Rachel: | But surely if you take it from the middle point to wherever it's going to still be six? |
| 64 | Teacher: | It depends what you call the base, doesn't it? If you want to call this, this the base then no you don't know it (*indicating the side drawn horizontally on Figure 12.5*) |
| 65 | Rachel: | No, well I'm calling either of these lines the base ... |
| 66 | Teacher: | You're calling that the base ... |
| 67 | Rachel: | In which case it would be six ... |

| 68 | Teacher: | So supposing you do know the base is six. |
| 69 | Rachel: | Six. |
| 70 | Teacher: | Now we've got to find the height, now it's not just the height is it? It's the? |
| 71 | Rachel: | So would we use something like trigonometry, as in with the angle, and so if this (*the angle between one of the radii and the chord*) was a right angle it would be ... |
| 72 | Teacher: | Ah, but it isn't. |
| 73 | Kerry: | It's not a right angle (referring to the angle between one of the radii and the chord). |
| 74 | Rachel: | Oh, it's not a right angle is it? |
| 75 | Kerry: | So we can't use ... (*pause*) |
| 76 | Teacher: | Let's assume that this is the base (*the chord*). |
| 77 | Rachel: | (*excitedly*) Oh, would you chop it in half? |
| 78 | Teacher: | (smiles) |
| 79 | Rachel: | Hey hey! |
| 80 | Teacher: | Now we've done something like that very recently haven't we? |
| 81 | Kerry: | In the test. |
| 82 | Rachel: | Yeah, we got something like it in our test. |
| 83 | Teacher: | Well, in the test ... and we did two questions like that in the homework. |
| 84 | Rachel: | Did we? (Starts looking in her exercise book) |
| 85 | Kerry: | Oh yeah we did. |
| 86 | Rachel: | Oh there, yeah. (Pointing to her exercise book). |
| 87 | Kerry: | There. |
| 88 | Teacher: | OK? (Starts to move away) |
| 89 | Kerry: | Yeah. Where you have to do inverse. |
| 90 | Rachel: | Oh yeah. ... so it has to be a (Rachel has labeled half of the chord 'a'; see Figure 12.6) equals six times tan fifteen isn't it? (Rachel, as the video later shows, is incorrectly assuming that the perpendicular bisector of the triangle has a length of six units) |
| 91 | Kerry: | I don't know ... |
| 92 | Rachel: | We better remind ourselves ... Look, see how we did it here? (*Turning back in her exercise book*). |
| 93 | Kerry: | 'Scusez moi, how *you* did it there! |
| 94 | Rachel: | Oh no ... |
| 95 | Kerry: | It's not, look ... |
| 96 | Rachel: | But that's different because we had to find the angle. |
| 97 | Kerry: | But this one, oh we had to find the angle on all of them, didn't we? |
| 98 | Rachel: | Look here's one, we had to divide it in half here ... |

*(continued)*

| 99  | Kerry:    | So it's tan fifteen equals ... |
| 100 | Rachel:   | Look, there you are, would we? Miss? (*works in book*) Would we do it like that? Because it's up there, would we do six times tan fifteen? |
| 101 | Teacher:  | So you half the angle? |
| 102 | Kerry:    | Which is fifteen ... |
| 103 | Teacher:  | So tan of fifteen ... Why is that six? (Referring to the perpendicular bisector of the triangle) |
| 104 | Kerry:    | It's not. |
| 105 | Teacher:  | It's not ... |
| 106 | Kerry:    | We don't know what it is. |
| 107 | Rachel:   | Oh ... (*pause*). |
| 108 | Teacher:  | It's this that's six, isn't it? The radii are six. |
| 109 | Rachel:   | Hmmm, so it'll be hypotenuse, oh dear (*unsure*) |
| 110 | Kerry:    | So it's not tan it's sine ... |

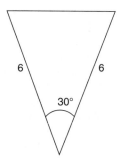

FIGURE 12.5. The labeled triangle.

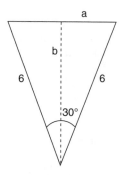

FIGURE 12.6. The annotated triangle.

In this extract, we see the group developing a collective understanding of how to calculate the area of a segment of a circle – by conceiving of it as a triangle removed from the sector of the circle. As with the group in the first extract, the students are focused, as we can see from their clear motivation (and indeed frustration). There is a sense of commitment to the problem and to wanting to understand the solution, rather than merely being able to produce an answer and move on. Although the students seek help from the teacher at times, they never merely ask for the answer, but instead look for a suggestion that might help them continue working together.

### ANALYZING MATHEMATICAL IMPROVISING

There are many interesting aspects to these two transcripts, and to the ways in which the students work collectively together. We wish to draw attention particularly to the interactional synchrony developed by both groups of students. Especially in the first extract, the discourse appears as though one person (rather than three) is speaking. The students complete one another's sentences – but, more than that, they seem to be speaking with one voice. Indeed, it is almost as though you could remove the names of the speakers in the transcript and read it as a monologue. Although not as marked, this is also true of the second group. When the actions and mathematical thinking seem to flow effortlessly from the group in this way, there is a sense of interactional synchrony being achieved and of the group of learners mathematically "striking a groove."

In these interactions, it is extremely difficult to discern how any one individual student's mathematical understanding is changing. Both groups of students, through carefully listening to each other, achieve moments of mathematical synchrony, where the emerging understanding is truly collective, and the contributions of each individual build on those of the others and facilitate a continued flow of appropriate mathematical actions. This claim echoes Sawyer's (2000) suggestion that "in an ensemble improvisation, we can't identify the creativity of the performance with any single performer; the performance is collaboratively created," and that although each individual is contributing something creative, these contributions only make sense "in terms of the way they are heard, absorbed, and elaborated on by the other musicians" (p. 182). When watching the videotapes, it is clear that the students genuinely listen to each other, and, more crucially, to the mathematical ideas proposed by their partners (whether those ideas are verbalized or represented in gesture or written form), and these *improvisational coactions* (Martin & Towers, 2009; Martin, Towers, & Pirie, 2006) allow the understanding to collectively flow and grow. As Becker (2000) noted of jazz performers "the improvisers are trying to solve a problem or perform a feat for its own sake or their own sake, because it is there to do and they have agreed to devote themselves collectively to doing it" (p. 174), something we suggest is true of both groups of students here. There is a powerful sense of collective purpose throughout both whole sessions (this comes through even more clearly when listening to the tapes) with the priority always being meaningful and useful engagement with the mathematics.

We now turn our attention to the three specific ideas, drawn from the improvisational metaphor, which, we suggested earlier, are key to this growth of collective mathematical understanding.

### The Potential for Many Pathways

In the first extract, when challenged to find the area of a parallelogram, the students began by proposing a variety of ideas for how to find the area. We see the students listening to each other's suggestions; no one idea is immediately collectively taken up, nor discarded. There is the potential for many different, equally appropriate actions to occur. At this stage there is no way to predict how the interaction will unfold, nor even what solutions will emerge from the co-actions of the group. Natalie takes the lead in measuring all the sides of the figure (line 4). Stanley and Thomas follow along. Thomas suggests multiplying as a strategy (line 9), which is briefly picked up by Natalie, who suggests dimensions to be multiplied (line 10), but no one seems satisfied that this will produce an appropriate solution. Suddenly, when Stanley adds two lines to the diagram (see Figure 12.1) saying "draw a straight line here and here, you get triangles and squares" (line 15), the energy of the group lifts; they collectively appear to recognize the potential of the strategy.

Similarly, the second episode is characterized by a sense of uncertainty rather than a simple progression from problem to solution. The students do not initially know how to find the area of the triangle; indeed, just prior to the extract offered here, the students had a way to find the area that did not involve the area of a triangle as such, but instead was simply some fraction of a square. Having been forced to discard this idea (as they realized it would not work for numbers that do not evenly divide 360, such as 22 degrees), they are now casting around to find some new approach that will let them move forward. The intervention of the teacher (line 50) helps the group to focus on the triangle, and there follows a period where the students try to determine firstly what is the base of the triangle (line 59–76), and then how to find its area. Similarly, later in the extract, they are not instantly sure of which trigonometric ratio to use, or of how to use it. They collectively search for previous examples that they can build on in the new context (line 92 onward).

Sawyer (2000) notes that "an improvisational transcript indicates many plausible, dramatically coherent utterances that the actors could have performed at each turn. A combinatorial explosion quickly results in hundreds of potential performances" (p. 183). We believe this to be true of the two examples presented here: Choosing to pursue any of the alternative ideas that are offered in the early stages of working would have led to the emergence of very different mathematical ideas.

## The Emergence of a Collective Structure

In both cases, we see a collectively created structure, a shared mathematical understanding, starting to emerge that "now constrains the actors for the rest of the scene" (Sawyer, 2000, p. 183). In the first extract, this can be seen from line 15 onward as the students decide to work with Stanley's idea. In the second extract, it takes a little longer as the group "plays" with the triangle – establishing what is the base, the height, and so on. However, once trigonometry has been determined as the way forward (line 71), the group then works only with this idea. At this point, the problem is not even one involving a circle in any way, but one of finding the height of a triangle. Of course we are not saying the collective structure instantly exists at these points in the episodes, but that the subsequent workings of the group are consistent with developing this idea into more than a potential understanding, and the groups do not introduce any new mathematical pathways after these points.

As suggested earlier, to remain coherent and to allow the improvisation to develop, subsequent actions must fit with and extend this emergent structure. In terms of the collective growth of understanding for these two groups, it would not likely be helpful for one student to suddenly argue for an alternate way of working (even if it were a correct one). To do so would run the risk of blocking the collective mathematical understanding now emerging within both groups, by shifting the focus back to one individual and their ideas rather than those of the "collective mind." Of course, there may be a point when an individual needs to be a catalyst for radically changing the approach of the group; but this would be most effective when a collective need arises and the group collectively realizes it is stuck. This has particular implications for the possible role of a teacher in maintaining improvisational flow; there is a fine balancing act between offering a possible way forward and simply telling the answer. When a collective structure is in place and working, if an individual – whether a teacher or a student – disturbs the synchronous flow of collective mathematical action, it is likely to inhibit rather than to facilitate the continued growth of mathematical understanding of the group.

### The Etiquette of Emerging Understanding

In our examples, there is a high level of attentiveness between the students in each group; they listen to each other and to the mathematics as it emerges from their engagement, an attunement that Becker refers to as improvisational etiquette. Becker (2000) comments that unless the performers listen carefully, and where necessary "defer" to the collective mind, the music will "clunk along" with each individual doing nothing more than playing their own "tired clichés" (p. 173). In both extracts, we see a deferring to a group mind, which allows a collective image to emerge; this includes a willingness to abandon personal motivations. For example, in the case of the second group, although Kerry seems initially unsure about where Rachel wants to take them (line 95), she is willing to go along with what seems to be an appropriate possibility, and to work with what the group feels is most useful at that moment. Becker (2000) noted that in jazz improvisation, everyone pays attention to the other players and is willing to alter what they are doing "in response to tiny cues that suggest a new direction that might be interesting to take" (p. 172).

By the end of each example, the two groups have collectively chosen which pathway to pursue, effectively rejecting all other previously offered ideas in favor of something that, for the moment, appears to be "better." In improvisation, when one person does something that is obviously better (in the view of the collective), "everyone else drops their own ideas and immediately joins in working on that better idea" (Becker, 2000, p. 175). In mathematics, judgments of "better" are based on whether the idea advances the group toward a solution, on whether the concept seems appropriate and useful in the present situation. Better ideas are those that lead to the continued growth of understanding.

In our first extract, Stanley's move (line 15) is clearly the critical moment in the episode – but only because the other students are prepared to "take the cue," to adapt their developing thinking to follow a new direction. However, as already noted, the group later recognizes that "doubling the area of the interior rectangle" is an incorrect solution, and they collectively work to develop a "better" solution. Their final solution (one that is consistent with the particular parallelogram offered in the question, but not generalizable) centers on the idea of the area of the interior rectangle being equivalent to four of the end triangles (see Figure 12.1).

In the second extract, Rachel suggests trigonometry as the way forward (line 71), and the group recognizes this suggestion as potentially "better" than their previous idea. Again, though, this is not an approach that she could have pursued alone. She needs Kerry to "take the cue" and follow this line of action. Indeed, it initially seems that Kerry is unsure about accepting this new proposal; for example, when Rachel says "See how we did it there?" Kerry replies "'Scusez moi, how *you* did it there!" (line 93). However, Kerry's actions following this (lines 97–110) suggest that she has agreed to follow this path. At the end of the extract, Kerry is the one who makes the critical suggestion to use *sine* rather than *tan* (line 110).

### DISCUSSION: TURNING TO TEACHING

In the preceding examples and analysis, our focus has very much been on the ways the students work together, and the mathematical understandings that emerge from this. In this section we turn our attention to the teacher, and the kind of role he or she might play in the improvisational emergence of collective understanding. By "teaching" we refer not just to the way the teacher chooses to interact with his or her students, but to the wider set of classroom practices that constitute an effective learning environment. Sawyer's introduction calls this *the learning paradox*: how a teacher can best organize his or her classroom to foster effective creative learning.

In the data extracts offered in this chapter, there are a number of identifiable factors that seem to contribute to the emergence of the three main elements of improvisational actions we identified as being observable in, and important for, the growth of mathematical understanding: the nature of the task; the nature of the group; and the nature of the teacher's interventions. It is to these possibilities that we suggest teachers might usefully attend and which they might seek to enact in their classrooms, and based on these, we propose teacher strategies that might enable collective improvisational actions and processes to occur.

### The Nature of the Task

First, in both cases, the question posed to the groups of students is open-ended and provides for a variety of responses. The questions appear to be very simple and are not situated in a real-world context. Indeed they appear almost stark, inviting nothing more than simple formulae as responses. However, in terms of mathematical thinking, we contend that for these students, they are rich tasks that open up possibilities for many different mathematical responses and pathways of action. For example, in the first extract, the solution chosen by the three students is not one that the interviewer expected, yet it allows for some powerful mathematical thinking to occur, which may not have emerged had the task been more structured or restrictive. In a similar way, the task in the second excerpt offers a wide range of mathematical opportunity for the group of learners, although again it might initially seem to be limited to discovering a rule that will solve the problem. As the extract shows, there are many choices made by Rachel and Kerry, both about what mathematics to draw on and how to apply this to the new problem. In both cases, students are engaged in a style of learning that is very different from working on a list of questions in a textbook that are designed to prescribe the content to be considered and learned. The fact that there is no one obvious answer to the posed problems is the catalyst for improvisational co-action to occur, and for what Sawyer (2000) calls a "combinatorial explosion" of potential pathways.

Second, in both cases, the task posed is at an appropriate mathematical level. It clearly is demanding enough to challenge the group – they cannot instantly "answer" the question – but also it is not so far beyond their existing mathematical understandings that they are unable to engage with the task. (See Krajcik & Blumenfeld, 2006 for a discussion of how "driving questions" can frame curricula units). It is essential for teachers to carefully match each task to the existing knowing and understandings of learners, because it creates a genuine need for shared action (see Csikszentmihalyi, 1996).

Third, it is important for students to work on a shared external representation of their developing understanding (Sawyer & Berson, 2004). In the first extract, the group had only one piece of paper that they shared as they were working (though each had ample writing tools). We observed another group in this same class who were given the identical task but who each had their own piece of paper. Because they each had their own paper, each student recorded their work separately; even when encouraged by the interviewer to work together, they continued to refer to their own workings and merely offered to each other contrasting solutions. The simple act of limiting the group to a shared document upon which to "pool" ideas has the potential to prompt improvisational co-action and collective mathematical understanding.

## The Nature of the Group

In these two extracts, mathematically appropriate ideas emerge at key moments (identified in lines 15 and 71, respectively), and no student thereafter offers either a new direction or an unhelpful piece of mathematics. Both groups are able to collaborate in ways that allow for the emergence of a collective understanding.

As with jazz musicians, there is perhaps much to be gained by having students of comparable ability work together. Such groupings may address the kinds of problems identified by Berliner (1994) including "deficient musicianship" and "incompatible musical personalities" (p. 395) where "significant disparity in individual preferences could threaten the entire group's foundation" (p. 396). In mathematics, differences in individual competencies might create such group disparities. We have yet to observe collective mathematical understanding emerging in a group made up of students of widely differing mathematical ability, though we do not contend that it cannot emerge in such groupings. We say this realizing that diversity of expertise has been shown to benefit collaboration when a group gets "stuck." Further research is warranted to help us understand more about the relationship between individual capacities and group capabilities in the domain of mathematical understanding.

Although our examples in this chapter were drawn from small groups working together, we also believe that improvisational collaboration can contribute to mathematical understanding in larger groups, even with a whole class of students. The development of a group mind would seem to be less likely (though not impossible) for a large number of learners. However, one of the principles of an improvisational performance is that not everyone is equally involved at any one moment. Sawyer (2001) notes the importance of "entrances" and "exits" of actors in improvisational theatre sketches, commenting that "the actors who are not actively participating in the current scene stand or sit at the back or sides of the stage; they don't want to interfere with the ongoing performance. But at the same time, they have to close enough to the action to hear the dialogue, so they can detect when it would be appropriate to enter the performance as a new character" (p. 55).

We believe there is, therefore, potential for the emergence of collective understanding within the whole class setting; although not every learner will actively be involved at every moment in the development of a collective understanding, there can still emerge something more than a set of individual understandings, and that with an appropriate improvisational etiquette in place there is still the potential for the establishment of a "group mind."

## The Nature of Teacher Interventions

In classrooms, the teacher is part of the emerging collective – a full participant, but one who makes judgments about when and how to intervene in the improvisation. In the second extract of data offered, what is striking in the transcript is that although the teacher participates in the discourse as it unfolds, she never takes over or simply tells the students what to do. Throughout the episodes described here, the teacher invites the students to explain their thinking so that she can better understand their current level of understanding ("Tell me what you think you are doing …", line 50). She problematizes the students' method ("Ah, but it isn't [a right-angle]", line 72), yet offers a new perspective ("Let's assume that this is the base", line 76) when the students had been struggling for some time working with one of the radii of the circle as the "base" of their triangle. Rather than continue with an explanation of why it would be better to use the chord of the circle as a base for the triangle, though, she simply smiles when Rachel recognizes the value of the suggestion ("Oh, would you chop it in half?", line 78), and instead prompts the students to access their own understandings of trigonometry to help them continue ("Now we've done something like that very recently, haven't we?", line 80). Such teaching requires a teacher to be willing to refrain from telling (at least immediately), and yet be responsive to the dynamical and improvisational nature of students' growing understandings. In such classrooms, teaching is a complex act of participation in unfolding understandings rather than a measured drip-feeding of information. This complex style of teaching is similar to the "inquiry mathematics" style that Cobb, Wood, Yackel, and McNeal (1992, p. 577) refer to as *orchestrated* to help the students "learn with what is typically called understanding" (p. 573) and that Towers (1998, 1999) describes as *shepherding*. Here, the teacher tends to intervene less, and when he or she does intervene, it is in more subtle ways. Such teaching also demands that a teacher develop a sophisticated capacity for professional noticing of students' mathematical thinking (Jacobs, Lamb, & Phillip, 2010), which includes the capacity for good judgment about when and how to act. Such orchestrated interventions are compatible with an improvisational view of mathematical understanding. They are helpful without disrupting the students' emerging understandings; they say "yes, and?" – a process recognized by Sawyer (2001) as the "First Rule of Improv," wherein strong improvisers support the emerging "storyline" by accepting the previously offered line and adding to it with their own contribution. The capacity to listen to the group mind – to pick up on innovations and say "yes, and" – is characteristic of improvisational co-action.

The outcome of the teaching-learning episode within such a classroom is emergent and "collectively determined" (Sawyer, 2004, p. 13). The teacher needs to be willing to share control, to allow events to unfold, and yet has a responsibility to act at critical moments. Knowing when and how to act in such a classroom requires a sophisticated improvisational competence that is unnecessary in a classroom dominated by more traditional modes of instruction – for example, the well-known IRE sequence, where a teacher deliberately funnels the talk and action in the classroom in such a way that there are a very limited number of possible responses to any question that is asked. In contrast, the teacher must continually listen to, and re-connect with, the improvisational actions of students, possessing a sophisticated capacity to step back until the collective action calls him or her forth.

## CONCLUSION

Understanding the improvisational character of collective mathematical understanding requires us to focus our analysis at the level of the group. As Sawyer (1997a) notes, "the central level of analysis for performance study is not the individual performer, but rather the event, the collective activity, and the group" (p. 4). Our two examples demonstrate that collective mathematical activity is an important and powerful part of learning and understanding mathematics, and one that merits a greater emphasis and recognition than presently exists in many classrooms, where the individual learner is still the dominant focus of curriculum, teaching, and assessment.

Clearly, a classroom in which there is little interaction is unlikely to function as an environment for the emergence of collective understanding. So how might we characterize the classroom in which collective mathematical understanding is likely to emerge and develop? As noted by Davis and Simmt (2003), "notions of teacher-centeredness or student-centeredness are not very useful for making sense of … collectives" (p.153), and most classrooms do not exist at either of these two extremes. Even in classrooms in which the teacher usually orchestrates the learning, there will inevitably emerge what Davis and Simmt (2003) term the "teachable moment – a cohering of many bodies in an instance of shared purpose and insight" (p. 164). These moments are always unpredictably emergent, and successfully taking advantage of them requires a teacher who is adept at enacting improvisational interventions. In these moments, there is the potential for collective mathematical understanding to emerge.

Recent years have seen a shift in classroom practices and teaching styles, with many teachers using group work. But just because a teacher has students work in groups does not necessarily imply that collective, improvisational co-action and understanding will emerge. Group work is too often viewed only as a technique to enhance individual learning, and is often embedded in broader classroom, school, curricula, and legislative contexts in which individual learning remains the focus. As Davis and Simmt (2003) note, "popular enactments of both traditional and contemporary teaching might ignore the complex possibilities of collective engagements as they focus on the qualities of single subjects" (p. 152). Focusing on the group allows us to better understand the collective processes that are always at play. In this chapter, we have shown how such processes can be understood as improvisational. Our intent has been to provide some clear suggestions for how teachers might think about, stimulate, and value collective mathematical understanding. Through doing this, we suggest that the practice of teaching is shifted into a space where expertise is characterized as the vital capacity to recognize and respond to the emerging understandings of students, and not just the facilitation of student competence as measured through standardized testing.

## REFERENCES

Becker, H. (2000). The etiquette of improvisation. *Mind, Culture, and Activity, 7*(3), 171–176.

Berliner, P. (1994). *Thinking in jazz: The infinite art of improvisation*. Chicago: University of Chicago Press.

(1997). Give and take: The collective conversation of jazz performance. In R. K. Sawyer (Ed.), *Creativity in Performance* (pp. 9–41). Greenwich, CT: Ablex Publishing.

Cobb, P., Wood, T., Yackel, E., & McNeal, B. (1992). Characteristics of classroom mathematics traditions: An interactional analysis. *American Educational Research Journal, 29*(3), 517–544.

Condon, W. S. & Ogston, W. D. (1971). Speech and body motion synchrony of the speaker-hearer. In D. L. Horton, & J. J. Jenkins (Eds.), *Perception of Language* (pp. 150–173). Columbus, OH: Charles E. Merrill.

Csikszentmihalyi, M. (1996). Creativity: Flow and the psychology of discovery and invention. New York: Harper Perennial.

Cuban, L. (1993). How teachers taught: Constancy and change in American classrooms, 1890–1990 (2nd ed.). New York: Teachers College Press.

Darling-Hammond, L. & Bransford, J. (Eds.) (2005). Preparing teachers for a changing world: What teachers should learn and be able to do. San Francisco: Jossey-Bass.

Davis, B. (1996). Teaching mathematics: Toward a sound alternative. New York: Garland.

Davis, B., & Simmt, E. (2003). Understanding learning systems: Mathematics education and complexity science. *Journal for Research in Mathematics Education, 34*(2), 137–167.

Department for Children, Family and Schools. (2006). *Primary framework for literacy and mathematics*. London: Department for Education and Skills.

Erickson, F. (2004). Talk and social theory: Ecologies of speaking and listening in everyday life. Cambridge: Polity Press.

Gordon-Calvert, L. M. (2001). Mathematical conversations within the practice of mathematics. New York: Peter Lang.

Hiebert, J., Carpenter, T. P., Fennema, E., Fuson, K. C., Wearne, D., Murray, H. et al. (1997). *Making sense – teaching and learning mathematics with understanding*. Portsmouth, NH: Heinemann.

Hiebert, J. & Stigler, J. (2000). A proposal for improving classroom teaching: Lessons from the TIMSS video study. *The Elementary School Journal, 101*(1), 2–20.

Jacobs, J. K., Hiebert, J., Givvin, K. B., Hollingsworth, H., Garnier, H., & Wearne, D. (2006). Does eighth-grade mathematics teaching in the United States align with the NCTM standards? Results from the TIMSS 1995 and 1999 video studies. *Journal for Research in Mathematics Education, 37*(1), 5–32.

Jacobs, V. R., Lamb, L. L. C., & Philipp, R. A. (2010). Professional noticing of children's mathematical thinking. *Journal for Research in Mathematics Education, 41*(2), 169–202.

Kieren, T. (2001). Set forming and set ordering: Useful similes in observing the growth of mathematical understanding? In R. Speiser, C. Maher, & C. Walter (Eds.), *Proceedings of the Twenty-Third Annual Meeting of the North American Chapter of the International Group for the Psychology of Mathematics Education, Vol. I* (pp. 223–233). Columbus, OH: Eric Clearinghouse for Science, Mathematics, and Environmental Education.

Krajcik, J.S. & Blumenfeld, P. (2006). Project-based learning. In Sawyer, R. K. (Ed.), *The Cambridge Handbook of the Learning Sciences* (pp. 317–334). New York: Cambridge.

Martin, L. C. & Towers, J. (2009). Improvisational coactions and the growth of collective mathematical understanding. *Research in Mathematics Education, 11*(1), 1–20.

Martin, L. C., Towers, J., & Pirie, S. E. B. (2006). Collective mathematical understanding as improvisation. *Mathematical Thinking and Learning, 8*(2), 149–183.

Matusov, E. (1998). When solo activity is not privileged: The participation and internalization models of development. *Human Development, 41*, 326–349.

NCTM (2000). *Principles and standards for school mathematics*. Reston, VA: National Council of Teachers of Mathematics.

No Child Left Behind Act of 2001, 20 U.S.C. § 6319 (2008).

Pressing, J. (1984). Cognitive processes in improvisation. In W. R. Crozier, & A. J. Chapman (Eds.), *Cognitive Processes in the Perception of Art* (pp. 345–366). New York: Elsevier.

Ruhleder, K., and Stoltzfus, F. (2000). The etiquette of the master class: Improvisation on a theme by Howard Becker. *Mind, Culture and Activity, 7*(3), 186–196.

Sawyer, R. K. (1997a). *Creativity in performance*. Greenwich, CT: Ablex Publishing. (1997b). *Pretend play as improvisation: Conversation in the preschool classroom*. Mahwah, NJ: Lawrence Erlbaum Associates.

(2000). Improvisational cultures: Collaborative emergence and creativity in improvisation. *Mind, Culture, and Activity, 7*(3), 180–185.

(2001). *Creating conversations: Improvisation in everyday discourse.* Cresskill, NJ: Hampton Press.

(2003). *Group creativity: Music, theatre, collaboration.* Mahwah, NJ: Lawrence Erlbaum Associates.

(2004). Creative teaching: Collaborative discussion as disciplined improvisation. *Educational Researcher, 23*(2), 12–20.

Sawyer, R. K. & Berson, S. (2004). Study group discourse: How external representations affect collaborative conversation. *Linguistics and Education, 15*, 387–412.

Stahl, G. (2006). *Group cognition.* Cambridge, MA: MIT Press.

Towers, J. (1998). Telling tales. *Journal of Curriculum Theorizing, 14*(3), 29–35.

(1999). Teachers' interventions and the growth of students' mathematical understanding. In J. G. McLoughlin (Ed.), *Proceedings of the Twenty-Third Annual Meeting* of the *Canadian Mathematics Education Study Group/ Groupe Canadien d'Étude en Didactique des Mathématique* (pp. 161–168). St. Catharines, ON.

# 13

## Conclusion: Presence and the Art
## of Improvisational Teaching

### LISA BARKER AND HILDA BORKO

In the introductory chapter of this volume (see Chapter 1), Keith Sawyer states that the goal for this book is "to present a new theory of professional pedagogical practice" (p. 13). At the core of this new theory is the premise that "balancing structure and improvisation is the essence of the art of teaching" (p. 2). The phrase "the art of teaching" suggests that teaching – like any interactive craft that includes collaboration or live performance (e.g., "the art of conversation") – entails two inter-related facets of expertise: mastery of a body of fundamental principles or methods governing the craft (i.e., "structure") and mastery of skills in conducting human activity (i.e., "improvisation"). The educational scholars represented in this book share this conception of teaching; they view teaching as an *improvisational activity*, and they contend that "what makes good teachers great" is *disciplined improvisation*. Each chapter either explicitly or implicitly address the question: How can the principles of artistic improvisation in theater, music, and dance be adapted for interactive educational contexts – from student learning in public school classrooms to teacher learning at the university level? In this chapter, we discuss this body of work through the lens of two additional guiding questions:

1. What does this multi-layered "theory of professional pedagogical practice" look like, and how does this theory contribute to our understanding of teaching, learning, and curriculum development?
2. What do this theory and these applied principles mean for teacher education?

To consider question (1), we draw on the literature on systems of instruction, and we discuss what the book chapters collectively seem to

In R. K. Sawyer (Ed.) (2011). *Structure and improvisation in creative teaching* (pp. 279–298). Cambridge: Cambridge University Press.

say about the essential qualities of effective teaching. To further illustrate these essential qualities, we offer an example of what they look like in one cross-curricular core instructional practice, the facilitation of classroom discussion. We then address question (2) by exploring the implications that these common themes and teacher qualities have for teacher preparation and professional development.

## THE THREE PARADOXES AND SYSTEMS OF INSTRUCTION

The three teaching paradoxes – the teacher, learning, and curriculum paradoxes – are reminiscent of features of educational systems that other scholars have identified. We first encountered a similar representation in the work of Joseph Schwab (1978), who identified students, teachers, curriculum, and context as the four "commonplaces" of schooling. More recently, in their analysis of resources related to student achievement, Cohen, Raudenbush, and Ball (2003) depicted a system of instruction as a triangle with three vertices – teacher, student, and content – embedded in a circle labeled "environment." As they explained, "Instruction consists of interactions among teachers and students around content, in environments" (p. 124). Effective instruction (i.e., teaching that results in student learning), therefore, requires a teacher's deft coordination of the complex interactions among herself, students, the content, and the specific community context. This coordination is similar to Sawyer's conception of teaching as balancing tensions within and between the teacher, learning, and curriculum; in this sense, the three paradoxes map onto the teacher, student, and content vertices of Cohen and colleagues' triangle.

Within and across each of these paradoxes, teachers are responsible for the dynamic management of the tension between structure and flexibility. The main contribution of this volume is that it provides a perspective on this tension by drawing comparisons to a similar tension in artistic genres of improvisation, whether in music, theater, or dance. Artistic improvisation excites audiences because there is a dance between predictable structures (e.g., the narrative arc of a story, the sixteen-bar form of a jazz standard) and uncertainty in the inevitable delicious moments that surface when humans are given freedom in a creative, collaborative task. The structure-flexibility tension is similar to Palmer's (1998) first paradoxical tension of pedagogical space – that the teaching space be both bounded and open. Palmer (2003) captures this tension in the question: "How ... does a good teacher hold together the apparent opposites of freedom and discipline, knowing that children, and learning, require both?" (p. 381). Ronald Beghetto and James

Kaufman raise similar questions in their chapter as they discuss how teachers can foster students' creativity in a rigorous standards-focused environment without encountering either curricular chaos or intellectual conformity. In their examination of the "curriculum-as-planned vs. curriculum-as-lived," they characterize the tension between structure and flexibility as finding the balance between utilizing enough structure to enable productive academic work and at the same time allowing for enough improvisation to encourage student creativity.

Sawyer sees this tension between structure and flexibility as central to a view of teaching as improvisation, and he cites research that has shown "that the most effective classroom interaction balances structure and script with flexibility and improvisation" (p. 2). The structure-flexibility continuum is central to understanding the use of improvisational tools and techniques in pedagogical contexts, and this continuum takes different forms in each of the three paradoxes elucidated in this book:

- While resolving the *teacher paradox*, a teacher nimbly moves along a continuum from structured plans and routines to improvised practice.
- While resolving the *learning paradox*, a teacher adjusts learning tasks along a continuum from carefully scaffolded exercises to more open-ended constructivist approaches.
- While resolving the *curriculum paradox*, curriculum designers plan sequences and activities along a continuum from scripted directions to suggestions that can be enacted more flexibly.

Each of these continua is a version of the broader structure-flexibility continuum, and each contributing author addresses one or more of the continua by situating one of Sawyer's paradoxes within the framework of specific improvisational forms, instructional contexts, or empirical studies.

## THE NECESSITY OF PRESENCE

Although the three paradoxes differ with regard to the form that the structure-flexibility continuum takes, they share one key feature: navigating the larger teaching paradox requires a teacher to be keenly *present*. In his introduction, Sawyer contends that both theatrical performance and effective teaching require "stage presence" (p. 4). In theatrical performance, this quality is often thought to mean a performer's ability to command an audience's attention through charisma, focus, expression, and confidence. In teaching, presence is necessary because of the relational and ever-uncertain nature of the work. The unique demands of teaching are such that teachers' practical knowledge must be situational, social, and personal-experiential (Elbaz, 1983). These demands are further complicated by the fact that "teaching is anything but certain, and teachers must learn to live with chronic uncertainty as an essential component of their professional practice" (Labaree, 2000, p. 231). Thus, good teaching – a complex, "contingent, interactive practice" (Grossman et al., 2009, p. 2056) – necessitates presence, and presence is the key to successful navigation of the teaching paradox.

Literature on improvisational theater offers an operational definition of presence. Seminal texts, such as *Improvisation for the Theater* (Spolin, 1963), *Impro* (Johnstone, 1979), and *Improv Wisdom* (Ryan Madson, 2005), suggest that successful improvisation requires players to make clear, specific verbal or physical *offers* – contributions to the unfolding narrative, such as lines of dialogue, gestures, movements, or facial expressions. They also must listen alertly for and to others' offers, and accept and apply these offers. In an improvised scene, the players co-construct a narrative by accepting and building on the verbal and physical offers of their fellow players (i.e., the "Yes, and" principle of improvisation). This kind of artful listening and nimble responsiveness is at the heart of what Sawyer calls "stage presence," and is a component of the teacher qualities that constitute classroom "presence."

Rodgers and Raider-Roth (2006) argued that the elusive but essential teacher quality of presence comprises three domains: (1) connection to self; (2) attunement to others; and (3) knowledge of subject matter, children, learning, pedagogical skills, and context. Their definition, which suggests that present teachers behave with "alert awareness, receptivity and connectedness" and respond to students intelligently and compassionately (p. 266), builds on related pedagogical ideals, including Dewey's (1933) notion of the teacher being "alive," Greene's (1973) "wide-awakeness," Buddhist ideas of "mindfulness," Schön's (1983) "reflection-in-action," Rud's (1995) "hospitality," and Palmer's (1998) "integrity."

Several of the chapters in this book discuss aspects of improvisational teaching that overlap with Rodgers and Raider-Roth's definition of presence. During Janice Fournier's discussion of how collaborative choreography offers a metaphor for the kind of facilitative work that good teachers do, she alludes to Dewey (1938) and Eisner's (2002) depiction of "flexible purposing." This improvisational aspect of intelligence corresponds to the intellectual and creative agility central to improvisational teaching; in Fournier's words, this agility includes not only the "ability to be flexible in one's goals, to be open to the potential in unexpected events to change the course of one's work" (p. 204), but also "an ability to change direction, to revise and refine one's aims when better options emerge in the course of one's work" (p. 187). This description of flexible purposing entails attunement to self and others – the first and second of Rodgers and Raider-Roth's domains of presence.

In his chapter on the use of improvisation in English as a Foreign Language (EFL) high school classrooms in Germany, Jurgen Kurtz contends that "improvisation encompasses attunement to a situational context … as well as spontaneous decision-making and problem-solving, openness and unpredictability" (p. 133). This notion of improvisation overlaps with the second and third domains of presence (attunement to others, and knowledge of subject matter) by emphasizing the importance of connection to others and attention to context. To illustrate these features of teaching, he describes *Bus Stop* and *Surprise Encounter*, improvisational activities that invite EFL learners to actively engage in meaningful, spontaneous talk. Unlike conventional role-plays, these activities offer learners "discourse lubricants" such as opening gambits and "communicative emergency exits" – structures that liberate discourse by ensuring language learners a series of safety nets that encourage communicative risk taking. Such activities also provide room for rigorous content-based work in the target language, such as idiomatic expressions, grammar, and cultural rules for polite exchange. In these ways, activities like *Bus Stop* and *Surprise Encounter* address the development of both content and community.

Annette Sassi's chapter attends to *content* and *community* as she discusses Making Meaning, a K-6 curriculum with a dual focus on reading comprehension and classroom community. Over the course of nine grade levels, Making Meaning employs a systematic, developmental approach to cultivating a variety of reading comprehension strategies as well as social values and skills. A core component of the approach is the use of productive classroom routines or "cooperative structures" (e.g., partner work and group brainstorming) within which students can collaborate (p. 218). Like Kurtz's chapter, Sassi's chapter straddles the second and third domains of presence (attunement to others and knowledge of subject matter) as she considers the extent to which curriculum and teaching address the tension between responsibility to disciplinary content and respect for rules of social engagement.

In the following, we delve further into the second and third of Rodgers and Raider-Roth's domains of presence – attunement to others and to one's professional knowledge base – because we believe these domains are central to the paradoxes discussed throughout the book. At the same time, we acknowledge that the first domain – knowledge of self – is fundamental to improvisational teaching, and we lean on the work of other authors to make links between "the personal and professional aspects of teaching"

(Meijer, Korthagen, & Vasalos, 2009, p. 297). We then apply these features of presence to one core instructional practice, the facilitation of large-group classroom discussion.

## The Second Domain of Presence: Attunement to Others

As suggested by the second domain of presence, improvisational teaching requires attention to the relational aspects of practice. As teachers attune to the needs and ideas of their students, two related (and often overlapping) tensions emerge. We call these tensions "shared control" and "the individual vs. the collective." *Shared Control* is the extent to which the teaching/learning interactions and the direction and flow of activities are shared by the teacher and students. *The Individual vs. the Collective* is a teacher's simultaneous and deft attention to the needs of individual students and the class as a whole. The chapters in this book address these tensions and the ways in which they complicate teachers' efforts to negotiate the teaching paradox.

### Shared Control

In artistic improvisation, players can share control of the performance in a variety of ways. While most improvisational performances are collaboratively created, the frequency, speed, and simultaneity of turn taking within the collaborative conversation can vary. Specific forms of improvisational theater and music, such as Theatresports and straight-ahead jazz, can be compared with respect to how control is shared because they often differ by the pace of turn taking within the collaborative conversation. Invented by Keith Johnstone in the 1970s, Theatresports is an example of short-form improv theater that employs a competitive format to enhance the dramatic effect. In Theatresports, narratives are typically co-constructed, often on a quick offer-by-offer basis. In contrast, straight-ahead jazz typically features an established sequence of solo improvisations derived from the song's melodic theme or chord progressions and accompanied by the other musicians. Although the music is co-constructed by all musicians, each soloist takes control of the musical direction; the other band members improvise in a way that is responsive to the ideas and emotions the soloist initiates. The conversation can consist of very brief musical contributions, with members responding to one another at a rapid give-and-take pace; more frequently, however, each member makes a lengthier contribution before another player responds, such as in a series of extended solos.

We characterize shared control in artistic contexts as a tension because artists are mindful of their own participation at the same time that they hold space for the offers of others. In improvisational theater, inviting another's offer can be done with a thoughtful pause, a gesture toward a fellow player, moving upstage (i.e., away from the audience) and thus foregrounding another player, or explicitly asking the audience for a suggestion. In jazz, such invitations may be communicated by a lowering of volume, a nodding gesture, or perhaps a solo musical flourish that invites audience applause as a way to transition to a new soloist.

Like musical and theatrical improvisation, teaching offers a context in which participants must mutually support one another through listening, accepting, and extending others' offers. In classrooms, the tension of shared control can be examined by considering the extent to which a teacher shares control of activities with her students. On one end of the continuum of teacher versus student control, a learning activity is fully teacher-directed, as might be observed during a direct-instruction lecture on a historical event; on the other end, students are autonomously driving the learning, such as in an inquiry-based science lesson. In their discussion of two cases of science teaching in K-1 laboratory school classrooms, Susan Jurow and Laura Creighton McFadden present a version of classroom control that, while tilted toward teacher-driven learning, includes key opportunities for students to influence the interaction. The students in these classrooms actively contribute to emergent instruction by bringing their ideas and questions to the interaction; the teachers, however, are the ones to provide direction and guidance for the activities.

Beyond notions of control as shared among a teacher and students, Pamela Burnard's chapter discusses a context in which classroom teachers share facilitative control during an in-school teacher-artist partnership. Through a review of relevant research and a description of the Creative Partnerships program in the United Kingdom, Burnard argues that artists have the most impact when they challenge teachers' pedagogic assumptions. Her stated goal for this chapter "is to understand how they resolve this tension to create a shared space for teaching" or "[w]hat takes them from teaching together, independently and side by side, to co-constructing an emergent pedagogy" (p. 54). In this way, Burnard suggests that teacher-artist partnerships require teachers and artists to navigate the productive tensions inherent to their distinct perspectives, expertise, and objectives. Burnard situates this discussion in a jazz metaphor to suggest that "creative learning is essentially polyphonic," dynamic, and multi-directional; as a result, during the teacher-artist partnership, "artists can adopt different stances and engage in different collaborative activities with teachers" (p. 58). In other words, such partnerships allow teachers to explore the tension of shared control with their artist partners.

*Attention to Both the Individual and the Collective*

At the same time that improvisation requires openness to shared control, it also demands a simultaneous and multi-directional attunement to the needs of individuals and the larger community. As a result, in any improvisational context, individual improvisers make offers within the framework of a set of central tenets that guide collaborative practice. When players in an improvisational theater troupe or jazz ensemble feel that they can trust their fellow players to honor the rules of improvisational engagement (e.g., the "Yes, and" maxim of improvisational theater), they are more likely to work collaboratively and to take the kind of creative risks that serve the artistic process. The individual artists work to honor this collective commitment to their fellow players, but they are also interested in their own performance and growth. As a result, they must manage a tension between their own artistic and learning objectives and those of the community of practice.

In classroom contexts, the management of the tension between individual and collective needs is the teacher's responsibility as she deftly shifts between emphasizing individual student learning and attending to the collective climate of the classroom. Palmer (1998) made a similar point with his third paradoxical tension of pedagogical space, that the teaching space should invite both the voice of the individual and the voice of the group. The authors of this book share this belief; they contend that improvisational teaching is a key to fostering both individual and collaborative creativity in students, and several chapters explicitly discuss the role of improv in balancing the tension between individual and collective creativity.

Lyndon Martin and Jo Towers, for example, frame the growth of mathematical understanding in a classroom as an improvisational process, and their research focuses on the collective mathematical actions, thinking, and learning that emerge when a group of learners work collaboratively on a mathematical task. Their chapter presents two episodes in which students work together to solve a mathematics problem – one in an elementary classroom and the second in high school – and then analyzes the episodes with respect to three central elements of improvisation: multiple potential pathways, the emergence of collectively created structures, and group norms or the "etiquette" of improvisation. Martin and Towers characterize their work as *improvisational co-actions* that enable understanding to collectively flow and grow. When one individual devises an approach that is compelling to the collective, others concede their ideas and join that person's efforts to move along that pathway toward a solution. The teacher periodically exerts control when the group seems stuck or headed down an unproductive path.

In this way, the teacher shares control with students as she manages the tension between the individual and collective student needs that surface during the mathematical task.

Whereas Martin and Towers examine the social phenomenon of mathematical problem solving, Anthony Perone explores the social phenomenon of language in an adult English language learning (ELL) context. His chapter explicitly examines the tension between individual and collective language learning, or, as Perone frames it, the conflict between "the individual versus the group" (p. 162). In his ELL class, Perone and his colleagues infused improvisational activities into the curriculum in order to invite students to be and become users and meaning makers of language. The learning context he describes is one of shared control as facilitators favor an atmosphere that values each participant's potential to teach and co-construct meaning. At the same time that they valued individuals' contributions, they were attentive to the group's learning. Drawing on the success of this approach, Perone devotes a section of his chapter to advocating for a more prominent role of the group in language learning. He contrasts this vision to the conventional language-learning context that "is primarily attentive to individual concerns and development" (p. 169).

### The Third Domain of Presence: The Role of Professional Knowledge

Improvisational presence requires a deep and flexible professional knowledge base. In improvisational theater, for example, this might mean that players exhibit practical expertise in fundamental acting skills related to body (e.g., clear pantomime) and voice (e.g., vocal projection) while accumulating knowledge of popular culture and current events that may inform their performance. Similarly, jazz musicians spend years building practical skills (e.g., breath control, manual dexterity) and mastering melodic themes and variations that fit the harmonic structure of canonical jazz "standards." Artistic improvisers apply their repertoire of practical skills and knowledge of a canon each time they discern what the story, song, or show needs in order to be successful; depending on the artistic form and context of the performance, "success" may mean a coherent musical feeling, a funny or moving moment of interaction, or a satisfying ending to a scene.

Like skilled artistic improvisers, expert teachers apply their professional knowledge and repertoire of instructional practices to their specific contexts. Ball and colleagues discussed two domains of professional knowledge unique to teaching: specialized content knowledge and pedagogical content knowledge (Ball, Thames, & Phelps, 2008). Specialized content knowledge is the disciplinary knowledge teachers draw on to help their students learn skills, procedures, and concepts specific to that discipline. In mathematics, for example, teachers must know more than which algorithm is needed to solve a problem; they must know why one algorithm works and another does not, and what variations on that algorithm might look like. They must also understand the various ways in which students are likely to approach a mathematical problem in order to follow the students' logic when they explain their solution strategies – whether correct, partially correct, or incorrect.

Pedagogical content knowledge (PCK) is the subject-specific pedagogical knowledge teachers draw on to foster student understanding (Shulman, 1986). Ball and colleagues separate PCK into two components. *Knowledge of content and teaching* integrates knowledge of content and knowledge of pedagogical strategies. Teachers draw on this type of knowledge, for example, to select tasks and to sequence classroom activities in order to facilitate student learning of a specific topic in developmentally appropriate ways. *Knowledge of content and students* integrates knowledge of subject matter and knowledge of students. Teachers draw on this type of knowledge, for example, to respond to students' novel approaches to a problem, to build on their thinking, and to determine whether students have complete and accurate understanding of a particular concept (Ball, Thames, & Phelps, 2008).

Recently, attempts to characterize the specific instructional practices that are central to good teaching have become prominent in scholarly discussions of teaching and learning to teach. As one example, Grossman and colleagues (e.g., Grossman, Hammerness, & McDonald, 2009; Grossman & McDonald, 2008) have begun to identify and describe "high leverage practices." These practices, such as providing clear instructional explanations and orchestrating classroom discussions, occur with high frequency in teaching, are enacted across different curricula or instructional approaches, are research-based, and have the potential to improve student achievement. Together, these domains of professional knowledge and core instructional practices constitute the expertise needed for improvisational teaching.

In sum, teacher presence requires: (a) simultaneous attunement to self, students, subject matter, and pedagogy within a given context; (b) openness to shared control; and (c) attention to individual students as well as the larger classroom community. Expert teachers apply these attributes to instruction through a blend of careful planning, artful listening, and nimble responsiveness.

## CLASSROOM DISCUSSION

To illustrate the three features of presence, we offer the example of one cross-curricular improvisational instructional practice – the facilitation of classroom discussion. Classrooms are dominated by teacher-directed didactic talk, and patterns of conversation most often take the form of teacher-centered Initiate-Respond-Evaluate (IRE). In this rhetorical structure, a teacher initiates a question and calls on a student, a student responds with a narrative, and the teacher offers an evaluative comment on this narrative (Mehan, 1979; Cazden, 2001). Discourse research reveals that IRE is a prevalent participation structure in classroom talk (Cazden, 1986). Many teachers "see instruction as a one-way transmission of knowledge from teacher and texts to students, and they typically assess students' knowledge for its congruence with curricular aims and objectives" (Nystrand & Gamoran, 1997, p. 30). Consequently, classroom discourse is overwhelmingly monologic and characterized by lecture, memorization, and recitation. Such participant structures are detrimental to the classroom, where rich, purposeful discussion is central in critically encountering mathematical tasks, scientific dilemmas, and literary, historical, and visual texts. In these contexts, students are often asked to demonstrate some form of "argument literacy," the ability to "listen closely to others, summarize them in a recognizable way, and make your own relevant argument" (Graff, 2003, pp. 2–3). Classroom discussion, when successfully facilitated, is a forum for exercising these skills of listening, synthesizing, and making new relevant offers.

This kind of rich, purposeful discourse is difficult to attain in practice. Many public school classrooms have thirty or more students, which makes large-group discussion difficult to prepare for and orchestrate. Moreover, as Cazden (1986) aptly asserted, "[t]he best laid plans may go awry because no lesson is under the teacher's unilateral control, and teacher behavior and student behavior reciprocally influence each other in complex ways" (p. 448). How do teachers honor both this complex mutuality and the targeted content as they prepare for classroom discussion? During discussion, what does teacher presence look like, and what can teachers do to cultivate argument literacy in and among students?

### Preparing for Discussion

Masterful facilitation of classroom discussion first requires thoughtful and structured planning. To prepare for large-group discussion, a teacher must select a rich text, such as a mathematical problem, an open-ended historical question, or a poem that is open to multiple interpretations. From there, she marshals her knowledge of her students to identify potential dilemmas, develop questions, and anticipate student responses, as well as to devise any pre-discussion activities, such as annotating a text based on a guiding question or brainstorming possible responses in a journal entry. At the same time, the teacher is doing the hard work of explicitly and/or implicitly establishing norms for participation and interaction during classroom discussion. In these ways, as a teacher prepares for discussion, she must consider both content and community.

To understand how a teacher can tackle both content and community in the context of classroom discussion, consider a Language Arts teacher who leads a text-based discussion with an underlying content objective (e.g., students will be able to make predictions and support them with evidence from a text). As the teacher prepares for this discussion, she outlines a series of explicit norms to guide how students engage with one another. These norms include both social rules for discourse (e.g., be aware of how often you contribute to the discussion.) and content-specific norms (e.g., support each claim by referencing a specific passage in the text.). Thus, the teacher's preparation exhibits attention to both a content objective and the needs of the learning community.

## Facilitating Discussion

As Frederick Erickson's examination of classroom discourse reveals, an improvisational perspective can help teachers understand how students negotiate the social, as well as academic, structures of the classroom. Using several examples from elementary school classrooms, Erickson illuminates the ways in which teachers and students improvise (and therefore navigate the learning paradox) during classroom discourse. He argues that the verbal and physical offers exchanged between teachers and students communicate information about both the subject matter of the lesson and the norms for social interaction. Thus, through their behavior, teachers and students simultaneously tackle the disciplinary content and "metacommunicate" implicitly and/or explicitly about the rules of the instructional and social contexts of the classroom (p. 117). This communication, Erickson contends, is similar to the kind of work improvising musicians do when they listen and adapt to each others' offers.

Christensen (1991) and Palmer (1998) also clarified notions of listening and response. Palmer contended that moments of creative tension (such as one might find in a discussion classroom) require heightened awareness. As part of this alertness and receptivity, discussion leaders must practice artful listening. Christensen asserted that during a discussion, "the teacher consciously grants total attention to each classroom speaker" (p. 165) – to gauge the student's grasp of content "and to assess the potential contribution of the comment to the group's continuing dialogue" (p. 164). This type of artful listening requires simultaneous attention to both individual students and the class as a whole, or what Palmer called "[listening] for what the group voice is saying" (p. 76). This notion of listening also informs skillful response, or what Christensen called "the art of the immediate" (p. 166). In the classroom, this means in-the-moment constructive action based on students' contributions, the particular objectives of the lesson, and the unique needs of the class.

During rich, purposeful, large-group classroom discussion, a teacher and students participate through verbal and physical offers (e.g., questions, gestures). At the same time, they must listen actively for and to others' offers. The way in which a teacher responds to student contributions (including, and perhaps especially, ideas that others may view as "wrong") influences both the content and nature of students' subsequent offers. Masterful discourse facilitators exhibit openness to allowing offers to modify the discussion and the deft incorporation of offers into subsequent questions. These instructional moves apply the "Yes, and" tenet of improvisational theater in the form of "uptake" – a discourse move in which teachers purposefully pick up on students' contributions during classroom discussion. Our definition of uptake encompasses active listening to student responses as well as two of Nystrand and Gamoran's (1997) dimensions of dialogic instruction: a teacher's openness to allowing a student response to modify the topic of discourse (what Nystrand and Gamoran labeled as "level of evaluation") and a teacher's incorporation of previous answers into subsequent questions (Nystrand and Gamoran labeled this "uptake").

Uptake can take a variety of forms and serve a range of functions. Suppose, for example, a history teacher is facilitating a discussion based on the question "Were the costs of the Civil War worth the results?" During this discussion, a student may make the following contribution: "Sort of. It made sense freedom-wise, but not money-wise." In an IRE rhetorical structure, a teacher's default response to this offer may be an unexplained evaluative statement (e.g., "Good, Gabi. Interesting.") followed by the next (often unrelated) question. In dialogic instruction that includes rich, purposeful uptake of student ideas, a teacher may encourage students to elaborate on their thinking (e.g., "Say more about that, Gabi.") or invite students to connect their thinking to others' offers and the subject matter (e.g., "What evidence can we offer to support Gabi's claim?"). When "mistakes" (e.g., a confused chronology of historical events) or disagreements surface, the skillful facilitator employs uptake to encourage students to clarify or extend their thinking.

We closely consider uptake in order to characterize the complexity of presence. Even in one teacher move (uptake) within one instructional practice (the facilitation of classroom discussion), expert teachers balance attention to content (e.g., the text being discussed, the objectives of the lesson) and community (e.g., the relationships with and among students in the classroom). A teacher's in-the-moment decision to employ uptake depends on the specific pedagogical objectives related to content and/or community. In one context it may be meaningful for a teacher to repeat a student's offer verbatim in order to affirm a student who is typically reluctant to participate during discussion (e.g., "Gabi says the war made sense 'freedom-wise, but not money-wise.'"); in another context, it may be more useful to revoice this same offer in order to model a mode of academic discourse (e.g., "I'm hearing Gabi say that the Civil War was morally, but not economically, defensible.").[1] Moreover, an instance of uptake can serve several content- and community-related functions simultaneously. For example, a teacher's offer during discussion could invite students to extend their thinking and seek textual evidence at the same time that it encourages students to listen to one another.

## IMPLICATIONS FOR TEACHER LEARNING

Aspects of the third domain of presence – knowledge of subject matter, knowledge of young people and how they learn, and knowledge of curriculum and pedagogy – constitute the primary, and often the sole, focus of coursework in teacher preparation programs. For the most part, novice teachers' initial opportunities to sharpen the second domain of presence – the contingent, interactive aspects of practice – do not occur until they are actually in the classroom (Grossman et al., 2009). In other words, novice teachers often do not explicitly encounter the paradoxes inherent to the profession until they are responsible for a group of students and their achievement. Delaying novice educators' preparation and support for the teacher, learning, and curriculum paradoxes is a disservice to teachers and the students they serve.

If masterful teaching is an art that requires multiple layers of expertise, then teacher preparation and professional development models must support

---

[1] "Revoicing" is a discourse move in which a participant paraphrases another person's offer to serve one or more functions; see O'Connor and Michaels (1996) for a more thorough definition of revoicing and the range of functions it serves.

this artistic development. Several chapters in the book explore the role of improvisation in teacher learning. Stacy DeZutter, for example, argues for explicitly including improvisation in teacher preparation programs – to help prospective teachers develop both an understanding of the improvisational aspects of teaching and the ability to use improvisational methods such as problem-based teaching. DeZutter contends that, given the importance of viewing teaching as an improvisational activity, the teaching profession must develop a body of knowledge that parallels the professional knowledge found in other improvisational communities and simultaneously prepare the next generation of teachers for improvisational teaching. Just as skilled improvisational performers must learn how to apply set of central tenets in addition to a deep understanding of relevant content, teachers must develop deep professional knowledge and a repertoire of instructional strategies, as well as the presence needed to apply this expertise in the classroom.

Carrie Lobman's chapter focuses on the use of theatrical improvisation in teacher professional development. She describes the Developing Teachers Fellowship Program (DTFP) – a year-long program for certified teachers working in New York City public schools – which is grounded in a Vygotskian perspective that learning leads, supports, and is inseparable from human development. In the DTFP, improvisation is both a pedagogical approach and a learning goal for participating teachers. Teachers participate in improvisational activity and learn to take risks, make mistakes, and support each other to "do what they do not yet know how to do" (p. 74). At the same time, they adapt and create improv activities that could be used to teach specific subjects and grade levels. Lobman concludes her chapter with the assertion, "As teacher educators it is critical that we find ways to help our teachers 'practice becoming'" (p. 89).

In their investigations of how people are prepared for relational professions – namely, the clergy, teaching, and clinical psychology – Grossman and colleagues (2009) suggested that one way to support teachers as they "practice becoming" is to structure opportunities for them to (1) observe, (2) unpack, and (3) try out aspects of real-world practice within the context of their professional learning experiences. The authors labeled the three components of this framework *representations*, *decomposition*, and *approximations* of practice, which they define as follows:

- Representations of practice comprise the different ways that practice is modeled in professional education and what these various representations make visible to novices.
- Decomposition of practice involves breaking down practice into its constituent parts for the purposes of teaching and learning.

- Approximations of practice refer to opportunities for novices to engage in practices that are more or less proximal to the practices of a profession. (p. 2058)

The authors further offered a continuum of authenticity along which one can array these approximations of practice (see p. 2079); this continuum ranges from less authentic practices (e.g., the analysis of case studies, live role-plays) to more authentic practices that allow the novice to enact practices in realistic contexts (e.g., student teaching in a classroom). In the programs they studied, they found that, while prospective teachers have multiple opportunities to approximate the pre-active (e.g., lesson-planning) and reflective (e.g., written self-critiques) aspects of practice, they "have fewer opportunities to engage in approximations that focus on contingent, interactive practice than do novices in [the clergy and clinical psychology]" (p. 2056). In other words, there are few opportunities in the context of university-based teacher preparation programs for prospective teachers to develop the relational (and, thus, improvisational) domain of presence. As a result, novice teachers enter the workforce with little preparation for the second facet of "the art of teaching" – how to conduct human social activity.

Similarly, many professional development programs focus on the pre-active aspects of practice, such as accumulating content knowledge and devising unit plans. Few programs, however, offer teachers the time, space, and emotional safety to approximate the instructional practices central to interactive teaching.

## Stanford Teaching Studio

To illustrate how one professional development model incorporates the concepts of core instructional practices and approximation of these practices, we discuss the "Stanford Teaching Studio: Secondary Literacy, Humanities, and the Arts," a professional learning partnership between Stanford University and teaching teams from San Francisco Unified School District and Stanford's partner schools. Stanford's Center to Support Excellence in Teaching (CSET) established the Stanford Teaching Studio with the goal of developing a cadre of teacher leaders to help improve instruction in literacy, humanities, and the arts. By including the word "studio" in the title, CSET likened teaching and learning to the kind of work artists and designers do, and therefore invited teachers to approach the partnership with the philosophy that professional learning, like design and art, involves access to rich resources and materials, creative collaboration with colleagues, and constant revision. Teaching as a design process incorporates both planned performance and skillful improvisation. CSET hoped that the Studio would be a place for teachers to see themselves as lifelong learners, and to collectively develop and rehearse instructional practices. Within this philosophical approach, the Studio focuses on the deepening of both specialized content knowledge and pedagogical content knowledge through thorough exploration of specific topics.

A central component of the Studio is a two-week summer institute during which San Francisco Bay-area teachers participate in one of a set of concurrent workshops. One such workshop is "Teaching Humanities: The Case of American Studies." Week one of the Teaching Humanities workshop includes an in-depth exploration of a rich historical topic through a range of literary, historical, and visual texts. In 2009, for example, participants examined the Japanese-American Internment during World War II, and, in 2010, new and returning participants explored the civil rights movement. During this first week, teachers build their historical and literary content knowledge while engaging in a multi-textual approach to teaching and learning the humanities.

In addition to the in-depth investigation of subject matter, the institute supports teachers' use of disciplined improvisation. Each institute day begins with a thirty-minute whole-group (i.e., teachers from all workshops) warm-up activity that explicitly targets improvisation principles that will serve the specific intellectual and social needs of the learning community (e.g., building ensemble, taking creative risks, embracing mistakes). Throughout the rest of the day, workshop activities explore how improvisation can inform instructional practices. For example, the Teaching Humanities workshop focuses on three core instructional practices: (1) teaching with primary historical source documents, (2) examining visual text, and (3) facilitating classroom discussion. Using these high-leverage practices, the instructional team devises a series of experiences that aligns with what teachers need to know and be able to do to flexibly incorporate these practices into their teaching. This series of experiences also follows Grossman and colleagues' three-part framework for understanding the pedagogies of practice in professional learning (i.e., representations, decomposition, and approximations of practice).

During the 2009 unit about internment, teachers participated in improvisation-based activities in order to explore possibilities for classroom discussion tethered to a story about a contemporary Japanese-American family visiting the site of a former camp (i.e., representation of content). The facilitator then provided teacher-participants with annotated plans for the session that elucidated both the specific steps followed and any in-the-moment choices informed by participants' offers (i.e., decomposition of practice). Upon receiving and reviewing these materials, participants worked in small groups to design and facilitate a brief discussion incorporating improvisational activities inspired by a different text about the internment (i.e., approximations of practice). After each group led a discussion, workshop participants collectively reflected on what worked and how they would modify and supplement activities for their own classroom contexts and content. This brief opportunity for approximating classroom discussion allowed teachers to collaboratively practice the pre-active, interactive, and reflective aspects of one core instructional practice.

As part of the unit on the civil rights movement, the 2010 Teaching Humanities workshop followed the same three-step framework for approximating classroom discussion, this time focused on specific teacher moves within discussion. Teachers participated in a discussion based on an iconic photograph from the 1957 desegregation of schools in Little Rock, Arkansas, and later received an excerpted transcript of this discussion, which they used to identify examples of types of questions and instances of uptake. Teachers then collaboratively planned, enacted, and reflected upon a brief discussion based on "Letter from a Birmingham Jail" by Martin Luther King, Jr. (1997).

As these examples illustrate, the Stanford Teaching Studio draws from research on teacher knowledge, high-leverage practices, and approximations of practice to structure learning opportunities designed to help teachers develop the expertise needed to incorporate new practices into their teaching of the humanities, and to use improvisation to improve the quality of text-based discussion. Although these approximations are inherently artificial (e.g., teachers are leading brief discussions among small groups of colleagues, which is quite different than facilitating extended large-group discussion with young people), such professional learning opportunities provide insight into the nature of teaching expertise and how we might develop it in teaching communities.

## CONCLUSION

*Structure and Improvisation in Creative Teaching* provides a convincing argument for viewing teaching and learning as improvisational activities, and the chapters work together as a response to Sawyer's question, "What makes good teachers great?" Their studies and stories suggest that skillful teaching with improvisation requires teachers to create and flexibly implement curriculum materials (i.e., the curriculum paradox); to scaffold individual student learning while being receptive to the needs and interests of the classroom community (i.e., the learning paradox); and to manage the tension between this responsiveness to students and the responsibility to plans, standards, and subject matter (i.e., the teacher paradox). It is our hope that the examples provided in these chapters will inspire teacher preparation and professional development programs to embrace the notion of teaching as improvisation, and to provide teachers with opportunities to explicitly examine, unpack, and approximate the instructional practices that draw on the kind of presence at the heart of the three paradoxes.

## REFERENCES

Ball, D. L., Thames, M. H., & Phelps, G. (2008). Content knowledge for teaching: What makes it special? *Journal of Teacher Education, 59*(5), 389–407.

Cazden, C. B. (1986). Classroom discourse. In M. C. Wittrock (Ed.), *Handbook of Research on Teaching* (pp. 432–463). New York: Macmillan.

(2001). *Classroom discourse: The language of teaching and learning.* Portsmouth, NH: Heinemann.

Christensen, C. R. (1991). The discussion teacher in action: Questioning, listening, and response. In C. R. Christensen, D. A. Garvin, & A. Sweet (Eds.), *Education for Judgment: The Artistry of Discussion Leadership* (pp. 153–172). Boston: Harvard Business School Press.

Cohen, D. K., Raudenbush, S. W., & Ball, D. L. (2003). Resources, instruction, and research. *Educational Evaluation and Policy Analysis, 25*, 119–142.

Dewey, J. (1933). *How we think.* Buffalo, NY: Prometheus Books.

(1938). *Experience & education.* New York: Collier Books.

Eisner, E. W. (2002). *The arts and the creation of mind.* New Haven, CT: Yale University Press.

Elbaz, F. (1983). *Teacher thinking: A study of practical knowledge.* London: Croom Helm.

Graff, G. (2003). *Clueless in Academe: How schooling obscures the life of the mind.* New Haven, CT: Yale.

Greene, M. (1973). *Teacher as stranger.* Buena Vista, CA: Wadsworth.

Grossman, P., Compton, C., Igra, D., Ronfeldt, M., Shahan, E., & Williamson, P. W. (2009). Teaching practice: A cross-professional perspective. *Teachers College Record, 111*(9), 2055–2100.

Grossman, P., Hammerness, K., & McDonald, M. (2009). Redefining teaching, re-imagining teacher education. *Teachers and Teaching: Theory and Practice, 15*, 273–289.

Grossman, P. & McDonald, M. (2008). Back to the future: Directions for research in teaching and teacher education. *American Educational Research Journal, 45*, 184–205.

Johnstone, K. (1979). *Impro: Improvisation and the theatre.* New York: Routledge.

King, M. L., Jr. (1997). "Letter from Birmingham Jail." In H. L. Gates, Jr. and N. Y. McKay (Eds.), *The Norton Anthology of African American Literature* (pp. 1854–1866). New York: Norton.

Labaree, D. F. (2000). On the nature of teaching and teacher education: Difficult practices that look easy. *Journal of Teacher Education, 51*(3), 228–233.

Mehan, H. (1979). *Learning lessons.* Cambridge, MA: Harvard University Press.

Meijer, P. C., Korthagen, F. A. J., & Vasalos, A. (2009). Supporting presence in teacher education: The connection between the personal and professional aspects of teaching. *Teaching and Teacher Education, 25,* 297–308.

Nystrand, M. & Gamoran, A. (1997). The big picture: Language and Learning in hundreds of English lessons. In M. Nystrand, A. Gamoran, R. Kachur, & C. Prendergast (Eds.), *Opening Dialogue: Understanding the Dynamics of Language and Learning in the English Classroom* (pp. 30–74). New York: Teachers College.

O'Connor, M.C. & Michaels, S. (1996). Shifting participant frameworks: Orchestrating thinking practices in group discussion. In D. Hicks (Ed.), *Discourse, Learning, and Schooling* (pp. 63–103). New York: Cambridge University Press.

Palmer, P. J. (1998). *The courage to teach: Exploring the inner landscape of a teacher's life.* San Francisco: Jossey-Bass.

  (2003). Teaching with heart and soul: Reflections on spirituality in teacher education. *Journal of Teacher Education, 54,* 376–385.

Rodgers, C. R. & Raider-Roth, M. B. (2006). Presence in teaching. *Teachers and Teaching: Theory and Practice, 12*(3), 265–287.

Rud, A. G., Jr. (1995). Learning in comfort: Developing an ethos of hospitality in education. In J. W. Garrison & A. G. Rud Jr. (Eds.), *The Educational Conversation: Closing the Gap* (pp. 119–128). Albany, NY: SUNY Press.

Ryan Madson, P. (2005). *Improv wisdom.* New York: Bell Tower.

Schön, D. (1983). *The reflective practitioner.* New York: Basic Books.

Schwab, J. J. (1978). The practical: Translation into curriculum. In I. Westbury and N. J. Wilkoff (Eds.), *Science Curriculum and Liberal Education: Selected Essays of Joseph J. Schwab* (pp. 259–286). Orlando, FL: Elsevier.

Shulman, L. S. (1986). Those who understand: Knowledge growth in teaching. *Educational Researcher, 15*(2), 4–14.

Spolin, V. (1963). *Improvisation for the theater.* Evanston, IL: Northwestern University Press.

# Index